OXFORD WORLD'S CLASSICS

—

JULES VERNE

Journey to the Moon

—

A new translation by
DAVID COWARD AND WILLIAM BUTCHER

OXFORD
UNIVERSITY PRESS

OXFORD
UNIVERSITY PRESS

Great Clarendon Street, Oxford, OX2 6DP,
United Kingdom

Oxford University Press is a department of the University of Oxford.
It furthers the University's objective of excellence in research, scholarship,
and education by publishing worldwide. Oxford is a registered trade mark of
Oxford University Press in the UK and in certain other countries

Published in the United States of America by Oxford University Press
198 Madison Avenue, New York, NY 10016, United States of America

British Library Cataloguing in Publication Data

Data available

Library of Congress Control Number: 2024952647

ISBN 9780198941781

Printed and bound in the UK by
Clays Ltd, Elcograf S.p.A.

The manufacturer's authorised representative in the EU for product safety is
Oxford University Press España S.A., Parque Empresarial San Fernando de Henares,
Avenida de Castilla, 2 – 28830 Madrid (www.oup.es/en).

Links to third party websites are provided by Oxford in good faith and
for information only. Oxford disclaims any responsibility for the materials
contained in any third party website referenced in this work.

The manufacturer's authorised representative in the EU for product safety is
Oxford University Press España S.A. of El Parque Empresarial San Fernando de Henares,
Avenida de Castilla, 2 – 28830 Madrid (www.oup.es/en or product.safety@oup.com).
OUP España S.A. also acts as importer into Spain of products made by the manufacturer.

JOURNEY TO THE MOON

JULES VERNE was born in Nantes in 1828, the eldest of five children in a prosperous family of French, Breton, and Scottish extraction. His early years were happy apart from the accidental drowning of his cousins and unrequited passions for his cousin Caroline and Herminie Grossetière. Literature always attracted him and while taking a law degree in Paris he wrote poetry and a large number of plays. His books *Journey to England and Scotland* and *Paris in the Twentieth Century* were not published in his lifetime. However, he published *The Salon of 1857* in 1857, and in 1862 the publisher Hetzel accepted *Five Weeks in a Balloon*, to be followed by sixty other novels covering the whole world and beyond; at the same time he insisted on radical changes to the structures and contents of the books. Verne travelled over three continents, before selling his yacht in 1886, following an attempt on his life by his favourite nephew, Gaston. Eight of the books appeared after his death in 1905—although in fact partly written by his son Michel.

DAVID COWARD writes widely on the history, literature, and culture of France. A regular contributor to the *Times Literary Supplement*, *London Review of Books*, and national newspapers, he won the Scott-Moncrieff Prize for Translation in 1996. He is the author of *A History of French Literature* (2002), and for Oxford World's Classics has translated and edited works by Dumas, Diderot, Sade, and Beaumarchais.

WILLIAM BUTCHER has taught languages and mathematics, notably at the École Nationale d'Administration and the University of Hong Kong. He is the author of *Jules Verne inédit: Les manuscrits déchiffrés* (The Unexpurgated Jules Verne, 2015) and *Jules Verne: The Biography* (2006 and 2020) and has published many translations and editions, including *Around the World in Eighty Days*, *Journey to the Centre of the Earth*, and *Twenty Thousand Leagues under the Seas* for Oxford World's Classics.

OXFORD WORLD'S CLASSICS

*For over 100 years Oxford World's Classics have brought
readers closer to the world's great literature. Now with over 700
titles—from the 4,000-year-old myths of Mesopotamia to the
twentieth century's greatest novels—the series makes available
lesser-known as well as celebrated writing.*

*The pocket-sized hardbacks of the early years contained
introductions by Virginia Woolf, T. S. Eliot, Graham Greene,
and other literary figures which enriched the experience of reading.
Today the series is recognized for its fine scholarship and
reliability in texts that span world literature, drama and poetry,
religion, philosophy and politics. Each edition includes perceptive
commentary and essential background information to meet the
changing needs of readers.*

CONTENTS

INTRODUCTION

FROM the Earth to the Moon (1865), written early on in the career of Jules Verne (1828–1905), ranks among a handful of his most successful and popular works. Its sequel, *Around the Moon* (1869), also belongs to the crucially creative first decade with Paris publisher, Jules Hetzel, which catapulted him from obscurity to international fame. With renewed interest in our only satellite expected in the 2030s and 2040s, the relevance of the pioneering and realistic two-volume *Journey to the Moon* can only increase.

Yet, despite its popularity and historical and literary importance, no critical edition has ever been published: the three surviving manuscripts remain largely unknown, and the necessary 'establishment of the text', including the identification of the best French edition issued by Hetzel, followed by the publication of an updated text, has not been carried out. This deficiency is in fact only part of a general problem: the best-known French writer has seldom benefited from a canonical edition of even his best-known works,[1] let alone his Collected Works, properly established on the basis of the last corrected texts. As a result, studies of Verne's work have often examined the novels in a defective edition. This essential groundwork on the texts was carried out long ago, however, for Flaubert, Stendhal, Balzac, and Proust.

The present volume will therefore explore aspects of the *Journey to the Moon* diptych including the references and allusions and the suppressed or modified handwritten text—in short, all the evidence, generally unpublished to date, that will enable us to better understand and appreciate this unparalleled marvel, this jewel of world literature.

In this Introduction in particular, after a brief examination of Verne's reputation, which still remains challenging to define, I will look at its characters, especially the intriguing Michel Ardan (double of the photographer and aeronaut Nadar). Verne's science, finally, will be examined, in particular the work's sources and its 'predictions' and 'errors'. The Explanatory Notes at the end of the volume will seek to clarify and reference obscurities and allusions; the profusion

---

[1] W.B. has made a few attempts for Gallimard Folio Classique and Oxford World's Classics.

of authorities cited by Verne is covered in Appendix 2: 'Proper Names
Cited by Verne'. In the general absence of information about the
lunar manuscripts, these three essential documents will be studied in
the context of the work's elaboration, to highlight not only where the
publisher changed the text but also the instances in which the contents
differ significantly from the known version (Appendix 1: 'Inception
and Development of the Novel'). Care will be taken to situate the
work in Verne's life ('A Chronology of Jules Verne') and in terms of
the exchanges with the publisher ('A Chronology of the Writing of
Journey to the Moon').

Voyage à la Lune fits into the mould of the first books under
Hetzel's direction: an audacious journey into an unknown domain of
prestige and mythical resonance, far from the too-familiar European
lands and deliciously empty of a human presence; with as much time
spent on the preparations as the journey itself; characters who are
stereotyped but striking; a thick underlay and solid veneer of science
and technology, done with so much accurate or credible information
as to become convincing, despite an essential implausibility. The first
volume of the diptych is lively, humorous, confident, and ambitious,
written in Verne's relief and joy of having finally found a publisher
and a national reputation. It exists on many levels, thanks to its psychological interplay, its scientific and technological expositions, its
plot twists; and to its wealth of metaphors, proverbial expressions,
images and reflections of contemporary social and political debate.

The mood of *Around the Moon* is less exuberant. Verne wrote the
volume after Hetzel had transformed, almost to destruction, *The
Adventures of Captain Hatteras* (begun in 1864) and *Twenty Thousand
Leagues under the Seas* (1868), including their heroic captains and
their ideologies and 'messages'.[2] These two masterpieces, together
with other works, lost some of their finest chapters in a paroxysm of
destructive editing that attacked their very cores, without any possibility of appeal. Be that as it may, although entertaining and enlightening, the second lunar volume, written after the worst editing traumas,
serves as a prelude to Verne's relative novelistic waning, from 1870 to
1905, where society is criticized more and literary form is experimented

---

[2] See William Butcher, *Jules Verne inédit: Les manuscrits déchiffrés* (Lyon: ENS
éditions and Institut d'histoire du livre, 2015), for chapter and verse of the changes the
publisher forced onto Verne's works.

with, but where less exhilarating themes are explored with reduced word-play and humour.

It is not easy to understand the enduring attraction exercised by *Journey to the Moon*, continuing since publication and operating across every continent. Part of the explanation may be in the very manner in which Verne tells the story, carrying it along with infectious excitement. Part may be in the revival of an age-old dream, although we now know that the journey has been accomplished in reality: humans have been to the Moon and lived to tell the tale. Travelling to the Moon represents the fulfilment of a reverie available to everyone, but one which is still hard to believe when contemplating the Moon's face in the constellation of the night sky.

Verne's books are invariably as developed when he is writing about the preparations for a journey as actually carrying it out, not only because he can work in the results of all his research, meaning that external constraints exist to structure the writing, but also because presenting the journey itself requires a great deal of imagination and inventiveness to keep the reader informed and entertained. Verne is in his element in synthesizing complex but familiar questions in precise but accessible language, in working towards a solution to concrete preparatory problems drawn from everyday experience.

In *From the Earth to the Moon* especially, the novelist can indulge himself to the utmost in selecting the launch site, choosing the propulsion method, and finally building the cannon, all in semi-technical language leavened with much good humour. Undoubtedly the quality of the writing, in the sense of clarity, coherence, and continuity, including details like rhythm, assonance, and vocabulary, all of which are highly polished, contributes greatly to the enjoyment of the volume.

The main themes of the first chapters, in particular, are the American character and the satirical showing up of the belligerence inherited from the Civil War. But much of their interest also comes from the interaction of the characters, each with his own foibles and weaknesses.

Genesis: dates of composition

Although we do not have many genetic documents for the years 1862 to 1867, it is clear that Hetzel often intervened, both in the choice of a plot for the novels and in the work of composing and revising. At the time his contribution was appreciated by Verne, who built up a fund of gratitude that would last his whole life, even after later works suffered significantly from the publisher's less constructive interventions; the Moon volumes straddle the turning point of 1867.

Around October 1864, Verne wrote to Hetzel to say that 'of course' he would use aluminium for the projectile and first experiment with animals: 'the dog will eat the squirrel'. Both volumes were serialized first in the daily newspaper the *Journal des débats politiques et littéraires* (henceforth *Débats*).[3] This was perhaps the reason they managed to mostly escape Hetzel's pedagogical and commercial straitjacket of being made suitable for a fragile young readership—a restriction that was to define Verne's writings for half a century—allowing him here to tackle more advanced 'adult' subjects with boldness and irreverence, as for example in his acid evocation of the 'bloody memories' of the Civil War: 'the cotton plants flourished in well-fertilized fields, [and] the mourning clothes were finally worn out together with the mourning' (p. 10); a peace that results in considerable exasperation among retired gunners:

'It's so depressing,' said good Tom Hunter one evening as his wooden legs slowly charred in the fire of the smoking room. '. . . Nothing to look forward to! . . . Whatever happened to the time when you were woken each morning by the noise of cannon-fire that gladdened the heart?' (p. 10)

Nevertheless, these robust remarks are already present in the manuscripts, when the author did not know how the novel would be published.

After Verne's writing of the fair-copy manuscript of the first volume in 1864, Hetzel read it closely as usual, giving the author the chance to review his corrections and comments; then repeated the process several times on the successive proofs in 1865 (for details see Appendix 1). In September and October 1866 *From the Earth to the Moon* appeared in serial form in the newspaper *Journal des débats politiques et littéraires*.

Verne penned the first manuscript of the second volume from November 1868 to February 1869, then the final manuscript between March and June of the same year. It seems that Hetzel sent it back to him twice in July, the first time annotated in blue pencil, the second

---

[3] Publication of the first volume in the *Débats* was only considered after the very first impression in spring 1865; it seems to have happened as a matter of course for the second volume, another indication of the inseparability of the two parts.

in black ink: each time the writer incorporated most of the suggested changes, while assuring the publisher that he had accepted them all. In the end, Verne declared himself satisfied with both its content and form,[4] although he rarely mentions the title itself of *Around the Moon*.

Rather than submit the text directly to the *Débats* for serialization, Verne again preferred to have the proofs prepared by Hetzel (letter of 25 July 1869); he reread them from September onwards and *Autour de la Lune* appeared in the *Débats* that November and December.

In the manuscript of *De la Terre à la Lune* the title is followed, in a second line and in an identical hand, by that of *Autour de la Lune*, which seems to imply that the basic idea for the second part dates from 1864 or 1865. In some other manuscripts, however, Verne wrote in the title long after the end of composition. In any case, the addition of the programmatic and spoiler second title does not seem to fit with the internal indications, which, even in the opening chapters of the second part, appear to foresee an actual arrival on the lunar surface.

The first volume seems deeper and richer because it can incorporate information from the Earth;[5] whereas the second volume has to generate its own narrative resources. One gets the impression that Verne embarked on writing *Journey to the Moon* as an amusement, a gamble, a way to fulfil his contracts. It appears unlikely that when he began, he was actually proposing to land on the Moon, if only because common sense implies that the projectile would crash into the surface. Even if one was to assume the use of retrorockets to achieve a soft landing, an idea absent from the first chapters of the diptych, there would still be all kinds of implausibility, such as the lack of food, water, and air. Another thorny problem, even for instinctive, improvisational writers like Verne, was to find a way of getting his travellers back—for if they failed to return how could he narrate the story of what had happened to them?

In short, he seems to have made a commitment without considering the ways and means of honouring it or the possibility that Hetzel would not allow him to launch his heroes into space without guaranteeing

[4] 'I have great hopes that the public, despite the strangeness and audacity of certain things, will accept and swallow the adventures of our three adventurers' [Sept. 1869]; 'My manuscripts are very much revised now, when I give them to the printer' [Sept. 1869].

[5] As just one small example, Verne semi-humorously converts the river system of North America into a single unbranching water course, and its 'orographic system' into two mountain chains.

their safe return. It may be that the publisher maintained the ambiguity about the ending for a few years, but eventually hardened his position. In the end Verne had to begin planning a trajectory which would bring the projectile back to Earth, and thus avoid a potentially infinite flight or a real Moon landing that would describe the surface in detail and so go far beyond contemporary knowledge. Faced with the danger of scientific inaccuracy, he seems to have eventually given up the objective of leaving the projectile, and thus of being able to do something new, to have genuine adventures, in a word for him to have enough interesting material to fill a second volume.

In the event, he came out it rather well: by dint of witty dialogues, debates on the trajectory, and informative exposés on the cosmology based as much on literary and historical culture as on science, an enjoyable 'novel about nothing' emerged, perhaps anticipating the spirit of the New Novelists of the mid-twentieth century, although not managing to come close to the number of words that the publisher required.

In sum, although there are indications that Verne did not do any serious work on *Around the Moon* before autumn 1867, very little is known about the date of his plan, if he wrote one at all. Nor do we know where the initial stimulus for the tale came from, whether the final plot was determined from the outset, or how Verne managed to finish writing the two volumes so quickly.

Precursors and sources

Back in December 1847, Verne had either composed or copied out a sonnet called 'The Moon', in which he attributed people's changeability, 'the ebb and flow of their moods', to lunar influence.

In 1854 the novelist Alexandre Dumas *père*, a friend of Verne's since 1848, published 'Voyage à la Lune' (Journey to the Moon), about an eagle-powered flight, a story that was reprinted in *L'Univers illustré* of 18 February 1865; that same year, an Alexandre Cathelineau anonymously published an ingenious way of getting the story back to Earth, in another 'Voyage à la Lune: D'après un manuscrit authentique projeté d'un volcan lunaire' (Journey to the Moon: based on an authentic manuscript expelled from a lunar volcano). From 26 January to 19 February 1864, a Charles Habeneck (1836–79) serialized a story about an interplanetary voyage called *La Légende du soleil* (The

Legend of the Sun) in the newspaper *Le Peuple*. In *Le Petit Journal* of 20 November 1865, this journalist pointed out similarities between his and Verne's stories: the use of a huge cannon to send a ball into space, the descriptions of the cannon, the effect produced by the launch detonation, and the presence of a 'scientific commission' inside the projectile. However, he charitably declared that he did not believe 'that M. Verne was inspired by my legend'.

Over the centuries, many other writers, too many to name, had imagined a fictional journey to the Moon, using a wide variety of distinctly unscientific methods. Although Verne himself mentions a few (p. 17), he apparently did not take them seriously and their influence on his own tale seems slight. He includes Edgar Allan Poe, although in his 1864 article, 'Edgar Poe et ses œuvres', he strongly criticizes the credibility of the American's story. In any case, Verne was the first novelist to present travel to the Moon in a relatively realistic way, describing in detail the methods used to launch the travellers, the craft, the ballistics, celestial mechanics, and the means of survival.

For the equations and calculations, Verne called on his first cousin, mathematician Henri Garcet, with the two men perhaps chatting in a café near the Lycée Henri IV in the Latin Quarter. He also seems to have had the first volume reviewed by mathematician Joseph Bertrand, who nevertheless found the story a little thin. It is not impossible that he sought further assistance from the astronomer Jules Janssen and the geologist Charles Sainte-Claire Deville, as claimed by his pioneering but unreliable biographer Marguerite Allotte de la Fuÿe.

As in all his first drafts, in order to aid later checking of details, Verne inserted page references in the margin of the first manuscript of the second volume, thus recording his documentary sources, nearly all of them astronomical works of quality.[6]

A honeymoon novel

It is not fashionable in academic circles to resort to biography; in any case, the novelist's life before 1870 remains largely unknown, with the links between the works and the biography in particular forming a neglected area. Nevertheless, as we shall see, Verne's semi-exotic

---

[6] The precision of the annotations makes it possible to identify the edition of the works consulted by Verne, some of which can be found in his library.

voyage of 1861 and the account of it constituted one important connection between his personal life and the writing of many of his stories.

In the late 1860s much of France's population was complaining about the arbitrary measures of the dictatorial and belligerent Napoleon III. In 1869 the nation was heading for disaster, continually provoking Germany into war: French people were optimistic about the final outcome but with little reason. When the Franco-Prussian War finally came in July 1870, Germany quickly overran and occupied much of the country, deposing the Emperor. The Paris Commune followed, fomenting violence and disrupting everyday life, including food supplies; Verne's cousin Henri Garcet died as a result of the privations.

Verne's new home in Amiens was commandeered and he served as a National Guard member (the type of French rifle that he was issued for the war is prominently mentioned in *Twenty Thousand Leagues*). But he suffered little except financially, for Hetzel's publishing house closed for the duration, and the second octavo volume of the marine novel only came out two years after the first one. However, the pugnacity of many French people at the time, including Verne's father, is surely reflected in the artillerymen's belligerence in *Journey to the Moon*.

It may be that Verne himself was not fully aware of the origin of the torrent of brilliant novels that poured out in the two years from 1864 to 1866: subsequently he would not be able to draw on so much inspiration, having to rely more on perspiration. Is the reason for the change to be found in the misfortunes of France, his personal life, or a subtle change in the world's atmosphere? After the initial honeymoon years, when Hetzel played a constructive role as co-creator and first reader, when the editor went on holiday in the south of France, Italy, and Germany with his protégé, even perhaps passing on his mistress, it is possible, as we have seen, that Hetzel's overbearing rewriting of Verne's output made him lose his balance, his confidence as a novelist. No longer daring to venture into the rarefied air of absurd inventions, crazy discoveries, and transgressive madness, Verne would stick henceforth to fixed trajectories on beaten tracks.

The first Vernian works, published from 1863 to 1869, are usually set in relation to a transcendent point, placing at the centre of their search an unexplored but highly symbolic point, an *ultima Thule*, a site located at the maximum distance from France, a distance that allows the heroes to encounter an increasing number of obstacles on the way to their goal, but which makes it problematic to close the novel without having the heroes either die or humiliatingly retrace their steps.

All these stories reflected the young author's life. Indeed, his own first trips abroad took him, first to the grandiose heart of the Scottish Highlands, haunted by the spirit of Walter Scott, and then to the dramatic natural spectacles of the Norwegian wilderness. Most of his early tales similarly transport us to poor, little-known, exotic lands with a rich history and culture, where the natives speak a language that goes back to the dawn of time, are isolated from the cultural mainstream, and are fierce but welcoming, independent-minded and rebellious. The geography of these two regions—not yet nations—is turbulent, chaotically diverse, made up of proud peaks reaching for the sky and enchanting, enticing valleys, inextricable networks of land and water, as if designed for getting lost and making unheard-of discoveries, ideal breeding grounds for rich fiction.

In a precursor work, the fascinating autobiographical fragment 'Joyeuses misères de trois voyageurs en Scandinavie' (Joyous miseries of three travellers in Scandinavia, 1861 or 1862), Verne explains his motivation, revealing his dreams and desires in the pre-Hetzel period and even his entire career plan: above all to maximize the geographical, linguistic, and cultural distance from Paris, now deemed too 'stifling'. This essential fragment foreshadows his destiny as a novelist when it expresses a laconic wish 'to see things that do not exist while on a journey'. Henceforth an irresistible urge will draw him 'to the hyperborean regions, like the magnetic needle to the North . . . I am temperamentally drawn to cold countries.'

The two northern trips, together with the writing of them, including that of 'Joyous miseries', in fact transformed Verne. By blending the Norwegian spray with the Scotch mist he had bottled in his innermost recesses, he finally found his voice: a potent mix of solid geographico-historical research, visual invention, and humorously self-mocking exaggeration, shaken together but not stirred. The two expeditions would thus generate several stories, to a certain extent autobiographical by contagion and therefore 'true', but at the same time bursting with imagination, madcap creativity, and boundless fiction: the early novels spawned by the two northern journeys emerge from their identical mould. The three heroes, a magical and practical number, as 'Joyeuses misères' explains, more or less Anglo-Saxon, are heroic and often Nordic, defined by a search for an absolute that is a stubborn physical fight against 'Impossible Odds' (as in the title of *Around the Moon*, chapter 19), wallowing in extreme conditions, verging on the miserabilist or the masochistic, as they strive to reach a *nec plus ultra*, a supreme inaccessible point, a culmination that is as topographical and metaphysical as it is allegorical, symbolic, and par-oxysmal: the heart of Africa, the North Pole, the centre of the Earth, the dark side of the Moon, later the bottom of the ocean, or, acciden-tally, the edge of the Solar System. All of these pilgrimages, governed by a quest for the extraordinary, create an ideal novelistic structure, with a gradual approach to the holy place, followed by a climax and, sometimes, insurmountable difficulties in retracing their steps across a now deflowered land, re-entering society, and returning derisorily to everyday reality.

After these two or three short years and this deluge of a quarter of a million enchanted words, Verne would never again find a compar-able combination of novelty, excitement, invention, and perfection of expression, of a happy sojourn in an age-old land, of union with the Earth, of extravagant escape without thought of tomorrow, of tran-scendence—he would have no more virgin domains to conquer.

As if to complement his two northern journeys, Verne turns to the New World from the middle of the 1860s. His vision of the United States is in fact less positive than perceived by most commentators— and by the comments of the author himself, when courteously receiving American journalists towards the end of his life.

The Floating City, the account of his experience on a whirlwind tour of the country in April 1867, contains less spontaneity and joy than his unrestricted leisure-time adventures in Scotland and Norway. This third foreign journey was made in the company of his brother Paul, who was probably less open-minded and creative than his previous companion, the composer Aristide Hignard; it seems to derive less from the desire to discover a country and find himself than the need to earn a living and find a subject for a story. While Scotland in particular was home to bilingual relatives and friends of friends, France's American tragedies must have been present in the minds of the two monolingual brothers—that of a continent which had become predominantly French and francophone, but now housed a seemingly less sophisticated, less refined nation.

Verne admired the pragmatism, energy, courage, technical and commercial know-how of Americans, but less so their materialism and naivety, the scarcity of fine architecture, respect for nature, scepticism, political discernment, cosmopolitanism, and perhaps even the absence from bookshops of his own four published novels, in French or English.

In sum, Verne loved the people, but not the culture; in an interview in the 1890s he said: 'Americans are undoubtedly the most practical people, but they sorely lack taste. Only look at their public buildings! Colossal, expensive, but no architecture.'

However, Verne's six North American days constituted a resounding success in literary terms, for more than thirty works featuring Americans or America grew out of the experience. In some of them, Fenimore Cooper's New World was still grandiose, lush—and full of engineers aching to tame it.

For example, *Humbug: The American Way of Life* (1905) echoes the saying of the unscrupulous showman Barnum, 'the American people like to be humbugged'. The first-person French narrator takes a steamboat upstream from New York, acerbically noting the idea 'of damming the Hudson and using its water to drive a coffee-mill'. The story focuses on the incredible discovery of the skeleton of a giant and satirizes modern publicity methods. Again, in *Around the World in Eighty Days*, probably first dreamt of in 1867, even the unobservant Phileas Fogg notices New Jersey's 'towns with ancient names, some with streets and trams but no houses' (ch. 31).

At the start of the lunar diptych, the 'heroes' are idle US artillerymen, brutal engineers punished in their bodies by their very ambition, murderous, warlike, and chauvinistic. Impey Barbicane, the only member of the Gun Club to remain in one piece, a projectile specialist, is austere and rigorous; the idea of launching the projectile into space comes from him. Sober and committed to facts, he shows his man-management skills and purpose through his scientific curiosity and competence. His virtual twin, Nicholl, man of detail, methodical and phlegmatic, committed to science, is a complementary armour specialist, a chronometer with an 'escapement' and 'eight holes', preoccupied with figures, eccentric, irascible. Accident-prone and combustible J. T. Maston is a loyal friend but lacks a cranium, so often falls down and cannot travel. All three, obsessed, egotistical, inhuman, fanatical, positivistic technologists rather than real scientists, overestimate their own abilities; but they come to life through their opinions and hobby horses. The plot is thus driven by their collective quest for scientific and other truth, which in turn shapes the novel when converted for dramatic purposes: a case in point being meteors, which allow the novelist plenty of opportunity for semi-learned expositions but also for dramatic plot turns and multiple cases of *deus ex machina*.

Michel Ardan

The forest is only burned by its own trees.
Michel Ardan

The unforeseen arrival of the eccentric and very Parisian *boulevardier*, Michel Ardan, lifts the mood of the novel. Sharing a first name with Verne's only son and three successive boats, closely related to his model, flight enthusiast Nadar, he is one of the author's great creations, along with Fogg, Nemo, Lidenbrock, and Hatteras, but perhaps the most complex of them all.

The initial description of the Frenchman, although slightly lengthy and self-indulgent, shows Verne's skill in conveying psychological traits through physical description:

A face, not long but broad at the temples, featured a moustache that bristled like a cat's whiskers and small yellowish growths of beard on the cheeks. Round eyes, a touch wild and faintly myopic, completed a physiognomy which was indisputably feline. But the nose was strong, the mouth unusually gentle, and the brow high, intelligent, and furrowed like a field which is never allowed to lie fallow. Finally, a well-developed torso set squarely on long legs, hefty arms, like powerful, well-anchored levers, a confident bearing—all combined to make this European a strapping and vigorous man, 'more forged in a smithy than cast in a mould', to borrow an expression from the iron-founder's art. The disciples of Lavater or Gratiolet would have had no difficulty reading the skull and physiognomy of this man and finding clear signs of combativity, that is of courage in the face of danger and a relish for overcoming obstacles; signs too of benevolence and openness to wonderment, an instinct which leads certain kinds of person to be drawn to the heroic . . . To complete the physical description of the *Atlanta*'s passenger, note must be taken of his capacious, loose-fitting clothes, with the material of both trousers and overcoat so generous that Michel Ardan nicknamed himself a 'ruination to cloth', a loose cravat, a shirt open at the collar through which rose a sturdy neck, and shirt cuffs invariably left unbuttoned, leaving his restless hands free to move. He gave the impression that even in the depths of winter, here was a man who never felt either the cold or fear. (p. 93)

His weaknesses and strengths adding to those of his companions, he is a brilliant and noisy daredevil, ardent and intuitive, charming and petulant, pacifist and carefree but resolute, independent but a camp-follower, 'a man you could take or leave', full of his own flamboyant optimism and genial genius. With an absurd imagination and a motto of 'no matter what', he proclaims himself a 'sublime ignoramus' and is an 'artist by instinct' with 'little concern for logic', but always landing on his feet. Without the bump of acquisitiveness, he adores elegance, eloquence, feeble puns and literary allusions, and sees 'everything in grand terms, except difficulties and men'. He despises US gun culture and the dry, opaque analyses of the scholars, 'people who keep the score while we play the game', outraging them with a skilful combination of fanciful common sense, pragmatism, pacifism, and humanism, of innocent wonder and mythomaniac combativeness, of adolescent demagogical appeals, of strategic ambiguity, of red herrings, of *reductio ad absurdum*.

In the second volume, the Moon-bound Ardan's lyrical musings and fantastic visions of Selenite constructions, full of desolate landscapes, stark ruins, and lonely sepulchres, stem from classical mythology and the death throes of Romanticism. In his zanier moments, Ardan provocatively extrapolates in elliptic, parabolic, or hyperbolic fashion, claiming that 'people will soon be travelling to the planets as rapidly as they wish' and that as a result 'distance is an empty word, there is no such thing as distance'. He resembles an authorial self-portrait, a self-deprecating representative of 'French agitation and loquacity'.

He sometimes plays the role of the ordinary reader, with his naive clairvoyance, his falsely ingenuous questioning of lunar data and the complex algebra governing trajectories. Unpretentious and childlike, Ardan, whose name in French sounds like 'ardent' and somewhat like Adam, is often restless and edgy, even feverish. But it is he who shows himself the creative scientist *par excellence*, confounding the experts with his heated flights of fancy, his ready-made primitive formulas and brilliant but hazardous ideas, such as the ideas of inhabiting the projectile, taking along a couple of dogs, or using rockets to modify the trajectory.

'Predictions'

Journey to the Moon has spawned a plethora of articles praising the accuracy of its prescience, described as 'forecasts' or 'predictions', or the number of ideas that would be reproduced in reality in the twentieth century. Even if some of Verne's details are erroneous, the presentations do often remain essentially correct or correspond to the events of subsequent decades, like the Apollo 8 and 11 missions. However, the majority of such articles, not based on a close reading of *Journey to the Moon*, are selective in their use of evidence: caution is called for in accepting their conclusions.

Much of the commentary focuses on the American spacecraft, to which some attribute an almost supernatural power of prophecy: its launch, carrying passengers, at a speed of 'twelve thousand yards per second', or just above 11 km/s, from coastal Florida, less than 140 miles from the Kennedy Space Center at Cape Canaveral, a place name featured in the original map of *From the Earth to the Moon*; or the location in Longs Peak, Colorado, of a telescope to track it. Certain aspects of *The Moon* are indeed surprisingly accurate: Verne's realization of the need to reach escape velocity; the duration of the flight; the effects of weightlessness; and the modification of the trajectory using retrorockets.

Verne appears to have been the first to conceive of a 'free return trajectory', the idea that it is possible to circumnavigate the Moon without landing, and then come back to Earth. For this return, he seems also to have been the first writer to use an ocean to cushion the impact, in the event the Pacific.

The accuracy of his vision can also be seen in a few specific ideas, like the one that the absence of refraction of light rays shows the lack of atmosphere on the Moon, and therefore also of water.[7]

In other ideas as well, Verne showed considerable far-sightedness: in the use of guncotton for propulsion; the 'cylindrical-conical' shape of the projectile, made of aluminium; gas heating, electric ignition, compressed meat and vegetables, the production of oxygen and elimination of nitrogen; a test launch using animals; the use of

---

[7] However, having observed some localized snow on the lunar surface, the voyagers deduce the corresponding presence of air (p. 269), since if liquid water cannot remain in the absence of an atmosphere, ice, but not snow, could subsist at the bottom of craters, a phenomenon whose existence was confirmed in 2009.

a 'count' for the launch, although not yet a countdown; the name of the cannon, the Columbiad; the complex mathematical calculations, such as those used to determine the influence of the gravity of the Earth and the Moon; the trajectories of objects in space; the absence of any sensation of movement; the appearance of the Moon when seen close up, including the predominance of chiaroscuro (the absence of shades of grey); rockets that can operate in a vacuum; the rescue by the US Navy; and the final tickertape procession through New York.

In a late interview, Verne correctly claimed that the basis of his book was more realistic than that of H. G. Wells's *The First Men in the Moon* (1900–1).

Some striking details of similarity may even stem from some of the real-life engineers adapting their work to align it with Verne's influential account. But mostly his genuine foresight derived from strongly-developed common sense combined with up-to-date scientific knowledge, which enabled him to become the first novelist to approach the question of space travel in realistic physical terms.

Errors

Much commentary on *Journey to the Moon*, relying on translations and so without in-depth knowledge of the French text, has also highlighted the scientific or technical 'errors' involved in Verne's 'anticipations', particularly in the trajectory. A full and fair understanding of the degree of accuracy of the novel requires an examination of many of the issues involved in its composition, including the use of sources and the changes pressed on Verne by his publisher.

Inevitably, in so much invention, such a profusion of information of all kinds, so much poetic licence, a few errors of detail crept in. However, many of the mistakes were shared by the majority of nineteenth-century scientists; and Verne often indicates his awareness of the inaccuracy of some of his ideas, but tries to find the least implausible solution or evade problems by means of literary 'three card tricks', especially by putting the more far-fetched ideas into Michel Ardan's mouth. The Frenchman's humorous dream of launching 'projectile trains' into space (p. 101), which gives rise to a striking illustration, where smoke is seen billowing from a train, has often been reproduced, further undermining Verne's scientific reputation.

Many of the alleged errors are in this way largely deliberate, required by the story and in any case placed in the mouths of the characters: two extreme examples are the collapsible water compartments to reduce the shock of the launch or Barbicane's idea that the projectile will not be melted or vaporized after take off since it will only spend a few seconds in the Earth's atmosphere (p. 44).

Certainly, some of the details in the novel remain inaccurate in the light of modern information. When dense molten metal is poured around and under a central core, as in the construction of the cannon, the core should float upwards; firing rockets in flight is difficult, even with custom-made holes to screw them into; the sun's heat comes from reactions in its interior (nuclear ones, we now know), rather than from the meteors falling on its surface; seeing the sun and stars at the same time is unlikely; since the same side of the Moon continuously faces the Earth, an observer on its visible surface will not see the Earth rising or setting on the horizon; gravity must surely have been acting from the birth of the universe; Verne ascribes the Tycho crater a height without mentioning the peak in its centre.

When the projectile is launched from the cannon, the objects in it would have been thrown to the ground and then, as soon as it encounters significant atmospheric resistance, flung upwards. The projectile has an external diameter of 3 metres, giving an internal diameter of about 9 feet: barely enough to contain what Verne presents as a table set for ten. Despite his assertion (p. 145), sound takes well under half an hour to travel from Florida to West Africa. Apart from the other coincidences involving the trajectory, undergoing two close encounters with celestial bodies in a ten-day journey is highly unlikely. As in Nemo's *Nautilus*, little provision is made for the removal of waste of all kinds. To dispose of the dog's body, the porthole is opened, which lets out 'barely a handful of molecules of air' (p. 195)! The corpse then flattens like deflated bagpipes, whereas it ought to inflate.[8]

According to Verne, the launch must satisfy three conditions: the declination and the phase of the Moon, which must be in perigee. In

[8] Belfast is right when he states that the launch site should be between 0° and 28° latitude north or south; but this figure of 28° is reached only in special circumstances, when the inclination of the Earth's axis (around 23°) and that of the Moon's orbit (around 5°) combine. Over Florida, the full Moon is not often at its zenith in winter, which rules out in particular the date specified of 4 December.

fact a declination at the zenith is the only necessary condition; it is not essential for the Moon to be at its perigee, and the perigee and zenith conditions will have only an imperceptible effect on the launch speed required. In any case, the calculations do not take into account the Earth's rotation; it is more economical and less dangerous to launch a projectile obliquely towards the east, from an east-facing coast close to the Equator.

The trajectories, whether projected or actually followed, are never very clear, and contain a number of other slips. The calculations of the time needed to reach the Moon for a projectile launched at a speed of 11 km/s do not take into account the respective attractions of the Earth and the Moon.

While humans can hardly withstand a sustained force of more than 10 gravities, or even briefly as much as 50 g, the acceleration needed to reach 11 km/s, although needed for the story, is more than 1,000 g: the passengers would be crushed. Admittedly, the effect is alleviated by Verne's face-saving idea of partitions, but not by much, since water is almost incompressible.

In any case, the use of gunpowder to launch the projectile would not give it enough speed,[9] without even taking into account the extra amount required by the weight of the passengers, dogs, and furniture.

When a close encounter deflects the projectile, it enters an elliptical orbit around the Moon. In fact, the Moon's capture of a body is virtually impossible (even in the case of the Earth, gravity in combination with the atmosphere can deflect bodies, but rarely capture them). As at the launch, the re-entry of the projectile into the Earth's atmosphere would vaporize it; and the impact with the ocean would crush it.

It is the protagonists who are sometimes responsible for oversimplifications and inaccuracies: 'modifying the movement of the projectile . . . by lightening it' by a few objects, says Nicholl, who omits to consider the direction of expulsion, would mean that 'the projectile . . . would move faster', while Michel asserts the opposite and Barbicane contradicts both statements: 'Neither faster nor slower' (p. 283). Similarly, when Ardan suggests a stroll outside the projectile, Barbicane replies that: 'as your density is less than that of the projectile,

---

[9] Achille Eyraud's *Voyage à Vénus* (1865) introduced the use of a gunpowder-powered rocket for space travel, although rockets were not very powerful at the time.

you would quickly stay behind' (p. 202), which shows a lack of understanding of the movement of bodies in a vacuum and is inconsistent with his view on the effect of lightening the projectile.

According to Verne's calculations, the speed of the projectile will be zero at the 'point' of equilibrium between the Earth and the Moon; but in that case it would not reach the Moon as planned. To arrive at such an equilibrium, the exact adjustment of the initial velocity is critical; but Verne forgets to take into account the air resistance, an oversight he finally recognizes in *Around the Moon*, where he estimates that the speed has been reduced by 'one third' (p. 165). We also understand later that by expelling the water in its collapsing partitions, the projectile has been lightened—which has the effect, by a very fortunate coincidence, of restoring its speed to exactly the revised value needed to leave Earth. Finally, Verne forgets that the final speed of the returning projectile, 16 km/s, should also be reduced a third due to the atmospheric resistance.

If Verne *is* innovative in describing the effects of weightlessness on the travellers, his understanding of the phenomenon remains incomplete. In no case, despite his idea, can the projectile remain at the 'neutral point' of gravity between the Earth and the Moon (which becomes a 'neutral line' in the second volume but should be a curved plane), because reaching it with zero speed is extremely improbable and would require an infinite time.

Verne is also mistaken in asserting that weightlessness only comes into play at the area of gravitational equilibrium between the Earth and the Moon, since it would in fact take effect as soon as the projectile is no longer undergoing deceleration, that is after leaving the atmosphere. Similarly, 'to hope that its velocity will be zero' (p. 288) at the neutral point on the way back is unrealistic, if only because it was not zero when it first passed through the point of equilibrium.

What is more, even at neutral gravity, Verne's liquids are not affected by weightlessness, as the travellers are able to pour and drink wine without incident. We now know that glasses cannot be filled in zero gravity conditions. Similarly, to say that 'the carbonic acid . . was massing towards the bottom of the projectile, because of its gravity' (p. 178) is incorrect.[10]

---

[10] 'What pleasure it would be to feel thus suspended in the ether' (p. 202), says Michel: because Verne realizes that weightlessness operates on the outside of the projectile, even

It is a slight exaggeration to assert that 'the light reflected by the Earth is . . . devoid of heat'; and fallacious to say that in a vacuum the projectile could be 'ignited by friction'; that any 'centrifugal forces' come into play when one object orbits another; that the reason for the scarcity of lunar atmosphere is probably its capture by the Earth; or that a body could be 'Held back by lunar attraction' (p. 255). The body of the dog would in fact continue to move away indefinitely after being thrown outside.

An elliptical orbit is not consistent with the speed of the projectile and its height above the lunar surface as given at various points; and would bring the projectile back to the same point in relation to the stars, but not to the Earth; in any case, after three days the neutral area would have moved about 40 degrees.

A body moves in an ellipse under the influence of a single central mass. But when revolving around the Moon, the influence of the Earth is also considerable: the orbit would not therefore be a simple ellipse (as modern astronauts have discovered).

Various aspects of the Moon itself, moreover, are not described entirely correctly. Although even at the time few people believed in active lunar volcanoes, Verne cannot resist including one. The production of bright explosions from volcanic eruptions would not imply the presence of oxygen.[11] It seems clear now—but only since the 1960s—that the craters were formed by impacts, not volcanic eruptions.

According to the 'latest observations of astronomers', claims Verne, but without naming them, the Moon retains 'a low, dense, thick atmosphere, at least in its deep valleys, and there streams and springs [cannot] be lacking'. Verne places air on the far side of the Moon, because the centre of gravity would be in the far hemisphere, given the Moon's egg-like shape, with a 'large end' and a 'small end'. We now know that the centre of lunar gravity is in fact located in the hemisphere closest to the Earth. His argument for the possibility of life on the Moon is based on an exaggerated observation 'that various

---

when not at the point of equilibrium, it would have been a small step to make the same deduction for objects inside. There are also a number of corresponding minor errors in the chapters where the Moon is orbited. As just one example, in the absence of atmospheric resistance, the projectile would not 'turn over' as it approaches the Moon.

[11] The belief that lunar volcanoes 'could themselves supply the oxygen necessary for combustion' was shared by few contemporary scientists.

aquatic insects, insensitive to temperature, are found . . . in springs of boiling water'. To temporarily illuminate the far side, Verne uses an exploding asteroid, even though in reality asteroids shatter only when they encounter an atmosphere or another object.

In sum, the book is far from free of scientific error, in both the details and the basic principles. Verne undoubtedly understands the improbability of some of his ideas, but surely prefers to retain them to make his story more dramatic and entertaining; his fiction remains surprisingly accurate overall, considering its date of composition.

In conclusion, then, it is for its literary values of entertainment and illumination of the human condition, rather than as a scientific treatise, that *Journey to the Moon* has survived and increased in popularity, as shown by the number of new editions.

If signs of satisfying literature are the depiction of conflict, for instance between the heroes and the elements, the use of witty dialogue, and an appropriate speed of delivery, then *Journey to the Moon* perfectly fits the bill. Many of the scientific expositions remain valid today; every scene with Ardan is entertaining; the density of literary allusion makes for a rich texture; and the story zips along, such is Verne's ability to turn scientific matters into vivid stories, and his memorable characters, his communicative enthusiasm, and his visual imagination (and so it must surely be eminently filmable?). Even some of the mistakes and misjudgements are amusing to spot in the light of modern knowledge. Written at the heart of Verne's most creative period, *Journey to the Moon* has entered the world's mythology. The reader who is new to the authentic story, published here in accurate, literary English, finally free from the Victorian accretions of most previous versions, is in for a treat.[12]

W.B.

[12] Thanks are due to Garmt de Vries for his scientific expertise and judicious advice; to Wim Thierens for his contribution to bibliography and to the circulation of scholarly work; and to Angel Lui for everything.

NOTE ON THE TEXT AND TRANSLATION

Any establishment of the text of *Journey to the Moon*, which must begin with a search for the 'best' edition published in Jules Verne's lifetime, unfortunately remains uncharted territory, as with almost all of his works.

The title of the present volume corresponds not only to what seems to be Verne's preferred form, '*Voyage à la Lune*', but also to his unwavering belief that the two published volumes, *From the Earth to the Moon* and *Around the Moon*, form a single unit, despite their fragmented publishing history. (Full information on the title and the unity of the work is provided in Appendix 1, 'Inception and Development of the Novel'.)

In the French editions to date, whether mass-market or specialized, the base text has always been a nineteenth-century grand-octavo edition published by Jules Hetzel, rather than one of his unillustrated sextodecimo (16mo) ones: a text that contains such eye-catching but wrong-headed images as 'lunar legions'—marching in formation across the '*the oceans of the* Moon' including their 'marshes'? The small-format editions, in contrast, can do no better than 'lunar regions', '*the oceans of the* Earth', and the 'tides' of the Moon (in French the term sounds similar to 'marshes'). The ultimate reason for the choice of the large-format edition (apart from simply borrowing Livre de Poche's first out-of-copyright edition of the 1960s) may be its fine engravings, lavish layout, and extensive promotion. However, the choice has never been justified in terms of the differences in the nineteenth-century texts.

For reasons explained in the section in Appendix 1 entitled 'The original editions' (pp. 318–19), the texts on which the present translation is based are the 10th 16mo edition of *From the Earth to the Moon* of 1871 and the 17th 16mo edition of *Around the Moon* of 1875.

The original versions of the work contain numerous spelling inconsistencies, including doublets such as 'Tallahassée' and 'Tallahassee' or 'pyroxyle' and 'pyroxile'. Spelling, above all that of the geographical and proper names, is corrected and modernized here, usually silently.

The numerous Author's Footnotes in the original editions, the majority of which add little for the modern reader, are omitted from the present edition.

This translation favours readability over a too-literal version: the aim is to employ the whole register of literary and spoken English, including formal and idiomatic expressions, as often as novels directly written in that language.

As regards terminology, historically the word '*météore*' included all smaller bodies visible in the sky. Verne also employs the term '*astéroïde*', which refers to a small body rotating around a planet or the sun. While these two terms are usually retained as such, '*bolide*', which strictly speaking means a small body entering the Earth's atmosphere and so becoming luminous, is translated here as 'meteor' or 'meteorite'.

Verne's mixture of 'imperial' and metric measures has been retained here. French feet are slightly larger than British ones but their miles are slightly shorter; Verne's leagues are usually 4 kilometres.

SELECT BIBLIOGRAPHY

Unless otherwise indicated, works are published in Paris or London; the publisher of pre-modern volumes is usually omitted.

Editions

Dahan, Jacques-Remi, *Autour de la Lune*, text established, presented, and annotated, in *'Voyage au Centre de la Terre' et autres romans* (Gallimard, Bibliothèque de la Pléiade, 2016) [useful notes and text-based presentation of the novel, but no establishment of the text and little study of its inception].

Dehs, Volker, translated and annotated, *Von der Erde zum Mond* (Artemis & Winkler, 2006) [generally accurate notes, but without information on the manuscripts or the editions, and some of the background material does not seem entirely relevant].

Ishibashi, Masataka, [*From the Earth to the Moon, Around the Moon,* and *The World Turned Upside-down* in Japanese], translated and annotated (Inscript, 2017), 978-4-900997-44-8 [publicity material claims the volume uses the last editions of the first two volumes; with intelligent notes and an informative presentation].

Miller, Walter James, translation, 'Introduction', 'Afterword', and notes in *From the Earth to the Moon* (New York: Crowell, 1978) [with excellent notes on the scientific aspects of the work, sometimes referred to here, but no knowledge of French studies. Although normally accurate, the translation occasionally adds extraneous material].

Scepi, Henri, *De la Terre à la Lune*, text established, presented, and annotated, in *'Voyage au Centre de la Terre' et autres romans* (Gallimard, Bibliothèque de la Pléiade, 2016) [as in this author's edition of *Twenty Thousand Leagues under the Seas*, judicious notes, but the presentation of the novel tends to the abstract; although the volume reproduces a few extracts from the manuscript of the work, the base text used is not the best one].

Verne, Jules, *Autour de la Lune* (Éditions des Saints Pères, 2019) [facsimile of the second manuscript of the second volume, but without any presentation material whatsoever].

Vierne, Simone, *De la Terre à la Lune* suivi de *Autour de la Lune*, 'Introduction', pp. 5–44, and 'Archives de l'œuvre' et 'Quelques jugements', pp. 444–53 (Garnier–Flammarion, 1978) [lively introduction but no other critical apparatus].

Studies

Badoureau, Albert, *Le Titan modern: Notes et observations remises à Jules Verne pour la rédaction de son roman 'Sans dessus dessous'* (Arles and Nantes: Actes Sud et Ville de Nantes, 2005), 64–73 [in 1888 this scientist sent Verne detailed notes on *From the Earth to the Moon* and *Around the Moon*: while failing to take into account the fictional nature of the tale, he is relatively critical of the scientific aspects, sometimes rightly so. His ideas are not incorporated into later Hetzel editions of *The Moon*; a few contribute to the endnotes of this edition].

Bradbury, Ray, 'Introduction', in William Butcher, *Verne's Journey to the Centre of the Self* (New York: Macmillan and St Martin's Press, 1990) [enthusiastic tribute to Verne's pioneering spirit].

Bulletin de la société Jules Verne, from the 1960s to the present. [Despite some fine articles, this periodical has been insufficiently 'broad-church'.]

Butcher, William, *Jules Verne inédit: Les manuscrits déchiffrés* (Lyon: ENS éditions and Institut d'histoire du livre, 2015), 137–45 and 205–18 [dense illustrated studies of the inception of *From the Earth to the Moon* and *Around the Moon*, especially the three manuscripts].

Charles, David, 'La Lune est dans le puits: une lecture politique de Jules Verne', *Romantisme*, 123 (2004), 95–104 [intelligent but ultimately doomed attempt to link the inception of *La Lune* with contemporary social and political events].

Clarke, Arthur C., 'Introduction', in *'From the Earth to the Moon' and 'Round the Moon'* (New York: Dodd, Mead and Company, 1962) [highlights Verne's inventiveness and pinpoints some errors].

Cook, David, 'En apesanteur dans le voyage de la Terre à la Lune', *Bulletin de la société Jules Verne*, 122 (1997), 40–3 [cogent analysis of the question of weightlessness].

Cook, David, 'Le Moment choisi pour faire tirer la Columbiad', *Bulletin de la société Jules Verne*, 117 (1996), 17–19 [lucidly presents errors].

Crovisier, Jacques, 'À propos de quelques sources pour la *Lune* de Jules Verne', *Verniana* 9 (2016), 43–56 [readable but unoriginal and incomplete].

Dahan, Jacques-Remi, '*Autour de la Lune*, ombres et lumières d'une genèse', *Revue d'histoire littéraire de la France* (2022, no. 4), 901–13 [informative and cogent, although the idea that the two volumes were written together is not entirely established].

Dumas, Olivier, and Eric Weissenberg, '*De la Terre à la Lune*, une prévision ignorée et accomplie', *Bulletin de la société Jules Verne*, 155 (2005), 53–7 [in the very first printing of *From the Earth to the Moon*, an ageing Lincoln is still president].

Ishibashi, Masataka, *Le Projet Verne et le système Hetzel* (Amiens: Encrage, 2015), *passim* [volume derived from a doctoral thesis that shows Hetzel's substantial role in the writing and promotion of the works: enlightening but slightly speculative and does not integrate into the main argument its groundbreaking transcriptions of extracts from Verne's manuscripts].

Lafleur, Laurence J., *Popular Astronomy*, 50 (1942), *passim* [accurate plot summary and good analysis of Verne's errors].

Martin, Charles-Noel, 'Les 9 erreurs de Jules Verne ou les jeux de la mécanique céleste', *Science et Vie, Magazine mensuel des sciences et de leurs applications à la vie moderne*, 115/618 (1969), 54–9 [description of mistakes in *Journey to the Moon*].

Sainlot, Claudine, 'Le Gun Club dans tous ses états', in *Jules Verne écrivain*, ed. Agnes Marcetteau-Paul (Nantes: Coffiard and Joca Seria, 2000), 51–65 [readable and well-informed analysis of the lunar manuscripts].

Vierne, Simone, 'Mais où sont les lunes d'antan? . . . ou la Lune et l'imaginaire chez Jules Verne', *Bulletin de la société Jules Verne*, 15 (1970), 142–51 [fine general study].

Main sources

In the margin of the first manuscript of vol. II, Verne cites these ten publications, apart from Guillemin's *La Lune*, in the edition noted here, while noting the page numbers of his borrowings. The volumes by Arago, Garcet, and Liais, as well as *Le Ciel* by Guillemin, were in Verne's personal library.

Arago, Francois, *Astronomie populaire* (Gide et Baudry) (vols 13–16 of his *Œuvres complètes*, ed. J.-A. Barral (Gide et Baudry, 1854–9 and 1862; contains 'La Lune', vol. 15, pp. 375–536).

Flammarion, Camille, *La Pluralité des mondes habités*, augmented edition (Didier, 1864; 1st edition Mallet-Bachelier, 1862).

Garcet, Henri, *Leçons nouvelles de cosmographie* (Dezobry et Magdeleine, 1853).

Guillemin, Amédée, *Le Ciel: Notions d'astronomie à l'usage des gens du monde et de la jeunesse* (Hachette, 1864).

Guillemin, Amédée, *La Lune* (Hachette, 1866).

Lecouturier, Henri, and Adolphe Chapuis, *La Lune: Description et topographie* (1860).

L'Illustration, no. 737 (1857), 'Tycho', pp. 234–8.

Liais, Emmanuel, *L'Espace céleste et la nature tropicale* (Garnier, 1865).

Moigno, Abbé François-Napoléon, *Physique moléculaire* (1868).

Vorepierre, Dupiney de, and Jean-François-Marie de Marcoux, eds, *Dictionnaire français illustré et encyclopédie* (1847–63, in two volumes; new edition, 1858–64).

Further Reading in Oxford World's Classics

Verne, Jules, *Around the World in Eighty Days*, ed. William Butcher.

Verne, Jules, *Journey to the Centre of the Earth*, ed. William Butcher.

Verne, Jules, *Twenty Thousand Leagues under the Seas*, ed. William Butcher.

A CHRONOLOGY OF JULES VERNE

1828 8 February: birth of Jules at 4 Rue Olivier de Clisson, Feydeau Island, Nantes. His parents are Pierre, a lawyer and son and grandson of lawyers, a reactionary and devout self-flagellator; and Sophie, née Allotte de la Fuÿe, Breton and artistic, from a shipowner and military line going back to an N. Allott, a Scottish archer ennobled by Louis XI.

1829 Birth of brother, Paul, later a naval officer then stockbroker; followed by those of sisters Anna (1836), Mathilde (1839), and Marie (1842).

1830 Jules hears the street battles of the July Revolution.

1833 First bucolic summer at probable former slave-runner Uncle Prudent Allotte's, together with the Tronson cousins, Henri, Edmond, Caroline, and Marie, all about the same age. Jules climbs trees with Paul; he will write 'invocations' (to God?) and dream of travel.

1834–8 Goes to boarding-school: the teacher, 67-year-old Marie-Élisabeth Sambin, is still waiting for her sea-captain husband after thirty years.

1836 Jules slips onto a three-master, breathes heady odours, and dreams of navigation. Henri and Edmond drown in the Loire River.

1837 The family rents a cottage overlooking the river in the village of Chantenay, where they will spend six months a year. Jules hires a leaky skiff and plays at Crusoe on a small island. With Paul, goes to St Stanislas boarding school, where he will receive merits in geography, translation from Greek and Latin, and singing.

1839 The boy perhaps runs away on board the *Octavia*, heading for 'the Indies', to be caught by his father at Paimbœuf.

1840 Boarding at St Donatien Junior Seminary, with friends Aristide Hignard and Adolphe Bonamy. Composes prayers, pastiches, acrostics, and poems. The family moves to Rue Jean-Jacques Rousseau.

1842 His father prints two poems about Jules's love for the Loire, envisaging a future for him as a 'scholar rather than a captain'.

1843–5 Attends Lycée Royal de Nantes, but falls a year behind. Is in love with cousin Caroline; the two families discuss marriage.

1846 Passes *baccalauréat* in humanities 'with credit'. Studies law at home, since his father wishes to pass his practice to him.

1847   Pierre does not allow Jules to sign up as a naval officer cadet. First-year law exams in Paris. Passion for Herminie Arnault-Grossetière, dedicating many poems to her. During this period, completes a novel, *A Priest in 1835*, and a tragedy, *Alexander VI*.

1848   Continues his law studies, sharing a room at 24 Rue de l'Ancienne-Comédie in the heart of the Latin Quarter. His uncle François Châteaubourg takes him to literary salons. Through the chiromancer Casimir d'Arpentigny, meets Alexandre Dumas *père* and *fils*.

1849   Passes law degree and avoids conscription.

1850   Has composed about twenty comedies and tragedies, including *La Conspiration des poudres*. 12 June: his one-act comedy *Les Pailles rompues* runs for fourteen nights at Dumas's Théâtre Historique and is published.

1851   Publishes 'Les Premiers navires de la Marine mexicaine' and 'Un Voyage en ballon'. Works as a bank clerk and private tutor. Is hired as a notarial clerk, but his employer immediately dies. Moves to Boulevard Bonne Nouvelle, opposite Hignard's room.

1852–5 Is appointed secretary of the Théâtre Lyrique. Publishes 'Martin Paz', 'Maître Zacharius', 'Un Hivernage dans les glaces', and the play *Les Châteaux en Californie*. His operetta *Le Colin-maillard* is performed to music by Hignard. Is rejected by a series of young women and visits brothels.

1856   Goes to a wedding in Amiens, and meets a young widow with two children, Honorine de Viane.

1857   10 January: marries Honorine; becomes an assistant stockbroker, and moves several times. Publication of art criticism *Salon de 1857*.

1859–60 Is greatly marked by a journey with Hignard to Edinburgh, the Highlands, and London. Writes *Voyage en Angleterre et en Écosse* and *Paris au XXᵉ siècle*.

1861–2 Birth of only child, Michel, while Verne is absent on a decisive trip to Norway. Writes *Joyeuses misères de trois voyageurs en Scandinavie*. The anglophile boys' writer Alfred de Bréhat introduces him to Jules Hetzel. The publisher orders proofs for his book about Britain, but then rejects it. Signature of a contract for 'Voyage en l'air', a work about ballooning.

1863   22 January: *Cinq semaines en ballon* is published. At this time, Hetzel categorically rejects *Paris in the Twentieth Century*.

1864   A second contract, Hetzel again keeping five-sixths of the profits. In his new *Magasin d'éducation et de récréation*, beginning of serial publication of *Aventures du capitaine Hatteras*, from which Hetzel deletes the Anglo-American duel on an ice-floe and the final suicide of the hero. (The endings of all Verne's famous novels are altered by the publisher, with many chapters deleted.) Publication of 'Edgar Poe et ses œuvres' and *Voyage au centre de la Terre*.

1865 *De la Terre à la Lune* and *Les Enfants du capitaine Grant*. At this time, visits Italy with Hetzel.

1866 Moves to the fishing village of Le Crotoy.

1867 Goes with brother Paul to Liverpool, then on board the *Great Eastern* to the United States.

1868 Has a boat built, the *St Michel*. Travels with Hetzel to Baden-Baden and to the Riviera. A fourth contract stipulates thirty volumes within ten years; Verne buys shares in Hetzel's company. Michel is proving difficult. Joins a lively musical dining club, the Onze sans Femmes.

1869 Rents a house in Amiens. *Vingt mille lieues sous les mers* and *Autour de la Lune*.

1870 Hetzel sharply criticizes *L'Oncle Robinson*. Sails up the Seine to see his mistress in Paris. In a manuscript, logs his intimate difficulties, together with the initial 'M'. During the Franco-Prussian War, Verne is in the National Guard at Le Crotoy.

1871 Briefly returns to the Stock Exchange. Father dies.

1872 Moves to 44 Boulevard Longueville, Amiens, and becomes member of the Académie d'Amiens. *Le Tour du monde en quatre-vingts jours*. Makes his ninth and tenth trips to the British Isles.

1873–4 *Le Docteur Ox*, *L'Île mystérieuse* and *Le Chancellor*. Begins collaboration with Adolphe d'Ennery on remunerative stage adaptations of *Le Tour du monde en 80 jours* and, later, *Michel Strogoff*.

1876–7 *Michel Strogoff*, *Hector Servadac*, and *Les Indes noires*, the publisher writing several chapters. Buys second and third boats, also called the *St Michel*. Gives huge fancy-dress ball. Wife critically ill, but recovers. Places Michel in a reformatory. Encouraged by Dumas *fils*, Verne dreams of membership of the French Academy.

1878 June–August: sails to Lisbon and Algiers.

1879–80 *Les Cinq cents millions de la Begum*, *Les Tribulations d'un Chinois en China*, and *La Maison à vapeur*. Verne sails to Edinburgh and visits the Hebrides. Settles Michel's debts while expelling him, to live with an actress.

1881 *La Jangada*. Sails to Rotterdam and Copenhagen.

1882 *Le Rayon vert*. Moves to a larger house at 2 Rue Charles Dubois, Amiens.

1883–4 *Kéraban-le-têtu.* Michel abducts a minor, and has two children
        with her within eleven months. Verne and his wife do a grand tour of
        the Mediterranean, and he is received by Pope Leo XIII.

1885   *Mathias Sandorf.* Sells the third *St Michel*.

1886   *Robur the Conqueror.* 9 March: his mentally-disturbed nephew
        Gaston asks for money. Verne refuses, and is fired at twice, laming
        him for life. Hetzel dies.

1887   Mother dies.

1888   Elected local councillor on a republican list. For the next fifteen
        years he will attend council meetings, administer the theatre and
        fairs, and give public talks.

1889   *Sans dessus dessous* (*Topsy-Turvy*) and 'En l'an 2889' (signed Jules
        Verne but written by Michel).

1892   *Le Château des Carpathes.* Pays debts for Michel.

1893–4 Sales fall.

1895   *L'Île à helice*, apparently the first European novel in the present
        tense and third person.

1896–7 *Face au drapeau* and *Le Sphinx des glaces*. Sued by chemist Turpin,
        who recognizes himself in *Face au Drapeau*, but successfully defended
        by Raymond Poincaré. Health deteriorates; brother dies.

1899   Verne is anti-Dreyfusard in the Dreyfus Affair.

1900   Moves back to 44 Boulevard Longueville. Sight weakens with
        cataracts.

1901   *Le Village aérien.*

1904   *Maître du monde.*

1905   Falls seriously ill from diabetes. 24 March: dies, and is buried in
        Amiens.

1905–14 On Verne's death, *L'Invasion de la mer* and *Le Phare du bout du
        monde* are in the course of publication. Michel takes responsibility
        and also publishes *Le Volcan d'or* (1906), *L'Agence Thompson and Co.*
        (1907), *La Chasse au météore* (1908), *Le Pilote du Danube* (1908), *Les
        Naufragés du 'Jonathan'* (1909), *Le Secret de Wilhelm Storitz* (1910),
        Hier et Demain (short stories, including 'L'Éternel Adam') (1910),
        and *L'Étonnante aventure de la mission Barsac* (1914); he wrote
        considerable sections of these works.

CHRONOLOGY OF THE WRITING
OF *JOURNEY TO THE MOON*

1864

January   A new contract between Hetzel and Verne does not mention *De la Terre a la Lune*.

12 Aug.   Verne writes to Hetzel 'I'm working hard to please you', implying that the original idea of *La Lune* may owe much to the publisher.

Aug. or Sept.?   He writes to Nadar: 'I'm portraying a man . . . with the best and boldest heart and, I beg your pardon, I've taken you as the model.'

About Sept.   Completion of the surviving manuscript of *From the Earth to the Moon*.

Oct.?   Verne has already thought of an aluminium projectile and a first 'animal experiment'.[1] 'How did M. Bertrand, to whom we told our story, not tell us that Newton had the idea of sending a projectile to the Moon?'[2]

Oct. and Nov.   The publisher writes comments on the manuscript, then adds further notes after Verne's revision.

After the turn of the year?   Preparation of the surviving proofs.

1865

Spring   1st impression (16mo), of a handful of copies.

15 Apr.   Assassination of Abraham Lincoln.

About 28 Apr.   'What a catastrophe! What are you doing about *The Moon*?'

19 May   Hetzel seems to have sent the French National Library a copy of the 1st printing.

20 May   *De la Terre à la Lune* announced in the *Bibliographie de la France*.

---

[1] 'Am I using aluminium! No choice! I've studied it—our cannonball's finished! It'll cost us 300,000 francs! . . . a ~~rabbit~~ dog and a squirrel . . . We'll talk about it.'

[2] Republican politician and specialist in number theory and thermodynamics Joseph Bertrand (1822–1900) was the author of *Les Fondateurs de l'astronomie moderne* (Hetzel, 1865), a work in Captain Nemo and Verne's libraries. It is not clear if both writer and editor ('we') spoke to Bertrand on this occasion. In an interview in 1887, Verne emphasized his assistance with his novels: 'Joseph Bertrand of the Institute had been his adviser on many occasions'. The manuscript similarly claims Newton thought of sending a cannonball to the Moon: in fact, *Principles of Natural Philosophy* (1687) merely discusses, in theoretical terms, the idea of firing a cannonball into orbit round the Earth.

26 May   End of the US Civil War.

May or June   Verne sends a copy to collaborator Charles Wallut, noting in it with reference to the passage about Lincoln: 'all this has been changed by the detestable assassination of the President'. Another copy is given to Camille Flammarion.[3]

14 Sept.–14 Oct.   *From the Earth to the Moon* appears in the newspaper *Journal des débats politiques et littéraires* (henceforth *Débats*).

25 Oct.   Publication of the 16mo edition.

Nov.   Hetzel stresses the novel's scientific aspects in the *Magasin d'éducation et de récréation*.[4]

11 Dec.   A contract between Hetzel and Verne refers to *From the Earth to the Moon*, but not to a second volume; the contract of 8 May 1868 will be similar.

1866

17 Feb.   While praising the book's literary aspect, reviewer André Lefèvre regrets that the plot does not go further.[5]

23 Aug.   In a review of Verne's first five novels, including *From the Earth to the Moon*, Victor Chauvin seems to have knowledge of the second lunar volume.[6]

1868

Nov. or Dec.   Verne begins writing the second volume.[7]

31 Dec.   He has already discussed it with Hetzel: 'I'm working like crazy . . . on our *Return from the Moon*.'

[3] Piero Gondolo della Riva, 'Camille Flammarion, lecteur de *De la Terre à la Lune*', *Bulletin de la société Jules Verne*, 122 (1997), 44.

[4] Vol. 4, p. 223. 'A writer . . . who puts as many treasures of imagination at the service of the most precise science as ten other novelists . . . There exists a readership eager for knowledge and for works that carry the imprint of modern times . . .'

[5] The 'successor' of Cyrano de Bergerac and Poe, he writes, 'is a pleasing scholar who strives to smuggle the most indisputable data of the exact sciences into youthful or idle brains' (*L'Illustration*, 107).

[6] He writes of the 'unforeseen obstacle' that stops the voyagers from reaching their original goal and their consequent 'semi-success': an accurate if brief description of the first encounter with a meteor in the 2nd volume? ('Voyages imaginaires', *Revue de l'instruction publique*, 326–7). Chauvin also wishes the journey can have a happy ending.

[7] Arguing that because Verne does not refer explicitly to the first manuscript of the second volume in his letters, because Ardan is often called 'Nadar' in it, and because the decisive encounter with the first meteor is a late addition, Dahan ('*Autour de la Lune*', 902) claims that the two volumes must have been drafted together.

1869

1st week of Jan.   'I'm immersed in the 2nd volume of *The Moon*, i.e. the return of our brave voyagers, and I'm so deeply plunged in it that I can't get out again . . . What strange and surprising things the subject throws up.'

17 Feb.   He is completely absorbed 'by the 2nd volume of *Twenty Thousand Leagues* and the 2nd volume of *The Moon*'. (Until mid-June, Verne will continue working hard on *Twenty Thousand Leagues*.)

About 21 Feb.   Completion of the first manuscript of vol. 1.

23 Apr.   'I'm slogging at [the fair copy of] *Return from the Moon*'.

7? June   Verne sends the second manuscript of vol. 2 to Hetzel: 'everything we know about [the Moon], all related questions, are covered. It's . . . often, I believe, very daring.'

28? June   He receives an encouraging and constructive letter from the publisher; but in his reply describes the volume as 'insufficiently serial-like'.[8]

30? June   While pointing out an instance in *Around the Moon* of '*May God preserve us*', Verne agrees to address a perceived lack of religion.[9]

1st week of July?   Hetzel sends corrections, which Verne describes as 'all . . . perfect'.

last week of July?   He incorporates many new suggestions from Hetzel.

Summer?   Henri Garcet[10] revises ch. 4 of the volume, and conceivably other parts.

Aug.   Verne sends the manuscript for typesetting.

1st half of Sept.?   He writes the missing last chapter; and corrects 16mo proofs.

Oct.   Verne has made the final corrections to the first ten chapters in proofs.

4 Nov.   *Around the Moon* begins to appear in the *Débats* (until 8 December).

1870

12 or 13 Jan.   Publication of vol. 2 in 16mo ('announced' in the *Bibliographie de la France* of 12 February—the grand-octavo edition

---

[8] Not light enough reading, not suitable for being cut into segments, or of too-variable chapter length (I 17 is one page long)?

[9] He will replace the phrase '*thanks to* the passage of time' with 'thanks to God . . .' (ch. 21). There are in fact several mentions of 'God' in the two volumes, but some imply that His Creation is imperfect or incomplete.

[10] Verne's first cousin (1815–71), Bertrand's collaborator, teacher of advanced mathematics at the Lycée Henri IV (then the Lycée Napoléon) and author of *Leçons nouvelles de cosmographie* (1853) and *Éléments de mécanique* (1856).

will come out only on 16 September 1872, preceded by 23 '*livraisons*' (issues) from about July).[11]

Mar.   Two unfavourable reviews of *De la Terre à la Lune* appear in Britain: 'The jokes . . . are unjustifiably heavy-handed'; 'M. Jules Verne almost goes beyond the proper limits of the ludicrous'.[12]

1st week of May?   Verne repeatedly requests acknowledgement of receipt for his corrections to the 'final proofs of the octavo *Around the Moon*'.

1872

End of the year   In his catalogue, Hetzel writes: '*From the Earth to the Moon* is a cheerful, humorous work which is also a book of impeccable positive science. There is nothing more engaging than the story of all the preparations for a visit to our satellite . . . [and] nothing more curious than the account of the return of the voyagers in the second part, *Around the Moon*.'[13]

1875

Early Nov.   Verne complains to Hetzel that the opera *Voyage à la Lune* by Albert Vanloo and Eugene Leterrier, with music by Offenbach, plagiarizes *Journey to the Centre of the Earth* and *From the Earth to the Moon*; but the matter is not pursued.

---

[11]   *Livraisons* were 8-page extracts from the illustrated octavo edition, published before the full volume.

[12]   *The Saturday Review* (5 Mar. 1870), 327–8; *The Westminster Review* (Jan.–Apr. 1870), 634.

[13]   Although here he presents *Around the Moon* as the 'second part'—while inserting a spoiler—later in the same catalogue he refers to 'two distinct . . . works'; his other catalogues sometimes describe the second volume as a 'sequel'.

JOURNEY TO THE MOON

CONTENTS

PART II. AROUND THE MOON

PART I

FROM THE EARTH
TO THE MOON

THE GUN CLUB

DURING the Federal War in the United States,* a new and highly influential club opened its doors in the town of Baltimore, in the heart of Maryland. Now, who does not know with what energy the military instinct flourished at the time amongst that people of shipowners, merchants, and engineers?* Ordinary shopkeepers leapt over their counters and changed into captains, colonels, and generals, without undergoing any military training at West Point. In 'the art of war',* they quickly proved a match for their counterparts of the Old Continent and, like them, they won victories by using lavish amounts of cannonballs, money, and men.

But where the Americans proved markedly superior to their European colleagues was in the science of gunnery. Not that the weapons they produced were more advanced, but they came in unusual dimensions, which meant that their ranges exceeded anything that had been witnessed before. As regards grazing and plunging fire, direct shelling, oblique, raking, and reverse-ricochet artillery fire, the British, French, and Prussians have nothing further to learn. But their cannons, howitzers, and mortars are not much more than pocket pistols compared with the mighty field-guns of the American artillery.

This should come as a surprise to no one. The Yankees—the finest artificers in the world—are engineers in the way the Italians are musicians and the Germans are metaphysicians: it is their birthright. So nothing could be more natural than to see them apply their daring inventiveness to the science of ballistics. Hence the gigantic cannons which, though far less useful than sewing machines, were no less astonishing—and even more admired. Among them, the prodigies of Parrott, Dahlgren, and Rodman[1] are well known and the likes of Armstrong, Palliser, and Treuille de Beaulieu were left with no choice but to yield to their transatlantic rivals.

As a result, in that terrible struggle between North and South, the gunners lorded it over the rest: the Union's journalists saluted their

---

[1] Details of authentic proper names, except where they are directly relevant to the Explanatory Notes, are grouped together in Appendix 2: 'Proper Names Cited by Verne'.

inventions with enthusiasm and there was no shopkeeper so mean, no booby so naive, but racked his brains night and day calculating preposterous trajectories.

Now when an American gets an idea, he looks round for another American to share it with. If there are three of them, they elect a chairman and two secretaries. When there are four, they appoint a clerk to keep the records and the office can function. If there are five, they call a general meeting and the club comes into proper existence. And so it came to pass in Baltimore. The first man to invent a new gun joined forces with the man who cast it and the man who bored out the barrel. This was the nucleus of the Gun Club. A month after it was set up, it had 1,833 full members and 30,575 corresponding subscribers.

One indispensable condition was imposed on anyone applying to join the association, which was that he should have designed a cannon, or at least improved the design of one. Or if not a cannon, then some other kind of firearm. To be frank, inventors of fifteen-shot revolvers, swivel guns, and combined pistol-sabres got short shrift. Artillery men were given precedence in every circumstance.

'The regard in which they are held', said one of the most learned members of the Gun Club, varies according to 'the bore of their cannon' and 'in direct ratio to the square of the distances attained by the shells they have fired'.

Anything more and it would have been Newton's law of universal gravitation* applied to the world of human affairs.

Once the Gun Club was established, what the inventive genius of the Americans produced may easily be imagined. Field guns attained colossal proportions and their projectiles exceeded permitted limits and sliced harmless walkers in half. All these inventions far outperformed the modest weapons used by European artillery. The reader may judge just how far from the following figures.

Once, 'in the good old days', at a range of 300 feet, a 36-pounder could cut through sixty-eight men and thirty-six horses side by side. But that was nothing. Since then, missiles have made huge strides. The Rodman gun, capable of firing a cannonball weighing half a ton over a distance of seven miles, could without difficulty account for 150 horse and 300 men. It was even mooted at the Gun Club that a full test-firing should be staged. But if the horses readily agreed to take part, the men unfortunately failed to step up to the mark.

Be that as it may, the impact of these guns was deadly and with every shot fired, swathes of combatants were mown down like grass beneath the scythe. Compared with such missiles, what is there to say about the famous cannonball which put twenty-five men out of action at Coutras in 1587, or the projectile which killed forty infantrymen at Zorndorf in 1758, or indeed about the Austrian cannon at Kesselsdorf in 1742, which flattened seventy enemies each time it was fired?* What to add about those amazing types of guns at Iena or Austerlitz* which decided the outcome of the battles in question? But a good many other guns were seen in action during the Federal War. At the Battle of Gettysburg,* a conical projectile fired by a rifled cannon mowed down 173 Confederate soldiers; and at the Crossing of the Potomac, a single Rodman cannonball dispatched 215 Southerners into the next and evidently better world. Mention should also be made of a formidable mortar invented by J. T. Maston,* a member of the Gun Club and its permanent secretary, the effect of which was lethal to a greater degree because, when first tested, it killed 337—by blowing up, it is true.

What more is there to say when these figures speak so eloquently for themselves? Nothing. And so we accept without demur the following calculation made by the statistician Pitcairn: dividing the number of victims killed by cannon fire by the number of members of the Gun Club, he found that each of them for his part had killed 'on average' 2,375 and a fraction men.

When we consider such a figure, it is perfectly clear that the sole concern of that learned society was the destruction of humanity, with a philanthropic end in view, namely the perfecting of weapons of war deemed to be instruments of civilization. It was a consortium of Exterminating Angels,* and they were in fact the nicest fellows you could hope to meet.

We should add that these Yankees, fearless in the face of any danger, did not confine themselves to theory but paid for their inventions with their lives. Among their number were officers of every rank, from lieutenants to generals, soldiers of all ages, some just setting out on their army careers and others growing old at their posts. Many had found their last resting places on the field of battle with their names inscribed on the Gun Club's roll of honour. Of those who returned, most bore the marks of their undeniable valour. Crutches, wooden legs, articulated arms, hooks for hands, rubber jaws, silver skulls, platinum noses, all were represented in the collection, and the afore-mentioned Pitcairn further calculated that in the Gun Club there was not quite one arm for every four men, and just two legs between every six of them.

But those dauntless gunners did not dwell on such things and felt justifiably proud whenever news of a battle reported lists of casualties that were ten times greater than the number of missiles fired.

But on one sad, grim day, peace was signed by the survivors of the conflict. The sound of explosions slowly died away, the mortars fell silent, howitzers were muzzled indefinitely and down-at-mouth can-nons were returned to artillery depots, missiles were piled high in parks, memories of bloodshed faded, the cotton plants flourished in well-fertilized fields, mourning clothes were finally worn out together with the grieving, and the Gun Club was plunged into a state of pro-found idleness.

Some keen types, of the beavering sort, went on devoting them-selves to ballistic calculations. They continued to dream of gigantic bombs, of shells in a class of their own. But without field trials, what was the point of their paper prototypes? As a result, meeting rooms became deserted, servants dozed in antechambers, newspapers were left to moulder on tables, dark corners rumbled with disconsolate snores, and the members of the Gun Club, once so exuberant but henceforth reduced to silence by the disaster that was peace, nodded off into dreams of Platonic forms of artillery.

'It's so depressing,' said good Tom Hunter one evening as his wooden legs slowly charred in the fire of the smoking room. 'Nothing to do! Nothing to look forward to! Life is so tedious! Whatever hap-pened to the time when you were woken each morning by the noise of cannon-fire that gladdened the heart?'

'Long gone,' answered the dashing Bilsby as he tried to stretch arms he no longer had. 'Those were the days! You invented your shell and no sooner was it cast than off you trotted to test it on the enemy. Then you came back with a pat on the back from Sherman or McClellan!* But today, the generals are back behind their shop coun-ters and instead of missiles they just dispatch harmless bales of cot-ton! By Jove, there's no future for guns and gunners in America!'

'Quite right, Bilsby,' exclaimed Colonel Blomsberry. 'It's all a cruel let-down. One day you abandon your quiet way of life, are trained to handle weapons, swap Baltimore for battlefields, behave like heroes and two or three years later, you reap none of the benefits of your efforts and have to slumber in a slough of god-awful indolence and keep your hands in your pockets!'

For all his talk, the valiant Colonel would have been quite unable to enact his indolence in that precise way, though it was not in pockets that he was deficient.

'And no sign of a war in prospect!' said the celebrated J. T. Maston as he used his iron hook to scratch his gutta-percha cranium. 'Not a cloud on the horizon despite there being so much still to be done in the science of ballistics! But I tell you now that this very morning I completed a design—with plan, section and elevation—for a mortar which will change the laws of war!'

'Really?' said Tom Hunter, as the thought of the last test conducted by the honourable J. T. Maston swam unbidden into his mind.

'Really!' came the reply. 'But what is the point of all these ideas even when they are tested successfully and all the problems have been ironed out? Is all the effort not an utter waste of time? The peoples of the New World seem to have come round to the view that we should live in peace, and the belligerent *Tribune* is already predicting imminent disaster caused by the scandalous growth of population!'

'Yet, Maston,' said Colonel Blomsberry, 'they are still going to war over in Europe to defend the idea of the nation.'

'Your point?'

'My point is that there may be an opening for us over there, and if our services were accepted . . .'

'Are you serious?' exclaimed Bilsby. 'You want us to continue working on ballistics so that foreigners can reap the benefit?'

'Better than abandoning ballistic work altogether!' retorted the colonel.

'Agreed,' said J. T. Maston, 'it would be better. But such a course of action is not to be contemplated.'

'And why not?' asked the Colonel.

'Because back in the Old World they have ideas about progress which are completely different to our American way of doing things. Over there, they cannot conceive that a man can become general-in-chief unless he has first served as a second lieutenant, which amounts to saying that a man cannot point a cannon unless he's cast it himself! So it's quite simply . . .'

'Absurd!' retorted Tom Hunter, whittling away at the arms of his easy chair with his Bowie knife.* 'But if that's the way things are, all that's left for us to do is plant tobacco or distil whale-oil.'

'What?' boomed J. T. Maston. 'Not spend the last years of our lives trying to make better firearms? Not have any new opportunity of testing how far our missiles will carry? Not light up the sky with the lightning of our cannons? Not have an international crisis that would allow us to declare war on some transatlantic power? Not witness the French sinking one of our steamships, or the British riding rough-shod over the law of nations, and hanging three of our nationals?'

'No, Maston,' answered Colonel Blomsberry. 'We'll have no such luck! No! Not one of those eventualities will arise and were it to, we should not gain by it. America's susceptibility is diminishing with every day that passes. We're going to the dogs!'

'Yes, we are doing ourselves down!' said Bilsby.

'We are being done down by others!' said Tom Hunter.

'All that is only too true,' replied J. T. Maston with renewed passion. 'There are many reasons these days for fighting and yet we are not fighting anybody! We have to make do without arms and legs and who has benefited? Why, those who already have more of both than they know what to do with! Look, I'm not scratching round for a reason for going to war, but did North America not once belong to the British?'

'Sure did,' said Tom Hunter as he poked the fire savagely with the end of his crutch.

'Well,' resumed J. T. Maston, 'why shouldn't it be Britain's turn to belong to the Americans?'

'That would be only right and fair,' said Colonel Blomsberry.

'But just you try telling that to the President of the United States,' cried J. T. Maston, 'and see how far you get!'

'Not very far at all,' muttered Bilsby, gritting the four teeth he had managed to bring back from the field of battle.

'By God!' said J. T. Maston, 'he can't count on my vote when election time comes round!'

'Nor on mine,' chorused the disabled veterans with one voice.

'In the meantime,' said J. T. Maston, 'and to conclude, if I am not given permission to try out my new mortar in a real battle, I shall resign as a member of the Gun Club, and go and bury myself in the grasslands of Arkansas!'

'And we'll follow you,' answered the audience of the intrepid J. T. Maston.

Things having reached that point, tempers rose higher and higher until the Club was staring imminent closure in the face when a totally unexpected event arose which averted that most unfortunate disaster.

The very day after this discussion took place, each Club member received a circular worded as follows:

Baltimore, 3 October,

The President of the Gun Club has the honour of giving notice to colleagues that at the meeting scheduled for the 5th instant, he will lay before them a matter which will be of considerable interest to all. Accordingly, he asks them to set aside all other business and accept the invitation to attend which is extended by this note.

Their faithful colleague,
Impey Barbicane*
President of the Gun Club

2

PRESIDENT BARBICANE'S ADDRESS

On 5 October, at 8 p.m., a great press of people crowded into the assembly rooms of the Gun Club at 21 Union Square. All the members who lived in Baltimore had responded to the invitation issued by their president. As for out-of-town members, express trains released them by the hundred onto the city's streets. But large as it was, the auditorium could not accommodate so numerous an influx of scientific experts. They overflowed into adjoining rooms, occupied hallways, and spilled out into outside courtyards. There they rubbed shoulders with ordinary citizens who crowded round the doors, each straining to get to the front* and all eager to hear President Barbicane's important statement, pushing, jostling, crushing each other with that freedom of action which characterizes the populace when it is raised on the idea of 'self-government'.

That evening, a casual stranger finding himself in Baltimore would not have been able at any price to get into the main hall, which was reserved for the exclusive use of members living locally or out of town. No one else was allowed in, and even the city's leading citizens, its councillors and elected officers had no choice but to join the throng of those they governed if they were to catch any stray crumb of whatever would be said inside.

However, the vast chamber alone was a most impressive spectacle. An immense space, it was magnificently suited to the purpose for which it was built. Tall columns made of cannons stacked one upon the other and resting on a base of heavy mortars supported the delicate ceiling arches, a series of exquisitely worked panels of cast-iron lacework. Ornate displays of blunderbusses, musketoons, arquebuses, carbines, and all manner of firearms ancient and modern were arranged trophy-like on the walls in eye-catching displays. Gaslight flared from innumerable revolvers got up to look like gasoliers while chandeliers made of pistols and candelabras formed of sheaves of muskets reinforced the intensity of the lighting. Models of cannons, specimens of bronze castings, gunsights dented by bullets, sections of steel plate pierced by Gun Club shot, assorted rammers and barrel brushes, racks of bombs, strings of missiles, garlands of shells, in short all the tools of the artilleryman's trade so struck the eye in this staggering exhibition that it prompted the thought that their ultimate function was more decorative than lethal.

In the place of honour, inside a splendid glass case, was part of a breech, shivered and twisted by gunpowder blast, a sacred relic of J. T. Maston's cannon.

At the far end of the hall, the president and four secretaries occupied a wide raised platform. His chair, set upon a carved gun-carriage, gave a general impression of the powerful outlines of a 32-inch mortar. It was set at an angle of 90° and suspended on trunnions in such a way that the president could, as with a rocking chair, set it seesawing in the most agreeable manner when the weather was hot. On his desk— an immense rectangle of sheet iron supported on six carronades— could be seen an inkstand of exquisite taste made out of a prettily chased cartridge case, and a shot-warning signal which, as and when required, would go off like a revolver. When discussions grew heated, however, this new-style bell could barely be heard over the voices of a company of over-excited gunners.

In front of the desk, rows of seats in zigzag formation—like the circumvallations of an entrenchment—made a succession of bastions and curtains where the members of the Gun Club took their seats, so it could be truly said that the place was bulging at the seams. The president was sufficiently well known for it to be clear to all that he would not have put colleagues to the inconvenience of attending without some very good reason indeed.

Impey Barbicane was a man of forty years of age, calm, cool, and austere, eminently serious and reserved; punctual as a stopwatch,* of imperturbable temperament and unshakeable character; not intrepid yet adventurous and applying practical ideas even to the riskiest enterprises. He was the embodiment of the New Englander, a Northern settler, a descendant of the Roundheads who had spelled death to the Stuarts, and the implacable foe of Southern gentlemen— the sometime Cavaliers* of the mother-country. In short, a Yankee through and through.

Barbicane had made a large fortune in the timber trade. Promoted to Director of Artillery during the Civil War, he had shown considerable inventiveness. Bold in his ideas, he made a massive contribution to the development of that branch of the armed services and gave unparalleled backing for experimental research in that area.

He was a man of average height and—a rare exception in the Gun Club—still had a full set of limbs. His strongly-marked features might have been made using a set square and a ruling-pen, and if it is true that a man's character may be known by examining his profile, then Barbicane, viewed from that angle, displayed the clearest signs of energy, boldness, and self-possession.

At that moment, he was sitting perfectly still in his chair, silent, engrossed, entirely lost in his thoughts under a tall top hat, one of those black silk cylinders which always look as if they have been screwed onto American heads.

Around him his colleagues were talking noisily but failing to catch his attention. They were asking questions of each other, launching into fields of speculation, and eyed their president as they tried—in vain—to penetrate the riddle of his inscrutable face.

But when the clock in the great hall thunderously sounded eight, Barbicane was suddenly on his feet as if released by some hidden spring. A general hush descended and the orator, affecting a somewhat formal tone of voice, began to speak in these terms:

'Esteemed colleagues, for too long now a barren peace has driven members of the Gun Club into a regrettable state of forced inactivity. After a period of a few years full of incident, we have been obliged to abandon our labours, brought to a standstill on the road to progress.

I do not hesitate to state publicly that any war which would call us to take up arms would be welcome . . .'

'Yes! War!' cried the combustible J. T. Maston.

'Quiet! Just listen!' he was told on all sides.

'But war,' said Barbicane, 'war is out of the question in the current climate. Whatever hopes my honourable heckler might have, many long years will pass before our cannons can thunder once more on the field of battle. We must therefore accept what we cannot change and seek another area of operations to satisfy our hunger for action.'

The entire room sensed that its President was about to reach the crux of his address and became increasingly attentive.

'For some months now, dear colleagues,' Barbicane resumed, 'I have been asking myself if, while staying within our area of specialization, we might not undertake some great venture worthy of the nineteenth century, and whether our advances in the science of ballistics might not allow us to make that venture a reality. I have therefore reflected, worked, and calculated and my studies have led me to the conclusion that we can succeed in an enterprise which would appear impossible to any other nation. This project, which has been long in the making, is the subject of my address. It is worthy of you, worthy of the Gun Club's history, and it will not fail to make some noise in the world.'

'A great noise?' cried one doting gunner.

'A very great noise—in the true sense of the word,' replied Barbicane.

'Stop interrupting!' came several voices.

'Please, colleagues,' resumed the President, 'please give me your full attention!'

A tremor ran through the audience. After settling his hat on his head with a swift gesture using one hand, Barbicane went on coolly with his speech:

'There is not one among you, colleagues, who has never seen the Moon, or at any rate heard of it. Do not be surprised if I now turn to talk to you about the Eye of Night. It could well be that we have been chosen to be the Christopher Columbuses of that unknown world. Listen closely to what I say, back me to the hilt, and I will lead you to its conquest and its name shall be added to those of the thirty-six states* that make up our great Union!'

'Three cheers for the Moon!' cried the Gun Club with a common accord.

'The Moon has been broadly studied,' went on Barbicane. 'Its mass, density, weight, volume, composition, motion, its distances from other heavenly bodies, its role in the Solar System have all been accurately measured. Selenographical maps have been drawn with an accuracy which equals, if it does not surpass, maps of the Earth. Photography has provided incontrovertible evidence of the incomparable beauty of our satellite. In short, we know everything about the Moon that mathematical sciences, astronomy, geology, and optics can teach us. But until now, no direct communication has ever been established with it.'

The speaker's last observation was greeted by a great surge of interest and surprise.

'But allow me,' he continued, 'to remind you briefly of the way in which some bolder spirits, launched on imaginary travels, claimed to have pierced the secrets of our satellite. In the seventeenth century, a man named David Fabricius* boasted of having seen inhabitants of the Moon with his own eyes. In 1649, a Frenchman called Jean Baudoin published a *Voyage to the World of the Moon, by Dominique Gonzales, a Spanish Adventurer.* At about the same time appeared Cyrano de Bergerac's famous expedition there, which was such a great success in France. Later, another Frenchman—the Moon holds a particular fascination for that nationality!—by the name of Fontenelle wrote his *The Plurality of Worlds*, considered a masterpiece in its day. But as science marches on, it tramples even masterpieces into the dust! In about 1835, a booklet translated from the *New York American* told how Sir John Herschel,* dispatched to the Cape of Good Hope to make astronomical observations, had, by means of a telescope made more efficient by an internal light, brought the Moon to an apparent distance of only eighty yards. At that point it seems he could distinctly make out caves where hippopotami lived, green mountains fringed with gold lacework, sheep with ivory horns, a species of white deer, and Moon people who had membranous wings like those of bats. This brochure was the work of an American named Locke* and proved immensely popular. But it soon became apparent that it was pure invention and the French were the first to sneer.'

'Sneer at an American!' cried J. T. Maston. 'Damn me if that isn't grounds for war!'

'There's no need to worry, my good friend. Before they did any sneering, the French were also completely taken in by our fellow countryman. But, to complete this brief historical overview, I will add that a man named Hans Pfaall* of Rotterdam ascended in a balloon filled with a gas derived from nitrogen and thirty-seven times lighter than air, and reached the Moon after a voyage of nineteen days. But like all the previous attempts, his flight was purely imaginary, the work of a popular American writer with a strange, brooding imagination. I refer to Edgar Allan Poe!'

'Three cheers for Edgar Allan Poe!' cried his listeners, thrilled by their president's words.

'I conclude my address,' Barbicane went on, 'with these experiments which I describe as purely literary and completely useless as a means of establishing any realistic connection with the Eye of Night. However, I must say a word about a number of practically-minded men who have tried to make actual contact with the Moon. For instance, a few years ago, a German geometer proposed to send a team of scientists to the Siberian steppes. There, on those endless plains, they would mark out colossal geometrical shapes using luminous reflectors*—including the square on the hypotenuse which French commonly call *le pont aux ânes*, meaning "donkeys' bridge", that is, "child's play". The geometer explained: "Any intelligent being will understand the scientific meaning of that figure. The inhabitants of the Moon, the Selenites—if they exist—will respond with a comparable symbol and once communications have been established, it will be easy to create an alphabet that will enable us to speak directly with the denizens of the Moon." Those are the words of the German geometer. But his scheme was never implemented and until now no direct link has been established between the Earth and its satellite. And so it has been left to our practical American genius to make that first contact with the world of the stars. The means of achieving that goal is simple, easy, assured of success, infallible, and it is the essence of my proposal.'

In the ensuing hubbub these words were greeted by a storm of raised voices. There was not one among those present who had not been won over, gripped, transported by the speaker's utterances.

'Listen! Listen there! Be quiet!' voices cried on all sides.

When the excitement died down, Barbicane resumed his interrupted speech in a more serious voice.

'You are aware,' he said, 'of the giant strides that the science of ballistics has made over these past few years and the great advances which would have been made in the development of guns and gunnery if the war had only lasted longer. You also know more generally that the strength of cannons and the expansive power of gunpowder are both unlimited. Well, using that as my starting-point, I asked myself if, by using a sufficiently powerful appliance, constructed to cater for pre-determined levels of explosive forces, it might be possible to fire a projectile all the way to the Moon!'

At these words, a great 'Oh!' of astonishment rose from countless heaving breasts. It was followed by a sudden moment of silence such as that which precedes a clap of thunder. And thunder there was— a thunder of applause, a clamour of raised voices which made the assembly hall shake. The president tried to speak, but could not. It was only after ten minutes had elapsed that he managed to make himself heard.

'Allow me to finish!' he said coldly. 'I have looked at the problem from all sides. I have approached it boldly and based on my incontrovertible calculations it emerges that any projectile with an initial velocity of 12,000 yards a second,* aimed at the Moon, could not fail to land there. I therefore have the honour, esteemed colleagues, to propose that we should attempt this modest venture!'

3

THE EFFECT PRODUCED
BY BARBICANE'S SPEECH

It is quite impossible to describe the effect of the honourable president's closing words. There was yelling, bellowing, and cheering and a whole string of great huzzas. There were hurrahs and 'hip-hips!' and all the onomatopoeias that flourish on American tongues. There are no words to convey the bedlam, the sheer uproar! Mouths bawled, hands clapped, and feet stamped, making the floors shake. All the weapons in that museum of guns, if fired simultaneously, could not have caused the sound waves to reverberate more loudly. This should come as no surprise. There are gunners who can make as much noise as their guns.

Barbicane remained calm in the midst of this outpouring of fervour. Perhaps he wished to say a few more words to his colleagues for the movements of his hands appealed for silence and his thundering shot-warning bell banged away in vain: no one even heard it. Soon, he was pulled from his chair and borne aloft in triumph and from the shoulders of his loyal comrades he was passed on to crowds who were no less seething with excitement.

Now there is nothing that can put an American out of countenance. It is often said that the word 'impossible' does not exist in French: clearly people have been using the wrong dictionary. For it is in America that everything is possible and practical difficulties melt away before they even arise. Between Barbicane's project and its implementation no true Yankee would even have allowed himself to anticipate any whiff of a hitch or snag. A case of 'no sooner said than done'.

The President's lap of honour continued throughout the evening, turning into a full-blown torch-lit parade. Irish, Germans, French, Scots—the motley mix which makes up the population of Maryland— all whooped in their native tongues and their acclamations, yells, and cheers combined to create an almighty paean of alleluias.

Right on cue, as if she knew she was the object of all the fuss, the Moon shone out, serene and magnificent, her intense luminescence eclipsing the attendant stars. All the Yankees looked up at her shining disc. Some waved with their hands, others called out to her using the fondest names, while yet others took her measure with a look or shook a challenging fist.

Between ten o'clock and midnight an optician on Jones Falls Street* made a fortune selling telescopes. The Eye of Night was stared at as though she was a lady of high degree. Those Americans treated her with familiarity, as if they owned her, as though pale Phoebe was the property of these bold conquistadores and already formed part of the territory of the Union. Yet they were only planning to send a projectile to the Moon, a rather forward way of starting a relationship, even with a satellite, though one widely practised among civilized nations.

Midnight had just struck and the mood of exuberance showed no sign of lessening. It remained at a high pitch amongst all classes of the population. The magistrate, the scientist, the merchant, the shop-keeper, the street porter, the educated and the unschooled, all felt stirred to their vitals. This was a national undertaking. The wealthy districts and the poor parts of town, the quaysides washed by the waters of the Patapsco and the ships held fast in their berths, all teemed with crowds drunk with joy, gin, and whisky. Every last citizen among them talked, held forth, declaimed, discussed, argued, approved, applauded, from the gentleman nonchalantly reclining on his bar room chesterfield with a glass of sherry-cobbler before him, to the boatman getting soused on rotgut spirits in the dimly-lit taverns of Fells Point.

But by two in the morning, the excitement had died down somewhat. President Barbicane managed to get back to his house, battered, ground-down, aching all over. The strongest of men could not have survived such a reception. Gradually the crowds drifted away from streets and squares. The railroads from Ohio, Susquehanna, Philadelphia, and Washington, all of which converge on Baltimore, scattered the out-of-towners to the four corners of the United States and the city slumbered in relative tranquillity.

But it would be a mistake to think that on that memorable evening Baltimore was alone in experiencing such mayhem. The great cities of the Union—New York, Boston, Albany, Washington, Richmond, the Crescent City, Charleston, Mobile—as from Texas to Massachusetts and Michigan to Florida, all surrendered to the hysteria. In fact all 30,000 members of the Gun Club had seen their president's letter and had looked forward no less impatiently to the famous speech on 5 October. Which was why, on that same evening, as the words were pronounced by the speaker, they also skeetered along the telegraph wires across the States of the Union at a speed of 248,447 miles per second. It may therefore be said with absolute certainty that at exactly the same instant, the entire United States of America, ten times the size of France,* gave a single cheer and that twenty-five million hearts, swollen with pride, beat as one.

The next day, fifteen hundred daily, weekly, fortnightly, and monthly publications took up the story.* They examined the project from every angle, physical, meteorological, economic, and ethical, and explored its political significance and the implications for civilization. They asked if the Moon was a world that was fully-formed and whether it would ever undergo further changes. Was it like the Earth had been before it had an atmosphere? What did the other, invisible side of the celestial sphere look like? Although nothing more than firing a projectile at the Eye of Night was as yet planned, everyone saw it as the starting point of a whole series of events. They hoped that one day America would pierce the ultimate secrets of that mysterious orb and some seemed even to fear that its conquest would significantly alter the balance of power in Europe.

Once the project had been comprehensively analysed, no newspaper or magazine ever suggested that it would not succeed. Revues, pamphlets, bulletins, newsletters, and journals published by scientific, literary, and religious societies all stressed its positive side and the Natural History Society in Boston, the American Society of Sciences and Arts in Albany, the New York Geographical and Statistical Society, the American Philosophical Society in Philadelphia, and Washington's Smithsonian forwarded thousands of letters of congratulation to the Gun Club, along with offers of immediate assistance and financial support.

It may safely be asserted that no proposal ever garnered such an array of backers. There was never any question of second thoughts, doubts or misgivings. As to the sarcasm, caricatures, and comic songs which would have greeted the idea of sending a projectile to the Moon in Europe—and particularly in France—they would have seriously damaged their proposer's chances. All the life-preservers in the world would not have saved him from the general opprobrium. But there are things in the New World at which no one laughs.

And so it was that, from that day forth, Impey Barbicane became one of the United States' most famous citizens, a kind of George Washington of science.* One incident out of many will demonstrate the depth of this sudden devotion of an entire nation to one man.

A few days after the famous meeting at the Gun Club, the manager of a travelling company of British actors advertised a performance of *Much Ado about Nothing* at Baltimore's theatre. But the city's population, seeing in the title an unflattering allusion to president Barbicane's plan, invaded the building, tore up the seats and forced the hapless fellow to change the billing. He bowed to the wishes of the public: being a man of wit, he replaced the unfortunately titled comedy with *As You Like It* and played to packed houses for several weeks.

4

THE RESPONSE OF THE OBSERVATORY
AT CAMBRIDGE, MASS.

MEANWHILE, Barbicane wasted no time amid the clamour of public adulation of which he was the object. His first task was to gather his colleagues together in the committee rooms of the Gun Club. There, after much discussion, it was agreed that astronomers should be consulted on the astronomical aspects of the enterprise. Once their reaction was ascertained, discussion could then begin on the mechanical means of embarking on the project. Nothing would be neglected to ensure the success of their great experiment.

A precisely-worded note containing specific questions was therefore drawn up and forwarded to the Observatory at Cambridge,* Massachusetts. This town, where the first university in the United States was founded, is justly famed for its astronomy department. It is there that scientists of the highest calibre are assembled; and it is there that is located the powerful telescope which allowed Bond to identify the Andromeda Nebula and Clark to discover the satellite of Sirius. This celebrated institution thus fully justified the confidence placed in it by the Gun Club.

And so two days later, its eagerly awaited response was delivered into the hand of President Barbicane.

It was written in these terms:

From the Director of the Cambridge Observatory to the President of the Baltimore Gun Club.

Cambridge, 7 October.

On receipt of your letter of the 6th inst. addressed to the Observatory at Cambridge on behalf of the membership of Baltimore Gun Club, our entire staff were immediately summoned and, after deliberation, agreed to respond as follows:

The questions put were these:

1. Is it possible for a projectile to be sent to the Moon?
2. What is the exact distance from the Earth to its satellite?
3. What would be the total travel time of a projectile released with adequate exit velocity; and, additionally, when precisely should it be launched so that it lands on the Moon at a predetermined location?
4. At precisely what time would the Moon be in the optimal position for a projectile to land on it?
5. At what area of the firmament should the cannon which fires the projectile be aimed?
6. What would be the exact position of the Moon in the firmament at the time when the projectile is fired?

In answer to the first question: '*Is it possible for a projectile to be sent to the Moon?*'

Yes, a projectile can indeed be sent to the Moon provided it is launched at an initial velocity of 12,000 yards per second. Our calculations show that such a speed is ample. The further a body travels from the Earth, the more the effect of gravity decreases in proportion to the square of the distance travelled. That is, for a distance three times greater, the effect would become nine times smaller. As a consequence, the weight of the projectile will fall rapidly and it is ultimately reduced to zero at the particular moment when the gravitational pull of the Moon is exactly equal to that of the Earth, that is, after it has reached a point which is forty-seven fifty-seconds ($^{47}/_{52}$) of the distance of its transit. At that point, the projectile will be without weight and, if it proceeds beyond it, it will be drawn towards the Moon powered only by the attractive force of lunar gravity. The theoretical viability of the proposed experiment is therefore proven beyond question. As to its practical success, that would depend entirely on the power of the propulsive device you have in mind.

Turning to question 2: '*What is the exact distance from the Earth to its satellite?*'

In its orbit around the Earth, the Moon does not describe a circle but an ellipse of which our planet occupies one of the *focuses*. As a result, the Moon is at certain times closer to the Earth and at others further away from it, or, in astronomical terms, at its *apogee* or *perigee*. The difference in distance between its furthest and closest points is consequently too great to be ignored. In precise terms, the Moon at its apogee is 247,552 miles (or 99,640 four-kilometre leagues) distant from us and at its perigee 218,657 miles* (88,010 leagues), a difference of 28,895 miles (11,630 leagues), or more than one-ninth of the overall distance. It is therefore the distance of the Moon in perigee which should be used as the basis for all calculations.

Question 3: '*What would be the total travel time of a projectile propelled with adequate exit velocity; and, additionally, when precisely should it be launched so that it lands on the Moon at a pre-determined place?*'

If the projectile maintained the inaugural velocity of 12,000 yards per second with which it was endowed at its launch, it would take only about nine hours to arrive at its destination. But in actual fact this initial velocity will steadily decrease. By our comprehensive computation, the projectile would take 300,000 seconds, or eighty-three hours and twenty minutes to arrive at the point where the gravitational forces of the Earth and Moon cancel each other out. From that moment on, it would reach the Moon in a further 50,000 seconds, or thirteen hours, fifty-three minutes, and twenty seconds.* It follows that the projectile would need to be launched ninety-seven hours, thirteen minutes, and twenty seconds before the Moon arrives at the point aimed at.

In reply to Question 4: '*At what time precisely would the Moon be in the optimum position for a projectile to land on it?*'

Having regard to what has been stated above, it is essential to select, first, a time when the Moon is in its perigee and, second, the exact moment when it is at its zenith.* This will have the effect of further reducing the distance of travel by an amount equal to the Earth's radius, viz., 3,919 miles.* This means that the final figure is 214,976 miles (86,410 leagues) to be travelled. But if the Moon arrives in perigee every month, it is not always at its zenith at the same moment. It is only at long intervals that these two conditions coincide. So it will be necessary to wait for a conjuncture of its passage at the perigee and its arrival at the zenith. Fortunately, it so happens that the Moon will meet both conditions on 4 December next year:* it will be at its perigee at midnight, which is to say at the shortest distance from Earth, and at the same time it will be at the zenith.

Answer to Question 5: '*At what part of the firmament should the cannon which fires the projectile be aimed?*'

If account is taken of the preceding remarks, the cannon should be pointed upwards at the zenith of the place where it is sited. This means that the line of fire will be perpendicular to the plane of the horizon with the result that the projectile will escape the effects of Earth's gravity more quickly. But if the Moon is to reach the zenith of a given location, that location must not be situated at a latitude higher than the Moon's declination. In other words it should be located between 0° and 28° latitude North or South.* In all other locations, the angle of fire must of necessity be oblique, which would reduce the chances of a successful outcome.

Finally, question 6: '*What would be the exact position of the Moon in the firmament at the time when the projectile is fired?*'

At the precise moment the projectile is launched into space, the Moon, which advances each day by 13° 10′ 35″, will be distant from the zenith by four times that figure: viz., by 52° 42′ 20″. This is the distance it will cover during the trajectory of the projectile. But some further account must be taken of the result of the deviation which the projectile will experience due to the rotation of the Earth. This means it will reach the Moon only after being deflected from its course over a distance equal to six times the radius of the Earth. When allowance is made for the Moon's orbit, this will be approximately eleven degrees.* These eleven degrees must be added to those which account for the Moon's delay as previously explained, which makes—in round figures—sixty-four degrees in all. This means that when the projectile is launched, the line of sight of the Moon will make an angle of sixty-four degrees with the vertical.

The above are the responses made by the Gun Club to the enquiries made to the Cambridge Observatory.

To sum up:

1. The cannon should be situated in an area between latitude 0° and 28° North or South.

2. It should be aimed at the zenith of its location.
3. The projectile should be launched at an initial velocity of 12,000 yards per second, sufficient for exit.
4. It should be fired on 1 December next year at 13 minutes and 20 seconds before 11 p.m.*
5. It will land four days later on the Moon, at exactly midnight, at the moment of its transit over the zenith.

Members of the Gun Club should therefore—without further delay—begin the work required for an enterprise of such a nature, and be ready to fire their cannonball on the date and at the hour specified above. For if they allow the date of 4 December to pass, they will not find the Moon in the same conjuncture of perigee and zenith for another eighteen years and eleven days.*

The personnel of the Observatory here at Cambridge remain entirely at their disposal for any queries regarding theoretical astronomy and by this letter they add their congratulations to those already extended by the rest of the United States.

On behalf of all colleagues,

J. M. Belfast*

Director of the Observatory, Cambridge.

5

THE ROMANCE OF THE MOON

At the time when the universe was still in its chaotic phase, an observer, possessing an infinitely acute vision and standing at the imaginary centre around which our globe now rotates, would have seen space completely filled with myriads of atoms. But little by little, over many centuries, a change came about. A law of gravitational attraction came into effect, governing all atoms which until then had enjoyed complete freedom of movement. Atoms now combined chemically, each according to its cohesive potential, became molecules, and formed the nebulous clouds with which the depths of the firmament are strewn.

Very quickly, these clusters acquired the ability to rotate round their central point. This centre, made up of loosely aggregated molecules, became progressively more concentrated and began to turn on its axis. Furthermore, obeying the immutable laws of mechanics, its density increased as its volume decreased, its spinning motion accelerated, and, these two phenomena continuing to operate, the result was the formation of one dominant star, the centre of the whole nebulous accretion.

Paying close attention, our observer would then have seen the other molecules in the accumulated mass behaving like the central star: they would first become denser each in its own manner, due to the progressively increasing speed of rotation, and would then gravitate around the main star as innumerable lesser stars. Thus was formed each *nebula*, of which astronomers have to date discovered almost five thousand.

Among these five thousand nebulae there is one—which we call the Milky Way—that contains eighteen million stars,* each of which has become the centre of a Solar System.

If, of these eighteen million stars, our observer had concentrated on one of the most modest and least brilliant, a star of the fourth order of magnitude which we have grandly called the sun, he could have followed the successive unfolding of all the events which were responsible for the formation of the universe.

In particular he would have seen that this sun, still at its gaseous stage and composed of freely moving molecules, was spinning on its axis and completing the process of densification. This rotation, in accordance with the laws of mechanics, would have speeded up as the volume was reduced. A moment would have come when the centrifugal force would have grown stronger than the centripetal force (which tends to drive molecules towards the centre).

Then as our observer watched, a further phenomenon would have occurred: molecules located on the equator, breaking off like stones from a sling whose strap has suddenly given way, would have formed concentric rings around the sun, like that of Saturn. In turn, these rings of cosmic matter, subject to a rotatory movement around the central mass of each, would have broken up and disintegrated into secondary nebulosities, that is, into planets.

If our observer had then given his full attention to those planets, he would have seen them behave exactly like the sun and give rise to one or more cosmic rings which were the origins of those lesser heavenly bodies that we call satellites.

And so, moving up from atom to molecule, from molecule to nebulous cloud, from nebulous cloud to nebula, from nebula to principal star, from principal star to sun, from the sun to planet and from planet to satellite, appears the entire sequence of changes undergone by heavenly bodies since the first days of the world.*

Our sun seems lost in the infinity of the world of the stars and yet it is linked, according to current scientific theory, to the nebula of the Milky Way. It forms the centre of a Solar System and, small though it seems in the depths of the ethereal regions, it is nevertheless enormous, for it is 1,400,000 times larger than the Earth.* Around it orbit eight planets it has begotten during the early days of creation. They are, from nearest to most distant, Mercury, Venus, Earth, Mars, Jupiter, Saturn, Uranus and Neptune.* In addition, Mars and Jupiter are orbited by other, smaller bodies which may be vagrant debris from a planet shattered into several thousand pieces, of which the telescope has, to date, discovered ninety-two.

Of these minions which the sun maintains, each in their elliptical orbit by the iron law of gravity, some in turn have their own satellites. Uranus has eight, Saturn eight, Jupiter four,* Neptune perhaps three, and the Earth, one. The latter, one of the least important in the entire Solar System, is called the Moon, and it is such a Moon that the daring genius of these Americans now sets out to conquer.

Given its comparative proximity and the relatively rapid recurrence of its various phases, the Eye of Night was the first, along with the sun, to attract the attention of Earth's inhabitants. But the sun is painful to the eye and the dazzling brightness of its light forces watchers to look away.

On the other hand, Bright Phoebe, more human, obligingly allows herself to be observed in all her modesty and grace. She is easy on the eye and unpretentious, although she is on occasion bold enough to eclipse her brother, shining Apollo, but without ever being eclipsed by him. Muslims acknowledge the debt they owed this faithful friend of the Earth and calculated their calendar on the phases of the Moon.

The earliest human peoples developed a distinctive religious cult based on this chaste goddess. For the Egyptians, it was Isis, and Astarte for the Phoenicians; the Greeks worshipped her as Phoebe, daughter of Latona and Jupiter, and they explained the eclipses as the secret visits of Diana to the beautiful youth, Endymion. If mythological legend is to be believed, the lion of Nemea* roamed the realms of the Moon before he appeared on Earth, and in his verses the poet Agesianax, as quoted by Plutarch, celebrated the doe eyes, captivating nose, and inviting mouth that seem to be pictured in the luminous areas of adorable Selene.

But if the ancients clearly understood the character, temperament, in short the spiritual ethos of the Moon from a mythological standpoint, even the most learned amongst them were highly ignorant in matters of lunar geography.

Nevertheless, a number of early astronomers in the dim and very distant past made certain discoveries which have been confirmed by modern science. If the Arcadians claimed to have inhabited the Earth before the Moon existed, if Simplicius believed that the Moon did not move and was anchored to the crystal vault of heaven, if Tatius regarded it as a fragment of the sun's disc, if Clearchus, a disciple of Aristotle, believed it was a polished mirror in which images of the oceans* were reflected, if yet others saw it as a mass of vapours exhaled by the Earth or a globe which was half fire and half ice and which turned on its axis—eventually certain learned men, not possessing optical instruments but relying upon shrewd observation, deduced most of the laws which govern the movements of the Eye of Night.

Thus it was that, 460 years before Christ, Thales of Miletus expressed the view that the Moon was illuminated by the sun. Aristarchus of Samos accurately explained its phases. Cleomenes* taught that the light it shone with was reflected. The Chaldean Berossus discovered that the time it took to rotate on its axis was equal to the time it took to make one orbital revolution and in this way taught us why the Moon always presents the same face. Finally, two centuries before the Christian era, Hipparchus discovered certain irregularities in the observed motions of the Earth's satellite.

These various intimations were subsequently confirmed and became of signal benefit to later astronomers. Ptolemy, in the second century, and the Arab, Aboul Wafa, in the tenth, completed the reflections of Hipparchus on the irregularities undergone by the Moon as it follows the wandering course of its orbit under the action of the sun. Then Copernicus in the fifteenth century and Tycho Brahé in the sixteenth gave a complete account of the universe and defined the role of the Moon in the interplay of the heavenly bodies.

By that stage, its motions were almost completely understood. But of its physical make-up precious little was known. It was then that Galileo explained certain phenomena of lunar light, which appeared in some of its phases, by the existence and effect of mountains to which he assigned an average height of 27,000 feet.

After him, Hevelius, a Danzig astronomer, brought the greatest elevations down to 15,600 feet. But his colleague Riccioli put them up again, to 42,000.

At the close of the eighteenth century, Herschel,* armed with a powerful telescope, significantly reduced all previous estimates. For the highest mountains he set a figure of 11,400 feet and brought the average height of the peaks down to a mere 2,400. But Herschel's calculations were still incorrect and it required the observations of Schröter, Louville, Halley, Nasmyth, Bianchini, Pastorff, Lohrmann, Gruithuysen, and not least the painstaking work of Messrs Beer and Mädler, to settle the question once and for all. Thanks to their labours, the height of the mountains of the Moon is now precisely established. Beer and Mädler have measured 1,905 peaks, of which six exceed 15,600 feet and twenty-two are over 14,400 high.* The highest summit of all rises over the surface of the lunar disc to an elevation of 22,806 feet.

At the same time, an accurate survey of the Moon was being finalized. It appeared to be riddled with craters and its essentially volcanic nature became more apparent with each observation. The lack of refraction in the rays of planets occluded by the Moon was taken as evidence that it had almost absolutely no atmosphere. The absence of air would also indicate an absence of water. It became clear therefore that if inhabitants of the Moon were able to live in such conditions, they must have a particular physical make-up and be markedly different from those who dwell on Earth.

Finally, thanks to new working methods, more powerful telescopes unremittingly scrutinized the Moon, leaving no point on its surface unexplored. And even though its diameter measures 2,150 miles, its surface area comprises one thirteenth of our globe's, and its volume is one forty-ninth part of that of the terrestrial spheroid, none of its secrets could escape the eyes of astronomers, and these highly skilled investigators took their prodigious ocular enquirings even further.

For instance, they observed that, when the Moon was full, certain parts of the lunar disc appeared to be marked with white lines and, during its phases, with black lines. Studying the matter with greater precision, they managed to arrive at an accurate account of the nature of these lines. They were long, narrow grooves running between parallel ridges and they generally ended on reaching the contours of craters. Their length was between ten and a hundred miles and they were some 4,800 feet wide. The astronomers called them 'furrows', but all they could do then was to find names for them. As for knowing whether or not these furrows were the dried-up beds of ancient rivers, they were unable to give a final answer. So now the Americans were hoping to determine the true nature of this geological feature in the next few days. They also aimed to be the first to explain the series of parallel 'ramparts' discovered on the surface of the Moon by Gruithuysen, a learned Munich lecturer, who believed them to be a system of fortifications built by Selenite engineers. These two issues—both still mysterious—together no doubt with a number of others, could not be settled once and for all except by means of close contact with the Moon.

As regards the intensity of its light, there was nothing further to discover in that regard. It was known to be 300,000 times weaker than sunlight* and to have no appreciable effect on the temperature of thermometers. As regards the phenomenon known as 'Earthshine', it is naturally explained as an effect of the sun's rays being reflected from the Earth's surface to the Moon where they give an appearance of completeness to the lunar disc when seen as a crescent in its first and last phases.

Such was the state of accumulated knowledge of the Earth's satellite that the Gun Club was bent on completing in all areas, cosmographical, geological, political and spiritual.

6

WHAT CAN NO LONGER REMAIN UNKNOWN OR BE BELIEVED IN THE UNITED STATES

THE immediate result of Barbicane's proposal* was to put all the astronomical facts about Bright Phoebe high on everyone's agenda. People began to study lunar data assiduously. It was as though the Moon had appeared on their horizon for the very first time, as if none of them had even glimpsed it up there, in the sky above, until that moment. The Moon became fashionable. It shot to top of the bill without making it any less simple and unaffected, and took its place in the ranks of the 'stars' of the hour without having its head turned. The press resurrected old stories in which this 'sun of the wolves'* played a part. They reminded readers of the different kinds of influence attributed to it by ignorance in times gone by. They sang its praises in every key. With a little more encouragement they would have quoted its wittiest sayings. The entire United States was seized by a fit of Moon madness.

The scientific journals dealt more particularly with matters relating to the Gun Club's plans. The response of the Observatory at Cambridge was published in their pages where it was extensively commented on and ratified without reservation.

In short, even the least literate Yankee was not allowed to remain ignorant of any facts relating to the satellite, nor were the most blinkered old matrons any longer permitted to harbour any of the superstitious beliefs associated with it. Scientific knowledge came to people in many forms: it reached them through eyes and ears until it was impossible for anyone to be a duffer in matters astronomical.

Up until then, most people had no idea of how anybody could have calculated the distance between the Moon and the Earth. Advantage was taken of this opportunity to teach them that it had been done by measuring the Moon's parallax. If the word parallax seemed to baffle them, they were told that it was the angle formed by two straight lines running from each end of the Earth's radius to the Moon. If they doubted the validity of this method they were given immediate proof that not only was the average distance 234,347 miles (or 94,330 leagues), but also that astronomers could not be mistaken in their calculations by more than a mere 70 miles (30 leagues)* either way.

For those unfamiliar with the way the Moon moved, newspapers demonstrated on a daily basis that it is endowed with two distinct types of motion. The first is known as rotation on its axis and the second as its revolution around the Earth, each taking exactly the same length of time to complete its cycle, which is twenty-seven and one-third days.

Rotatory motion is the type which creates day and night on the surface of the Moon. However, there is only one day and only one night per lunar month and they are each 354⅓ hours long.* But fortunately for the Moon, the face which is turned to the terrestrial globe is lit by it with an intensity equal to that of fourteen Moons. As

for its other face, which is permanently invisible to us, it consequently has 354 hours of totally dark night relieved only by 'that pale
brightness that drops down from the stars'.* This phenomenon is
due entirely to the fact that both kinds of motion—rotation and
revolution—complete their sequences in precisely the same length
of time, a mechanism which it shares, according to both Cassini and
Herschel,* with the satellites of Jupiter and very probably all other
satellites too.

Certain well-meaning but somewhat obtuse parties did not immediately grasp that if the Moon always showed the same face to the
Earth as it turned around it, it was also itself revolving on its own
axis and taking the same time to do it. Those people were told: 'Step
into your dining-room and walk around your table while keeping
your eyes fixed on its centre. When you have completed your circular
tour, you too will have turned one complete revolution because your
eyes will have observed all parts of the room one after the other as
you went round. Well, the room is the sky, the table is the Earth and
the Moon is you!' And the doubters would go away delighted with
the comparison.

It is a fact, therefore, that the Moon constantly presents the same
face to the Earth. But to be accurate, it should be added that as a result
of some rocking or swinging north to south and west to east, known
as *libration*, it does allow a little more than half of its disc, to be exact
57 hundredths,* to be displayed.

Once the ignoramuses understood as much as the Head of the
Observatory at Cambridge himself knew about the rotation of the
Moon on its axis, they began to worry about its orbiting motion
around the Earth and a score of scientific journals wasted no time in
keeping them informed. So now they learned that the firmament,
with its infinite number of stars, may be thought of as one immense
dial around which the Moon moves showing the true time to all the
inhabitants of the Earth; that it is according to this movement that the
Eye of Night reveals its various phases; that the Moon is full when it
is *in opposition* to the sun, that is when the three bodies form up in
straight alignment, with the Earth situated in the middle; that the
Moon is *new* when it is *in conjunction* with the sun, which is to say
when it is located between it and the Earth; and lastly that the Moon
is in its first or last quarter when it forms a right angle with the Earth
and the sun of which it is at the apex.

From all this, a handful of perceptive Yankees inferred the following effect, viz. that eclipses could only occur at moment of *opposition* or *conjunction*, and their reasoning was correct. In conjunction, the Moon is able to eclipse the sun, whereas in opposition, it is the Earth's turn to eclipse it, and if these eclipses do not occur twice per *lunation*,* it is because the plane over which the Moon moves is inclined towards the *ecliptic*, in other words, towards the plane along which the Earth travels.

With regard to the altitude which the Moon can reach above the horizon, the Observatory's response had explained the matter comprehensively. Everyone now knew that this height will vary with the latitude of the place from which the observation is made. But the only regions of the Earth's surface where the Moon is sometimes at its zenith, viz. where it can be stationed directly over the heads of its observers, must of necessity be situated between the Equator and one of the two twenty-eighth parallels. Hence the express recommendation that the experiment be undertaken at a location in that particular area of the globe, so that the projectile can be launched vertically and thus escape the pull of gravity more quickly. This was a primary condition for the success of the enterprise and it did not fail to catch and preoccupy the public's entire attention.

As for the path taken by the Moon in its orbits around the Earth, the Observatory at Cambridge had sufficiently made clear, even to the ignorant in all countries, that this line is a re-entrant curve, not a circle, but an ellipse of which the Earth occupies one of the focuses. Such elliptical orbits are common to all planets, as they are to all satellites, and theoretical mechanics proves rigorously that it could not be otherwise. So it was fully understood that the Moon was further from the Earth at its apogee and closer at its perigee.

This, then, amounted to more or less all that every American knew and could not decently admit not knowing. But if these incontrovertible truths spread rapidly amongst the public, many errors and some unfounded fears were less easily uprooted.

It was thus, for example, that some good folk argued that the Moon was an erstwhile comet which, as it pursued its ellipsoid course around the sun, had come near to the Earth and become trapped in its gravitational field. These armchair astronomers reckoned this could account for the charred appearance of the Moon as an irreversible mishap, for which they placed the blame squarely on the heat of the sun. However, when it was pointed out to them that comets have an atmosphere and that the Moon has little or none, they were at a loss for an answer.

Others, members of the lily-livered brigade, expressed certain fears concerning the Moon. They had heard somewhere that, according to lunar observations made at the time of the Caliphs,* its orbital motion was accelerating at some rate or another. From this they inferred, quite logically it is true, that an increase in this motion must correspond to a reduction in the distance between the two bodies and that if this twin effect were to continue indefinitely, the Moon would one day end up falling onto the Earth. But they were made to put their apprehensions to one side and to stop worrying about future generations when it was explained to them that, according to the calculations of Laplace, an eminent French mathematician, any such acceleration in the orbital motion was confined to very strict limits and that a matching reduction would follow promptly. And so the equilibrium of the Solar System would not be upset in the centuries to come.

There remained only one final category of ignoramuses. Those people who, not content with not knowing what is true, know everything that is false. And where the Moon was concerned they knew a very great deal. Some believed its disc was a polished mirror in which people in various places on Earth could see each other and exchange thoughts. Others claimed that of every thousand New Moons observed, nine hundred and fifty had brought about noteworthy changes, such as cataclysms, revolutions, earthquakes, floods, and so forth. In other words, they believed in the mysterious power of the Eye of Night to influence human destinies. They considered it to be the 'authentic counterpart' of our existence and thought that each Selenite was linked to an inhabitant of Earth by a bond of sympathy. Following Dr Mead, they maintained that the entire system of life is wholly subservient to the Moon, stubbornly insisting that boys are born mostly during a New Moon and girls during its last quarter,* etc., etc. But in the end they were obliged to abandon these mindless ideas and accept the unvarnished truth. And if the Moon, shorn of her influence, fell in the estimation of some interested parties and others turned their backs on her, the vast majority came out in her favour. As for the Yankees, they now had only one ambition: to claim possession of the new continent in the sky above and to plant on its highest peak the star-spangled banner of the United States of America.

7

A PAEAN OF PRAISE TO THE CANNONBALL

In its memorable letter of 7 October, the Cambridge Observatory had discussed the problem from the astronomical point of view. The question now was how to solve it mechanically. At this juncture the practical difficulties might well have seemed insurmountable in any other country. But in America, they were child's play.

Wasting no time, President Barbicane had appointed an implementation committee from within the Gun Club. The Committee was directed to clarify the three great issues: the cannon, the cannonball, and the propulsive powder. It was composed of four members who were experts in these areas: Barbicane, who had the casting vote should opinion be divided, General Morgan, Major Elphiston, and lastly the inevitable J. T. Maston on whom fell the duties of recording secretary.

The Committee met on 8 October at the home of President Barbicane at 3 Republican Street. Since it was vital that any sounds and alarums emanating from empty stomachs should not be allowed to trouble the discussion of such serious matters, the four members of the Gun Club took their seats at a table laid with sandwiches and substantial teapots. J. T. Maston screwed his pen into his iron hook and the meeting got under way.

Barbicane opened the proceedings:

'My dear colleagues,' he said, 'we are charged with solving one of the major problems of ballistics, queen of the sciences, which is concerned with the movement of projectiles through the air, that is, of bodies fired into space by some propulsive power and then allowed to go freely on their way.'

'Ah! Ballistics, ballistics!' cried J. T. Maston, his voice quivering with emotion.

'Perhaps it might have appeared logical', Barbicane resumed, 'to devote the whole of this first meeting to a discussion of the propulsive appliance to be used . . .'

'Hear, hear!' said General Morgan.

'However,' Barbicane continued, 'after much reflection, it seemed to me that the problem of the projectile should take precedence over that of the cannon, since the dimensions of one will be determined by the dimensions of the other.'

'I would like to be heard!' cried J. T. Maston.

He was given the floor with the promptness called for by his magnificent record.

'Dear friends,' he began in an inspirational voice, 'our President is quite right to give priority to the projectile over everything else! The cannonball which we are about to fire at the Moon will be our messenger, our ambassador, and I ask your permission to think of it in that broader spiritual light.'

This new way of looking at a projectile tickled the curiosity of the members of the Committee and they gave their full attention to the words spoken by J. T. Maston.

'Worthy friends,' he went on, 'I shall be brief. I will leave to one aside the physical cannonball, the cannonball that kills, and consider only the mathematical cannonball, the cannonball of righteousness. For me, the cannonball is the most striking manifestation of man's power which it fully encapsulates. It is in its creation that Man has come closest to the Creator!'

'Well said!' commented Major Elphiston.

'And,' the speaker proceeded, 'if God made the stars and the planets, man made the cannonball, that standard by which terrestrial speeds are measured, that small-scale model of the stars wandering through space, which are actually projectiles! Grant God the speed of electricity and of light, the speed of the stars and the comets and the planets, the speed of satellites, of sound and of the wind! But accord Man the speed of the cannonball which is one hundred times greater than the speed of the fastest trains and the swiftest horses!'

J. T. Maston was transported. His voice acquired accents of poetry as he sang this sacred paean of praise to the cannonball.

'You need figures?' he went on. 'Here are some figures that speak for themselves! Just take the humble 24-pounder. It may travel 800,000 times more slowly than electricity, it may be 640,000 times slower than the speed of light,* and seventy-six times slower than the speed of the Earth around the sun—yet as it leaves the cannon's mouth, it exceeds the speed of sound, travelling at 1,200 feet a second, 12,000 feet in ten seconds, fourteen miles a minute, 840 miles an hour, 20,160 miles a day, which is the same speed as every point on the equator in the rotatory motion of the globe, and 7,336,500 miles in a year. So, to get to the Moon it would take eleven days, twelve years to reach the sun, three hundred and sixty years to reach Neptune at the outer limit of our Solar System. And that is what a modest cannonball, the work of the human hand, is capable of! So what will happen if we multiply its speed by a factor of twenty and launch it at a speed of seven miles a second? O cannonball transcendental! Projectile sublime! I foresee that thou shalt be received on high with all the honour due to an ambassador from Earth!'

Cheers greeted this ringing oration and J. T. Maston, much moved, sat down amidst the congratulations of his colleagues.

'And now that we have given poetry a proper hearing,' said Barbicane, 'we should give our full attention to the question before us.'

'We are ready,' replied the members of the Committee as each ingurgitated half-a-dozen sandwiches.

'You are aware of the problem we have to solve,' the President went on. 'We have to find a way of firing a projectile at a muzzle velocity of 12,000 yards per second. I have every confidence that we can do it. But for now, let us review the speeds which have been achieved to date. General Morgan will be able to enlighten us on this subject.'

'And the best placed man to do so,' replied the General, 'since I was a member of the Trials and Tests Board during the war. So I can tell you that the Dahlgren hundred-pounder, which had a range of 5,000 yards, fired its missiles with an exit velocity of 500 yards a second.'

'Good,' said the President. 'What about the Rodman Columbiad?'

'Rodman's Columbiad, first trialled at Fort Hamilton near New York, fired a projectile weighing half a ton a distance of six miles at a muzzle velocity of 800 yards per second, a result never matched by Armstrong and Palliser in England.'

'Oh, the British!' barked J. T. Maston and he brandished his fearsome hook in the direction of the eastern horizon.

'So 800 yards a second,' said Barbicane, 'is the maximum velocity achieved until now?'

'Yes,' said Morgan.

'But I would point out,' said J. T. Maston, 'that if my mortar had not burst . . .'

'But burst it did,' replied Barbicane amiably. 'Let us take this exit velocity of 800 yards a second as our starting point. It will have to be increased twentyfold. I suggest we keep discussion of the means of reaching that target to a later meeting and direct the attention of colleagues to the dimensions the projectile should have. As you can imagine, we are not talking now of cannonballs weighing at most half a ton!'

'Why not?' asked the Major.

'Because,' retorted J. T. Maston, 'the projectile must be big enough to be noticed by the inhabitants of the Moon if, that is, there are any.'

'Quite,' Barbicane answered, 'although there is another and even more important reason.'

'What do you mean, Barbicane?' asked the Major.

'I mean that it is not enough to fire off a projectile and then forget all about it. We must track it during the entire flight until the moment it reaches its goal.'

'Really?' said the General and the Major, somewhat taken aback by the idea.

'Of course,' said Barbicane, in the tones of a man who knew his mind, 'of course! Otherwise, our experiment would serve no purpose.'

'If that is so,' replied the Major, 'are you proposing to make a projectile of an enormous size?'

'No, not at all. But hear me out. You are aware that modern optical instruments are now very advanced. With some telescopes, it has been possible to enlarge objects by a factor of 6,000, enough to bring the Moon to within what appears to be about forty miles. Now, at that distance, objects sixty feet in size are perfectly visible. If we have not increased the magnifying power of telescopes any further it is because enlargement is achieved at the expense of clarity and the Moon, which is only a reflecting mirror, does not emit light strong enough for it to be possible to take the process beyond that limit.'

'Well? What do you intend to do?' asked the General. 'Are you proposing to build a projectile with a diameter of sixty feet?'

'No, no!'

'Then are you thinking of making the Moon brighter?'

'Exactly.'

'But that's perfectly absurd!' exclaimed J. T. Maston.

'No, it's perfectly simple,' replied Barbicane. 'Now, if I can reduce the density of the atmosphere through which the Moon's light must pass, do I not make its light more luminous?'

'Obviously.'

'Well then, to achieve that effect, all I have to do is position the telescope on some high mountain top. And that is exactly what we shall do.'

'I give up, I surrender,' said the Major. 'You have a way of making everything sound simple . . .! But what order of magnification do you hope to get by such a course of action?'

'Magnification in the order of 48,000 times. That will bring the Moon nearer, so that it looks as if it is no more than five miles away and objects will need to have a diameter of only nine feet to be seen clearly.'

'Excellent!' cried J. T. Maston. 'So our projectile will need a diameter of just nine feet?'

'Quite.'

'But allow me to say,' said Major Elphiston, 'that it would still weigh so much that . . .'

'Please, Major,' replied Barbicane, 'before we start discussing weight, I would point out that our forefathers worked wonders in this field. It is not my intention to suggest that ballistics has not made significant advances. But it is worth reminding ourselves that even in the Middle Ages, surprising results were achieved which, I venture to say, were more astonishing than ours.'

'Really?' replied Morgan.

'Prove it!' demanded the Major.

'Nothing simpler,' Barbicane replied. 'I can quote many examples to support my claim. For instance, at the siege of Constantinople by Mahomet II in 1453, solid stone balls weighing 1,900 pounds were fired, which means that they must have been very large.'

'By Jove!' said the Major. 'Nineteen hundred pounds! That's a very high figure!'

'At Malta, in the time of the Knights of St John, there was a gun at Fort St Elmo* that fired stone balls that weighed 2,500 pounds.'

'It's not possible!'

'And according to one French historian, a mortar in the reign of King Louis XI fired an explosive charge weighing just 500 pounds. But that shell was shot from the Bastille, a place where the mad lock up the wise, and landed at Charenton,* a place where the wise lock up the mad.'

'Well put!' cried J. T. Maston.

'And since then, what have we witnessed? Armstrong cannon use 500-pound cannonballs and Rodman's Columbiads* shoot projectiles weighing half a ton! So it would seem that what missiles have gained in range they have lost in weight. Now, if we bend our best efforts in that direction, we must, given the advances made by science, get to the stage of being able to multiply by ten the weight of Mahomet's stone balls and those Maltese missiles.'

'Obviously,' said the Major. 'But what metal have you got in mind for the projectile?'

'Plain cast iron,' said General Morgan.

'Surely not cast iron!' exclaimed J. T. Maston in a tone of utter disdain. 'That's simply not good enough for a cannonball intended to reach the Moon!'

'Let's not overdo it, my friend,' replied Morgan. 'Cast iron will fit the bill nicely.'

'Quite,' went on Major Elphiston, 'but since the weight of the projectile is in proportion to its volume, a cannonball made of cast iron nine feet in diameter would be unthinkably heavy!'

'True—if it is solid,' said Barbicane, 'but not if it's hollow.'

'Hollow? You mean it is to be a shell?'

'And you could send letters and dispatches in it,' said J. T. Maston, 'together with samples of goods made here on Earth!'

'A shell, yes,' said Barbicane, 'it must be. A solid cannonball measuring nine feet, or a hundred and eight inches, would weigh upwards of 200,000 pounds, which is evidently far too much. However, as we need to give our projectile a certain degree of stability I propose that we should limit its weight to 20,000 pounds.'

'And how thick will the casings need to be?' the Major asked.

'If we use regulation tolerances,' Morgan went on, 'a diameter of 108 inches would call for the casing to be at least two feet thick.'

'That's far too much,' said Barbicane. 'Bear in mind that this will not be a shell designed to pierce armour-plate. So it will be enough to have an outer casing that is strong enough to withstand the pressure created by the gases released by the explosive charge. So this is the issue: how thick does the casing of a shell made of cast iron need to be so that it weighs no more than 20,000 pounds? Our mathematical maestro, our worthy Maston, will give us the answer forthwith.'

'Nothing simpler,' said the Committee's honourable secretary.

And so saying, he scribbled down several algebraic formulas on a sheet of paper where his pen quickly traced various symbols, notably π and x^2. He even appeared, with pen poised, to extract one cubic root before saying:

'The casing will have to be just under two inches thick.'

'Will that be enough?' asked the Major doubtfully.

'No,' said Barbicane, 'clearly not.'

'Well, what's to be done now?' said Elphiston in a puzzled voice.

'Use a different metal rather than cast iron.'

'Copper?' asked Morgan.

'No, it would still be too heavy. But I have something better to suggest.'

'What?' said the Major.

'Aluminium,' said Barbicane.

'Aluminium?' exclaimed the President's three colleagues.

'Yes. As you know, in 1854 a distinguished French chemist named Henry Sainte-Claire Deville succeeded in obtaining aluminium in a compact mass.* This valuable metal is white, like silver, and has the durability of gold, the toughness of steel, the fusibility of copper, and the lightness of glass. It is easily worked, is widely distributed throughout nature since alumina forms the basic component of most rocks, is three times lighter than iron, and seems to have been expressly created to supply us with the material for our projectile!'

'Bully for aluminium!' cried the Committee's secretary, a man always boisterous in moments of enthusiasm.

'But Chairman,' the Major said, 'is the market price of aluminium currently not extremely high?'

'It was,' replied Barbicane. 'Immediately after, it was discovered, aluminium cost between 260 and 280 dollars a pound (about 1,500 francs).* Then it fell to 27 dollars (150 francs) and today it sells at nine dollars (48 francs and 75 centimes).'

'But nine dollars a pound,' snorted the Major, not a man to give ground easily, 'is still a very hefty price!'

'True, Major, but not unaffordable.'

'So what would be the weight of the projectile?'

'Here is the result of my calculations,' replied Barbicane. 'A shell with a diameter of 108 inches and a twelve-inch-thick casing would weigh, if made of cast iron, 67,440 pounds. If made of aluminium, its weight would be reduced to 19,250 pounds.*'

'Capital!' cried Maston. 'That fits in perfectly with our plans!'

'Capital!' repeated the Major. 'But are you aware that at eighteen dollars a pound,* the projectile would cost . . .'

'Exactly 173,250 dollars (928,437 fr. 50 cents). Yes, I know. But there's no cause for concern, my friends, I do assure you: there will be no shortage of money for our project.'

'The money will pour in!' said Maston.

'Well?' said the President. 'What do you think of aluminium?'

'Motion carried *nem con*!' said all three members of the Committee.

'As for the design of the shell,' Barbicane continued, 'it need not delay us overmuch because, once it is free of the Earth's atmosphere, the projectile will be in empty space. So I propose we make it spherical, so that it can rotate, if needs be, and behave exactly as it sees fit.'

On that note, the first meeting of the Committee came to a close. The issue of the projectile had been settled once and for all and J. T. Maston took great pleasure at the thought of loosing off an aluminium shell aimed at the land of the Selenites.

'That should give them a pretty lively idea of the kind of people who live on Earth!'

8

THE CHRONICLE OF THE CANNON

THE decisions taken at that first session of the Committee produced a great sensation in the world outside. The faint of heart were apprehensive at the prospect of a cannonball weighing 20,000 pounds being fired at the sky. They wondered what sort of cannon could ever impart sufficient initial velocity to so fearsome a mass. The minutes of the second meeting of the Committee would provide convincing answers to all their questions.

On the evening of the very next day, all four members of the Gun Club sat down in front of an absolute mountain of sandwiches beside an ocean of tea. Discussion resumed where it had left off, this time with no preamble of any kind.

'Dear colleagues,' began Barbicane, 'we shall now turn our attention to the gun we have to build—its length, its shape, what it is to be made of, and its weight. It seems likely that we shall eventually conclude that it should be colossal in size, but whatever difficulties lie in our way, our industrial ingenuity will triumph over them. So please, if I could have your attention—but don't hesitate to fire away with your objections. I have nothing to fear from them.'

'Let us remind ourselves,' said Barbicane, 'of where we got in yesterday's meeting. Our problem now is the following: how to provide muzzle velocity of 12,000 yards a second for a shell 108 inches in diameter and a casing weighing 20,000 pounds.'

'Quite so, that is exactly the problem,' nodded Major Elphiston.

'Let me continue,' resumed Barbicane. 'When a projectile is fired into space, what happens? It is subject to three quite distinct forces: the resistance of its environment, the Earth's gravity, and the impulse force which has been imparted to it.* Let us consider these three forces. The resistance of its environment, that is of the air, will be negligible. The Earth's atmosphere extends for a mere forty miles* (about sixteen leagues). At a speed of 12,000 yards a second, the projectile will be clear of it in five seconds, a time short enough for air friction to be deemed insignificant. Let us move on to the pull of the Earth's gravity, in other words, the weight of the projectile. We know that its weight at the beginning will decrease in inverse proportion to the square of the distance travelled. Now here is what physics tells us: when a body left to its own devices falls towards the surface of the Earth, it drops fifteen feet in the first second. If that same body were sent on a journey of 247,542 miles—in other words, the distance from here to the Moon— its fall in the first second would be reduced to about one twelfth of an inch,* or 2.25mm. Which means it would be virtually static. So our problem is how to overcome progressively the effect of gravity at the start. How can we achieve it? By the force of propulsion.'

'Yes, and that's the real issue,' said the Major.

'Indeed it is,' said the President. 'But we shall solve it! For the propulsive force that is needed will be created by the length of the cannon and the amount of powder we use—the latter being limited only by the stress-proof strength of the former. So let us direct all our attention today to the size that our cannon shall have. It goes without saying that we can give it levels of anti-shatter strength that can have more or less no limit, since the gun will not have to be manoeuvred.'

'All of which of goes without saying,' growled the Secretary.

'Up to the present,' said Barbicane, 'the longest cannons—our giant Columbiads—have not exceeded a length of twenty-five feet. We will astonish everyone with the dimensions we shall have no choice but to adopt.'

'I should think we will!' cried J. T. Maston. 'Speaking for myself, I should want a gun at least half a mile long!'

'Half a mile!' exclaimed the Major and the General in unison.

'Yes, half a mile—and even then it would still be too short by half.'

'Hold on, Maston,' replied Morgan, 'you're exaggerating.'

'I'm not!' retorted the combustible secretary. 'And I cannot think why you say I am.'

'It's because you go too far!'

'I'll have you know, sir,' said Maston, adopting his grandest manner, 'that a gunner is like a shell: he can never go too far!'

The discussion was beginning to turn personal, but the President stepped in.

'Come, gentlemen, let's keep calm and think this matter through! We obviously need a cannon with a huge range since its length will increase the explosive release of the gases massed behind the projectile. But it is pointless to exceed certain limits.'

'Quite,' said the Major.

'Now what are the norms that apply in such cases? As a rule, the length of a cannon is twenty or twenty-five times the diameter of the shell, and weighs between 235 and 240 times its weight.'

'That won't be enough,' cried J. T. Maston impulsively.

'I agree with you, my friend, and indeed, were we to follow that formula for a projectile nine feet wide that weighed 30,000 pounds,* the cannon would be just 225 feet long and weigh only 7,200,000 pounds.'

'Absurd!' snapped J. T. Maston. 'Might just as well use a pistol.'

'I'm of the same mind,' replied Barbicane, 'which is why I propose we quadruple the length and build a cannon 900 feet long.'*

The General and the Major both raised a few objections but nevertheless the proposal, lustily seconded by the secretary of the Gun Club, was finally accepted.

'And now,' asked Elphiston, 'how thick should we make its walls?'

'Six feet,' replied Barbicane.

'I assume you're not thinking of installing anything as big on a gun mounting?' the Major asked.

'What a wonderful idea!' said J. T. Maston.

'But impractical,' said Barbicane. 'No, I'm thinking of burying the gun in the ground, strengthening it with wrought iron hoops and collars and, finally, encasing it in a thick aggregate of concrete so that it becomes part of the shock resistance of the surrounding terrain. When the device has been cast, its bore must be meticulously reamed and calibrated to prevent windage and thus prevent any escape of gas and ensure that the totality of the expansive force of the charge is used for propulsion.'

'Bravo! Well done!' cried J. T. Maston. 'We have our cannon!'

'Not quite,' said Barbicane, calming his friend's impatience with a gesture of his hand.

'Why not?'

'Because we have yet to discuss its type. Is it to be a cannon, a howitzer, or a mortar?'

'Cannon,' replied Morgan.

'Howitzer,' snorted the Major.

'Mortar!' cried J. T. Maston.

A fresh and rather lively debate was about to begin, with each member promoting his favoured option, when the President put a sudden end to it.

'Friends!' he said. 'I can put to you something on which you can all agree: our Columbiad will have characteristics of all three fire-pieces. It will be a cannon because the powder chamber will be of the same diameter as the bore. It will be a howitzer because it will fire a shell. Finally, it will be a mortar since it will be levelled at an angle of ninety degrees and because, being anchored to the ground with no shock possible, it will give the projectile the full benefit of the propulsive force that builds up behind it.'

'Motion carried *nem con*,' cried the Committee members.

'One thought, however,' said Elphiston, 'will this cannon-cum-howitzer-cum-mortar be rifled?'

'No,' said Barbicane, 'it will not. We require very high initial velocity and, as you know, shells fired from rifled cannon are slower off the mark than from the smooth-bored type.'

'Quite true.'

'At last, this time we've got it!' J. T. Maston said again.

'Still not quite,' said the President.

'Why not?'

'Because we do not yet know with what metal it should be cast.'

'We should settle that question without further delay.'

'I was about to suggest it.'

All four members of the Committee tucked in to a dozen sandwiches washed down with lashings of tea, and the discussion resumed.

'Colleagues,' said Barbicane, 'our cannon must be extremely tough and durable, unaffected by heat, insoluble and unoxidizable by the corrosive action of acids.'

'There can be no doubt on that score,' replied the Major, 'and since we shall need to use a considerable quantity of it, we won't exactly be spoiled for choice about which one to pick.'

'Well, in that case,' said Morgan, 'I propose we use for the manufacture of our Columbiad the finest alloy yet known, by which I mean one hundred parts of copper, twelve parts tin and six of brass.'

'Friends,' answered the President, 'I fully agree it is an admixture which has given excellent results. But in the present case, it would cost far too much and would be very difficult to work with. So I think we should adopt a high quality but low priced material such as cast iron. Wouldn't you agree, Major?'

'Totally,' replied Elphiston.

'In fact,' said Barbicane, 'cast iron costs ten times less than bronze, is simple to cast, for it flows easily into sand moulds, and is quick to work—which is why it saves both time and money. Moreover, it is excellent as a material and I recall that during the war, at the siege of Atlanta,* there were iron cannon that each fired a thousand rounds every twenty minutes and were none the worse for it.'

'Still, cast iron is liable to shatter,' said Morgan.

'True, but it is also very durable. But it won't burst—you can take that from me.'

'A man's mortar can burst but he can still be an honest fellow,' said J. T. Maston sententiously.

'Very true,' answered Barbicane. 'And I shall now invite our excellent secretary to work out the weight of a cast-iron cannon nine hundred feet long, with a bore of nine feet and walls six feet thick.'

'Give me a minute,' said J. T. Maston.

And just as he had done the previous evening, he lined up his formulas with conspicuous dexterity and one minute later said:

'The cannon will weigh 68,040 tons (68,040,000 kilograms).'

'And at 2 cents a pound (10 centimes), what would it cost?'

'2,510,701 dollars (13,608,000 francs).'

J. T. Maston, the Major, and the General all gave Barbicane anxious looks.

'Well then, Gentlemen!' said the President. 'I shall repeat what I told you yesterday evening. Don't you worry! The millions will come rolling in!'

And with that assurance from their President, the Committee went their separate ways, having arranged for their third meeting to be held on the evening of the next day.

9

THE MATTER OF THE PROPELLANT

ALL that remained to be settled now was the choice of powders. The public waited anxiously for the Committee's final arbitration. Now that the size of the projectile and the length of the cannon had been announced, how much gunpowder would be needed to create the required propellant thrust? This fearsome agent, whose worst effects have, however, been tamed by Man, was about to be called upon to play its customary role—but to an unprecedented degree.

It is generally believed, and widely repeated, that gunpowder was invented in the fourteenth century by a monk named Schwartz* who paid for his great discovery with his life. But it is now more or less proven that this story should be ranked among the myths of the Middle Ages. Gunpowder was not invented by anybody. It derives directly from 'Greek fire', which was also composed of sulphur and saltpetre.* However, since those distant times, such mixtures and blends, which were merely combustible amalgams, have been turned into explosive compounds.

While experts are well acquainted with the fanciful history of gunpowder, few ordinary people understand its mechanical power. Now this is precisely what must be grasped if the importance of the question submitted to the Committee is to be understood.

A litre of gunpowder weighs approximately 2 pounds (900 grams). As it burns, it produces 400 litres of various gases. These gases, when released by exposure to a temperature of 2,400°C, will occupy a volume equivalent to 4,000 litres. The ratio of the volume of gunpowder to the volume of gas produced by combustion is therefore 1 to 4,000. It may be imagined then how terrifying is the build-up of pressure of such gases when they are constricted to a space four thousand times too small for them.

Each member of the Committee was, of course, conversant with all this when their meeting began the next evening. Barbicane gave the floor to Major Elphiston, who had been director of explosives production during the war.

'My good friends,' said the distinguished chemist, 'I shall start with some unimpeachable figures which we can use as a basis for our discussion. The twenty-four-pound shell of which the honourable

J. T. Maston spoke to us so poetically the day before last, is released from the muzzle of its ordnance by just sixteen pounds of gunpowder.'

'You are sure of that figure?' asked Barbicane.

'Quite sure,' replied the Major. 'The Armstrong cannon uses only 75 pounds of explosive for a projectile weighing 800 pounds, and the Redman Columbiad a mere 160 pounds to fire its half-ton shell a distance of six miles. These facts cannot be disputed: I got them myself from the minutes of the Board of Ordnance.'

'Quite!' observed the General.

'Well,' the Major continued, 'the following is the conclusion to be drawn from these figures: the amount of explosive does not increase with the weight of the projectile. So, for the sake of argument, say that if 16 pounds of gunpowder are required for a 24-pound shell, ordinary cannons should use a quantity of gunpowder equal to two-thirds of the weight of the projectile—yet in practice this ratio is not constant. Do the calculation and you will see that for a half-ton shell the quantity of gunpowder is not 333 pounds but falls to just 160.'

'And your point?' asked the President.

'But Major,' interjected J. T. Maston, 'if you follow your theory to its logical conclusion, you will end up saying that if your shell is big enough, you won't need to use any gunpowder at all!'

'My good friend Maston allows his sense of humour to get the better of him even when dealing with serious matters,' the Major rejoined. 'But he need not worry. I will shortly provide specific quantities of gunpowder that will satisfy his artilleryman's professional pride. I would merely point out that during the war, in the case of the biggest guns, the weight of gunpowder was reduced by trial and error to one tenth of the weight of the shell.'

'Absolutely correct,' said Morgan. 'But before we decide the weight that will be required to provide the required muzzle velocity, I think it would be useful to agree on the type of gunpowder we need to use.'

'We shall choose a coarse-grained powder,' said the Major. 'It burns more rapidly than the mealed, pulverized variety.'

'True,' said Morgan. 'But it is liable to cause shattering and over time damages the bore of the cannon.

'I do not doubt it, but what constitutes a disadvantage in a piece of ordnance designed for lengthy service is irrelevant in the case of our

Columbiad. There will be no risk of a burst barrel and we must have a powder that will ignite instantaneously so that we achieve the most effective mechanical result.'

'We could make several priming holes,' said J. T. Maston, 'so that the powder could be touched off at various points simultaneously.'

'We could,' said Elphiston, 'but that would only make the firing operation more complicated. I stand by my coarse-grained powder which avoids all these difficulties.'

'Agreed,' said the General.

'When Rodman loaded his Columbiad,' the Major went on, 'he used powder in the form of mammoth grains the size of chestnuts, made using willow charcoal and torrefaction in cast-iron pans. It came in the shape of a hard, shiny powder, left no trace on the hand, contained a high quotient of hydrogen and oxygen, ignited instantaneously, and, though extremely disruptive, did not noticeably damage the inside of a cannon's barrel.'

'Well now,' answered J. T. Maston, 'my sense is that there is no need to beat about the bush as our choice has been made for us!'

'Unless you'd prefer to use gold dust!' said the Major with a laugh that brought a threatening wave of the hook of his prickly friend.

Up to this point, Barbicane had taken no part in the discussion. He allowed others to speak and listened. It was clear that he had an idea of his own. But all he said was:

'And now, friends, what amount of gunpowder are you thinking of using?'

The three members of the Gun Club glanced briefly at each other.

After a moment, Morgan said: '200,000 pounds.'

'500,000,' said the Major.

'800,000,' cried J. T. Maston.

This time, Elphiston did not dare accuse his colleague of exaggerating. The fact was that they needed—no less—to send a projectile to the Moon that weighed 20,000 pounds and which had to be given an exit velocity of 12,000 yards a second. Hence the brief silence that followed the three bidding proposals advanced by the three colleagues.

The silence was finally broken by President Barbicane.

'My friends,' he said in an unhurried voice, 'I start from the premise that there will be no limit to the resistant strength of our cannon when it is built according to the specifications we have agreed upon. So I shall surprise the honourable J. T. Maston by saying that he has been too modest in his estimate and propose that we double his 800,000 pounds of gunpowder.

'1,600,000 pounds!' said J. T. Maston, leaping out of his seat.

'That much.'

'But in that case we shall have to re-think my idea of a cannon half a mile long.'

'Clearly,' agreed the Major.

'One point six million pounds of gunpowder,' the Committee's secretary went on, 'will fill a space of about 22,000 cubic metres. Now, given that your cannon has an overall capacity of 54,000 cubic metres, it will be half full and the barrel will cease to be long enough for the detonation of gases to provide the projectile with adequate thrust.'

There was no answer to this. What J. T. Maston had said was true. All eyes turned to Barbicane.

'And yet,' said the President, 'I stand by that amount of powder. Think a moment! 1,600,000 litres of powder will generate six billion litres of gas. Six billion! Just think of that!'

'But how can it be done?' asked the General.

'Quite simply. We must reduce the huge amount of powder while maintaining its mechanical power.'

'Right! But how?'

'I am about to tell you,' replied Barbicane coolly.

The Committee members stared at him intently.

'Indeed, nothing could be simpler,' he resumed. 'We make the mass of powder four times smaller. You are all familiar with a remarkable substance of which the basic matter of plant life is made. It is called cellulose.'

'I've got it!' said the Major. 'I can see what you're driving at, my dear fellow!'

'This substance,' said the President, 'is found in its purest state in various life forms, but especially in cotton which is actually just the fibres that grow on the seeds of the cotton plant. Now cotton, when combined with nitric acid at low temperatures, changes into a substance that is highly insoluble, highly combustible, eminently detonatable. A few years back, in 1832, it was discovered by a French chemist named Braconnot who called it xyloidine. In 1838, another Frenchman, Pelouze, studied its various properties, and finally, in 1846, Schonbein, Professor of Chemistry at Basle, recommended it as an explosive powder for military use. That powder is nitric cotton . . .'

'Or pyroxyle,' noted Elphiston.

'Otherwise guncotton,' added Morgan.

'So is there not a single American name than can be linked to this discovery?' cried J. T. Maston, moved by his strong sense of national pride.

'Alas no,' was the Major's answer.

'But to put Maston out of his misery,' said the President, 'I can say that the researches of one of our fellow Americans can be added to the study of cellulose because collodion, which is one of the main elements in the photographic process, is simply pyroxyle dissolved in alcohol-enriched ether and was discovered by Maynard who, at the time, was a medical student in Boston.'

'Well, it's bully for Maynard and bully for guncotton!'* exclaimed the Gun Club's loudmouthed permanent secretary.

'I come back to pyroxyle,' Barbicane continued. 'You are familiar with its properties which make it invaluable for our purposes. It is very easy to prepare: cotton is soaked for fifteen minutes in fuming nitric acid, then thoroughly washed in water and finally dried and it's done.'

'Indeed, what could be simpler?' said Morgan.

'Added to which, pyroxyle is unaffected by humidity, a crucial property from our point of view, since it will take several days to load the cannon. It becomes flammable at 170° instead of 240° and its combustion is so rapid that it can be ignited on top of ordinary gunpowder, which does not have time to begin to burn.'

'It's ideal,' said the Major.

'However, it is expensive.'

'That don't signify,' said J. T. Maston.

'Lastly, it gives shells four times more velocity than gunpowder. I will even add that if it is mixed with 80 per cent of its weight of potassium nitrate, its expansive power is further boosted very considerably.'

'Will that be necessary?' asked the Major.

'I think not,' replied Barbicane. 'Anyway, instead of 1,600,000 tons of gunpowder, we shall use just 400,000 pounds of guncotton. And since 500 pounds of guncotton can be safely stowed into a space of twenty-seven cubic feet, it will fill no more than 180 feet of the Columbiad. In this way, the shell propelled by six million litres of gas will have at most seven hundred feet of bore to travel through before it flies out and up towards the Eye of Night!'

At this high point, J. T. Maston could no longer contain his feelings. He threw himself into the arms of his friend like a shell bursting and would have completely done for him had Barbicane not been built to withstand such firepower.

This incident brought the third sitting of the Committee to a close. Barbicane and his bold colleagues, for whom nothing seemed impossible, had well and truly settled the highly complex problem of the projectile, the cannon, and the propellant powder. Now that their plans were sewn up, all that remained was to carry them out.

10

ONE ENEMY VERSUS TWENTY-FIVE MILLION FRIENDS

THE American public took an intense interest in the smallest details of the Gun Club's project. They followed the Committee's deliberations on a daily basis. The simplest measures taken for the Great Experiment, the questions that arose about figures and numbers, the mechanical problems that needed solving, in a word the whole 'cranking up' process, was what fascinated people to such a tremendous degree.

More than a year was to go by between the start and the finish of the work. But the passage of time would not happen without its moments of high excitement: deciding the location of the cannon's deployment, constructing the mould, casting the Columbiad, the dangerous business of loading—each and every phase never failed to draw the curiosity of the public. Once launched, the projectile would be out of sight in a few tenths of a second. Thereafter, what happened to it, how it behaved in space, how exactly it reached the Moon, were things that only a handful of privileged individuals would see with their own eyes. It was understandable, then, that the preparations for the great experiment and the detail of how it would be done should become the focus of interest.

However, public fascination with the enterprise was suddenly raised beyond the purely scientific level to an even higher pitch by an unexpected development.

It was widely known that Barbicane's project had earned him, personally, whole legions of admirers and friends. But however honourable and unusual their adulation, the majority view proved not to be unanimous. One man, just one in all the States of the Union, voiced his opposition to the Gun Club's initiative. He used every opportunity to attack it ferociously and, such is human nature, Barbicane was more deeply affected by the opposition of this single man than by the applause of the rest.

Moreover, he was very well aware of the cause of this animosity, the source of this solitary antagonism, the reason why it was personal and long-standing and, lastly, the professional rivalry from which it stemmed.

The President of the Gun Club had never met this persistent foe—fortunately, because any meeting between the two men would inevitably have had disastrous consequences. This rival was a man of science like Barbicane and was possessed of a proud, unflinching, stubborn, combustible nature—a Yankee born and bred. His name was Captain Nicholl and he lived in Philadelphia.

Now, few people can be unaware of the strange enmity that broke out during the Federal War between the cannonball and the armour of metal-plated ships, the former being designed to pierce the latter and the latter being determined not to be pierced by the former. It was the cause of a radical transformation in the navies of the nations of both continents. Cannonball and armour-plate embarked on a vendetta with unprecedented bitterness, the one getting steadily bigger as the other grew proportionately thicker. Ships armed with redoubtable guns sailed into battle shielded by their impregnable carapace. Vessels like the *Merrimac*, the *Monitor*, the *Ram Tennessee*, and the *Weehawken** fired enormous cannonballs after being freshly clad in iron to withstand those of the enemy. They did to others that which they did not want others to do to them, an immoral principle but the one on which rests the whole art of war.

Now Barbicane was a great founder of cannonballs and Nicholl was a great forger of armour-plating. The one cast night and day in Baltimore and the other forged day and night in Philadelphia, each pursuing a goal diametrically opposed to the other's.

No sooner did Barbicane invent a new kind of cannonball than Nicholl would create a new kind of armour-plating. The President of the Gun Club spent his time blowing holes in metal; the captain spent his trying to stop him succeeding. Thus began an unremitting rivalry which soon turned personal. Nicholl loomed large in Barbicane's dreams in the shape of an impenetrable suit of armour against which he tilted and by which he was painfully repulsed, while Barbicane, in Nicholl's dreams, was a cannonball which went clean through him.*

However, although they followed divergent paths, both these experts must surely—despite all the laws of geometry to the contrary—have met sooner or later, though it would have been only to fight a duel. Fortunately for these two upright citizens who had so well served their country, they were kept apart by a distance of fifty or sixty miles and their friends littered the road between them with obstacles, thus ensuring that they never did come face to face.

Now, no one was entirely clear about which of the two had outdone the other: the results obtained made it difficult to provide a definitive answer. However it seemed that in the last analysis armour-plating would have to give way to cannonball. Nevertheless, doubts remained in the minds of those in a position to judge. In the final trials that were held, Barbicane's cylindro-conical projectiles had ended up sticking like pins in Nicholl's solid plating. That day, the Philadelphian forger believed that victory was his and did not have scorn enough to heap on his rival. But when his opponent subsequently used plain 600-pounders instead of conical shells, the captain was obliged to change his tune. For the alternative projectiles, though fired at only a middling velocity, smashed, holed, and completely shattered plate made of the finest metal.

Things had reached this point, with the winner seeming to be the cannonball, when the war ended, on the very day that Nicholl was putting the final touches to a new kind of armour-plate for which he used forged steel! It was the crowning point of the entire history of armour-making. It would withstand all the projectiles in the world. The captain had it shipped to the experimental range in Washington and summoned the President of the Gun Club to come and smash it. But the war was over and Barbicane did not take up the challenge.

Nicholl was incensed and offered to expose his new armour to the fire of the most improbable cannonballs, solid, hollow, round, or conical, a proposal rejected out of hand by the President, who was most reluctant to compromise his belated success.

Nicholl, infuriated by such unspeakable intransigence, tried to tempt Barbicane by stacking the odds in his favour. He suggested setting up his armour-plate two hundred yards from the cannon. Barbicane dug his heels in deeper. One hundred yards? No, not even seventy-five!

'Then make it fifty!' bawled the captain in the pages of the news-papers. 'My plating at twenty-five yards!—And I'll stand behind it!'

Barbicane let it be known that even if Captain Nicholl stood in front of the target, he still wouldn't shoot at it.

When Nicholl heard this answer, he was beside himself with fury. He descended to personal vituperation, insinuated that funk was funk wherever you found it; that a man who would not even fire a cannon-ball was tantamount to running scared; in short, that modern gunners who do battle at a range of six miles had craftily exchanged individual courage in favour of waging war by mathematical workings on paper and that, moreover, there was as much gallantry involved in waiting quietly behind a sheet of armour-plating for a cannonball to land on it as there was in firing it in strict observance of the instruction manual.

Barbicane never replied to any of these insults. Perhaps he was not aware of any of them, for by that time his mind was entirely taken up by his great enterprise.

The day he delivered his famous address to the Gun Club, Captain Nicholl's fury rose to a paroxysm of rage. In it were elements of intense envy which coexisted with feelings of total impotence. How could he invent anything to compete with a Columbiad nine hundred feet long? No armour-plating could possibly stand up to a projectile weighing thirty thousand pounds! For the moment, Nicholl was left feeling crushed, annihilated, broken by the barrage of publicity. But then he picked himself up and promised himself that he would demolish Barbicane's proposal with the sheer weight of argument.

He began by launching vitriolic attacks on the deliberations of the Gun Club. He published a number of letters which newspapers were not loath to reprint. He attempted to undermine the scientific basis of Barbicane's undertaking. Once his private war had begun, all was grist to his mill and it must be said that some of the arguments he called on were specious and of dubious quality.

First, Barbicane's figures were viciously attacked. Pointing out that since one mathematical slip leads to another, Nicholl sought to show that his calculations were wrong and accused him of ignorance of the first principles of ballistics. Among his errors, as Nicholl used his own calculations to demonstrate, was his quite impossible claim that any object could be given a velocity of 12,000 yards per second. He further argued, algebra at the ready, that even if such speed could be generated, such a heavy projectile would never escape the limits of the Earth's atmosphere. It would struggle even to reach an altitude of twenty-five miles (eight leagues)! And there was more. Even assuming that this velocity was both achievable and adequate for the purpose, the projectile would never withstand the pressure developed by the explosive combustion of 1,600,000 pounds of gunpowder, and even if it did, it would not tolerate the high temperature but melt as it left the Columbiad's mouth and rain down in a red-hot shower on the heads of misguided spectators.

Barbicane disregarded these attacks, did not bat an eye, and carried on with his labours.

At this juncture, Nicholl resorted to an entirely different tactic. Passing silently over the question of the utter folly of the proposal, he portrayed it as highly dangerous both for the members of the public who legitimized so reprehensible a spectacle by their presence, and for towns situated anywhere near the abominable cannon. He also pointed out that if the projectile failed to reach its target—which it would not—it would inevitably fall back to Earth where the impact of such a mass multiplied by the square of its velocity would have a devastating effect on any part of the globe. Therefore, given these circumstances and without in any way infringing the rights of free citizens, here was one of the cases where the government should intervene. For the safety of all can never be sacrificed to the whims of one individual.

Such hyperbolic exaggeration shows all too clearly that Captain Nicholl had let himself be carried away by such exaggerated hostility. But he remained alone in his opinions. Accordingly no notice was taken of his bilious soothsaying. He was thus allowed to state his case until he was hoarse, since that was what he wanted. He appointed himself the defender of a cause that was lost from the outset. He was heard, but no one listened, and he failed to alienate a single admirer of the Gun Club's President, who, incidentally, never bothered to counter any of his rivals' arguments.

Having exhausted all expedients and unable even to lay down his life for his cause, he decided instead to lay out his money for it. In the columns of the Richmond *Enquirer*,* he drew up a series of wagers conceived in these terms and on a rising scale.

The bets were as follows:

1. That the funds vital for the Gun Club's experiment will not be forthcoming $1,000
2. That the operation of casting a cannon 900 metres long will prove impractical and fail $2,000
3. That it will not be possible to load the Columbiad and that the guncotton will ignite spontaneously and prematurely under the weight of the projectile $3,000
4. That the Columbiad will burst when fired for the first time $4,000
5. That the projectile will not travel six miles but will fall back to Earth within seconds of being fired $5,000

As can be seen, Captain Nicholl was risking a large sum of money in his pig-headed obstinacy—no less than $15,000.

Yet, despite the size of the stake, he received on 19 May* a sealed envelope with a message written with admirable brevity:

Baltimore, 18 October,
Done.
Barbicane

11

FLORIDA AND TEXAS*

YET there was one last question outstanding which had yet to be decided: the choice of the most suitable siting for the experiment. According to the recommendation of the Cambridge Observatory, the shot had to be fired vertically in relation to the plane of the horizon, that is toward the zenith. Now, the Moon rises to the zenith solely at locations situated between latitude 0° and 28°, in other words, its declination is only 28°. So what was now required was to determine exactly where on the Earth's surface the Columbiad should be cast.

On 20 October, the Gun Club met in open session. Barbicane brought a copy of the magnificent Z. Belltrop* map of the United States. But without even giving him time to unfold it, J. T. Maston requested the floor with his customary fiery fervour and spoke in these terms:*

'Honourable colleagues, the question before us today is of truly national importance, and it is about to furnish us with an opportunity to perform a great act of patriotism.'

The members of the Gun Club looked at each other, not knowing what the speaker had in mind.

'Not one of you here present', he went on, 'would ever dream of doing anything to tarnish the honour of his country. Now, if there is one right to which the Union can legitimately lay claim it is the right to keep the Gun Club's most powerful cannon within its borders. So, in the present circumstances . . .'

'Well said, Maston, but now . . .' said the President.

'Let me explain what I mean,' said the speaker. 'In the present circumstances, for the experiment to be performed in the most favourable conditions, we have to choose a location not too far distant from the equator . . .'

'Perhaps you would . . .' said Barbicane.

'I insist on the free discussion of ideas,' barked the volatile J. T. Maston, 'and I here state my view that the place from which our glorious projectile shall rise must be situated within the Union.'

'Quite right!' cried several members.

'Now, because our frontiers do not extend far enough downwards, because to the south the sea forms an impassable barrier and because we shall be forced to look for this 28th parallel outside the United States, in another country with which we share a border, we have a situation which constitutes a legitimate *casus belli*! I propose, therefore, that we declare war immediately on Mexico!'

'No! Out of the question!' came cries for every corner of the auditorium.

'No?' replied J. T. Maston. 'No? Now there's a word I never thought I should hear within these walls!'

'But listen a moment . . .'

'Never! Never!' cried the hot-blooded speaker. 'This war is set to break out at any time and I vote that it should start no later than this very day!'

'Maston!' said Barbicane, setting off his shot-warning bell with an ear-shattering clangour, 'you no longer have the floor!'

Maston tried to reply but a few of his colleagues succeeded in restraining him.

'I agree,' said Barbicane, 'that the experiment cannot and must not be attempted anywhere but on the soil of the Union. But if my impatient friend had only allowed me to speak, if he had cared to glance at any map, he would have known that it would be quite pointless to declare war on our neighbours, since certain frontiers of the United States do extend down beyond the 28th parallel. Just look and you will see that we have at our disposal the entire southern parts of both Texas and Florida.'*

The incident was quickly forgotten, though it was not without regret that J. T. Maston allowed himself to be convinced. So it was decided that the Columbiad would be cast and laid in the soil of either Texas or Florida. But it was a decision that created a rivalry without precedent between the towns of the two States concerned.

The 28th parallel, at the point where it encounters the American coast, crosses the peninsula of Florida, dividing it into two almost equal parts. Then, proceeding into the Gulf of Mexico, it subtends the arc formed by the coasts of Alabama, Mississippi, and Louisiana. Next, making land in Texas, off which it slices a corner, it carries on through Mexico, crosses the Sonoran desert, skips over Baja California, and continues on its own way over the waters of the Pacific Ocean. So there were only parts of Texas and Florida, both situated below the parallel, that met the latitudinal criteria stipulated by the Cambridge Observatory.

The southern half of Florida boasts no settlements of any great size, though it bristles with forts built to defend against marauding Indians. Only one place, Tampa, was in a position to make a case for selection and to put itself forward on the basis of its location.

In Texas, on the contrary, towns are both more numerous and larger. Corpus Christi, in Nuecos County, and all the towns on the banks of the Rio Bravo,* Laredo, Comalites, San Ignacio in Webb County, Roma and Rio-Grande City in Starr County, Edinburg in Hidalgo County, Santa Rita, El Panda, Brownsville in Cameron County, together were mighty impressive competition against the claims of Florida.

As a result, the choice had barely been made known when representatives from Texas and Florida began flocking to Baltimore by the quickest routes available. From that moment on, President Barbicane and the more senior members of the Gun Club were bombarded night and day with powerful proposals. If seven Greek cities contend for the honour of being the birthplace of Homer, two entire States threatened to come to blows over a cannon.

These 'rival brothers' armed themselves and were seen parading in the streets of the town. Whenever they met, violence was much to be feared, for it would have had disastrous consequences. Fortunately, the prudence and diplomatic skills of President Barbicane averted that particular danger. But these physical demonstrations became public when they found their way into newspapers published in various States. Thus the *New York Herald* and the *Tribune* both supported Texas while the *Times* and the *American Review** came down in favour of the cause of Florida. Members of the Gun Club reached the point where they did not know which side to believe.

Texas was proud to have the backing of its twenty-six counties, which were lined up like big battalions. But Florida in reply said that twelve counties in a State six times smaller counted for far more than those twenty-six.

Texas made a great deal of its 330,000 inhabitants but Florida, being smaller, claimed that with 56,000 people it was the more densely populated. Furthermore, it accused Texas of harbouring swamp fevers which in an average year cost it the lives of several thousand citizens. And Florida was not wrong.

In turn, Texas replied that in the matter of swamp fevers Florida was in no position to lecture anybody and that it was, to say the least, unwise to call other places disease-ridden when you yourself had the honour of having chronic levels of *vomito negro*.* And Texas was right.

'Besides,' said the Texans through the pages of the *New York Herald*, 'people should show some respect for a State which grows the finest cotton in the whole of America, a State that produces the best green oak for ship-building, a State that has reserves of high-grade oil and of iron ore that yields fifty per cent of pure metal.'

To this, the *American Review*'s reply was that the soil of Florida, though less rich, furnished the best conditions for moulding and casting the Columbiad, as it was mainly composed of sand and clayey soil.

'But,' said the Texans, 'before anything can be cast in a place, you have first to be able to get there. Now, communications with Florida are difficult whereas the coast of Texas has Galveston Bay which has a shoreline of fourteen leagues and could hold all the ships of all the navies in the entire world.'

Newspapers which supported Florida hit back with: 'Really? But you're selling a pig in a poke: your Galveston Bay is situated *above the twenty-ninth parallel*! We on the other hand can offer the Bay of Espiritu Santo* which opens out exactly on the 28th degree of latitude and from which ships can sail directly up to Tampa.'

'Some bay!' retorted Texas. 'It's half silted up!'

'Silted up yourself!' cried Florida. 'Are you trying to make out that I am a land inhabited by savages?'

'Well, you still have the Seminoles running around all over your prairies!'

'Hark who's talking! Do you call your Apaches and Comanches civilized?'

The war of words had been raging along these lines for several days when Florida attempted to draw its adversary onto different ground. One morning, the *Times* implied that the enterprise being 'fundamentally American', it could not be attempted anywhere except on ground that was 'fundamentally American'.

To these words Texas responded with alacrity: '*American*! We're every bit as American as you! Were not Texas and Florida both added to the Union in 1845?'

'Of course,' said the *Times*. 'But we have belonged to the Americans since 1820!'

'That I fully believe,' replied the *Tribune*. 'But having being Spaniards and British for two hundred years, you were *sold* to the United States for five million dollars!'

'So what?' said the Floridians. 'It's nothing to be ashamed of. In 1803, Louisiana was bought from Napoleon for sixteen million dollars!'

'It's a disgrace!' cried the representatives from Texas. 'A miserable spit of land like Florida dares compare itself to Texas, which never sold itself to anybody, carved out its independence unaided, kicked out the Mexicans on 2 March 1836 and declared itself a federative republic after the victory won by Samuel Houston over Santa Anna's soldiers on the banks of the San Jacinto! In other words, a territory which joined the United States of America of its own free will!'

'Because it was running scared of the Mexicans!' said Florida.

Scared! The day that word, which was frankly too strong, was pronounced, the situation became intolerable. People would not have been surprised to see both parties cutting each others' throats in the streets of Baltimore. It became necessary to keep a strict eye on all the representatives.

President Barbicane did not know which way to turn. Notes, documents, and threatening letters rained down on his house. On which side should he come down? As to the acquisition of a suitable site, ease of communications, speed of transportation, the claims of both states were evenly balanced. As for the politicians, they had nothing to do with the matter.

This state of uncertainty, of indecision had already lasted some considerable length of time when Barbicane finally resolved to end it. He summoned his colleagues and the solution which he put to them was eminently sensible, as will be seen.

'Given,' he began, 'what has been going on between Florida and Texas, it is quite clear that exactly the same problems will be repeated between the towns of whichever State is preferred. The rivalry will descend from the genus to the species, that is, from State to town, and that is the fact of the matter. Now Texas has eleven towns which meet the prescribed conditions. All of them would fight each other for the honour of hosting our undertaking and all of them would create new difficulties for us. Whereas Florida has just one that is suitable. Ergo, we choose Florida and Tampa!'

When this decision was announced, the representatives from Texas were utterly devastated. They became indescribably angry and issued individual challenges to various members of the Gun Club. For the burghers of Baltimore, there was only one course of action to take and they took it. They chartered a special train, the Texans were rounded up, packed into it, and in that manner left town at a rate of thirty miles an hour.

But despite the breakneck speed at which they departed, they still had time to hurl one final sarcastic threat at their opponents.*

Referring to the lack of breadth of Florida, a flimsy peninsula situated between two seas, they said it would not survive the blast when the projectile was launched and would explode the first time the cannon was fired.

'If it explodes, it explodes!' replied the Floridians, with a dry understatement worthy of ancient times.

12

URBI ET ORBI

ALL difficulties astronomical, mechanical, and topographical having been settled, there now arose the question of money. An enormous sum had to be raised, sufficient to finance the project. No one individual, nor even one State could have sufficed to furnish the necessary millions.

President Barbicane therefore resolved—though the enterprise was an American initiative—to make it a matter of universal interest and to invite the cooperation of the people of each and every nation. It was both the right and the duty of the entire terrestrial globe to have a hand in a matter which concerned its satellite. To this end, the subscription would open in Baltimore and be extended to the whole world, *urbi et orbi*.*

The subscription succeeded beyond all hopes even though the sums advanced were to be gifts, not loans. The operation was entirely disinterested in the literal sense of the word since it offered no prospect of profit whatsoever.

The impact of Barbicane's address to the Gun Club had not stopped at the frontiers of the United States. It had crossed the Atlantic and the Pacific, sweeping simultaneously across Asia and Europe, Africa and Oceania. Observatories within the Union got in touch immediately with their counterparts in foreign countries. Some observatories, those in Paris, Saint Petersburg, Cape Town, Berlin, Altona, Stockholm, Warsaw, Hamburg, Buda,* Bologna, Malta, Lisbon, Benares, Madras, and Peking, sent their compliments to the Gun Club. The rest, less enthusiastic, held out lower expectations.

As to the observatory at Greenwich, its response, backed by all twenty-two of Great Britain's other astronomical establishments, was unequivocal. It rejected outright any possibility of success and endorsed theories of Captain Nicholl. Moreover, when learned bodies elsewhere promised to send delegates to Tampa, the Greenwich scientists met in formal session, bluntly set aside Barbicane's proposal, and moved to pass on to other business. It was nothing more or less than pure, true-blue British jealousy.

But overall, the impact on the scientific world was entirely gratifying, and from there it spread to the masses, who, on the whole, took a keen interest in the enterprise. This was a fact of critical importance since the common people were about to be called up to subscribe huge sums.

On 8 October, President Barbicane had launched a confident manifesto in which he appealed 'to all men of good will on Earth'.* This document, translated into all languages, proved to be a great success.

The public subscription was opened in the major cities of the Union with its head office in Baltimore, at 9 Baltimore Street. Banks for subscribers were opened in the various countries of both continents, as follows:

Vienna, S. M. de Rothschild
Petersburg, Stieglitz and Co.
Paris, Credit Mobilier
Stockholm, Tottie and Arfuredson
London, N. M. Rothschild and Son
Turin, Ardouin and Co.
Berlin, Mendelssohn
Geneva, Lombard, Odier and Co.
Constantinople, The Ottoman Bank
Brussels, J. Lambert
Madrid, Daniel Weisweller
At Amsterdam, Netherlands Credit Co.
Rome, Torlonia and Co.
Lisbon, Lecesne
Copenhagen, Private Bank
Buenos-Aires, Maua Bank
Rio de Janeiro, ditto
At Montevideo, ditto
At Valparaiso, Thomas La Chambre and Co.
At Mexico, Martin Daran and Co.
Lima, Thomas La Chambre and Co.

Three days after President Barbicane's manifesto appeared, four million dollars had already been deposited in banks in various cities of the Union. With such immediate backing, the Gun Club could begin operations at once.

But a few days later, advices were received in America which revealed that foreign subscriptions were being taken up with great enthusiasm. Some countries were notable for their generosity; others were less ready to undo the purse-strings. It varied according to national temperament.

Still, figures speak louder than words. Here is the certified official final statement of the sums paid into the Gun Club's account after the subscription was closed.

Russia's contribution amounted to the colossal sum of 368,733 roubles. If this figure should come as a surprise, it is only because people underestimate the keen interest that Russians take in science and the progress they have made in the study of astronomy through their numerous observatories, the largest of which was built at a cost of two million roubles.

At the outset, France took a supercilious view of brash American bombast. The Moon was used as a pretext for innumerable tired old puns and a score of comic songs in which bad taste vied with ignorance. But whereas the French had once paid heavily for singing a song,* this time, when they had done laughing, they readily paid up, raising subscriptions for a sum of 1,253,930 francs. At that price, they were entitled to have their fun.

Austria proved suitably generous despite its financial crisis. Its share of the overall public contribution was 216,000 florins, a most welcome offering.

Sweden and Norway jointly donated 52,000 riksdalers, a considerable amount given the size of their populations. But it would have been certainly more if a subscription bureau had been opened in Christiania* as well as in Stockholm. For some reason, Norwegians dislike sending money to Sweden.*

Prussia, by sending 250,000 thaler, expressed its hearty approval of the enterprise. Its various observatories were quick to subscribe a large sum and were President Barbicane's most enthusiastic supporters.

Turkey behaved generously. Of course it had a particular interest in the undertaking, for the cycle of the Moon regulates its calendar and fixes the date of the holy month of Ramadan. It could hardly donate less than the 1,372,640 piastres, which it produced with a promptness, however, that indicated some pressure on the part of the government of the Sublime Porte.*

Belgium stood out in leading all second-ranking countries with its gift of 513,000 francs, the equivalent of about twelve centimes per head of population.

The interest of Holland and its colonies in the venture was expressed by its grant of 110,000 florins, though it was made with a request for a 5 per cent discount for paying cash.

Denmark, though territorially somewhat restricted,* nevertheless offered 9,000 fine gold ducats, thereby demonstrating the Danes' passion for scientific expeditions.

The German Confederation pledged 34,385 florins. No one could have asked for more, though in any case they would not have given it.

Despite being strapped for cash, Italy managed to come up with 200,000 lire by turning the pockets of its people inside out. If Italy had had Venetia, she would have fared better. But Venetia did not belong to Italy.

The Papal States did not feel it could send less than 7,000 Roman scudos, while Portugal put a figure on its devotion to science by offering 30,000 cruzados, no less.

In the case of Mexico, it was the widow's mite: just 96 piastres. Still, fledgling empires invariably have little cash to spare.*

The sum of 257 francs was Switzerland's modest stake in the American project. To be perfectly frank, Switzerland saw no practical point in the venture. It simply could not understand how firing a cannonball at the Moon could lead to the establishment of profitable business relations with the Eye of Night. They therefore did not think it prudent to invest capital funds in so risky an operation. Still, maybe Switzerland was right.

On the other hand, Spain could not scrape together more than 210 reals. Ostensibly, the reason given was that it had to finish building its railways. But the truth is that science is not highly regarded in that country, which is still rather backward. Moreover, some Spaniards—and not the worst-educated of them—had no clear idea of the size of the projectile compared with the mass of the Moon. They were afraid it would upset its orbit, disrupt its functions as a satellite, and cause it to crash down onto the surface of the terrestrial globe. In the circumstances, it seemed best to have nothing to do with the scheme. Which is what, to within a handful of reals, it did.

That left England and we know the sneering antipathy which had greeted Barbicane's proposal there. The British have just one soul for all twenty-five million inhabitants who live in the British Isles. They let it be known that the Gun Club's proposal was contrary to 'the principle of non-intervention'* and consequently contributed nothing, not one farthing.

When they heard the news, the Gun Club merely gave a shrug and returned to matters in hand. When South America—Peru, Chile, Brazil, the provinces of La Plata and Colombia—had come up with its contribution and handed over the sum of 300,000 dollars, the Gun Club found itself with a considerable capital sum to its name, broken down as follows:

United States Subscriptions	$4,000,000
Foreign Subscriptions	$1,446,675
Total	$5,446,675

So five million, four hundred and forty-six thousand, six hundred and seventy-five dollars had been paid into the Gun Club's accounts.

No one should be surprised by the immensity of this sum. The casting and forging; the masonry; the dispatch of workers to a virtually uninhabited area; the construction of furnaces and workshops; the installation of mechanized plant; the gunpowder; the projectile; overheads—the estimates told the tale—would run through it almost down to the last penny. During the Federal War, a volley from some cannons had cost a thousand dollars; every time one of President Barbicane's cannons, unique in the annals of artillery, was fired, the price tag might well have been five thousand times greater.

On 20 October, a contract was signed with the foundry at Cold Spring,* near New York, which had manufactured Parrott's finest cast-iron cannon during the war.

It was stipulated between the contracting parties that the factory at Cold Spring would undertake to supply and deliver to Tampa in southern Florida the requisite materials for casting the Columbiad.

The whole operation should be completed by 15 October of the following year at the latest, and the cannon delivered in full working order. Failure to comply would incur a penalty of one hundred dollars per day until the Moon should appear again in the same position, which was to say, following an interval of eighteen years and eleven days.

The recruitment of workers, their pay and the oversight of the entire operation would be the responsibility of the Cold Spring Company.

This contract, executed in duplicate and made in good faith, was signed by I. Barbicane, President of the Gun Club, for the first part, and J. Murchison, director of the Cold Spring works, for the second part, who each approved its terms.

13

STONE'S HILL

Ever since the decision of the members of the Gun Club that went against Texas, the whole of America, where everybody can read, felt it their duty to inform themselves of the geography of Florida. Bookshops had never sold so many copies of Bartram's *Travels in Florida*, of Roman's *Natural History of East and West Florida*, Williams's *Territory of Florida*, and Cleland's *On the Culture of the Sugar-Cane in East Florida*.* New editions had to be brought out. They flew off the shelves.

But Barbicane had better things to do than spend his time reading. He was eager to see the terrain with his own eyes and decide on the spot where the Columbiad would be sited. And so, not wasting a moment, he advanced the Observatory at Cambridge the funds it would need to build a telescope and negotiated with the firm of Breadwill & Co., of Albany, for the constructing of a projectile in aluminium. Then he left Baltimore accompanied by J. T. Maston, Major Elphiston, and Cold Spring's managing director.

The next day, the four travelling companions reached New Orleans. There they immediately boarded the *Tampico*, a dispatch boat belonging to the federal Navy which the government had placed at their disposal. Steam was up to full pressure and soon the coast of Louisiana dropped out of view.

Their passage was not a long one. Two days and 480 miles later, the *Tampico* was within sight of the coast of Florida. As they drew nearer, Barbicane made out a low, flat stretch of apparently barren country. After running along a series of creeks abounding in oysters and lobsters, the *Tampico* entered the Bay of Espiritu Santo.

The Bay is divided into two elongated roadsteads, Tampa Bay and Hillsborough Bay, both reached by a narrows through which the steamer passed quickly. Soon, the low batteries of Fort Brooke showed across the water and the town of Tampa appeared, casually nestling at the head of the small natural harbour formed by the mouth of the Hillsborough River.

It was there, at seven in the evening of 22 October, that the *Tampico* dropped anchor. Its four passengers disembarked immediately.

Barbicane felt his heart race as he set foot on the soil of Florida. It seemed as if he were testing it with his boot, as an architect might do when assessing the soundness of a house. J. T. Maston jabbed the ground with the end of his hook.

'Gentlemen,' said Barbicane, 'there's not a second to lose. Tomorrow morning we will acquire horses and start exploring the country.'

The moment Barbicane had set foot on dry land all three thousand inhabitants of Tampa came out to meet him, an honour worthy of the President of the Gun Club which had so favoured them by its decision. They greeted him with great bursts of cheering. But Barbicane cut short the ovation, made his way to a room at the Hotel Franklin and refused to receive visitors. The celebrity style of life was clearly not for him.

The very next day, 23 October, a number of small Spanish thoroughbreds, high-stepping and eager, were pawing the ground spiritedly beneath his windows. But instead of just four, there were fifty of them, all with riders. Barbicane went downstairs with his three companions and was mightily taken aback to find himself in the middle of a cavalcade. He also noted that each rider had a carbine slung slantwise across his back and pistols in his saddle holsters. The reason for this display of force was promptly supplied by a young Floridian who said:

'Sir, it's on account of the Seminoles.'

'Seminoles?'

'Savages who roam the prairies. To be on the safe side, we thought we'd give you an escort.'

'What nonsense!' snorted J. T. Maston as he climbed into the saddle.

'Anyway,' the Floridian went on, 'it's just a precaution.'

'Gentlemen,' said Barbicane, 'thank you for your concern. But now, we ride!'

The small cohort moved off at once and disappeared in a cloud of dust. It was five in the morning; the sun was already shining brightly and the thermometer read 84°. But a fresh breeze off the sea kept the worst of the heat away.

Leaving Tampa behind, Barbicane bore south and followed the coast, a route that took him to Alifia Creek. This small river flows into Hillsborough Bay, some twelve miles below Tampa. Barbicane and his escort hugged its right bank as they rode eastwards. Soon the waters of the Bay disappeared behind a fold in the terrain and thereafter all there was to see was the landscape of Florida.

Florida is divided into two parts, one to the north, more densely populated and less backward, with Tallahassee as its capital and also Pensacola, one of the United States' major naval bases. The other, wedged between America and the Gulf of Mexico,* which hold it fast it in their watery embrace, is little more than a narrow peninsula scoured by the current of the Gulf Stream, a spit of land lost in the middle of a small archipelago, a headland incessantly rounded by numerous vessels proceeding from the Old Bahama Channel. It is the advance guard that stands on the edge of the Gulf where the great hurricanes drive in.

The surface covered by this State is 38,033,267 acres, and it was somewhere in that area that Barbicane had to find a location below the 28th parallel that was suitable for their great undertaking. Accordingly, as he rode along, he paid great attention to the lie of the land and its particular configuration.

Florida, discovered by Juan Ponce de León on Palm Sunday 1512, was first christened *Pascua florida*. Such a charming name seemed scarcely justified by its arid, sun-scorched shore. Yet within a few miles of the coast, the terrain began to change slowly and the country now lived up to its name. The ground was crisscrossed by a network of creeks, *ríos*, streams, pools, and small lakes. It was like being in Holland or Guyana. But the land soon rose noticeably and gave way to cultivated plains where a wide range of northern and southern crops were grown. The vast fields, the sun of the Tropics, and the water stored in the heavy clay soil ensured the successful growth of the great sweeps of pineapple, yams, tobacco, rice, cotton, and sugar-cane which stretched away into the distance in an exuberant display of effortless abundance.

Barbicane appeared well satisfied with the way the land rose progressively and J. T. Maston questioned him on the subject:

'My good friend,' said the President in reply, 'we have every reason for wanting to cast our Columbiad on high ground.'

'To be nearer the Moon?' asked the Gun Club's secretary.

'No,' smiled Barbicane. 'Would a few yards here and there make any difference? Of course not. But in high country, our work will proceed more easily. We won't need to worry about water and that means no long, costly drainage pipes, which is a consideration if we're going to have to bore a shaft nine hundred feet deep.'

'You're right,' said Murchison,* who was an engineer. 'We'll have to avoid water insofar as possible when we're digging. But if we do encounter springs, it will not matter for we have the equipment to pump them dry or divert them. We're not talking here of artesian wells, narrow and dark where drilling, boring, shoring up, and the rest of the well-borer's work is all done blind. We shall be operating in daylight with pick-axe and mattock and, with the help of blasting powder, we'll have the job done in no time.'

'Even so,' said Barbicane, 'if on account of the height or nature of the land we can avoid having to cope with underground water, we shall progress more quickly and with better results. So we must try to dig our trench on a site which is a thousand or two feet above sea-level.'

'You are right, sir. And unless I am very much mistaken, it won't be long before we find a suitable spot.'

'And I do most heartily wish we were at the point where I could see the first pick being swung,' said the President.

'And I the last!' cried J. T. Maston.

'We'll do it, gentlemen,' said the engineer, 'and, believe me, Cold Spring won't have to pay you any penalty for late completion.'

'By Jove, you're right!' answered J. T. Maston. 'Did you know that a hundred dollars a day until the Moon is again in the right position, that is for eighteen years and eleven days, would come to 658,100 dollars?'*

'No, sir, we did not,' replied the engineer, 'and it's something we won't ever need to know.'

By about ten in the morning, the small party had covered a dozen miles and fertile country now gave way to an area of forest that was home to a wide variety of life forms, proliferating with tropical extravagance. The forests, which were virtually impenetrable, were full of the competing colours and scents of pomegranates, oranges, lemons, figs, olives, apricots, bananas, and hanging lianas of vines. In the sweet-smelling shade of those magnificent trees was a world of brilliantly-plumaged birds which sang and flitted hither and thither. Particularly noticeable amongst them were crab-catchers, whose nests would have to be jewel cases to be worthy of such dazzling, feathered brilliance.*

Confronted by such opulence of nature, J. T. Maston and the Major could not but marvel at its splendours and beauties. But President Barbicane, not being as open to such impressions, was eager to press on. This lush country offended him here by its very lushness. Though no dowser, he could sense water under his feet and he looked around in vain for palpable signs of aridity.

On they went. Several times they had to ford rivers, not without danger, for they were infested with caimans fifteen to eighteen feet long. J. T. Maston boldly threatened them with his fearsome hook but succeeded only in scaring pelicans, teals, and tropic-birds, wild residents of those river-banks, while tall red flamingos stood looking vacantly at him. Eventually, it was the turn of these denizens of wetlands to be left behind. The trees, smaller now, grew more scattered in woodland that became less dense. A few isolated clumps stood up on the endless plains across which passed herds of startled deer.

'At last!' cried Barbicane, standing up in his saddle, 'pine country!'

'Injun country too,' said the Major.

Indeed, a few Seminoles appeared just then on the horizon. They became excited and rushed around each other on their quick-footed ponies, brandishing long lances and shooting in the air, the crack of their muskets muted by distance. But in the event, they settled for these shows of defiance and did not otherwise trouble Barbicane and his companions.

At that juncture, the party had reached the middle of a rocky plain, a vast open area covering several acres on which a burning sun beat down. It was formed by a wide bulge or raised fold of the land and looked to the Gun Club to meet all the conditions required for the location of their Columbiad.

'Halt!' cried Barbicane as he came to a stop. 'Do people here have a name for this place?'

'It's called Stone's Hill,'* answered one of the Floridians.

Without saying a word, Barbicane swung down from his horse, laid out his instruments and began taking his exact position with scientific precision. The small party gathered round him and watched in complete silence as he worked.

At that moment, the sun passed the meridian. Barbicane waited a few moments, then quickly scribbled down the result of his observations and said:

'This place is 1,800 feet above sea-level* at latitude 27° 7´ and longitude 5° 7´ west. To my mind, this arid, rocky terrain fully meets the conditions required for our purpose. It is therefore here, on this plain, that we shall build our magazines, workshops, furnaces, and accommodation for our workers, and it is from this very spot,' he repeated, stamping his boot on the summit of Stone's Hill, 'that our projectile will soar up and away into the outer regions of the solar system!'

14

WITH PICK AND TROWEL

BARBICANE and his companions returned to Tampa that same evening, and Murchison the engineer again boarded the *Tampico* and sailed back to New Orleans. His task was to hire an army of workers and return with most of the materials they needed. The members of the Gun Club stayed behind in Tampa to organize the start of operations with the help of the local population.

A week after his departure, the *Tampico* was back in the Bay of Espiritu Santo accompanied by a flotilla of steam vessels. Murchison had assembled a group of fifteen hundred workers. In the bad old days of slavery, such a mission would have been a waste of his time and effort. But since America, land of liberty, no longer nurtured any except free men in its bosom, hands now flocked to wherever there were well-paid jobs for the asking. Now the Gun Club was not short of funds. It offered its employees high wages, and substantial bonuses where appropriate. When the Florida project was completed, a man hired for it could count on having a round sum of money deposited in his name in a Baltimore bank. So Murchison did not need to seek very far and could set strict levels of intelligence and skill for applicants. It can safely be said that he filled the ranks of his work force with the very finest mechanics, stokers, miners, foundrymen, limeburners, brick-makers, and men with trades of all kinds, black and white with no distinction of colour. Many of them brought their families. It was in effect a migration.

At 10.30 on the morning of 31 October, this contingent debouched onto the wharves of Tampa. It is not difficult to imagine the commotion and activity which prevailed in that little town whose population doubled in just one day. And there is no question that Tampa gained enormously from the Gun Club's activity, not so much from the number of workers who were dispatched at once to Stone's Hill but from the crowds of sightseers who travelled to the Florida peninsula from every part of the world.

The first few days were taken up with the task of unloading the cargo shipped in by the flotilla—machines and provisions as well as a large number of prefabricated dwellings in the form of metal sheets numbered for ease of assembly. While this was proceeding, Barbicane laid the first sleepers for a railway fifteen miles long that would connect Stone's Hill with Tampa.

The approach to building railways in America is well-known. There a railroad—unpredictable in its twists and turns, bold in its gradients, scorning parapets and bridges and tunnels, climbing hillsides, clattering through valleys—rushes blindly on, without a care for the direct route. It is not expensive to build nor does it cause much disruption, but its trains do jump the rails and unrestrainedly jar and jolt their passengers. The line from Tampa to Stone's Hill was a trifling thing, and its construction did not call for much in time and money.

Meanwhile, Barbicane was the moving spirit of the body of men who had answered the call. He was its driving force, he fired it with energy, enthusiasm, and commitment. He was everywhere as if endowed with the gift of ubiquity, and with J. T. Maston always at his side, like a buzzing fly. His practical turn of mind produced all manner of ingenious innovations. For him, there were no obstacles, no insurmountable difficulties, and he was never at a loss. He was a miner, mason, mechanic, as well as an artillery man, and he had a solution for every problem. He stayed regularly in touch with the Gun Club and the Cold Spring company while day and night the lights stayed on and steam was kept up to pressure in the *Tampico*, which rode at anchor in Hillsborough Bay awaiting his orders.

On 1 November, Barbicane left Tampa with a crew of workmen and the very next day a village of sheet-metal houses sprang up around Stone's Hill. They surrounded it with a fence and soon, judging by its activity and energy, it could have passed muster as one of the great cities of the Union. Inside the precinct, life was subject to strict discipline and work now began according to a set routine.

Carefully conducted test bore-holes had revealed the composition of the soil, and the start of digging operations was scheduled for 4 November. On that day, Barbicane assembled all his foremen and told them:

'Now, friends, you all know why I have brought you to this wild part of Florida. Our object is to cast a cannon with a bore of nine feet and walls six feet thick, to be encased in a stone sheath to a thickness of nineteen and a half feet. Which means that we shall need to sink a shaft sixty feet wide and nine hundred feet deep. This enormous task must be completed in eight months' time. In short, you have 2,543,400 cubic feet of earth to extract in 255 days or, in round figures, 10,000 cubic feet to dig out each and every day. Now this would not be much of a challenge for a thousand men working in the open air, but it will be much harder in a relatively confined space. Nevertheless, because this work must be done, done it shall be and I am counting as much on your spirit as on your skill to see it through.'

At eight o'clock that morning, the first pick was driven into the earth of Florida and from that moment on that splendid tool did not lie idle in miners' hands for a single moment. Labourers were relieved every six hours.

But however colossal the task, it never asked more of men than human strength could give. Far from it. How many even more formidable challenges, some needing to combat the hostile elements, have, over the ages, been brought to a successful conclusion! To mention only comparable undertakings, it will suffice to quote Father Joseph's Well dug near Cairo by Sultan Saladin* in an age before machines increased the power of man a hundredfold. It goes straight down to the level of the Nile 300 feet below! Or that other well sunk at Coblenz for John, Margrave of Baden, which reached a depth of 600 feet! And what did this new venture involve? It meant tripling that depth and sinking a shaft ten times wider—which would incidentally make the work of excavation that much easier! There was not one foreman or labourer who doubted the success of the operation for a single moment.

An important decision made by the engineer Murchison and endorsed by President Barbicane was another factor which helped to speed up the work further. A clause in the contract stipulated that the Columbiad was to be fitted with wrought-iron hoops welded on hot. This was an unnecessary precaution since the cannon clearly would not need these strengthening collars. The clause was therefore cancelled and dropping it saved a great deal of time. It meant they could use the new method of digging wells, then widely adopted, in which the stone-work could be put in place while the shaft was still being sunk. Thanks to this very simple procedure, it is no longer necessary to shore up the sides with struts and braces—the masonry-work gives them solid support and as it descends it is held in place by its own weight.

But that phase would not begin until the picks had exposed the bedrock below the Earth.

On 4 November, fifty men began work at the centre of the fenced-off area—that is to say, at the top of Stone's Hill—digging a circular hole with a diameter of sixty feet.

First, the picks encountered a kind of blackish leaf-mould six inches deep which they quickly disposed of. After this layer of earth came two feet of fine sand which was carefully removed, for it would be used in the casting process.

After this sand appeared fairly dense white clay, not unlike British marl, which lay in tiers, one below the other, for the next four feet.

Next the picks struck sparks from the hard bed of the soil, a type of rock made of petrified shells, very dry, very hard, of which they would never get to the end. At this point, when the hole was six and a half feet deep, the masons could begin their work.

They then installed a heavy-duty circular 'well base' of oak which filled the floor of the well, a kind of disc strengthened with bolts to make it solid and unbreakable. At its centre was a hole with a diameter equal to the external diameter of the Columbiad. It was on this 'base' that the first layers of masonry were set, its hydraulic cement holding the stones together in an inflexible grip. Once they had filled the space from circumference to centre with masonry, the workmen were left occupying a well twenty-one feet wide.

Once this stage was complete, the miners shouldered picks and mattocks and started cutting the rock away under the base, taking good care to support it on strong, solid props as they went. Each time the hole became two feet deeper, these props were removed one after the other, so that the curb sank slowly taking the circular plug of masonry with it. On the layer above, the masons laboured constantly, taking care to leave vent holes to permit the escape of gas during the casting operation.

This kind of work demanded of the workmen high levels of skill and unflagging alertness. Those working in the space beneath the curb could be dangerously, sometimes fatally injured by flying debris of stone. But their dedication never failed for a single moment, day or night—by day when, a few months later, the sun scorched those frazzled parts with ninety-nine degrees of heat, and by night as they laboured on in the white glare of the electric light. The noise of pick on stone, the firing of shot, the clanking of machinery, the scattered clouds of smoke rising into the air, created over Stone's Hill a halo of terror which the herds of bison or parties of Seminoles dared not brave.

And yet the work progressed steadily. Steam cranes accelerated the removal of spoil. There were few unexpected problems, only difficulties that had been anticipated and were speedily overcome.

The first month passed and the shaft had reached the depth set for that length of time, namely 112 feet. In December, that figure was doubled and it trebled in January. During the month of February, the workers had to deal with water from underground springs which broke through the Earth's crust where they had breached it. Powerful pumps and compressed air equipment had to be brought in to drain the water before the source could be sealed off with concrete, the way a leak is stopped on a ship. In the end, they solved the problem of springs of unwanted water. However, because there had resulted some settling in the ground, the curb tilted unevenly and caused a section of the masonry to come away. It is not difficult to imagine the crushing weight of this colossal block of masonry 450 feet high! The incident cost the lives of several workmen. For three weeks, the men had to be diverted to the work of shoring up the masonry plug, underpinning it and restoring the base to its original sound state. But very largely due to the skill of the engineer and the power of the machines used, the structure—briefly compromised—regained its equilibrium and the digging resumed.

Subsequently, no further setbacks delayed the forward march of the operation and on 10 June, twenty days before the expiry of the deadline set by Barbicane, the shaft, fully lined with its supporting stonework, had reached a depth of 900 feet. At that level, the masonry block rested on a solid cube thirty feet thick, while at the top it emerged flush with the surface of the surrounding ground.

President Barbicane and the members of the Gun Club heartily congratulated the engineer Murchison. His cyclopean labours had been brought to a successful conclusion with quite exceptional speed.

For eight months, Barbicane had never once left Stone's Hill. While keeping a close eye on the excavation of the shaft, he never wavered in his concern for the well-being and health of his workers. He had been very fortunate in warding off outbreaks of those diseases common to large groups of men living closely together which can be devastating in parts of the world which are exposed to the influence of tropical climates.

It is however true that a number of men paid with their lives for the risk-taking which is an integral part of all dangerous undertakings of this kind. Such fatal accidents cannot be prevented and Americans are not unduly worried by them. Their concern is more with human kind in general than with the individual in particular. But Barbicane's principles maintained the opposite view and he applied them on all occasions. As a result, thanks to his care, his intelligence, his vital contribution in moments of crisis and his acute, humane judgement, the number of serious mishaps did not exceed the average figure for countries overseas noted for the wealth of the precautions they took, among which was France, where the accident rate is one for every 200,000 francs worth of work.

15

CELEBRATING CASTING DAY

DURING the eight months spent excavating the shaft, preliminary work on the casting operation had proceeded simultaneously and at breakneck speed. A visitor to Stone's Hill would have been amazed by what he saw.

Six hundred yards from the lip of the shaft and arranged in a circle around it, 1,200 reverberatory furnaces had been installed, each six feet wide and separated from the others by a gap of three feet. These 1,200 furnaces formed a circle of circumference two miles long. All were built to the same design, with square chimneys, and together they created the most striking effect. J. T. Maston considered this architectural layout to be quite splendid. It reminded him of Washington's public monuments. For him, there was nothing finer anywhere, not even in Greece, 'though', he added, 'I've never been there'.

The reader will recall that at its third meeting, the Gun Club opted to use cast iron for the Columbiad, and specifically 'grey iron'. This type is actually tougher, more malleable, softer; it is easily drilled and suitable for all types of metal founding and, when smelted with coal, it has the best quality for high-resistance castings, such as cannons, steam-engine boilers, hydraulic presses, and so on.

Now when the casting process involves a single smelting, the result is rarely sufficiently homogenous. It takes a second fusion to purify and refine the metal by removing the last remaining soil deposits.

Therefore, before it was shipped to Tampa, the iron ore, treated in Cold Spring's blast furnaces with added coal and silicon* heated to a high temperature, had been carbonized and converted into cast iron. After this first stage, the product was to be dispatched to Stone's Hill. But 136,000,000 pounds of cast iron would be needed in total, an amount far too expensive to move by rail: the transport charges would have doubled the cost of the freight. It seemed preferable to charter ships in New York and load them with cast iron in the form of ingots. This called for the hire of no fewer than sixty-eight vessels, each of a thousand tons, a virtual fleet which, on 3 May, set off down the fairway of New York harbour, headed out towards the ocean, followed the American coast, passed through the Bahama Channel, and sailed round the tip of Florida. On the tenth day of the same month, it steamed into the Bay of Espiritu Santo and, having incurred no damage in transit, dropped anchor in the port of Tampa. There the cargo was transferred from the ships to the rolling-stock of the Stone's Hill Railway and, by the middle of January, the enormous quantity of cast iron had reached its destination.

It will now be easily understood that twelve hundred furnaces were not too many for the 136 million pounds of cast iron which would have to become molten at the same time. Each furnace could contain more than 114,000 pounds of metal. They had all been built on the same lines as those which had been used to cast the Rodman cannon. They were trapezoidal in form and very bluntly arched. The fire chamber and the chimney were at opposite ends of each furnace, which was thus evenly heated along its length. Built of fire-brick, these furnaces consisted solely of a grating where coal was burned, and a 'sole' or bed-plate on which the cast-iron bars were laid. This plate, set at an angle of twenty-five degrees, allowed the molten metal to flow into catchment pans. From there twelve hundred converging drainage channels guided it towards the central shaft.

The day after the work of excavation and masonry was finished, Barbicane proceeded directly to the business of casting the inner mould. This meant building up—in the centre of the shaft and along its axis—a cylinder nine hundred feet long and nine feet in diameter, which would exactly fill the space planned for the inside bore of the Columbiad. This cylinder consisted of a mixture of clayey soil and sand to which hay and straw were added.* The gap left between the mould and the masonry would be filled by the molten metal which would form the six-feet thick walls of the cannon.

To ensure that the cylinder remained vertical, it needed to be reinforced with iron bands and braced at intervals by cross-pieces securely embedded in the stone lining. During the casting, these cross-pieces would melt and be amalgamated into the liquid metal,* and would thus pose no problem.

This phase of the operation was concluded on 8 July and running the metal was scheduled for the next day but one.

'The casting ceremony will be a very grand occasion', J. T. Maston told his friend Barbicane.

'So it will,' replied Barbicane, 'but it will not be a public occasion.'

'What? You're not going to throw the gates of the site open to the general public?'

'Certainly not, Maston. Casting the Columbiad is a very delicate, not to say dangerous business, and I would much rather it happened behind closed doors. The day the projectile is fired, we'll put on a show if you wish, but not before.'

The President was right. The process might throw up unforeseen dangers and the presence of a large influx of spectators would hinder efforts to deal with them. It was essential to maintain complete freedom of action. So no one was allowed onto the site except a delegation of members of the Gun Club who travelled to Tampa. Among them were observed the dashing Bilsby, Tom Hunter, Colonel Blomsberry, Major Elphiston, General Morgan, and various others, who all took a personal interest in the casting of the Columbiad. J. T. Maston was their self-appointed guide. He spared them no detail and showed them around everywhere, the powder magazines, the workshops and the machine shops, and made them inspect all 1,200 furnaces one after the other. By the time they were inspecting the twelve-hundredth, each man had had more than enough.

The casting was to take place at noon exactly. The previous day, each furnace had been filled with 114,000 pounds weight of metal in bars arranged crosswise in layers to enable the hot air to circulate freely between them. From early morning, all twelve hundred chimneys belched great bursts of flame into the air and the ground was shaken by muffled tremors. Casting that weight of metal called for an equal weight of coal to be burned. That meant 68,000 tons of coal, which obscured the face of the sun with a thick curtain of black smoke.

The heat soon became unbearable inside the ring of furnaces, which made a racket like the crashing of thunder. Powerful fans added a continuous roar as they saturated every glowing fire-chamber with oxygen.

To be successful, the casting process needed to be carried out quickly. On a signal given by firing a cannon, each furnace would simultaneously release its molten metal until it was completely drained.

When everything was in place, foremen and all hands gathered round, waiting for the signal with impatience and no little excitement. There was no one inside the ring now and every casting overseer stood at his post by the nozzles of the runnels.

Barbicane and his colleagues, who had taken up a position on rising ground close by, watched the operation. In front of them was a cannon primed to fire when the engineer gave the signal.

A few minutes before noon, the first drops of metal began to flow. The catchment pans slowly filled and when the reduced metal was fully molten, it was held back for a brief moment to facilitate the removal of impurities.

Then it was noon. Suddenly the shot came from the cannon, its lurid flash lighting up the air. The outlets of twelve hundred runnels were opened simultaneously and twelve hundred fiery serpents, unwinding their incandescent coils, swarmed toward the central shaft. Into it they poured with an ear-splitting roar and dropped to a depth of 900 feet. It was a magnificent, heart-stopping sight. The earth shook while the molten flow blasted great swirls of smoke skywards, vaporized the moisture in the mould, and expelled it in dense exhalations through the vents in the stonework lining. These spiralling, unnaturally thick clouds unfurled as they rose to an altitude of 3,000 feet. Any native of the place roaming beyond the horizon might well have believed that a new crater was being born in the heart of Florida, and yet there was no eruption nor whirlwind nor storm nor brawling elements, nor any of the terrible phenomena which nature is capable of unleashing. No! Man alone had created these ruddy vapours, the gigantic flames worthy of a volcano, ground tremors which reverberated like the shocks of earthquakes, and the great boomings which could challenge hurricane and tempest! It was the hand of man which, having dug out a pit, had poured a Niagara of molten metal into it!

16

THE COLUMBIAD

Had the casting operation gone as planned? All concerned were reduced to mere conjecture. Yet everything pointed to its success, for the mould had swallowed up the entire mass of the metal that had been liquefied in the furnaces. In any case, it would not be possible for some time to have any certainty on the outcome.

Indeed, when Major Rodman cast his cannon weighing 160,000 pounds, he had had to wait no less than two weeks before it cooled. So for how long would the giant Columbiad, wreathed in clouds of vapour and wrapped in its own intense heat, continue to elude the gaze of its admirers? It was difficult to say with any accuracy.

During that period of waiting the patience of the members of the Gun Club was sorely tested. But it could not be helped. J. T. Maston's devotion to duty almost got him roasted alive. A fortnight after the casting operation, a huge column of smoke was still rising into the open sky and the ground burned the feet within a radius of two hundred paces around the top of Stone's Hill.

The days passed, the weeks grew in number. There was no way to cool that immense cylinder—it was impossible to get anywhere near it. There was nothing to do except wait and the Gun Club's members chafed at the bit.*

'Today is 10 August,' J. T. Maston said one morning. 'It's barely four months between now and 1 December! We still have to remove the inner core, calibrate the bore of the barrel, and load the Columbiad for firing—we have all that yet to do! We'll never be ready in time! We can't even get anywhere near the cannon! What if it never cools? Now wouldn't that be a cruel joke!'

They tried to calm down the hot-headed secretary but failed. Barbicane said nothing but his silence hardly hid his irritation. To see himself stopped in his tracks by an obstacle that only time could overcome—Time, a formidable enemy in the present circumstances—and to be subject to the will of that or any enemy was anathema to all warriors.

But daily readings pointed to a measure of change in the state of the ground. By 15 August, the quantity of vapour discharged had reduced significantly and grown less concentrated, less dense. A few days later, the area was giving off no more than a light mist, the last gasp of the monster shut up in its sarcophagus of stone. Little by little, the earth tremors faded and the circle of ground giving off heat grew smaller. The more impatient observers could now get closer. One day, they gained six feet, the next twelve, and on 22 August, Barbicane, his colleagues and the engineer were all able to stand on the thin sheet of cast-iron plate that lay on the top of Stone's

Hill—most certainly an exceedingly healthy spot, for there was no danger of getting frozen feet there!

'At last!' cried the President of the Gun Club with a huge sigh of relief.

They resumed work that same day. They proceeded at once to extract the core of the mould so that the bore of the barrel would be cleared. Pick, mattock, perforating tools began and went on working without respite. The clayey earth and sand had been baked extremely hard by the intense heat. But with the help of mechanical extractors, work was not stopped by this mixture that was still blisteringly hot from its contact with the cast-iron wall. The extracted material was then quickly taken away on steam-driven wagons. So well was work done, such was the enthusiasm for it, so urgent were Barbicane's words of encouragement, so forceful were his exhortations, backed as they were by the persuasive power of overtime dollars, that on 3 September all trace of the core had disappeared.

The work of boring out the inside of the barrel then began. Machines were set up without delay to drive powerful drilling bits with cutting edges that ate away the rough corrugations of the cast iron. A few weeks later and the surface of the inside of the immense tube was perfectly cylindrical and the bore of the cannon had acquired the smoothest polish.

Finally, on 22 September, less than one year after Barbicane had delivered his famous address, the enormous cannon, accurately calibrated and, as attested by the most delicate instruments, exactly vertical, was ready for service. Nothing more now needed to be done except wait for the Moon, though there was no question of its failing to keep its appointment.

J. T. Maston's joy knew no bounds and he narrowly escaped a horrible fall when he was staring down into the 900-foot barrel. Had it not been for Blomsberry's right arm, which the worthy Colonel fortunately still had, the Gun Club's Secretary, like some modern Herostratus,* would have met his end at the bottom of the Columbiad.

The cannon was now finished. There were no remaining doubts about the faultless way it had been constructed. And so, on 6 October, Captain Nicholl, though he might grind his teeth, duly paid his debt to President Barbicane, who entered in his accounts, under 'receipts', the sum of two thousand dollars. It may well be supposed that the captain's fury was pushed to its limits and that it all made him ill.

However, he still had three bets on, for three, four, and five thousand dollars, and provided he won two of them his venture would not turn out badly, though not brilliantly. But money did not really enter into his calculations, for the success of his rival, who had cast a cannon against which armour-plate sixty feet thick would have been useless, was a terrible blow to him.

From 23 September, the Stone's Hill site had been largely open to the public and what attracted such large crowds of visitors will be readily understood.

For vast numbers of sightseers from every part of the United States now converged on Florida. The town of Tampa had grown prodigiously during the year which had been entirely devoted to the labours of the Gun Club, and now had a population of a hundred and fifty thousand souls. After ringing Fort Brooke with a network of streets, it now spread along the tongue of land separating the two roadsteads of the Bay of Espiritu Santo. New neighbourhoods, new squares, a whole forest of private houses had grown up on previously deserted shores in the warm American sunshine. Development companies had been set up to build churches, schools, and private dwellings and within a year the town's area had increased tenfold.

Now it is well known that Yankees are born businessmen. Wherever fate may lead them, from the icy poles to the torrid tropics, their zest for making money finds practical outlets. That was why ordinary sightseers, people who had come to Florida and whose only purpose was to observe the Gun Club's progress, had no sooner settled in Tampa than they were drawn into various commercial activities. The ships chartered to bring in materials and men had made the port exceptionally busy. Soon, other vessels of every shape and size, loaded with provisions and merchandise, were sailing into the Bay and both its roads. Shipowners built enormous premises, chandlers opened their doors in the town, and each day the *Shipping Gazette* registered new arrivals in the port.

While new roads spread out around Tampa, the town—given the huge expansion of its population and commercial activity—was also at last linked by rail to the southern States of the Union. A railroad ran from Mobile to Pensacola, the great naval base of the South. Then, from that major location, it headed for Tallahassee. A small section of track twenty-one miles long already existed there which connected Tallahassee with St Marks on the coast. It was this short line that was now extended clear through to Tampa and as it went it revived and regenerated dead or dormant areas of central Florida. And so, due to the marvels of commercial activity which had grown one day from an idea in the brain of one man, Tampa now had every right to assume the ways and style of a metropolis. It was already being called 'Moon City' and it sent the official capital of Florida into an eclipse which was total and visible from every point of the globe.

It will now be clear to all why the rivalry between Texas and Florida had been so fierce and why the Texans had been so incensed to have their case rejected by the Gun Club's decision. With canny foresight, they had realized what a territory might stand to gain from Barbicane's experiment and what benefits might flow from a shot fired from such a cannon. Texas had lost a potentially vast commercial centre, railways, and a considerable increase in its population. Instead, all those benefits had gone to the trifling Floridian peninsula, that sea wall thrown up between the waters of the Gulf and the breakers of the Atlantic. As a result Barbicane acquired a share of the hatred Texans felt for General Santa Anna.

However although Tampa was now subject to the new commercial hysteria and industrial frenzy, its population took great care not to lose sight of the exciting activities of the Gun Club. On the contrary. They lapped up the smallest details of the operation, the lightest tap of a pick on rock. There was a constant toing and froing of people between the town and Stone's Hill in what was like a procession—no, more: a pilgrimage.

It was already clear that by the day the test finally took place, the crowd of spectators would be numbered in millions, for they were already arriving from all parts of the world and converging on that narrow peninsula. Europe was emigrating to America.

But thus far, it must be said, the curiosity of the multitude of new arrivals had been left pretty much unsatisfied. Many had been counting on casting day to provide something spectacular, but all they had seen was smoke. It was poor fare for hungry eyes. But Barbicane had refused to allow anyone in to see the operation. The result was ruffled feathers, discontent, and disgruntlement. The President got the blame. He was accused of being autocratic and his handling of the matter was said to be 'un-American'. There was a near-riot outside the fence ringing the top of Stone's Hill. But Barbicane, as we have seen, stood by his decision.

However, when the Columbiad was finally and definitively finished, the embargo on entry could not be maintained. Besides, it would have been churlish to keep the gates shut and frankly unwise to alienate public opinion. So Barbicane now opened the site to all-comers. But true to his practical turn of mind, he thought he could make some money out of people's curiosity.

It was of course quite something to be allowed to see the enormous Columbiad from close up, but to descend into its depths . . . now, that was in American eyes the *nec plus ultra* of earthly joys. Indeed, there was not a single thrill-seeker who did not yearn to treat himself to the pleasure of inspecting the chasm of metal from the inside. Baskets let down by steam winch enabled spectators to satisfy their curiosity. It became all the rage. Women, children, old men, they all made a point of going down to the bottom of the colossal cannon and exploring its mysteries. Tickets were priced at five dollars per person and, though this was thought rather steep, throughout the two months leading up to the launch, the rush of visitors was such that the Gun Club were able to bank almost five hundred thousand dollars.

It hardly needs saying that the first to go down into the Columbiad were the members of the Gun Club, a privilege rightly accorded to that illustrious company. This solemn occasion took place on 25 September. President Barbicane, J. T. Maston, Major Elphiston, General Morgan, Colonel Blomsberry, Murchison the engineer, and other distinguished members of the distinguished club, about ten in all, were winched down in a special gondola. It was still very warm at the bottom of the immensely long metal tube and they sweltered somewhat! But oh, what joy! What delight! A table set for ten had been placed on the massive stone block which supported the Columbiad now lit up like day by a beam of electric light. A long succession of exquisite dishes, which seemed to descend from on high, arrived in front of the guests one after the other and the finest French wines flowed generously during that splendid dinner served nine hundred feet underground.

The occasion grew very festive, even noisy. Toasts galore were proposed and seconded. Bumpers were drunk to planet Earth and to its satellite, glasses were raised to the Gun Club, the Union, the Moon, Phoebe, Diana, Selene, the Eye of Night, and the 'peaceful courier of the heavens'!* The cheers, borne aloft by the sound waves in that gigantic acoustic tube, emerged from its mouth with the noise of thunder, and the crowd that had gathered around Stone's Hill added their jubilation and voices to those of the ten table companions hidden from view at the bottom of the huge Columbiad.

J. T. Maston was beside himself. It would be hard to say if he yelled more than he waved his arms or if he drank more than he ate. But either way, he would not have given up his seat for an empire, no, 'not even if the cannon had been loaded, primed and fired at that moment, and were to blast him in small pieces into outer space!'

17

A TELEGRAM

THE major works undertaken by the Gun Club were now virtually at an end. And yet two more months still had to pass before the projectile would be fired at the Moon. Two months which to an impatient world would seem like two years! Thus far, every slight detail of the operation had been reported in the newspapers day in, day out, had been eagerly, voraciously seized by the public. But it looked as if henceforth this 'loyalty stimulant' applied to the public might well become significantly reduced and ordinary people feared that they would no longer be able to get their daily dose of thrills.

Nothing of the sort happened.

For at this juncture, a most unexpected, extraordinary, unbelievable, and unlikely event occurred which once more galvanized their breathless spirits and left the whole world in the grip of thrilling anticipation.

One day—it was 30 September—at 3.47 in the afternoon, a telegram sent by the cable that runs undersea from Valentia (Ireland) to Newfoundland and down the coast of America* arrived in Tampa. It was addressed to President Barbicane.

President Barbicane tore open the envelope and read the wire. For all his considerable powers of self-control, his lips turned pale and his eyes became clouded as he re-read the twenty or so telegraphed words.

FRANCE, PARIS.

30 September, 4 a.m.

Barbicane, Tampa, Florida, United States.

Replace spherical shell with cylindrico–conical projectile. Shall be
inside at launch. Arriving on steamer *Atlanta.**
  MICHEL ARDAN*

18

THE PASSENGER ON THE *ATLANTA*

IF, instead of winging its way along the electric wires, this astonishing piece of news had simply arrived through the post, in an envelope
duly stamped and sealed, and if various telegraphy clerks in France,
Ireland, Newfoundland, and America had not clearly read the contents of the telegram, then Barbicane would not have hesitated for
a single moment. He would have said nothing, as a precautionary
measure, but also to avoid the risk of compromising his work. The
wire, coming as it did from a Frenchman, might well be a cover for
a hoax or a prank. What chance was there that any man could have the
nerve even to think of such a venture? And if there really was such
a man, he must be insane and should be shut up in a padded cell, not
put in an outsized cannonball!

  But the contents of the telegram were already public knowledge
because this method of transmission is by definition not private, and
hence Michel Ardan's statement was already doing the rounds of
various States of the Union. There was thus no reason why Barbicane
had to hold his tongue. So he gathered together the colleagues who
happened to be in Tampa and, without revealing his opinion or discussing the degree to which the telegram could or could not be
believed, he simply read out the terse message.

  'Impossible!'
  'Never heard the like of it!'
  'It's a joke!'
  'What do they take us for?'
  'Ridiculous!'
  'Absurd!'

For several minutes, there followed a comprehensive litany of reactions expressing doubt, disbelief, derision, and insult, accompanied
by much waving of arms, as is customary at such moments. Each man
followed his nature and smiled, giggled, shrugged his shoulders, or

hooted with laughter. J. T. Maston was the only one to come up with a majestic thought:

'But it's a splendid idea!'

'Yes,' retorted the Major, 'but if a man may sometimes be permitted to have ideas like that, it is only on the understanding that he does not seriously believe that they can be put into practice!'

'But why ever not?' snapped the Secretary of the Gun Club, only too ready to argue the case in question. But no one wished to take the notion any further.*

However, the name of Michel Ardan had already begun to circulate in the town of Tampa. Newcomers and natives alike exchanged looks, raised eyebrows, and joked, not about this European—a mythical, chimeral character—but about J. T. Maston who was foolish enough to believe in the existence of this legendary being. When Barbicane had suggested sending a projectile to the Moon, everyone believed that such an undertaking was quite natural and eminently feasible, a simple matter of ballistics. But when a man seemingly in his right mind offered to take a place inside the projectile and embark on such an improbable journey, then the proposal seemed to be playful, a joke, and, to use a word for which the French have an exact equivalent in their colloquial speech, a piece of *humbug*.

The jeering continued uninterrupted until evening and it may be stated that the entire Union was convulsed with laughter, something that cannot be said to be usual in a land where impossible ventures can always find takers, practised hands and supporters.

However, Michel Ardan's proposal, like all new ideas, continued to trouble some people. It parted company with the usual ways of thinking: 'Why, it never crossed our minds!' Because it was so strange, the incident soon became an obsession. Much thought was given to it. How many things dismissed out of hand yesterday turn out to be true tomorrow? Why shouldn't a voyage to the Moon actually happen some day? Still, all things considered, the man prepared to risk his neck in this way was clearly mad and, moreover, since his proposal could not possibly be taken seriously, he should have kept quiet about it and stopped bothering the whole population with his ridiculous, crackbrained schemes.

But was there actually such a person? Good question! Still, the name 'Michel Ardan' was not unknown in America. It belonged to a European widely renowned for undertaking bold ventures. And then there was the telegram which had arrived via the depths of the Atlantic, the name of the vessel on which the Frenchman claimed to have booked his passage, and the indication of his impending arrival— all these details gave his proposal a certain air of plausibility. People felt that they had to get to the bottom of the whole thing. Soon isolated individuals formed groups, the groups became more tightly knit, bound by the power of curiosity the way atoms come together through molecular attraction, and eventually there resulted a dense crowd, which headed for the residence of President Barbicane.

Since receiving the telegram, Barbicane had made no public utterance. He had allowed J. T. Maston's opinion to circulate freely without expressing either approval or comment. He remained silent, resolving to wait upon events. But he had reckoned without the impatience of the public and was not best pleased when he saw much of the population of Tampa forming a crowd beneath his windows. It was not long before the dissatisfied muttering and growing clamour forced him to make an appearance. And so it was that Barbicane acquired all the obligations and drawbacks of fame.

Finally he emerged. The crowd fell silent and one citizen, speaking for the others, put to him the following point-blank question: 'Is the man named as Michel Ardan in the telegram now on his way to America: yes or no?'

'Gentlemen,' replied Barbicane, 'I know no more than you do.'

'We have to know,' cried several impatient voices.

'Time will tell us in due course,' the President replied calmly.

'Time has no right to keep an entire country in suspense,' the speaker added. 'Have you modified the design of the projectile along the lines set out in the telegram?'

'Not yet, gentlemen. But you are quite right. We need to know where we stand. Telegraphy caused all this uncertainty and telegraphy should end it by sending details.'

'To the telegraph office!' roared the mob.

Barbicane went down to them and, at the head of the huge crowd, led the way there.

A few minutes later, a telegram was sent to the agent of the shipping company at Liverpool. It asked for answers to the following questions:

'What kind of vessel is the *Atlanta*? When did it leave Europe? Did it have on board a French passenger named Michel Ardan?'

Two hours later, Barbicane received information so precise as to make any further doubt impossible.

'The steamer *Atlanta*, of Liverpool, sailed on 2 October—bound for Tampa—with on board a Frenchman named on the passenger list as Michel Ardan.'

On getting this confirmation of the first telegram, the President's eyes suddenly lit up, he tightly clenched his hands, and he was heard to murmur:

'It's true then! So it *is* possible! This Frenchman is real! And two weeks from now, he will be here! But he is mad! He is a death-or-glory hothead . . .! I'll never go along with it . . .'

And yet that same evening he wrote to Breadwill & Co. asking them to suspend casting the projectile until further notice.

And now, how to describe the excitement which gripped the whole of America; how to speak of the impact that was ten times greater than that produced by Barbicane's original address; how to relate what was said by the country's press, what the newspapers made of the news, and how they celebrated the arrival of this hero from the Old Continent; how to depict the state of feverish excitement in which every citizen lived as they counted the hours, the minutes, the seconds; how to give some idea, however faint, of the wearying obsession of so many minds all gripped by a single thought; how to show all other occupations being replaced by this one preoccupation, with work stopping, commerce being suspended, ships that were ready to leave remaining at their moorings so as not to miss the arrival of the *Atlanta*, trains arriving full and leaving empty, the Bay of Espiritu Santo being constantly churned up by steamers, packet boats, pleasure craft, and flyboats* large and small; how to put a figure on the thousands of sightseers who, in the space of a fortnight, quadrupled the population of Tampa and were forced to live under canvas like a campaigning army—this is a task to which the human hand is not equal and should not even be attempted without considerable temerity.

At nine in the morning on 20 October, semaphore stations on the Bahama Channel reported seeing thick smoke on the horizon. Two hours later there was an exchange of acknowledgement signals between the stations and a large steamer. Its name—the *Atlanta*—was immediately sent on to Tampa. At four, the British ship entered the Bay of Espiritu Santo. At five, it sailed briskly through the entrance of Hillsborough Bay. At six, it berthed in the port of Tampa.

Before the anchor was fast in the sandy sea bed, five hundred boats had surrounded the *Atlanta* and the steamer was taken by storm. Leading the way, Barbicane climbed aboard and, in a voice whose excitement he tried in vain to control, cried out:

'Michel Ardan!'

'Present!' replied a man standing on the poop deck.

With arms crossed, questing eyes, and tight lips, Barbicane stared at the passenger on the *Atlanta*.

He was a man of forty-two years of age, tall, and already slightly stooped, like the Caryatids who bear the weight of balconies on their shoulders. At intervals his impressive head, as powerful as a lion's, would toss a shock of unruly red hair like a mane. A face, not long but broad at the temples, featured a moustache that bristled like a cat's whiskers and small yellowish growths of beard on the cheeks. Round eyes, a touch wild and faintly myopic, completed a physiognomy which was indisputably feline. But the nose was strong, the mouth unusually gentle, and the brow high, intelligent, and furrowed like a field which is never allowed to lie fallow. Finally, a well-developed torso set squarely on long legs, hefty arms, like powerful, well-anchored levers, a confident bearing—all combined to make this European a strapping and vigorous man, 'more forged in a smithy than cast in a mould',* to borrow an expression from the iron-founder's art.

The disciples of Lavater or Gratiolet would have had no difficulty reading the skull and physiognomy of this man and finding clear signs of combativity, that is of courage in the face of danger and a relish for overcoming obstacles; signs too of benevolence and openness to wonderment, an instinct which leads certain kinds of person to be drawn to the heroic. On the other hand, acquisition bumps, indicating the urge to amass and possess, were totally absent.

To complete the physical description of the *Atlanta*'s passenger, note must be taken of his capacious, loose-fitting clothes, with the material of both trousers and overcoat so generous that Michel Ardan nicknamed himself a 'ruination to cloth', a loose cravat, a shirt open at the collar through which rose a sturdy neck, and shirt cuffs invariably left unbuttoned, leaving his restless hands free to move. He gave the impression that even in the depths of winter, here was a man who never felt either the cold or fear.

There on the deck of the steamer, amongst the crowd of people, he paced this way and that, never settling in the same spot, 'dragging his anchor', as sailors say, gesticulating, exchanging friendly words with one and all and biting his nails with nervous energy. He was one of God's freakish originals whom the Creator casts in playful moments and then immediately breaks the mould.

The character of Michel Ardan indeed offered the analyst a broad field for study. This amazing man lived in a constant state of hyperbole and had yet to grow out of the habit of superlatives. Objects appeared on his eye's retina in wildly exaggerated forms. This led to the growth of correspondingly over-sized ideas. He saw everything as being larger than life—except difficulties and other people.

Moreover, his was a rich and inventive nature. He was artistic by instinct, a witty man who did not keep up a running fire of banter but was more of a sharpshooter. In discussion, caring little for logic and resistant to syllogisms, both alien to his character, he had his own methods. No respecter of rules, he would throw back into opponents' faces personal comments with deadly effect, and he loved nothing better than fighting tooth and claw for hopeless causes.

Amongst his other oddities, he claimed to be 'a sublime ignoramus'* like Shakespeare, and professed utter contempt for experts of all kinds, who he said were 'people who keep the score while we play the game'. He was, as they say, 'a man you could take or leave'. He was in fact a bohemian from the Realm of Mountain and Miracle, a swashbuckler but not a buccaneer, a daredevil, a Phaeton driving the chariot of the sun at full tilt, an Icarus* with a spare set of wings. He was prepared to risk his neck and ready to take the falls. He threw himself into madcap schemes with his eyes wide open, he burned his boats behind him with more gusto than Agathocles,* and did not hesitate to risk broken bones at the drop of a hat yet invariably ended up falling on his feet, like those little figures of elder wood that children play with.

To sum up, his motto was: 'I'll try it, whatever the odds', while love of the impossible was, to use Pope's fine words, his 'ruling passion'.*

But this adventurous man also had the defects of his qualities. Nothing ventured, nothing gained, they say. Ardan often ventured but had gained nothing! Money burned holes in his pocket, a bottomless pit. He had no axes to grind and was as likely to follow his heart as to act with his head. Ever helpful and chivalrous, he would not have signed the death warrant of his own worst enemy and would have sold himself into slavery to buy a black person's freedom.

In France and throughout Europe, everyone had heard of this brilliant and exuberant man. Was he not for ever being talked about by the many voices of Fame which had grown hoarse in his service? Did he not live in a house of glass, making the whole world a party to his most intimate secrets? But did he also not have a fine collection of enemies among those whom he had mercilessly offended, insulted, and pushed aside as he elbowed his way through the crowd?

But overall he was greatly liked and people treated him as they would a spoilt child: indulgently. He was, as they say, 'a man you could take or leave', and people generally took him. Everyone was fascinated by his daring plans and watched his progress with an anxious eye. They all knew that he was shamelessly bold. Whenever a friend tried to restrain him, saying that he was headed for certain disaster, he would say: 'The forest is only burned down by its own trees',* smile pleasantly, and not realize for one moment that he was quoting the pithiest of Arab proverbs.

And there you have the passenger on the *Atlanta*, never still, perpetually ebullient and burning with some inner force, constantly excited not by what he had come to do in America—that was furthest from his mind—but as an effect of his febrile constitution. If two men ever provided a vivid contrast, they were the Frenchman Michel Ardan and the Yankee Barbicane, though both were enterprising, bold, and audacious in their own ways.

The thoughts which filled the mind of the President of the Gun Club* on being confronted with this rival, who had pushed him out of the limelight, were quickly interrupted by the hurrahs and bravos of the crowd. Their cheering even became so frenzied and their enthusiasm found such personal expression that Michel Ardan, after shaking innumerable hands and almost losing all his fingers in the process, was forced to take refuge in his cabin.

Barbicane, without saying a word, followed him in.

'You, I presume, are Barbicane?' asked Michel Ardan the moment they were alone, in the tone he would have used when speaking to a friend he had known for twenty years.

'I am,' replied the President of the Gun Club.

'Well, Barbicane, and how are you? Well, I assume? Capital! That's good to hear!'

'May I take it,' said Barbicane, coming directly to the point, 'that you are still certain you want to go?'

'Absolutely certain.'

'Nothing will change your mind?'

'Nothing. Have you modified the projectile along the lines indi-cated in my telegram?'

'I have been waiting for you to get here. But,' asked Barbicane, again insistent, 'have you fully thought this through?'

'Thought it through! You think I have time to waste? The chance of a trip to the Moon has come my way and I'm making the most of it, that's the long and the short of it. It doesn't seem to me something that warrants a great deal of thinking about.'

Barbicane eyes were fixed on this man who spoke of the journey he was contemplating with such a casual lack of concern and complete absence of nerves.

'But at least,' he said, 'you must have a plan, some ideas of how to set about it . . . ?'

'Excellent ideas, my dear Barbicane. But if you will allow me to say something first: I would much prefer to tell my story once, to all and sundry, and get it over with. It avoids me having to repeat myself. So unless you have a better idea, summon all your friends and colleagues, the population of Tampa, all Florida, the whole of America if you like, and tomorrow I will be ready to set out my ideas and to respond to whatever objections are raised. Don't worry, I shall be one hundred per cent ready for them! How does that suit you?'

'It suits me very well,' said Barbicane.

Upon which note the President strode out of the cabin and addressed the crowd, outlining Michel Ardan's proposal. His words were greeted with stamping of feet and cries of delight and smoothed away any remaining difficulties. It meant that next day they would be able to feast their eyes on the hero from Europe. Some of the more insistent spectators, however, refused to leave the deck of the *Atlanta* and spent the night on board ship. J. T. Maston was among them. He had clamped his iron hook onto the rail of the poop and it almost took a capstan to free it.

'The man's a hero! A hero!' he cried, his voice rising above the others. 'And compared to this European, we are no better than milk-sops and jellyfish!'

Meanwhile the President, after intimating to the visitors that it was time to leave, returned to the passenger's cabin and did not emerge from it until the ship's bell sounded the midnight watch.

But at that time, the two rivals in popularity were warmly shaking hands and Michel Ardan could not have been on friendlier terms with President Barbicane.

19

A MASS MEETING

THE next morning the sun rose much too late for the taste of an impatient public. This conduct was thought too casual by half for a sun which was due to shine down on such an occasion. Barbicane, fearing that awkward questions might be put to Michel Ardan, would have preferred to restrict his audience to a small number of informed persons—his colleagues, for example. But it would have been easier to halt the Niagara Falls. So he was forced to abandon his plans and let his new friend take his chances with a public lecture. The hall of Tampa's new Stock Exchange, for all its immense size, was judged inadequate for the occasion, since the planned gathering was already assuming the proportions of a mass public meeting.

The location chosen was a huge field situated outside the town. In a matter of hours, the site had been protected against the sun's glare. Ships in the port, having plentiful sails, rope, spare masts, and yard-arms, furnished the materials needed for the erection of a colossal tent. Soon, a vast canopy of canvas had spread across the scorched prairie and shielded it from the direct heat of the day. Three hundred thousand people gathered there and braved the stifling temperature for several hours while waiting for the Frenchman to arrive. Of this multitude of spectators, a third could see and hear, another third could barely see but not hear, while the remaining third could not see or hear anything at all, but were not any the less stinting in their applause.

At three o'clock, Michel Ardan made his appearance flanked by the senior officials of the Gun Club. He had President Barbicane on his right and J. T. Maston on his left, who, glowing brighter than the noon-day sun, beamed almost as ruddily.

Ardan climbed onto the platform and from its height looked out over a sea of black hats. He did not seem at all nervous. He did not strike a pose but looked totally at home, cheerful, friendly, affable. He responded to the reception he was given with a gracious wave. Then calling for silence with a gesture of his hand, he began speaking, in perfect English, as follows:

'Gentlemen,' he began, 'although it is very hot, I shall take a few moments of your time to give some idea of an undertaking which seems to interest you greatly. I am no orator, nor am I a scientist, and I was not intending to speak in public. But my friend Barbicane told me that you would be pleased if I did, so I am making the effort. Hear me out then, with each of your six hundred thousand ears, and be kind enough to overlook the shortcomings of the speaker.'

These straightforward opening remarks were well received by his listeners who showed their appreciation with a huge murmur of satisfaction.

'Gentlemen,' he went on, 'no expression of your approval or disapproval is forbidden. Now that this is clear I shall begin. First point: never forget that you are dealing with an ignoramus, whose ignorance runs so deep that he does not know what difficulties lie ahead. So it seemed to this numbskull that it was a simple, natural, straightforward thing to get a berth on a projectile and go to the Moon. Such a journey is bound to happen sooner or later, for whatever means of transport we use invariably follows where the law of progress leads us. Man began by moving about on four limbs, then one fine day on two, and then by cart, wagon, rattletrap, stagecoach, and now by rail. Don't you see! The projectile is the vehicle of the future. In fact, the planets are projectiles, cannonballs loosed off by the hand of the Creator. But to return to our vehicle.

'Now, gentlemen, some of you may well have been led to believe that the velocity at which it is to be launched is excessive. This is not the case. All heavenly bodies travel faster and as the Earth itself orbits the sun, it is carrying us at three times that speed. I shall give you a few examples, only I would ask your leave to express the distances in leagues because I am not very familiar with the American system of measurement and I do not wish to get lost in my calculations.'

The request seemed simple enough and it raised no objection. The speaker then resumed:

'Here, then, are the speeds of the various planets. I have to admit that despite my ignorance, my knowledge of these small astronomical particulars is actually pretty accurate. But two minutes from now you will know as much as I do. So first, Neptune travels at 5,000 leagues an hour; Uranus, 7,000; Saturn, 8,858; Jupiter, 11,675; Mars, 20,011; the

Earth, 27,500; Venus, 32,190; Mercury, 52,520; and some comets reach 1,400,000 leagues in their perihelion!* We, on the other hand, are mere strollers in no particular hurry, and our speed will be no greater than 1,900 leagues an hour—and it will steadily decrease! I ask you, is there anything in all that to concern us? In any case, isn't it obvious that one day those values will be exceeded by still greater speeds, for which light or electricity will probably supply the mechanical power.'

No one seemed prepared to doubt Michel Ardan's contention.

'But gentlemen,' he went on, 'if you listened to some dim people—and dim is the word for them—the human race would be confined inside a circle of Popilius,* never able to step outside it, and thus doomed to vegetate on this globe of ours and never venture into interplanetary space! But it is not so! We shall go to the Moon, we shall go to the planets, we shall go to the stars, just as today we travel from Liverpool to New York, easily, quickly, and safely, and the oceans of space will soon be crossed like the oceans of the Earth. Distance is a relative concept and in the end it will be reduced to naught.'

His audience, predisposed as they were in favour of the French hero, were somewhat taken aback by this bold theory, as Michel Ardan seemed to understand.

'You do not appear to be convinced, gentlemen,' he went on with a pleasant smile. 'So let's look at some facts. Do you know how long it would take an express train to get to the Moon? Three hundred days—no more. A matter of 86,410 leagues, but what's that? It's not even nine times around the Earth, and there are no even mildly adventurous sailors or voyagers who have not covered greater distances during their lifetimes. So just bear in mind that I shall be travelling for a mere ninety-seven hours! Ah, I see that you're telling yourselves that the Moon is a long way from Earth and that a man should think twice before having a crack at it! But what would you say if we were talking of going to Neptune which orbits the sun at a distance of 1,147 million leagues! Now that's a trip that not many people could manage even if it cost only five sous a kilometre! Even Baron de Rothschild, who is worth a billion, could not afford the fare and being 147 million short,* he'd have to get off somewhere along the way.'

This kind of talk seemed to please the audience. Moreover, Michel Ardan, now getting into his stride, went at it hammer and tongs, with tremendous gusto. He sensed that he had his listeners where he wanted them and resumed with total confidence.

'Well, my friends, even the distance from Neptune to the sun is insignificant when it is compared with the distance between us and the stars. Indeed, to estimate how far away they are, we will need to deal in breathtaking numbers of which the smallest has nine zeroes and the basic unit is the billion. You must forgive me for being so well-up on this question but it is such a fascinating subject. Hear me out and then you can decide for yourselves! Alpha Centaurus is 8,000 billion leagues away, Vega and Sirius 50,000 billion, Arcturus 52,000 billion, the North Star 117,000 billion, Capella 170,000 billion,* and the other stars are thousands, millions, or billions of billions of leagues away! And people go on about the distances which separate the planets from the sun! But how can anyone believe that these distances are real? They are wrong! Distance is a fallacy, an aberration of the senses! Do you know what I think about the system which starts with the sun and reaches its furthest point with Neptune? Shall I tell you my theory? It is very simple. For me, the solar system is one solid, homogenous body. The planets of which it is composed are pressed together, they touch and cohere, and the space between them is the same as the space which separates molecules in the densest metals, such as silver, gold, or platinum. So I am right to say categorically, and I repeat it now with a conviction which I know you will share: distance is a meaningless word. There is no such thing!'

'Well said! Bravo! Hooray!' cried the entire audience with one voice, thrilled by the speaker's gestures, his rhetoric, and the boldness of his vision.

'It's true!' bawled J. T. Maston more passionately than the rest. 'There's no such thing as distance!'

Then, carried away by the vigour of his contortions and the thrashing of his limbs which he found difficult to control, he almost fell off the high platform onto the ground. But he just managed to regain his balance, thus avoiding a fall which would have proved to him that distance is incontrovertibly not an empty word. Meanwhile, the speaker resumed his message:*

'Friends,' he said, 'I think that the question has now been settled. If I have failed to convince all of you, it is because I was not bold enough in putting my point across and inept in my arguments, and you must lay the blame for that on the shortcomings of my theoretical studies. Be that as it may, I say again: the distance from the Earth to its satellite is really unimportant and quite undeserving of the attention of serious minds. As a result, I do not think that I am getting too far ahead of myself when I say that the time will come when whole trains of project-iles will run from the Earth to the Moon and allow the journey to be made in comfort. There will be no accidents, collisions, or derailments to be feared and passengers will reach their destination quickly and without fatigue by a direct, straight route, 'a bee-line', if I may use an expression from the language of your trappers. Within twenty years, half of the Earth's population will have been to the Moon!

'Hooray! Hooray! Let's hear it for Michel Ardan!' cried his listeners, even those who were least convinced.

'And for Barbicane too!' the speaker responded modestly.

This expression of gratitude towards the original begetter of the enterprise was greeted by universal applause.

'And now, my friends,' resumed Michel Ardan, 'if any of you have questions for me, you will be putting a man as ignorant as I am on the spot. But I will do my level best to answer you.'

Up to this point, the President of the Gun Club had had every reason to be pleased with the turn the discussion had taken. It had covered speculative theories which Michel Ardan, carried away by his sparkling imagination, had dealt with quite dazzlingly. But now he would have to be prevented from straying into practical areas where he would probably perform much less well. Barbicane stepped in and took the floor. He began by asking his new friend if he thought that the Moon or the planets were inhabited.

'That's a very broad question you put to me, Mr. President,' said the speaker with a smile. 'However, unless I am very much mistaken, very intelligent men, amongst them Plutarch, Swedenborg, Bernardin de Saint-Pierre,* and many others, have answered in the affirmative. If I take the standpoint of natural philosophy, I would be inclined to accept their view. I would say to myself that in this world nothing exists that is entirely without purpose. So to reply to your question with another, my dear Barbicane, I would say that if worlds are inhab-itable, then either they are inhabited or they have been or will be.'

'Well said!' cried the spectators sitting in the front row whose opin-ion dictated that of the people at the back.

'The answer could not be more logical or fair,' said the President of the Gun Club. 'So the question comes down to this: are those worlds inhabitable? I myself believe that they are.'

'And I am quite sure of it!' replied Michel Ardan.

'Nevertheless,' cried someone in the audience, 'there are arguments against their being fit for habitation. It is obvious that on most
of them the conditions for life will be different. So, limiting ourselves
to the planets, we would roast on some and freeze on others, according to whether they were nearer or further away from the sun.'

'I regret,' replied Michel Ardan, 'that I do not have the honour of
knowing my worthy challenger personally, for I must try to give him an
answer. His objection is not without merit, but I think that it can be
answered with some success, as can all those which have focused on the
inhabitability of other worlds. If I were a physicist, I would say that if
less caloric is released on the one hand by the planets near the sun and,
on the other, more caloric on those further away, this simple phenomenon alone would be enough to balance the heat and keep the temperature of all those worlds bearable for living creatures organized as we are.
If I were a naturalist, I would tell him what many illustrious men of
science have said, namely that here on Earth nature furnishes us with
examples of animals living in varying conditions in a range of habitats;
that fish can breathe in an environment lethal to other animals; that
amphibians lead double lives which are difficult to explain; that some
denizens of the sea are able to maintain life at great depths, tolerating
pressures of fifty or sixty atmospheres without being crushed; that various aquatic insects, unaffected by temperature, may be found both in
springs of boiling water and on the icy polar expanses; that, in a word,
we must acknowledge in nature the diversity of its processes which
often appear incomprehensible but are nonetheless very real and may
even seem to verge on omnipotence. If I were a chemist, I would say to
him that aeroliths—bodies obviously originating from outside our terrestrial globe—have on analysis revealed indubitable traces of carbon,
a substance that can only derive from the bodies of living organisms
and which, according to Reichenbach's experiments, must of necessity
be of animal origin.* Finally, if I were a theologian, I would say that
according to Saint Paul, divine redemption seems to apply not only
here on Earth but in all celestial worlds.* But I am neither a theologian,
chemist, naturalist, nor a physicist. Moreover, being entirely ignorant
of the great laws which govern the universe, I shall confine myself to
answering: 'I do not know if other worlds are inhabited, and since I do
not know, I shall go there and see for myself!'

Did the man who had challenged Michel Ardan's theories venture
further objections? It is impossible to say, for the frenzied roar of the

crowd would have prevented opinions of any sort being heard. When silence was restored in even the most distant parts of the audience, the all-conquering orator was content merely to add the following remarks:

'My Yankee friends, you may well think I have barely scratched the surface of such a great question. But I did not come here to deliver a lecture or put forward a particular view on this vast subject. There are a number of other views which favour the inhabitability of distant worlds which I set to one side for now. But allow me to insist on just one point. To those who maintain that planets are not inhabited, I would answer: you may be right, if it can be demonstrated that the Earth is the best of all possible worlds,* but that is not the case, whatever Voltaire may have said. It has just one satellite, whereas Jupiter, Uranus, Saturn, and Neptune each have several at their service, an advantage which is not to be underestimated. But what above all makes our world particularly unwelcoming is the way it shifts on its axis during its orbit. It is why our nights and days are not equal. Hence too the disagreeable variations of the seasons. On our wretched spheroid it is always too hot or too cold. We freeze in winter and burn in summer. Ours is the planet of colds, coryzas, and bronchitis while on the surface of Jupiter, for example, whose axis is barely inclined, its inhabitants could enjoy temperatures that never vary. There, they have a zone of perpetual spring, a zone of perpetual summer, and permanent zones for autumn and winter, with every 'Jovian' able to choose the climate which suits him best, where he can spend his entire life protected against fluctuations of temperature. You will have no difficulty in recognizing the superiority in this matter of Jupiter over our own planet—to say nothing of its years, each of which lasts twelve of ours! Moreover, it is obvious to me that under its auspices and in such admirable living conditions, the inhabitants of that happy world must be superior to us, that learned men there are more learned, that artists are more artistic, the wicked less wicked, and the good are better. Alas! in what is our spheroid lacking that it does not reach this level of perfection? Not much! Only an axis that tilts less in relation to the plane of its orbit.'

'If that's so,' came an excited voice, 'let's pool our efforts, build the machines we need, and straighten up the Earth's axis!'*

A torrent of applause greeted this proposal which was made, and could only have been made, by J. T. Maston. It seems likely that the hot-blooded Secretary had been carried away by his engineering instincts to propose such a thing. But it must be said, for it is true, that many in the crowd shouted out their seconding of his motion, and it is likely that, if they had had the fulcrum called for by Archimedes,* those Americans would have built a lever capable of raising the world and setting its axis to rights. But the fulcrum is precisely what those reckless artificers did not have.

Nevertheless, this 'eminently practical' idea had a great success. Discussion was suspended for a good quarter of an hour and for long, long afterwards throughout the United States of America, men went on talking of the proposal put forward by the Perpetual Secretary of the Gun Club.

20

ATTACK AND RIPOSTE

THIS incident seemed likely to put an end to all discussion. It was 'the last word' and it could not have been bettered. Yet when the excitement had died down, a strong, insistent voice was heard saying:

'Now that the speaker has finished giving such free rein to fantasy, will he now return to the subject, stop talking theory, and deal with the practical aspects of his expedition?'

All eyes turned towards the man who spoke these words. He was thin, gaunt, with an assertive face and a beard which grew thickly, American-style, under his chin. Taking advantage of various fluctuations in the movement of the crowd, he had gradually worked his way up to the front. There, arms crossed, with a clear, bold look in his eye, he stood staring calmly at the man of the hour. Having asked his question, he did not speak again and seemed unaware of the thousands of looks focused on him or the murmur of disapproval provoked by his words. An answer being slow in coming, he put his question again in the same clipped accent, then added:

'We are here to talk about the Moon, not the Earth.'

'You are quite right, sir,' replied Michel Ardan, 'the discussion has drifted from the point. Let us return to the Moon.'

'Sir,' the stranger resumed, 'you claim that our satellite is inhabited. Perhaps it is. But if indeed Selenites do exist, they must of necessity live without breathing for—and I warn you for your own sake—there is not the faintest molecule of air on the surface of the Moon.'

At this assertion, Ardan shook back his lion's mane. He was well aware that battle was about to be joined with this man on the nub of the question. He stared back at him, then said:

'So there is no air on the Moon! And who, pray, claims that to be the case?'

'The scientists.'

'Really?'

'Really.'

'Sir,' Michel Ardan went on, 'joking apart, I have the greatest respect for scientists who know their business but utter contempt for those who do not.'

'Do you know any of the latter sort?'

'Assuredly. In France, there is one scientist who claims that "mathematically" birds cannot fly, and another whose theories prove beyond doubt that fish are not made to live in water.'*

'Sir, we are not talking of such as those and I could, in defence of my argument, give you names which you could not possibly object to.'

'If you do so, sir, you would seriously embarrass a poor ignoramus* who only asks to learn!'

'So why do you engage in scientific matters if you have never studied them?' the stranger asked with brutal directness.

'You ask why?' retorted Michel Ardan. 'For the very good reason that a man who has no idea of danger is always a brave man. I know nothing, it's true. But it is my weakness which is the source of my strength.'

'But your weakness is tantamount to folly,' cried the stranger ill-humouredly.

'Then so much the better,' countered the Frenchman, 'if my folly takes me all the way to the Moon!'

Barbicane and his colleagues gawked at the stranger who had set his countenance so boldly against their enterprise. None of them knew who he was, and the President, hardly reassured by where such a frankly expressed debate was taking them, glanced up at his new friend with a degree of apprehension. The audience was listening attentively and somewhat anxiously, for this dispute was having the effect of focusing attention on the danger or even the very infeasibility of the entire venture.

'Sir,' continued Michel Ardan's opponent, 'there are many unanswerable reasons which prove the total absence of an atmosphere on the Moon. I would even say *a priori* that if an atmosphere ever existed there it must have been siphoned off by the Earth. But I prefer to put up unassailable facts against you.'

'Put them up, sir,' said Michel Ardan, perfectly politely, 'put up as many as you like!'

'You must know,' said the stranger, 'that when light rays pass through a medium such as air, they are deflected from a straight line or, to use another word, they are refracted. Well, when stars are occulted by the Moon, their light skims the edge of its disc without undergoing the slightest deflection or giving the smallest hint of refraction. From that follows the self-evident conclusion that the Moon is not enveloped by an atmosphere.'*

All eyes turned to the Frenchman, for once this point was conceded, the rest followed logically on.

'That,' said Michel Ardan, 'is your strongest, not to say your only argument, and a scientist might well be hard put to answer it. For myself, I will merely say that it is far from conclusive because it assumes the annular circumference of the Moon is perfectly even, which is not the case. But let us proceed. Tell me, sir, if you admit the existence of volcanoes on the Moon's surface.'

'Extinct volcanoes, yes; active volcanoes, no.'

'So I may be allowed to believe, without straining logic, that these volcanoes were once active over a given period of time?'

'It was certainly the case, but since they themselves were able to supply the oxygen required for combustion, the mere fact that they erupted in no way proves the existence of a lunar atmosphere.'

'Then let us move on from that line of argument,' answered Michel Ardan, 'and come to direct observation. But I warn you that I intend to quote names.'

'Name your names.'

'I shall. In 1715, as the astronomers Louville and Halley observed the eclipse of 3 May, they noticed flickerings of a curious nature. These bursts of light, rapid and frequently repeated, were attributed by them to thunderstorms generated by the Moon's atmosphere.'*

'In 1715,' replied the stranger, 'the astronomers Louville and Halley mistook for lunar phenomena effects which were in fact purely terrestrial,* such as meteors and the like which may flare up in our own atmosphere. That was the view expressed by other scientists at the time and I fully endorse it.'

'Let's press on,' replied Ardan appearing quite unperturbed by the stranger's rejoinder. 'Now, did Herschel in 1787 not observe a large number of small lights on the surface of the Moon?'

'He did, but offered no explanation for the origin of those luminous points. Herschel himself never used their appearance as evidence in favour of a lunar atmosphere.'

'Well said, sir!' cried Michel Ardan, complimenting his opponent. 'I see that you are well versed in selenography.'

'Extremely well versed, sir, and I would add that the finest observers, Messrs Beer and Mädler, who have studied the Moon most closely, are in absolute agreement that there is no air whatsoever on its surface.'

A ripple ran through the crowd which seemed shaken by the arguments put forward by this remarkable stranger.

'But we should move on,' replied Michel Ardan, as cool as a cucumber, 'and come to a most important point. When a very able French astronomer, Monsieur Laussedat, observed the eclipse of 18 July 1860, he noted that the horns of the solar crescent* were rounded and truncated. Now such a phenomenon could not have been produced except by refraction of the sun's rays through the Moon's atmosphere. He has no other possible explanation for the facts.'

'But are the facts confirmed?' the stranger broke in.

'Absolutely.'

A contrary ripple brought the crowd back to favour their blue-eyed hero, whose adversary did not respond. Ardan spoke again and without exploiting his advantage merely said:

'So you see, my dear sir, that you really ought not to say categorically that there is no atmosphere on the surface of the Moon. Its atmosphere is probably not very dense, even ultra-tenuous, but nowadays science generally admits that it is there.'

'But not on its mountains, in case you forget,' retorted the stranger, unwilling to give way entirely.

'Not there, but in its valley bottoms and even then not above a height of a few hundred metres.'

'Even so, you would be well advised to take precautions, for such air as there is will be very rarefied.'

'My dear fellow, there'll always be enough for one man on his own. Actually, once I get up there, I shall do my best to eke it out and breathe only on important occasions!'

A great burst of laughter rang against the ears of the mysterious stranger, who let his gaze sweep across the crowd, braving them, proud and defiant.

'And since,' went on Michel Ardan in an easy tone of voice, 'we are agreed on the existence of a certain amount of air, we are forced also to acknowledge the presence of a certain quantity of water. It is a logical consequence and for my part I am delighted that it is so. But I would ask my honourable opponent if he would allow me to put one other observation to him. We know only one face of the Moon's disc, and if there is very little air on the side which is presented to us, it is possible that there may be a great deal on the other side.'

'Why should that be?'

'Because under the influence of the Earth's gravitational pull, the Moon has acquired the shape of an egg. What we see is the smaller end. From this discovery, which we owe to the calculations of Hansen, it follows that its centre of gravity is located in its other hemisphere. From that deduction the conclusion in turn follows that the mass of both air and water must have been drawn to the distant side of our satellite during the first days of its creation.'

'Pure fantasy!' snapped the stranger.

'Not at all! Pure theory, which is rooted in the laws of mechanics, and, to my mind, would be most difficult to refute. I therefore appeal to this assembly and call for a vote on this motion: "Is life as it exists here on Earth possible on the surface of the Moon?" '

Three hundred thousand listeners joined forces to approve the proposition. Michel Ardan's opponent tried to speak but was unable to make himself heard above the clamour and threats which descended on him like hail.

'We've had enough of you!' some cried.

'Get that man out of here!' roared the angry mob.

But he stood firm, holding onto the platform, not budging from where he was, and allowed the storm to blow over. It would have assumed alarming proportions if Michel Ardan had not calmed it with a gesture. He was far too much of a gentleman to abandon his opponent to such a predicament.

'Did you wish to add a few words?' he asked most graciously.

'Yes! A hundred thousand!' the stranger replied heatedly. 'Or rather, just one! To persevere with this folly, you must be . . .'

'Reckless! But how can you say that to me? Did I not ask my friend Barbicane for a cylindro-conical projectile so that I would not be tossed around like a squirrel on a wheel?'

'But, foolish man, the brutal shock of the launch will smash you to smithereens before you've got anywhere!'

'My dear fellow, you have just put your finger on the real, the only problem. However, I have far too good an opinion of the industrial genius of the American people to think them unable to come up with a solution.'

'But what about the heat generated by the velocity of the projectile as it passes through the layers of the Earth's air?'

'Its walls are thick and I shall soon have left the Earth's atmosphere.'

'But what will you eat? What about water?'

'I have calculated that I could take enough with me to last a whole year—and my journey will last for just four days.'

'And air to breathe while you are on your way?'

'I shall produce some using chemical processes.'

'And your descent onto the Moon, supposing you ever get there?'

'It will happen six times more slowly than it would on Earth since everything weighs six times less on the lunar surface.'

'But it will still be enough to smash you like glass.'

'But what's to stop me slowing my descent by using rockets suitably positioned and fired at the right moment?'

'But ultimately, assuming that all the problems have been solved and all obstacles overcome, and fixing the odds in your favour and conceding that you arrive on the Moon safe and sound and in one piece, how will you get back again?'

'I shan't be coming back!'

When they heard this reply, almost sublime in its simplicity, the assembled crowd fell silent. But its silence was more eloquent than any amount of fanatical cheering would have been!

The stranger took the opportunity to make one last appeal.

'You will inevitably be killed,' he cried, 'and your death will be that of a madman and of no use whatsoever to knowledge!'

'Please continue, kind sir! For truly you prophesy in such an agreeable style!'

'Oh, this is too much!' exclaimed Michel Ardan's adversary. 'I don't know why I'm having this absurd conversation! Go ahead with your insane scheme! But you're not the one who's to blame for all this!'

'Feel free to carry on.'

'No, it's someone else who will carry the responsibility for what you do!'

'And who might that be? Pray tell!' said Michel Ardan in a commanding voice.

'The ignoramus who organized this mission which is as impossible as it is absurd!'

The attack was direct. Ever since the stranger had appeared on the scene, Barbicane had been making strenuous efforts to control his feelings and 'burn off his smoke', like certain boiler furnaces. But now, on hearing himself singled out so odiously, he leapt to his feet and was about to march right up to the man who had challenged him so openly, when he suddenly saw that they had been separated.

The platform had been wrenched free by a hundred strong arms and the President of the Gun Club found himself having to share the glory of the day with Michel Ardan. The shield of honour on which they were borne aloft was heavy but bearers came in continuous relays, all of them competing, straining, battling in their eagerness to lend the power of their shoulders to its grand progress.

But the stranger had not taken advantage of the confusion to make himself scarce. Could he even have done so in the middle of such a packed crowd? Probably not. But still, there he stood, in the front of the crowd, arms crossed and glowering at Barbicane.

The President did not lose sight of him for an instant and the eyes of both men remained locked like two straining swords.

The noise of the vast crowd remained at maximum intensity for the duration of the march of triumph. Michel Ardan fell in with the mood and enjoyed it all immensely. His face beamed with delight. From time to time, the platform seemed to pitch and roll like a ship on a heavy sea. But the two heroes of the mass meeting had their sea legs: they kept their footing and their vessel reached the port of Tampa without incident.

Fortunately, Michel Ardan was able to disentangle himself from the final farewells of his enthusiastic admirers and fled to the Hotel Franklin where he went straight up to his room and slipped quickly into his bed, while an army of a hundred thousand men kept watch under his windows.

Meanwhile, a short, intense, decisive scene was being played out between the mysterious stranger and the President of the Gun Club.

Barbicane, his freedom of movement at last restored, marched straight up to his opponent.

'Come with me!' he said curtly.

The man followed him along the quayside and soon both found themselves alone at the entrance to an open wharf near Jones Falls.

There the two enemies, each still unknown to the other, stared at one another.

'Who are you?' asked Barbicane.

'Captain Nicholl.'

'I thought as much. Until now, fate has never made you cross my path . . .'

'I came here now.'

'You insulted me!'

'In public.'

'And you will give me satisfaction for the insult.'

'Straightaway.'

'No. I wish what happens between us to remain secret. There is a wood three miles from Tampa: Skersnaw Wood. You know it?'

'I know it.'

'Would you care to venture into that wood, on one particular side, tomorrow morning at five o'clock?'

'Yes—if at the same time you venture into it, on its further side.'

'And you won't forget your rifle?' said Barbicane.

'No more than you will forget yours,' replied Nicholl.

And with those icily exchanged words, the President of the Gun Club and the captain went their separate ways.

Barbicane returned to his house but instead of resting for a few hours, he spent the night trying to work out how to eliminate the shock effect inside the projectile and to find a solution to the difficult problem raised by Michel Ardan during the discussion at the meeting.

21

HOW A FRENCHMAN SETTLES
AN AFFAIR OF HONOUR

WHILE the conditions of the duel were being decided upon by the President and the captain—a terrible, savage encounter in which each opponent would become a man-hunter—Michel Ardan rested from the fatigues of his triumph. But resting is hardly the right word. American beds can sometimes compete in hardness with tables made of marble or granite.

In fact, Ardan slept quite badly, tossing and turning in the material serving as sheets, and he was thinking he would have to install a more comfortable bunk in the projectile when a loud noise tore him from his dreams. There was a furious knocking on his door. The noise seemed to be made by some kind of metal instrument. A loud voice added to the racket, too early in the morning.

'Open the door!' someone shouted. 'In the name of God, open the door!'

Ardan had no reason to comply with an order so roughly expressed. He got up nevertheless and opened the door just as it was about to give way beneath the onslaught of his determined visitor.

The Secretary of the Gun Club burst into his bedroom. A bomb lobbed inside would not have made a less ceremonious entrance.*

'Last night,' J. T. Maston started explosively, 'our President was publicly insulted during the meeting. He called out his man who was none other than Captain Nicholl. They are due to fight each other this morning in Skersnaw Wood! I learned about this from Barbicane himself. If he's killed, it means the end of all our plans! We must stop this duel. But there's only one man in the entire world who has any influence over Barbicane and could persuade him to stop, and that man is Michel Ardan!'

While J. T. Maston was saying this, Michel Ardan did not even try to interrupt, but had got into his capacious trousers and, two minutes later, the two friends were heading hotfoot towards the outskirts of Tampa.

As they hurried along, Maston brought Ardan up to date with the situation. He told him of the real causes of the bitter enmity between Barbicane and Nicholl, explaining that it went a long way back and that it was thanks to common friends that the President and the captain had never previously met face to face. He added that their enmity arose solely from a disagreement about the respective merits of armoured plate and cannonballs and that the scene at the meeting had been no more than the opportunity Nicholl had long been looking for to settle old scores.

Now, there is nothing more savage than the proposed kind of duel, unique to America. Two opponents hunt each other through a patch of woodland, taking cover in the undergrowth and lying in wait for the other, and then shooting at him between the trees like a wild animal. It is at such times that a man envies the amazing gifts so natural to the plains Indians: quick intelligence, astute cunning, the ability to track and get the scent of an enemy. A mistake, a moment's hesitation, one false step can end in death. In these encounters, Yankees are regularly accompanied by their dogs and, as both hunter and prey, they can keep going for hours on end.

'Damnit, what sort of people are you?' cried Michel Ardan when his companion had finished forcefully outlining the scenario.

'It's the way we are,' said J. T. Maston simply. 'But come on, we mustn't waste time!'

However, it was no good. Though Michel Ardan and he raced over the plain, still wet with dew, tramped over rice-fields, negotiated creeks, and cut corners, they were unable to get to Skersnaw Wood before half past five. Barbicane must have entered the forest half an hour earlier.

Close by an old woodsman was busy making up bundles of firewood from trees he had cut down with his axe.

Maston ran over to him calling:

'Have you seen a man armed with a rifle go into the trees, Barbicane, the President . . . my best friend?'

The good Gun Club Secretary naively assumed that everybody on Earth must know the President. But the woodsman did not seem to understand.

'A hunter,' said Ardan.

'A hunter? Yes,' said the woodsman.

'Long ago?'

'About an hour since.'

'We're too late!' cried Maston.

'Have you heard a rifle shot?' asked Ardan.

'Nope.'

'None at all?'

'Not a one. It don't seem that hunter of yours has had much luck.'

'What are we to do now?' said Maston.

'We must go into the wood and risk getting a bullet that wasn't intended for us.'

'Oh!' cried Maston in a tone which could not be mistaken. 'I'd sooner have ten bullets in my head than one in Barbicane's.'

'Then let's not waste any time!' said Ardan seizing his companion's hand.

Moments later, the two friends disappeared into the stand of trees, a dense growth of giant cypresses, sycamores, tulip trees, olive bushes, tamarinds, oaks, and magnolias, their branches twisted and knotted in an inextricable tangle barely penetrable to the eye. Michel Ardan and Maston advanced side by side, moving silently through the tall vegetation, forcing their way past clinging vines, peering into bushes or under branches hidden in the darkness of their foliage and at every step expecting to hear the terrible blast of a rifle. Although Barbicane must have left signs of his progress through the wood, they found it impossible to detect them, and blundered blindly along virtually inexistent paths, where an Indian would have trailed an enemy step by step.

After an hour spent searching in vain, the two friends came to a halt. Their anxiety mounted.

'It must be all over,' said Maston unhappily. 'A man like Barbicane won't have tried to stalk his man or set a trap or tried to outflank him! He is too open, too straightforward for that. He will have marched right in, looking danger in the eye, somewhere most likely too far from the woodsman for the sound of a rifle shot to carry on the wind!'

'But what about us?' said Michel Ardan. 'In all the time we've been in this wood, surely we would have heard . . .'

'But what if we got here too late?' cried Maston with despair in his voice.

Michel Ardan could find nothing to say.

He and Maston resumed their interrupted progress. At intervals they called out, shouting the names of Barbicane and Nicholl. But neither of the two adversaries answered their halloos. Startled by the sounds, flights of cheerful birds disappeared among the branches and a few frightened deer fled at full speed through the trees.

The search continued for another hour. Most of the wood had by now been explored. There was nothing to indicate the presence of the duellists. They were beginning to doubt what the woodsman had said, and Ardan was about to give up the idea of continuing any longer with such a pointless exercise, when Maston suddenly stopped.

'Sh!' he said. 'There's somebody over there!'

'Who?' said Michel Ardan.

'Yes! It's a man! He doesn't seem to be moving. He's not holding a rifle. What on Earth is he doing?'

'Can you make out who it is?' asked Michel Ardan, whose short-sightedness did him a disservice in such circumstances.

'Yes! He's turning this way . . .' answered Maston.

'Who is it?'

'Captain Nicholl!'

'Nicholl!' exclaimed Michel Ardan, his blood suddenly running cold.

And Nicholl with no rifle! Did that mean he no longer had anything to fear from an opponent?

'Let's get closer,' said Michel Ardan, 'and then we'll know where we stand.'

But he and his companion had not gone fifty yards when they halted to get a closer look at the captain. They imagined they would find a man with his thirst for blood slaked and replete with satisfied revenge. They were dumbfounded by what they saw.

A fine-meshed net had been slung between two huge tulip trees. In the middle of it, a small bird, its wings entangled, was struggling to free itself and squawking its distress. The bird-catcher who had hung this deadly net was not a human being but a venomous spider, found only in that country, as big as a pigeon's egg and equipped with enormous legs. This hideous creature, as it was about to pounce on its prey, had been forced to retreat and seek safety in the upper branches of the tulip tree, because it in turn was being threatened by a fearsome enemy.

Captain Nicholl, his rifle laid on the ground and heedless of the danger of his situation, was busy trying, as gently as he could, to rescue the victim which had been caught in the net of the monstrous arachnid. When he was done, he released the little bird, which, happily fluttering its wings, flew off and disappeared.

Nicholl, looking pleased, was watching it fly off into the foliage when he heard the following words spoken with genuine feeling:

'You are a good man!'

He turned. Michel Ardan was standing in front of him saying in the same tone:

'And a kind-hearted one!'

'Michel Ardan!' cried the captain. 'What on Earth brings you here?'

'A wish to shake your hand, Nicholl, and to prevent you from killing Barbicane or being killed by him.'

'Barbicane!' cried the captain. 'I've been looking for him for two hours and not seen hide nor hair of him. Where's he hiding?'

'Nicholl,' said Michel Ardan, 'mind your manners! You should always respect your opponent. But there's no need to worry. If Barbicane is alive, we shall find him, it will be so much easier now—unless, that is, he has been indulging himself liberating oppressed birds—because he is also looking for you. But when we've found him, I, Michel Ardan, guarantee that there'll be no more talk of duels between the pair of you.'

'Between President Barbicane and myself,' Nicholl replied grimly, 'there is such rivalry that only the death of one of us . . .'

'Stuff and nonsense,' Michel Ardan went on. 'Men of your calibre might once have been at loggerheads, but they respect each other too. You won't fight.'

'I shall fight, sir!'

'No, sir, you won't!'

'Captain,' J. T. Maston broke in earnestly, 'I am the President's friend, his alter ego, his second self. If you are quite determined to kill somebody, shoot me, it amounts to the same thing!'

'Sir,' said Nicholl, his hand clutching his rifle with an involuntary movement of his hand, 'this is no time for joking . . .'

'Brother Maston is not joking,' replied Michel Ardan, 'and I fully understand why he should want to get himself killed to save his friend! But neither he nor Barbicane will die by the gun of Captain Nicholl, because I have a proposal to put to you two rivals which is so attractive that you will fall over yourselves to accept it.'

'What proposal might that be?' asked Nicholl, visibly incredulous.

'All in good time,' replied Ardan. 'I can only reveal what it is when Barbicane is present.'

'So let's go and find him,' exclaimed the captain.

The three men set off at once. The captain, after uncocking his rifle, slung it over one shoulder and moved off on fitful feet and not saying another word.

For a further half hour, their search proved fruitless. Maston was seized with a sinister presentiment. He kept a stern eye on Nicholl. wondering if he had already taken his revenge, and if the unfortunate Barbicane, a bullet in him, was not lying lifeless in some blood-smeared thicket. It seemed that Michel Ardan was also having the same thought and both were staring questioningly at Captain Nicholl when Maston stopped dead in his tracks.

The torso of a man sitting with his back against an enormous catalpa was visible not twenty paces away, half-hidden by the under-growth.

'It's him!' said Maston.

Barbicane was motionless. Ardan looked straight into the eyes of the captain, who did not turn a hair. Ardan moved several steps forward and called:

'Barbicane! Barbicane!'

There was no reply. Ardan hurried towards his friend but just as he was about to grip him by the arm, he came to a sudden stop with an exclamation of surprise.

Barbicane, a pencil between his fingers, was jotting mathematical formulae and geometrical numbers in a notebook while his uncocked rifle lay on the ground.

Lost in his work, this other man of science had also forgotten his duel and all thought of revenge, and had neither seen nor heard a thing.

But when Michel Ardan put his hand on his, he bounded to his feet and stared at him with a look of surprise.

'Ah!' he cried, 'It's you! Here at last! My friend, I've done it! I've got it!'

'Got what?'

'A way!'

'What way?'

'A way of countering the shock effect when the projectile is launched!'

'Really?' said Michel glancing at the captain out of the corner of his eye.

'Yes! Water! Just water. It will provide a cushion!—Ah, Maston,' exclaimed Barbicane, 'you here too?'

'In person,' said Michel Ardan, 'and may I at the same time present the distinguished Captain Nicholl?'

'Nicholl!' cried Barbicane* who got instantly to his feet. 'My apologies, Captain. I had forgotten . . . I am ready!'

Michel Ardan stepped in, giving no time to the two adversaries to resume hostilities.

'Great heavens,' he said, 'it's as well that the two of you didn't run into each other sooner! If you had we would now be shedding tears for one or the other of you. But thanks to God, we now have nothing more to fear. When a man forgets to hate and instead turns his mind to problems of mechanics or the tricks he can play on spiders, then his hatred ceases to be dangerous to anyone.'

And Michel Ardan told the President how they had found the captain.

'So I would ask you,' he said, as he finished, 'were two good men such as yourselves really put on this Earth to blow each other's heads off with rifles?'

There was something in the situation that was almost farcical and so unexpected that Barbicane and Nicholl did not know how they should behave towards each other. Michel Ardan sensed it and he found a quick way of restoring peace.

'Dear friends,' he said allowing his most friendly smile to play over his lips, 'all that's ever been between you is a misunderstanding. That's all. Well, to prove it's all over and done with, and because you are both men who are not averse to putting your lives on the line, I sincerely hope you will accept the proposal I am about to put to you.'

'Say your piece,' said Nicholl.

'Barbicane here believes his projectile will fly straight to the Moon.'

'It will,' said the President.

'And Nicholl is convinced it will fly up and crash back down on *terra firma*.'

'I'm sure of it,' said the captain.

'Right, then' said Michel Ardan. 'Now, I do not claim I can make you see eye to eye but I say to you in all seriousness: "Come with me, and see if we come a cropper."'

'What?' said J. T. Maston, stunned.

As they heard this unexpected proposal, both rivals looked up and observed each other closely. Barbicane waited for the captain to reply. Nicholl waited to hear what the President would say.

'Well?' said Michel in his most winning voice. 'There's nothing to fear now: there'll be no shock or surprises!'

'Agreed!' said Barbicane.

But quickly though he spoke, Nicholl said the word at the exactly same instant.

'Bravo! Well done! Hip, hip hooray!' cried Michel Ardan and he held out his hand to both adversaries. 'And now, friends, since everything is settled now, you must allow me to behave like a Frenchman. I invite you to have breakfast with me!'

22

A NEW CITIZEN OF THE UNITED STATES

THE same day, the whole of America learned of both the challenge between Captain Nicholl and President Barbicane and its singular outcome. The role played in their duel by the gallant European, his unexpected proposal which resolved the unpleasantness, its simultaneous acceptance by both rivals, the conquest of the continent of the Moon towards which France and the United States were proceeding arm in arm—all this combined to carry the popularity of Michel Ardan to new heights. The hysterical way Yankees can have of becoming infatuated with a given individual is well known. In a country where sober-sided holders of public office may harness themselves to the carriage of a dancer and bear her along in triumph,* it may easily be imagined what fervour was unleashed by the dashing Frenchman! If his horses were not unhitched, it was probably because he did not have any, but he was given all the other marks of public adulation. There was not a single citizen who did not identify with him body and soul! *E pluribus unum,** as the emblematic motto of the United States puts it.

From that day on, Michel Ardan did not have a moment's peace. Deputations arrived from all parts of the Union and plagued him without let or hindrance. He was obliged to receive them, whether he wanted to or not. The hands he shook and the backs he slapped are too numerous to put a figure on. Soon he was worn to a frazzle. His voice, grown hoarse by the countless speeches he gave, allowed only unintelligible whispers to pass his lips and he almost went down with gastro-enteritis after the series of toasts he was forced to drink to all the counties of the Union. Such success would have gone straight to the head of a lesser man, but he managed to carry on in a kind of state of charming, witty half-tipsiness.

Among the deputations of all kinds which harassed him, those made up of 'lunamaniacs' particularly acknowledged the huge debt they owed to the future conqueror of the Moon. One day, a few of these poor deluded people, who are quite numerous in America, came to him and asked if they could go with him back to 'the country of their birth'. Some of them claimed to be able to speak 'Selenite' and tried to teach him to speak it too. Michel Ardan happily went along with their harmless obsession and readily agreed to take messages from them to give to their friends on the Moon.

'It's weird! They're deluded!' he said to Barbicane after he had waved them goodbye. 'And deluded in the way that often affects the very intelligent. One of our foremost scientists, Arago, told me that many people who ordinarily take a quiet, sane, conservative view of things are prone to peculiar fixations and believe the strangest things whenever they think of the Moon. You don't believe the Moon has the power to influence the disorders of the body, do you?'

'Hardly,' replied the President of the Gun Club.

'Nor do I. Yet history records facts that are rather surprising. In 1669, during an epidemic, the largest number of deaths occurred on 23 January, when there happened to be an eclipse. The celebrated Bacon regularly fainted during lunar eclipses and only got his wits back after the Moon was full again. In the year 1399, King Charles VI went mad on six occasions when the Moon was either new or full.* Some physicians have included the falling sickness among the forms of illness that follow the phases of the Moon. Nervous disorders have seemingly been influenced by it too. Mead speaks of a child who had convulsions whenever the Moon went into opposition and Gall observed that heightened states among the feeble-minded grew worse twice every month, during new and full moons. There are thousands of observations of this kind relating to fainting fits, malignant fevers, sleepwalking, and so on, which tend to suggest that the Eye of Night does in fact exert some sort of mysterious influence over the health of Earthlings.'

'But how?' asked Barbicane. 'And why?'

'Why?' said Ardan. 'Well, I'd have to give the same reply Arago gave nineteen centuries after Plutarch, who said: "Perhaps it's because it isn't true!" '*

In the midst of his triumph, Michel Ardan could not escape the irksome duties that inevitably come with fame. Those who make money out of famous names were eager to turn him into an exhibit. Barnum* offered him a million for the right to take him on a tour of cities throughout the United States and display him, like some out-landish animal. Michel Ardan told him he was a vulgar elephant driver and told him to his face to go run up a shutter.

But while he refused to satisfy the curiosity of the public in this way, pictures of him circulated throughout the world and occupied a place of honour in scrapbooks everywhere. They came in all forms and shapes, from life-size to the smallest format on postage stamps. Every man, woman, and child had his likeness in all imaginable poses:* head, head and shoulders, full length, full face, profile, the three-quarters view, and seen from the back. More than a million and a half were produced and a wonderful opportunity fell into his lap: if he chose to, he could have auctioned off parts of himself as relics. But he did not seize the moment. Yet if he'd just sold the hairs of his head at a dollar apiece, he could have made a fortune!

But to tell the truth, he did not dislike all the attention he was given. On the contrary, he made himself available to his public and replied to letters from all over the globe. His witticisms were repeated and circulated everywhere, especially ones he had never uttered. For as always happens, these were bestowed on him, as people lend to the rich—and he was certainly rich in that regard.

Not only did he have the men on his side but the women too. He might have made any number of 'good marriages' if only the fancy had taken him and he had been minded to 'settle down'. Older ladies, particularly those who had been withering on the vine for forty years, dreamed night and day surrounded by photographs of him.

He could certainly have acquired wives by the hundred even if he had made it a condition that they fly off with him up into the empyrean. Women can be intrepid when they are not afraid of everything. But his intention was not to put down roots on the lunar continent and settle it with a people that was a mixture of French and American. So he refused all offers.

'What!' he said. 'Go all that way to be a new Adam with a daughter of Eve? No thanks! I'd be sure to find serpents up there . . .'

As soon as he could tear himself away from the incessant celebrations of his triumph, he went with his friends to inspect the Columbiad. He felt it was the least he could do. Besides he had become something of a ballistics expert since he had been living in the company of Barbicane, J. T. Maston and the rest of them. His greatest pleasure was to keep telling those excellent artillerymen that they were basically genial, highly qualified murderers. He never wearied of teasing them along such lines. The day he went to see the Columbiad, he praised it to the skies and was lowered to the bottom of the barrel of the gigantic mortar which would soon send him on his way to the Moon.

'At least,' he said, 'this is a cannon which won't hurt anybody, which is not something you often hear said about a cannon. But don't talk to me about guns that destroy and burn and wreck and kill, and especially never tell me that they have a "soul", for I won't have it!'

Mention must be made of a proposal concerning J. T. Maston. When the Secretary of the Gun Club heard Barbicane and Nicholl accepting Michel Ardan's proposal, he had decided that he must join them and make up a 'foursome'. One day, he asked if he could be included on the flight. Barbicane, hating to say no, gave him to understand that the projectile was not built to carry that number of passengers. In desperation, Maston went to see Michel Ardan, who suggested that he should resign himself and added various arguments *ad hominem*.

'Look, my dear Maston,' he said, 'don't take my words the wrong way but really, just between ourselves, you are too . . . incomplete to go to the Moon.'

'*Incomplete?*' exclaimed the lion-hearted war veteran.

'Absolutely, my dear fellow. Just think: if, when we get there, we find that it is inhabited. Would you want to give those inhabitants a grim picture of what goes on here on Earth, telling them what war is like, showing them that we use most of our time gobbling each other up, going at it hammer and tongs, breaking each other's arms and legs, and all that on a planet which could feed a hundred billion people at a time when there are barely one billion two hundred million there now? You do see, my friend, that you'd get us kicked out of the place!'

'But if when you got there you were in bits,' replied J. T. Maston, 'you'd all be just as *incomplete* as me!'

'True,' said Michel Ardan, 'but we won't arrive in bits.'

And indeed a test trial, on 18 October, had produced excellent results which provided well-grounded hopes of success. In an effort to have some idea of the effect of shock inside a projectile when it was fired, Barbicane sent for a 32-inch mortar (75 cm)* from the arsenal at Pensacola. It was set up on the shore of Hillsborough Bay, so that the shell would fall into the sea and the impact thus be minimized. His intention was to test the blast at launch and not the effect of a landing.

A hollow shell was got ready with the greatest care for this unusual experiment. A thick padding applied over a network of springs made of the finest steel was used to line the inside of the casing. It then resembled a meticulously wadded nest.

'Such a pity I can't get into it!' said J. T. Maston, lamenting the fact that he was too big to take part in the test.

Into this comfortable shell, which was sealed with a screw-down lid, were put a large cat, and then a squirrel belonging to the Perpetual Secretary of the Gun Club of which J. T. Maston was particularly fond. They wished to know how an animal not subject to dizziness would be affected by this experimental voyage.

The mortar was primed with a hundred and sixty pounds of gun-powder, the shell was placed in the breech, and then it was fired.

The shell rose quickly in a majestic parabola, reached a height of about one thousand feet and then, in a graceful curve, went and dived beneath the foaming waves.

Without wasting a moment, a small open boat headed towards its point of entry. Skilled divers leapt into the water and attached cables to the handles of the shell which was quickly hauled on board. Five minutes had passed between the moment the two animals had been shut inside and the time when the lid of their prison was unscrewed.

Ardan, Barbicane, Maston, and Nicholl were in the boat for the recovery operation and looked on with a degree of interest which may be readily imagined. The moment the shell was opened, the cat leapt out, looking rather cross but otherwise perky enough and giving no indication of having just returned from an aerial expedition. But there was no squirrel.* They looked. But there was no sign of it. They were forced to acknowledge the truth. The cat had eaten its travelling companion.

J. T. Maston was greatly saddened by the loss of his poor squirrel and proposed that its name be added to the martyrology of science.

Be that as it may, after this experiment all doubt and all fear vanished. Moreover, Barbicane's final plans for the projectile included further improvements to be made, including measures to eliminate the effects of shock almost completely. All that now remained was to set off.

Two days later, Michel Ardan received a message from the President of the Union,* by which he was particularly moved.

Following the precedent set for his noble compatriot, the Marquis de La Fayette, the government conferred on him the title of citizen of the United States of America.

23

THE PASSENGER PROJECTILE

AFTER the completion of the Columbiad, public interest now turned to the projectile, the new type of conveyance which was to transport the three bold adventurers through space. No one had forgotten that in his telegram of 30 September, Michel Ardan had requested some modification to the plans drawn up by members of the Committee.

At the time, President Barbicane had rightly believed that the shape of the projectile was of little importance since, having left Earth's atmosphere in a matter of seconds, its passage would there-after take place in a complete vacuum. The Committee had there-fore opted for a sphere, so that the projectile could revolve and behave freely. But once it had been turned into a vehicular convey-ance, the matter took on a different aspect. Michel Ardan did not care to travel like a squirrel in a box. He intended to ride with his head held high, his feet on the floor, with as much dignity as if he were travelling in the basket of a hot-air balloon—though much faster, of course—but without being tossed and flung about in the most unseemly fashion.

So new plans were forwarded to Albany, to the firm of Breadwill & Co., with instructions that the changes should be implemented with-out delay. The projectile, duly modified, was cast on 2 November and immediately transported to Stone's Hill by the eastern railway system.

It arrived safely at its destination on the tenth. Michel Ardan, Barbicane, and Nicholl had been waiting with the greatest impatience for this object, this passenger projectile, in which they would take their seats for their voyage of discovery of a new world.

It cannot be disputed that it was a magnificent piece of work, a metallurgical production which did the greatest honour to American industrial genius. It was the first time that aluminium had been used in such a large quantity and the result had every right to be regarded as a prodigious achievement. The exquisite projectile gleamed in the sun's rays. To see it with those impressive lines and its cone-shaped prow, it could easily have been mistaken for the kind of substantial turrets shaped like pepper-pots which medieval architects used to hang on the corners of fortified castles. All it lacked were slits for archers and a weather-vane.

'I fully expect', said Michel Ardan, 'to see a man-at-arms stepping out of it wearing chainmail and carrying an arquebus. When we're inside her, we'll be like feudal chiefs and, with a modicum of artillery, we could hold our own against the Selenite armies—if, that is, there are any on the Moon!'

'So you like the vehicle?' Barbicane asked his friend.

'Oh yes, of course!' replied Michel Ardan who looked it over with an artist's eye. 'My only criticism is that its lines were not made more slender and the cone more graceful. Really, they should have finished it off with a flourish of guilloche enamel decoration with, say, a mythological beast or a gargoyle or a salamander emerging from the flames with wings outstretched and jaws wide open . . .'

'What on Earth for?' said Barbicane, for his practical mind was not very attuned to artistic beauty.

'What for? My dear Barbicane, if you need to ask the question, I'm afraid you will never understand the answer!'

'Tell me anyway, my friend.'

'Well, to my way of thinking we should always add a dash of art to whatever we do. Do you know an Indian drama called *The Little Clay Cart*?'*

'Not even by name.'

'I'm not surprised,' said Michel Ardan, 'so listen. In the play there is a thief who, just as he is breaking through the wall of a house, pauses and wonders if he should give the hole he was making the shape of a lyre, a flower, a bird, or an amphora. Now, tell me, Barbicane, if you had been a member of the jury at his trial, would you have found that man guilty?'

'Without a moment's hesitation,' said the President of the Gun Club. 'Breaking and entry.'

'And I would have acquitted him! That's why you'll never understand me!'

'And I, my artistic friend, would never dream of trying to.'

'But at least,' said Michel Ardan, 'since the outside of our passenger projectile is something of a let-down, might I be allowed to design the interior as I see best and with a level of luxury that befits ambassadors from Earth?'

'In that area, my dear Michel,' replied Barbicane, 'you shall be free to act as the fancy takes you and we shall let you get on with it as you please.'

But before moving on to the *dulce*, the President of the Gun Club had attended to the *utile*, and the practical means he had invented of softening the effects of the shock were even then being installed by first-class minds.

Barbicane had concluded, with good reason, that no spring could be strong enough to absorb the initial shock, and during his celebrated perambulation through Skersnaw Wood, he had finally solved the problem in the most ingenious way. He was counting on water to do this essential job for him. Here's how:

The projectile would be filled with water to a depth of three feet. Over it would be laid a wooden disc fitting so snugly as to be perfectly watertight yet still capable of moving smoothly up and down against the inside walls of the projectile. It was on this raft of sorts that the passengers would take their places. The volume of water was divided by horizontal partitions which would be collapsed in rapid succession by the shock of departure. At that point, each quantity of water, bottom, middle, and top in turn, being forced up in a rising sequence through overflow pipes into the upper part of the projectile, would act like springs and the disc, fitted with powerful shock-absorbers, was prevented from hitting the floor of the projectile until it had smashed through all three partitions in turn. Of course, the passengers would still experience a further shock effect after the total evacuation of the mass of water, but the initial impact would be almost completely neutralized by this ultra-powerful form of shock-absorption.

True, three feet of water over a surface of fifty-four square feet would weigh almost 11,500 pounds. But the sudden release and accumulation of explosive gases in the breech of the Columbiad would, according to Barbicane, be enough to compensate for this increase in weight. Furthermore, the shock would expel all the water in less than one second, and the projectile would promptly revert to its normal weight.

That was the sequence of events which the President of the Gun Club had foreseen and his solution to the serious question of the shock effect. His scenario, most intelligently grasped by the engineers at Breadwill, was masterfully translated into reality. Once the initial shock had been absorbed and the water forced out, the passengers would have no problem disposing of the remains of the shattered wooden partitions and dismantling the sliding disc on which they had been supported for the launch.

The projectile's upper walls were covered with a thick cushioning of leather attached to spirals of the finest steel as pliant as watchsprings. The outflow pipes were hidden under this leather wall-cladding and their existence was undetectable.

Thus every imaginable precaution had been taken to absorb the effects of the initial shock. Given this fact, said Michel Ardan, if they were pulverised, it would only be because they themselves were made of 'wishy-washy stuff'.

The projectile was 9 feet wide at its external circumference and 12 feet tall. In order to avoid exceeding the stipulated weight, the thickness of the walls had been slightly reduced but they had strengthened the bottom, which would have to bear the full blast of the gases released when the guncotton was detonated. The base, of course, is always the thickest part of missiles and cylindro-conical shells.

Entry to this metal tower was through a narrow opening which, made in the side of the cone, resembled the 'manholes' in steam boilers. It was hermetically closed by an aluminium hatch secured on the inside by powerful pressure bolts. When the voyagers reached the Moon, they would thus be able to leave their mobile prison whenever they liked.

But it was not enough that they should go: they would need to see out as they went. This posed no problem. Under the leather cladding were four portholes made of thick lentiform glass, two let into the circular wall of the projectile, a third into its base, and the fourth into its cone at the top. During the flight, the passengers would be able to observe the Earth which they had left, the Moon which they were approaching, and the star-filled space of the heavens. However, these portholes were protected against the initial blast-off by solidly housed metal plates which could easily be swung open outwards by unscrewing them from inside. In this way, no air in the projectile would escape and observations in all directions could be made.

All these mechanical systems and instruments, admirably installed, were easily operated and the engineers had not been any less intelligent in fitting up the inside of the projectile.

Lockers were solidly incorporated which held the drinking water and provisions the three voyagers would need. For fire and light they could use a special container of gas kept under a pressure of several atmospheres. All they had to do was to turn a tap and for six days their congenial projectile would be lit and warmed. As can be seen, it lacked nothing that was necessary to life and even comfort. Moreover, at the behest of Michel Ardan, the agreeable was added to the useful in the form of *objets d'art*. Had the space been available, he would have turned the projectile into an artist's studio. But it would be a mistake to suppose that three men thrown together would feel cramped in their metal tower. They had a space ten feet high and an area of about fifty-four square feet. It was enough to give the occupants a degree of freedom of movement. They would not have felt more at home in the most comfortable railway carriage in the United States.

The matter of provisions and lighting was thus settled. There now remained the supply of air. It was obvious that the air contained at the outset inside the projectile would not be enough to last the passengers for four days. One man in an hour or so uses up all the oxygen contained in a hundred litres of air. Over a period of twenty-four hours, Barbicane and his companions, plus the two dogs they intended to take with them, would thus consume 2,400 litres of oxygen, a weight of about seven pounds. The air inside the projectile would therefore have to be replaced. How was it to be done? By using the simple process devised by Messrs Reiset and Regnault which Michel Ardan brought up during a meeting.

Now it is a well-known fact that air is made up mainly of 21 parts oxygen and 79 parts nitrogen. What exactly happens when a man breathes? A very simple phenomenon occurs. From the air, he absorbs the oxygen which is essential to life and exhales the nitrogen intact. The air breathed out has lost approximately 5 per cent of its oxygen and contains an almost equal volume of carbonic dioxide produced by the combustion of elements in the blood caused by the oxygen inhaled. So in a closed environment after a certain length of time, all the oxygen in the air is replaced by carbon dioxide, a harmful gas.

At this point, the problem boils down to the following. Given that the nitrogen survives unchanged, (1) how can the oxygen which has been used be replaced? (2) how can the carbon dioxide which has been exhaled be eradicated? Both actions are easily achieved by using potassium chlorate and caustic potash.

Potassium chlorate is a salt which occurs in the form of white flakes. When heated to temperatures above 400 degrees centigrade, it changes into potassium chloride and releases its entire oxygen content. Now, eighteen pounds of potassium chlorate will yield seven pounds of oxygen, which is to say the amount the passengers would need for a period of twenty-four hours. That took care of replacing the oxygen.

Turning now to the caustic potash. It is a substance which readily interacts with the carbon dioxide present in the air and it needs only to be agitated for it to extract it and be changed into potassium bicarbonate. That is how the carbon dioxide could be absorbed.

By combining both processes, it was possible to restore to air that is bad all its lost life-giving properties. That is what the experiments of the two chemists, Messrs Reiset and Regnault, had successfully demonstrated.

But the fact was that their experiments had been carried out using only animals. For all its scientific accuracy, no one knew what effect the process would have on human beings.

This complication was drawn to the attention of the meeting at which the whole issue was discussed. Michel Ardan insisted that there should be no doubt about whether it was possible or not to live by breathing artificial air and volunteered to test theory before they set off.

But the honour of putting the question to the trial was energetically claimed by J. T. Maston.

'Since I shall not be going,' said the brave gunner, 'at least I might be allowed to live inside the projectile for a week.'

It would have been ungracious to refuse his request, which was granted. A sufficient quantity of potassium chlorate and caustic potash was made available to him along with provisions for a week. Then, on 12 November, at six in the morning, after shaking hands with his friends and making it absolutely clear that they were not to open his prison door before the twentieth, at six in the evening, he entered the projectile. The hatch was hermetically sealed.

What went on inside it during the week that followed? It was not possible to say. The thickness of the walls of the projectile prevented the escape of any sound.

On 20 November, at exactly 6 p.m., the hatch was opened. J. T. Maston's friends could not help feeling somewhat anxious. But they were quickly relieved when they heard a jovial voice delivering a loud 'Hooray!'

And then the Secretary of the Gun Club appeared at the top of the cone both arms raised in triumph.

And he looked fatter!

24

THE TELESCOPE IN THE ROCKIES

On 20 October of the previous year, after subscriptions closed, the President of the Gun Club had supplied the Observatory at Cambridge with the funds it needed to build a gigantic optical instrument. Either a field-glass type or a telescope, it would have to be powerful enough to allow an object no wider than nine feet to be seen on the surface of the Moon.

There is a fundamental difference between the reflecting field glass and the refracting telescope, and we cannot pass up this chance of reminding ourselves of it here. The refracting type is a tube which has a convex lens known as an *objective* at the front end, and a second lens at the back end through which the observer looks and is called the *ocular* or eye-piece. Light emanating from a luminous source enters through the objective, is refracted, and becomes its inverted image at its focal point. This image is observed at the eye-piece, which enlarges it exactly as would a magnifying glass. The tube of the refracting telescope is sealed at both ends, by the objective and the eye-piece respectively.

On the other hand, the tube of the reflecting telescope is open at the front end. Light from the object being observed enters freely and falls on a concave, or convergent, metal mirror. There its reflection is redirected to a small mirror which relays it to the eye-piece, whose function is to enlarge the image thus produced.

The operating principle of a closed-field glass is refraction, whereas in telescopes it is reflection, hence the name of 'refractors' for the first type and 'reflectors' for the second. By far the thorniest part of building the two kinds of optical instrument lies in the grinding of the lenses, both the objective and the eye-piece.

However, at the time when the Gun Club was embarking on its great experiment, these instruments had already reached an advanced stage of sophistication and were giving some amazing results. The time was long past when Galileo observed the stars with a primitive refracting telescope which had a magnifying power of seven at most. Since the sixteenth century, optical instruments had grown considerably in circumference and width and they allowed stellar space to be scrutinized at distances undreamed of until then. Among the refracting instruments in use at that time, the most celebrated were the one used at the observatory at Poulkowa in Russia, with an objective 15 inches (38 centimetres) wide, the telescope of the Frenchman Lerebours, which was equipped with one of equal size, and last but not least the Cambridge Observatory's own refractor, which boasted an objective 19 inches (48 centimetres) in diameter.

As to reflecting telescopes, two in particular were known for their remarkable power and immense size. The first, built by Herschel, was 36 feet long and had a 54-inch mirror with a magnifying power of six thousand. The other was sited in Ireland, at Birr Castle, in Parsonstown Park, and belonged to Lord Rosse. The length of its tube was fully 48 feet and the width of its mirror, 6 feet (1 m 93 cm). Its magnifying power was 6,400 and a massive stone building had to be erected to accommodate the machinery which allowed the telescope, weighing 28,000 pounds, to be manoeuvred.

Now it is clear that despite their tremendous size, the magnifications obtained did not exceed 6,000 in round terms. But a magnifying power of 6,000 will only bring the Moon to within an apparent distance of 39 miles (16 leagues) when only objects with a diameter of 60 feet will be visible on its surface—unless they are very, very long.

Now the object in hand was a projectile just 9 feet wide and 15 long. So the Moon had to be brought nearer, to at least 5 miles (2 leagues), which meant achieving a magnification of 48,000 times.

This had been the problem put to the Observatory at Cambridge. The problem would not be any lack of finance. No, the difficulty lay in the material difficulties of its construction.

First a choice had to be made between refractors and reflectors. Reflectors have distinct advantages over the refractors. Assuming the objectives of both are identical, the former enable higher magnifications to be obtained because light which passes through a lens loses less of its intensity than when it is reflected by the metal mirror of a telescope. But there are limits to how thick a lens can be made because if it is too thick it will not allow light rays to pass through it at all. Moreover, the manufacture of these huge lenses is extremely problematic and requires a considerable length of time measurable in years.

And so, although the image was brighter in a refractor—a considerable advantage in observing the Moon whose light is already reflected—it was decided to use a reflector, which can be made more quickly and allows higher magnifications to be obtained. However, since light rays lose much of their intensity as they pass through our atmosphere, the Gun Club decided to locate the instrument on one of the highest mountains in the Union. This would reduce the density of the layers of the Earth's air.

In reflectors, as we have seen, the eye-piece is the enlarging lens to which the observer puts his eye, whereas the objective, which provides the greater magnification, has the larger diameter and longer focal length. To provide a level of 48,000 times magnification, it would be necessary to exceed markedly the objectives made by Herschel and Lord Rosse. That was where the difficulty lay, for grinding the mirrors is an extremely difficult process.

Fortunately, a few years earlier, an expert at the Institut de France named Léon Foucault had found a quick and easy way of polishing lenses by replacing the metal mirror with another made of silvered glass. It consisted simply of preparing molten glass in the quantity required and then treating it with a silver compound. It was this process, which gives excellent results, that was used to make the objective.

For the overall assembly of parts, the method devised by Herschel for his telescopes was adopted. In the great instrument built by the astronomer of Slough, the image of objects, reflected by the mirror set at an angle at the bottom of the tube, was sent to the other end where the eye-piece was located. Thus the observer, instead of being placed at the lower end of the tube, would be installed at its higher end and, using his magnifying glass, could look directly down into the gigantic cylinder. This combination had the advantage of eliminating the need for the small mirror which relayed to the eye-piece the image, which now underwent a single reflection instead of two. As a result less light was absorbed and the image was less weakened. This meant, in other words, that greater clarity was achieved, a precious advantage given the kind of observations which would have to be made.

Once these decisions had been made, work began. According to the calculations made by the Observatory at Cambridge, the tube of the new reflector would need to be 280 feet long and the mirror sixteen feet in diameter.* Enormous though such an instrument might be, it could hardly be compared to the telescope 10,000 feet long (3½ kilometres) which a few years ago the astronomer Hooke said should be built. Even so, the construction of such an instrument presented considerable difficulties.

On the question of where it should be located, a decision was quickly taken. They had to choose a high mountain and there are not many high mountains in the United States.

In effect, the orographic system of that great country is reduced to two mountain ranges of modest elevation and between them flows the magnificent Mississippi, which Americans—if they recognized any form of royalty at all—would call 'the king of rivers'.

To the east are the Appalachians, whose highest point, in New Hampshire, does not exceed 5,600 feet, which is modest enough.

To the west, on the contrary, are to be found the Rocky Mountains, an immense chain which begins at the Straits of Magellan, follows the west coast of South America, where it is called the Andes or Cordilleras, crosses the Panama isthmus, then runs up the length of North America until it reaches the shores of the polar seas.

These mountains are of no great altitude: the Alps or the Himalayas would look loftily down on them with unfeigned contempt. Indeed, their highest peak measures just 10,700 feet, while Mont Blanc rises to 14,439 feet and Kangchenjunga to a height of 26,776 feet above sea level.*

But since the Gun Club insisted that like the Columbiad the telescope should be sited within the United States of the Union, they had to make do with the Rockies. So all the materials that would be needed were sent up to the summit of Longs Peak in Missouri Territory.*

Pen cannot tell or words describe the difficulties of every kind that the American engineers had to overcome, nor the prodigies of nerve and skill they displayed. It was an amazing feat. Enormous stone blocks, heavy pre-cast metal parts, angle clamps of fearsome weight, enormous sections of the cylinder, the objective, which alone weighed 30,000 pounds, all this they had to haul up and beyond the permanent snow line to an altitude of more than 10,000 feet, after having already dragged and manhandled it across empty prairies, through impenetrable forests, over terrifying rapids, far from centres of population, traversing untamed regions where every aspect of life became an almost insoluble problem. Yet American genius overcame these countless problems. Less than one year after the work began, in the last days of the month of September, the enormous reflector was aiming its 280-metre-long tube at the sky above. It had been slung on a huge ironwork scaffolding. An ingenious mechanism enabled it to move effortlessly. It could be pointed at any part of the sky and follow the stars from one horizon to another as they progressed through space.

It had cost more than 400,000 dollars.

The first time it was trained on the Moon, observers approached it with an emotion that was a mixture of curiosity and apprehension. What were they about to discover in the field of this telescope which magnified the object observed 48,000 times? People, flocks of lunar animals, towns, lakes, oceans? No, they saw nothing except what science already knew, and everywhere they looked on the Moon's disc, the volcanic nature of the Moon was confirmed with absolute precision.

But before the telescope in the Rocky Mountains was handed to the Gun Club, it rendered immense services to astronomy. Thanks to its enormous penetrative power, the depths of the heavens were probed to the limits of its range, the apparent diameter of large numbers of stars was accurately measured, and Mr Clark, of the Institute at Cambridge, decomposed the Crab Nebula in the constellation of Taurus, which Lord Rosse's reflector had never been able to resolve.

25

FINAL PREPARATIONS

IT was now 22 November. The long-awaited departure was scheduled to take place ten days later. One last operation still needed to be carried out, a delicate and dangerous procedure that needed to be handled with utmost care. Indeed, it was against its successful completion that Captain Nicholl had laid his third bet: the no small matter of loading the Columbiad with 400,000 pounds of guncotton. Nicholl had believed, and not without good cause, that manhandling such a large quantity of pyroxylin would end in a terrible catastrophe and, moreover, that such a large amount of highly inflammable material would self-ignite under the pressure of the projectile.

The danger was seriously increased by the careless, casual attitude of Americans who, during the Federal War, never thought twice about loading bombs with a lighted cigar between their teeth. But Barbicane was determined to succeed and not fall at the last fence. He therefore chose his best workmen, directed their efforts himself, kept a constant eye on them and, taking every care and precaution, ensured that all the odds of success were on his side.

Before all else, he made sure that all the charge was taken directly to the enclosure on top of Stone's Hill. He had it brought there in instalments, in secure powder chests. The 400,000 pounds of pyroxylin had been divided into batches of 500 pounds, making in all 800 sealed crates which had been made with great care at Pensacola by its most skilled artificers. Each powder chest could contain ten crates and they arrived at intervals by train from Tampa. It follows that there were never more than 5,000 pounds of pyroxylin in the enclosure at any given time. On delivery, each chest was unloaded by workmen who wore no footwear,* and each crate was taken to the mouth of the Columbiad, into which it was lowered by a crane operated by man-power. No steam-driven machinery was allowed on site and no flame was permitted within a radius of two miles. Even in November, there was more than enough risk from the heat of the sun with such quantities of pyroxylin. For this reason they preferred to work at night by light generated in a vacuum, using the lamps invented by Ruhmkorff. In this way, they created artificial daylight at the bottom of the Columbiad shaft. There the crates were stacked in order and connected to each other by metal wires designed to send the electric signal to the middle of each one of them simultaneously.

In other words, a battery would be used to deliver the spark that would set off the charge of the accumulated guncotton. All these separate wires, fully insulated, were gathered into a single cable which was fed through an aperture at a suitable height, corresponding to the waiting projectile. From there, this cable would pass out through the thick cast-iron wall and continue up to the surface through one of the vents in the stone lining designated for this purpose. When it reached the summit of Stone's Hill, the cable, supported on poles over a length of two miles, was connected via a switch mechanism to a powerful Bunsen battery. All that was needed, therefore, was to move the switch with one finger for the circuit to be instantly completed and for a spark to ignite 400,000 pounds of guncotton. It scarcely needs to be said that the battery would not be activated until the very last moment.

By 28 November, the 800 sealed crates were all stowed in the base of the Columbiad. This part of the operation had gone smoothly but at the cost to President Barbicane of much trouble, stress, and strain!

He had struggled in vain to block all entry to Stone's Hill, but every day sightseers climbed over the fences and some, carrying reckless-ness to the point of folly, lit up and smoked as they stood next to the mound of guncotton. Barbicane was in a constant state of frustration. J. T. Maston did what he could to help, furiously chasing out inter-lopers and picking up the still-lighted cigar ends that the Yankees dropped everywhere. It was no easy task, for more than three hun-dred thousand people crowded around the enclosure. Michel Ardan had volunteered to escort the crates as they were moved to the mouth of the Columbiad. But when he himself was caught with a large lighted cigar in his mouth as he ejected trespassers, for whom he set such a bad example, the President of the Gun Club realized that he could not rely on this inveterate smoker and had no choice but to have a special eye kept on him.

But there is a God for gunners. Nothing blew up and the loading operation was brought to a successful conclusion. Captain Nicholl's third bet had thus been a bet too far. There remained now only to insert the projectile into the Columbiad and position it on top of the bed of guncotton.

But before this process could begin, everything needed for the journey had to be stowed shipshape fashion in the capsule. There was quite an amount of it, and if Michel Ardan had been given his head, there would soon have been no room left for the passengers. It is impossible to imagine everything that the affable Frenchman wanted to take to the Moon, a whole ragbag of useless things. But Barbicane stepped in and only items which were strictly necessary were allowed on board.

A number of thermometers, barometers, and binoculars were put into the instrument chest.

The voyagers would be anxious to study the Moon during the voyage and, to facilitate their scrutiny of this new world, they also took with them the excellent map made by Beer and Mädler, the *Mappa selenograhica*, published as four engraved plates and rightly acknowledged as an authentic masterpiece of observation and patience. It reproduced with meticulous accuracy the smallest details of that part of the satellite which is permanently turned towards the Earth: its mountains, valleys, basins, craters, peaks, and rilles could all be picked out with their exact measurements, correct oriehtation, and names, from the Doerfel and Leibnitz ranges whose highest points rise in the eastern portion of the Moon's disc,* to the *Mare frigoris* which extends across the north in the circumpolar regions.

It was a precious document for the voyagers who could study the land before they set foot on it.

They also took three rifles and three patent hunting guns which used explosive shells, together with a supply of gunpowder and a very large quantity of lead shot.

'We don't know what or who we'll be dealing with,' said Michel Ardan. 'Men or beasts might object to our going to call in on them! So we must take precautions.'

So to those weapons of self-defence were added mattocks, pick-axes, saws, and other essential tools, not to mention clothes to suit all temperatures, from the cold of the polar regions to the heat of the torrid zone.

Michel Ardan would have liked to take a certain number of animals on the expedition—though not two of every known species. But he saw no point in arranging for serpents, tigers, alligators, and other dangerous creatures to be acclimatized to the world of the Moon.

'Absolutely not,' he told Barbicane, 'but some beasts of burden, ox or cow, mule or horse, might do nicely on the land there and could come in very handy.'

'I dare say, my dear fellow,' replied the President of the Gun Club, 'but our capsule is not Noah's Ark. It has neither the capacity nor is that its purpose. We should remain within the bounds of the possible.'

In the end, after long discussions, it was agreed that the voyagers would settle for taking an excellent hunting dog that belonged to Nicholl and a prodigiously strong Newfoundland. Several boxes of the most useful type of seeds were among the objects deemed indispensable. If Michel Ardan had had his way, he would also have insisted on adding a few bags of soil to sow them in. But he did manage to take a dozen bushes which were carefully wrapped in straw and stowed in a corner.

Then there was the all-important matter of provisions, because they had to consider the possibility that they might land on an absolutely sterile part of the Moon. Barbicane managed this so well that he succeeded in assembling enough supplies to last them a year. But it should be added, by way of explanation, that these stores, consisting of preserved meats and vegetables, were reduced in volume by strong hydraulic pressure to their most compact state and that they contained a high percentage of nutritious elements. These victuals may not have offered much variety but no one who embarks on such a venture can afford to be choosy. There was also a supply of brandy, around fifty gallons, plus enough water for six months. Actually, according to the latest astronomical observations, no one doubted the existence of a certain amount of water on the surface of the Moon. As for edibles, a man would have to be mad to believe that Earthlings would be unable to find anything at all up there to eat. Michel Ardan had no doubt whatsoever on that score. If he had, he would have decided not to go.

'Anyway,' he told his friends one day, 'we won't be completely abandoned by friends and colleagues here below. They will ensure that we are not forgotten.'

'That we will,' replied J. T. Maston.

'What do you mean?' asked Nicholl.

'It's quite simple,' replied Ardan. 'The Columbiad will always be there, won't it? Well then, every time the Moon is at its zenith—if not its perigee—and favourable conditions allow it to be seen, which is to say about once a year, why can't they send us projectiles filled with supplies which we can look forward to on the appointed day?'

'Bravo,' cried J. T. Maston, like a man who has just been struck by a first-rate idea. 'Well said! But of course, dear friends, it goes without saying that we shall never forget you!'

'I'm counting on it!' said Ardan. 'So you see, we shall receive regular news from Earth, while we, in turn, will be very dense indeed if we cannot come up with some way of communicating with our good friends back home!'

The words breathed such confidence that Michel Ardan, with his air of determination and dazzling self-assurance, might well have carried the entire Gun Club with him. What he said seemed so simple, so straightforward, so easy, so sure to succeed, that a man would have needed to be ploddingly attached to this wretched terraqueous globe* of ours not to want to follow the three voyagers on their lunar expedition.

When all the various items had been stowed in the projectile, the water intended to absorb the shock of departure was pumped into the three compartments, and the gas that would provide lighting was stored under pressure in its container. As for the potassium chlorate and caustic potash, Barbicane, making allowance for unforeseen delays during the journey, took sufficient quantities of both to replenish the oxygen and absorb the carbon dioxide for two months. A most ingenious, self-operating apparatus took over the function of purifying the air and restoring its vivifying qualities. The projectile was thus now ready and all that remained now was to lower it into the Columbiad, an operation fraught with many difficulties and dangers.

The enormous projectile was brought to the top of Stone's Hill. There it was hoisted by powerful cranes and held suspended over the metal shaft.

It was a tense moment. If the chains were to break under the enormous weight, the fall of such a mass would inevitably cause the guncotton to explode.

Fortunately nothing of the sort happened, and a few hours later, the passenger projectile, having been gently lowered into the barrel of the cannon, was resting on the guncotton eiderdown of its bed of pyroxylin. The only effect of its weight was to pack the charge in the Columbiad more tightly.

'I've lost my bet,' said the captain as he handed Barbicane the sum of three thousand dollars.

Barbicane did not wish to take the money from a travelling companion. But he was forced to yield by the stubborn insistence of Nicholl, who was determined to settle all his debts before leaving Earth.

'Since that's the way of it,' said Michel Ardan, 'I have only one thing to wish for you.'

'What?' said Nicholl.

'That you also lose your two other bets! If you do, we cannot fail to have a straight run all the way!'

26

FIRE!

THE first day of December had dawned, the fateful day! For if the projectile was not launched that very evening, forty-six minutes and forty seconds past ten o'clock precisely, it would be another eighteen years* before the Moon again appeared in the same conjunction of zenith and perigee.

The weather was quite splendid. Despite the approach of winter, the bright sun shone down warm and radiant on the Earth which three of its inhabitants were about to exchange for a new world.

How many people slept badly the night before the day whose coming they had so impatiently looked forward to! How many spirits were weighed down with the heavy burden of expectation! Every heart beat anxiously except that of Michel Ardan. That nerveless man came and went with his customary briskness but nothing about him indicated that he had any kind of unusual concerns on his mind. He had slept peacefully, as Turenne had once slept on a gun carriage the night before a battle.

By early morning, vast crowds covered the prairies around Stone's Hill which stretched away as far as the eye could see in all directions. Every fifteen minutes, trains from Tampa brought more sightseers until this great movement of people was soon growing at a fantastic rate. During that memorable day, according to figures published by the *Tampa Observer*, five million spectators trampled the good earth of Florida.

For a month now, most of the crowds had been camped around the Stone's Hill enclosure, and had laid the foundations for a settlement that has since been known as Ardan's Town. Huts, cabins, shanties, and tents were scattered all over the plain and those temporary dwellings gave a roof to a population large enough to be the envy of the biggest cities of Europe.

Every nation on Earth was represented there, at any given time every language in the world could be heard spoken. It brought to mind the tangle of tongues, as reported in the Tower of Babel in biblical times. The various classes of American society all mingled on a footing of absolute equality. Bankers, farmers, sailors, agents, brokers, cotton planters, merchants, boatmen, magistrates rubbed shoulders with casual familiarity. Louisiana settlers fraternized with tenant farmers from Indiana; gentlemen from Kentucky and Tennessee and haughty Virginian dandies passed the time of day with barely civilized trappers from the Great Lakes and cattlemen from Cincinnati. They wore white broad-brimmed beaver hats and classic panamas, blue cotton trousers from the mills of Opelousas, smart unbleached linen jackets and brightly coloured half-boots. Around their necks they sported frothing batiste jabots, and added sparkle to shirt-fronts, cuffs, ties, fingers, even their ears with a whole assortment of rings, pins, diamonds, chains, buckles, and trinkets, whose value was equalled only by their sheer bad taste. Women, children, servants, all in equally expensive outfits, accompanied, followed, preceded, and encircled their husbands, fathers, and masters, who were to a man like tribal chieftains surrounded by their enormous families.

At meal times, it was a sight to see all these people fall on dishes peculiar to the Southern States and, with an appetite that threatened Florida's food supplies, wolf down items which would turn European stomachs, such as fricasseed frog, braised monkey, fish chowder, roast sarigue, opossum cooked rare, or raccoon steaks.*

And what a variety of spirits and other drinks there were to help down this indigestible food! And such excited voices that combined to create the inviting hubbub which filled bar-rooms and taverns glinting with glasses, tankards, flasks, carafes and unusually shaped bottles, mortars for crushing sugar in pestles, and packets of straws!

'Here's that mint julep!' yelled one of the barmen.

'One claret sangria!' screamed another.

'And your gin-sling,' yelped the first man.

'Cocktail and brandy mash!' bawled the second.

'Who wants to try the latest line in authentic mint julep?' shouted out canny hucksters, who, with a hey presto! movement of the hands filled glass after glass with the sugar, lemon, green mint, crushed ice, water, cognac, and fresh pineapple juice that went in to that refreshing drink.

But that was not all. Throats parched by hot, spicy food were encouraged to drink by the usual goadings which ricocheted, competed, and produced the most almighty din.

Yet on that day, 1 December, there was not much in the way of whooping and yelling. The proprietors of the dram-shops would have shouted themselves hoarse in vain trying to drum up custom. No one gave a second thought to eating or drinking and, at four in the afternoon, many of the spectators who drifted with the crowd had not even had their lunch yet! A more telling symptom still: the great American passion for sport and gambling had been stifled by the excitement. The sight of ten-pins lying on their sides, of the dice rolled in crap games sleeping in their shakers, the roulette wheel stilled, the cribbage boards abandoned, the decks of cards used for *vingt-et-un*, red and black, cribbage and faro* quietly intact in their unopened wrappers—the sight was enough to show that the great event of that day had cancelled all other priorities and left no time for anything else.

Until evening fell, a dull stir spread, unbroken by raised voices like the lull that precedes some great catastrophe, and it descended all over the nervously expectant crowd. An indescribable unease filled people's minds, an apprehensive lassitude, an indefinable feeling gripped their hearts. Everyone wished it was all over and done with.

But around seven o'clock, this heavy silence suddenly drained away: the Moon was rising on the horizon. Several million hurrahs greeted its appearance. It was exactly on time. The sound of cheering voices rose into the air. Applause broke out on all sides while Bright Phoebe shone peacefully in the clear night sky, caressing the crowd intoxicated by her tender moonbeams.

At that moment, the three intrepid voyagers appeared. At the sight of them, the clamour doubled in intensity. Unanimously and instantly, the United States national anthem burst from every heaving bosom and *Yankee Doodle*,* taken up by a chorus of five million voices, rose like a wall of noise that soared clear away to the outer reaches of Earth's atmosphere.

After this overwhelming outpouring of feeling, the national anthem came to an end, the last notes faded slowly, and all noise died away, save a vanishingly-muffled buzz that hung over the mass of the deeply moved spectators.

By this time, the Frenchman and the two Americans had entered the special enclosure around which the vast crowds were densely packed. They were accompanied by members of the Gun Club and deputations sent from various European observatories. Barbicane, cool and collected, calmly gave his final instructions. Nicholl, tight-lipped, his hands clasped behind his back, walked with firm and measured steps. Michel Ardan, debonair as ever, was dressed like the model voyager: legs encased in leather gaiters, a game bag hanging by his side, easy in his loosely fitting suit of brown velvet, a cigar between his lips, vigorously shaking hands with lordly generosity as he walked. He overflowed with endless zest and good humour, laughing, joking, playing schoolboy jokes on the worthy J. T. Maston—in a word, he was being 'French' and worse, 'Parisian', right up to the last moment.

Ten o'clock struck. The moment had come to take their places in the projectile. The operations required for moving down the barrel to reach it, closing and securing the hatch, removing the cranes, and clearing scaffolding from the mouth of the Columbiad would take some time.

Barbicane had set his chronometer to within one tenth of a second against the time shown by the engineer Murchison's, who would be responsible for igniting the gunpowder charge using the electric spark. The voyagers inside the projectile could thus watch the movement of the implacable hand which would show the exact second for their departure.

The time for farewells had now come. It was a touching scene. For all his feverish high spirits, Michel Ardan was genuinely moved. J. T. Maston had found lurking somewhere in a corner under his desiccated eyelids an aged tear which he had very likely saved up just for this occasion. He shed it. It dropped on the brow of his dear comrade, the good Barbicane.

'Can I come too?' he said. 'There's still time!'

'It's not possible, Maston, old friend.'

Moments later, the three travelling companions settled down in the projectile after they had screwed down the inside bolts securing the hatch, and the mouth of the Columbiad, now completely clear, was entirely open to the sky above.

Nicholl, Barbicane, and Michel Ardan had at last been locked into their metal capsule.

There are not words enough to describe the feelings shared by all, which had now reached their highest pitch.

The Moon moved across the pure, clear sky, extinguishing in its progress the twinkling lights of the stars. It was now passing through the constellation of Gemini and was already almost at the halfway stage between the horizon and the zenith. By this time, it was clear to each and every watching person that the projectile was being aimed at a point ahead of the target rendezvous, just as a hunter aims at a spot in front of the hare he wishes to shoot.

A dreadful silence bore down on the scene. Not a breath of wind passed over the land! Not a breath of air escaped from any waiting breast! Hearts did not dare to beat! Every eye was fixed in awe on the gaping maw of the Columbiad.

Murchison kept his eye on the moving hand of his chronometer. There now remained only forty seconds before the launch, but each of those seconds seemed as long as a year.

With twenty seconds to go, a generalized tremor ran through the crowd as each person realized that the courageous voyagers inside the projectile would also be counting off those last terrifying seconds. Voices were raised on all sides:

'Thirty-five! Thirty-six! Thirty-seven! Thirty-eight! Thirty-nine! Forty!!'

At that instant, Murchison raised his finger, pressed the switch on the transmitter, completed the circuit, and sent the electric spark into the breach of the Columbiad.

Instantly, there was an almighty, unprecedented, unearthly explosion of which nothing can convey the faintest idea, not the blast of thunderbolts nor the boom of volcanic eruptions. A vast sheaf of fiery flames leaped from the entrails of the earth as if spewed from a crater. The ground shook and only the smallest fraction of those present were vouchsafed the briefest glimpse of the projectile as it shot triumphantly into the air through the cloud of blazing smoke and fumes.

27

THE WEATHER CLOSES IN

As the great incandescent firestorm climbed up to a prodigious height in the sky, the glare of the flames lit up the whole of Florida and for a brief moment night became day over a large swathe of the country. The immense plume of fire was visible for a hundred miles out to sea, both in the Gulf and out in the Atlantic, and more than one ship's captain recorded the sighting of a gigantic meteor in his log.

The detonation that launched the Columbiad was accompanied by a virtual earthquake: Florida was shaken to its very core. The gases from the gunpowder, expanded by the heat, vaporized whole layers of the atmosphere with unequalled violence, creating an artificial hurricane which turned a hundred times faster than any regular tornado, and passed through the air like a whirlwind.

Not a single bystander was left standing. Men, women, and children were left flattened, like corn after a storm. All was chaos and confusion. Large numbers of people were injured and J. T. Maston, who had most imprudently insisted on getting too near, was blown back nearly forty yards, shooting like a bullet over the heads of his compatriots. Three hundred thousand people were temporarily deafened and left looking stunned.

After it had overturned huts, smashed cabins, uprooted trees within a radius of twenty miles, and blown the trains all the way back to Tampa, the atmospheric chaos swooped down on the town like an avalanche, destroying a hundred houses and buildings including St Mary's Church, and the new Stock Exchange, which developed a great crack which ran from one end of it to the other. Ships in the harbour were smashed against each other and sank like stones and a dozen vessels anchored in the roadstead were blown onto the shore when their moorings snapped like cotton thread.

But the circle of devastation spread wider yet and extended beyond the borders of the United States. The effects of the after-shock, aggravated by westerly winds, were felt out in the Atlantic, three hundred miles from the American coast. A storm, man-made and totally unexpected and which Admiral Fitzroy could not have foreseen, struck his ships with unprecedented violence. Several were hit by fearsome whirlwinds before they had time to furl their sails and were lost. They included the *Childe Harold*,* out of Liverpool, a most unfortunate occurrence which became the subject of fierce protests from the British.

Finally, to complete the record, there is the statement made by the local population, but for which there is no confirmation, that half an hour after the launch of the projectile, inhabitants of Gorée and Sierra Leone claimed that they had heard a muffled rumble, the last gasp of the turbulence in the sound waves which, after crossing the Atlantic, finally expired on the coast of Africa.

But to return to Florida. The moment the havoc ended, the injured, the deafened, all the mass of people came to life and wild cries—'Hooray for Ardan! Hooray for Barbicane! Hooray for Nicholl!'—broke out and rose into the air. Several million people, noses pointing skywards, hands gripping telescopes, field-glasses, and opera-glasses, scanned the heavens, forgetting their bumps and bruises and all they had been through, and concentrating all their attention on the projectile. But they looked in vain. It was no longer visible and they had no choice but to resign themselves and wait for the telegrams which would come from Longs Peak. The director of the Observatory at Cambridge was at his post there in the Rockies and it was to that patient, persistent astronomer that all observations had been entrusted.

But one unforeseen event—though not unforeseeable, and nothing could have been done to prevent it—then occurred which would soon test the public's patience sorely.

The weather, fine up to that point, suddenly deteriorated. The sky darkened and was obscured by cloud. How could it have been otherwise after that brutal displacement of whole layers of the atmosphere and the dispersal of the huge quantity of vaporous fumes produced by the detonation of 400,000 pounds of pyroxylin? The natural order had been disrupted. This should come as a surprise to no one because during naval battles it has often been observed that atmospheric conditions can be suddenly changed by the discharge of many cannons.*

The next day, the sun rose out of a horizon laden with thick cloud that formed a dense, impenetrable curtain between sky and land and which, unfortunately, spread as far as the region of the Rockies. It was bound to happen! A chorus of protest was heard from every part of the globe. But nature would not give an inch: if men had chosen to interfere with the atmosphere by creating such an explosion, they would have to suffer the consequences of their action.

During that first day, everyone tried to find some way of seeing through the opaque veil of cloud, but they were wasting their time. For they all made the mistake of looking up into the sky while, as a consequence of the daily rotation of the Earth, the projectile was in fact speeding away on the opposite side of the globe.

Be that as it may, when night came it wrapped the Earth in deep, impenetrable gloom, so that when the Moon had risen once more on the horizon, it was impossible to see it. It was as though it was deliberately hiding from the gaze of the men who had had the temerity to shoot at it. Therefore observation was out of the question and dispatches from Longs Peak amply confirmed this annoying turn of events.

However, if the experiment had succeeded, the voyagers, who had left at forty-six minutes and forty-two seconds after ten in the evening on 1 December, should by rights reach their destination at midnight on the 4th. So until then—and because it would have been difficult in those conditions to observe a body as small as the shell they had fired—people decided to be patient and not complain too much.

On 4 December between the hours of 8 p.m. and midnight, it might have been possible to follow the progress of the projectile, which would have appeared as a black dot against the luminous disc of the Moon. But the sky remained stubbornly hidden and this exasperated the public beyond measure. They even started shouting insults at the Moon for refusing to put in an appearance. A sorry return to business as usual in the here below!

Desperate for news, J. T. Maston left for Longs Peak, wanting to see for himself. He had no doubt that his friends had reached their journey's end. At least there had been no news that the projectile had crashed at any point on any islands or on any of the Earth's continents and J. T. Maston refused to admit for one moment the possibility that it had come down in any of the oceans which cover three-quarters of the globe.

On the 5th, the same conditions persisted. The great telescopes of the old world, those of Herschel, Rosse, and Foucault, were permanently trained on the Eye of Night, for the weather was particularly good in Europe. But the comparative weaknesses of their lenses made their observations useless.

On 6 December, no change in the weather. Impatience consumed three-quarters of the globe. People came up with all sorts of wild ideas for dispersing the clouds which still clogged the sky.

On 7 December, the sky seemed to lighten a little. Hopes were got up but they did not stay up and by the evening thick clouds again hid the starry canopy of the heavens from human eyes.

But now the situation was becoming critical. On the morning of the 11th, at eleven minutes past 9, the Moon was due to enter its last quarter. After that it would begin to wane and even if the sky became clear again the chances of observing anything would be considerably reduced. For from then on the Moon would display only a decreasing fraction of its disc until it became new, that is, it would set and rise at the same time as the sun whose light would make it virtually invisible. They would then have to wait until 3 January, at four minutes past noon, for it to be full again before they could start observing.

The newspapers wrote extensively about these matters and commented endlessly and they did not hide from readers that they would have to arm themselves with the patience of saints.

On the 8th, nothing. On the 9th, the sun reappeared to cock a snook at the Americans. It was greeted with boos and jeers and, doubtless offended by such a welcome, kept its hand in the pocket where it kept its beams.

On the 10th, no change. J. T. Maston was almost out of his mind with worry and there were fears for the good man's brain, which, until now, had been well-preserved under his gutta-percha cranium.

But on 11 December, one of those great storms that devastate semi-tropical regions developed in the atmosphere. Terrific winds swept away the clouds which had for so long crouched overhead and that evening the half-decayed disc of the Moon sailed majestically over the pellucid constellations of the heavens.

28

A NEW CELESTIAL BODY

THAT same night the astonishing news so impatiently awaited burst like a bolt of lightning across all the States of the Union and from there, skipping across the ocean, it sped along telegraph wires throughout the world. The projectile had been sighted, courtesy of the giant reflector at Longs Peak.

Here is the note, written by the director of the Cambridge Observatory. It summarizes the scientific conclusions to be drawn from the Gun Club's great experiment:

Longs Peak
   12 December
   To all Members of Staff of the Cambridge Observatory.
   The projectile launched by the Columbiad at Stone's Hill was observed by J. Belfast and J. T. Maston on 12 December, at 8.47 p.m., the Moon then entering its last quarter.
   The projectile did not reach its targeted destination but passed to one side of it. It was, however, sufficiently close to be captured by the Moon's gravitational pull.
   As a result its linear course was changed to a circular trajectory of high velocity which set it on an elliptical orbit around the Moon,* of which it has become, effectively, a satellite.
   Exact details of this new celestial object have yet to be established. Both its new movement of translation and its orbital speed are not known, but its distance from the surface of the Moon can be estimated at 2,833 miles (or 4,500 leagues).
   Two hypothetical possibilities might now enter into play and modify the current state of things.
   Either (1) the Moon's gravitational power will assert itself and the voyagers will achieve the goal of their mission;
   or (2) held in position by the power of an immutable orbit, the projectile will continue to circle the lunar disc until the end of time.

Which it will be, only future observations will tell us. But at present, the Gun Club's endeavour has had no result other than to add a new celestial body to our Solar System.

J. Belfast

This unexpected outcome left so many questions unanswered! How many advances which create new mysteries did the future hold in store for scientific investigation? Thanks to the courage and perseverance of three men, the seemingly futile undertaking of sending a cannonball to the Moon had produced a hugely important result which had incalculable implications. Though the voyagers now imprisoned in a new satellite had not done what they set out to do, they were now at least part of that lunar world: they were orbiting the Moon and for the first time human eyes were able to behold its mysteries. The names of Nicholl, Barbicane, and Michel Ardan would henceforth be famous in the annals of astronomy, since those bold explorers, so eager to widen the circle of human knowledge, had had the audacity to launch themselves into space and had gambled with their lives by taking on one of the strangest challenges of modern times.

Be that as it may, once the report from Longs Peak was made public, a sense of astonishment and horror sprang up all over the world. Would it be possible to go to the rescue of those three bold inhabitants of Earth? Very probably not, for they had left the realm of humankind by breaching the limits that God lays down on Earth's creatures. They would have air to breathe for two months and enough food for two years. But then what? Even the stoniest hearts began to beat faster at the very thought of it.

Just one man refused to accept that the situation was hopeless. Only one man remained optimistic. And that man was their friend, as devoted, bold, and resolute as they were: the worthy J. T. Maston.

He never lost sight of them. His home was now the observatory at Longs Peak, and his horizon the huge mirror of its famous reflector. The moment the Moon rose on the skyline, he framed it in the telescope's field. He did not take his eyes off its disc for one single moment and followed it assiduously as it progressed across the starry heavens. With inexhaustible patience he watched the projectile traverse the silver face of the Moon. So it would be true to say that the worthy Maston remained in regular contact with his three friends, whom he never gave up hope of seeing again some day.

'We'll be in touch,' he would say to anyone who cared to listen, 'when circumstances permit. We'll get news from them and we'll send them our news! Anyway, I know them! They are an ingenious group of men! When they flew out into space they took between them the whole range of resources of art, science, and industry. With all that in their baggage, they can achieve whatever they put their minds to. You'll see, they'll come through right as rain in the end!'

PART II

AROUND THE MOON

PRELIMINARY CHAPTER: WHICH SUMMARIZES THE FIRST PART OF THIS WORK AND SERVES AS A PREFACE TO THE SECOND

DURING the course of the year 186–, the whole world was uncommonly excited by a scientific experiment totally unprecedented in the annals of science. The members of the Gun Club, an association of artillerymen founded in Baltimore at the end of the American War, had conceived the idea of establishing communications with the Moon, yes, the Moon, by sending a projectile to it. Barbicane, its president and instigator of the project, consulted with astronomers at the Observatory at Cambridge and took all the measures necessary to ensure the success of this extraordinary venture, which was then declared practicable by a majority of the competent Club membership. Having set in motion a public subscription which raised some thirty million francs, Barbicane set to work on his gigantic labours.

According to the report by members of the Observatory's staff, the cannon which would launch the projectile would have to be located in an area situated between 0 and 28 degrees of latitude north or south, so that the Moon could be targeted when it was at the zenith.

The projectile would have to be fired at an initial muzzle velocity of 12,000 yards per second. Launched on 1 December at thirteen minutes and thirteen seconds before 11 p.m., it would in theory reach its destination four days after its departure, that is, on 5 December, at midnight precisely—the exact moment when the Moon would be in perigee, that is, at its closest point to Earth, a distance of 86,400 leagues.

The leading members of the Gun Club, President Barbicane, Major Elphiston, its secretary J. T. Maston, and other specialized experts held several committee meetings in which they discussed the design and material composition of the missile, the siting and nature of the cannon, the quality and quantity of propulsive gunpowder that would be needed. It was resolved:

(1) that the projectile should be a round shell made of aluminium, have a diameter of 108 inches, walls twelve inches thick, and weigh 19,250 pounds;

(2) that the cannon should be a Columbiad type made of cast iron, 900 feet long, which would be run directly into a mould in the ground;

(3) that the charge to be used should be 400,000 pounds of guncotton which, generating six billion litres of gas at the rear of the projectile, would more than suffice to propel it all the way to the Eye of Night.

With these matters settled, President Barbicane, assisted by the engineer Murchison, selected a site situated in Florida at latitude 27° 7′ north and longitude 5° 7′ west.* It was at that location, on completion of stupendous labours, that the Columbiad was successfully cast.

Matters had reached this point when an incident occurred which increased the interest generated by these great endeavours by a factor of a hundred.

A Frenchman, a Parisian with a fanciful turn of mind, an artist as witty as he was bold, asked to be allowed to ride in the projectile so that he could go to the Moon and make observations of the Earth's satellite. This intrepid adventurer was named Michel Ardan. He arrived in America, was greeted with rapture, held public meetings, carried the day triumphantly, reconciled President Barbicane with his mortal enemy, Captain Nicholl, and, to seal the outbreak of amity, proposed that they should both go along with him.

His proposition was accepted. The design of the projectile was modified, and became a hollow, conical cylinder. What was now a kind of aerial carriage was fitted with powerful springs and collapsible partitions designed to deaden the concussive effect of departure. The voyagers were supplied with provisions for a year, water for several months, and gas to last several days. An automatic appliance made air to breathe and supplied it to the three passengers.

While all this was proceeding, the Gun Club financed the construction, on one of the highest peaks of the Rocky Mountains, of a gigantic telescope that would allow the progress of the projectile to be tracked through space.

Everything was now ready.

On 30 November, at the appointed hour, watched by an extraordinary gathering of spectators, the launch took place and for the first time three human beings left the Earth, and soared into interplanetary space, virtually certain that they would reach their goal.

These bold voyagers, Michel Ardan, President Barbicane, and Captain Nicholl, were scheduled to complete their journey in ninety-seven hours, thirteen minutes, and twenty seconds. Consequently, their landing on the surface of the Moon's disc would not take place until midnight on 5 December, at the precise moment when the Moon was full, and not on the 4th, as a few ill-informed newspapers had announced.

But an unforeseen circumstance occurred: the explosion produced by the launch of the Columbiad had the immediate effect of disrupting the Earth's atmosphere by releasing an enormous quantity of water vapour into it. This phenomenon brought howls of indignation all over the world because the Moon was completely obscured from watching, straining eyes for several nights running.

The worthy J. T. Maston, the most devoted of the three voyagers' friends, left for the Rocky Mountains to join the honourable J. Belfast, director of the Cambridge Observatory, and arrived at the site on Longs Peak where the telescope had been erected. It brought the Moon close, to an apparent distance of two leagues.

The build-up of cloud in the atmosphere made it impossible to see anything on 5, 6, 7, 8, 9, and 10 December. There was even talk that any attempt at observation would have to be put off until 3 January, at the start of the following year, for the Moon, entering its last quarter on 11 December, would until then display only a decreasing area of its disc, insufficient for anyone to track the projectile.

Eventually, much to everyone's relief, a violent storm wiped the atmosphere clean on the night of 11–12 December, and the Moon, half-illuminated, then showed up clearly against the darkness of the night sky.

That night, J. T. Maston and J. Belfast sent a telegram from the Longs Peak site to members of staff of the Cambridge Observatory.

And what did this telegram say?

It stated that on 11 December, at 8.47 p.m., the projectile launched by the Columbiad at Stone's Hill had been seen by J. Belfast and J. T. Maston; that, deflected by some unknown cause, it had not reached its target but had instead passed close enough to it to be captured by the Moon's gravitational field; that its linear course had been changed to a circular trajectory; and that, drawn into an elliptical orbit around the Moon, it had become its satellite.

The dispatch added that the details and properties of this new heavenly body had yet to be calculated; and that at least three sightings of the projectile, each made at different times, would have to be made before its position could be established. Then it further indicated that the distance between the projectile and the surface of the Moon was calculated to be in the order of 2,833 miles, or 4,500 leagues.

In conclusion, it put forward two possibilities. Either the Moon's gravity would prevail and the voyagers would reach their target; or else the projectile, held in a permanently fixed orbit, would circle the lunar disc until the end of time.

Given these two alternatives, what would be the fate of the voyagers? They had sufficient provisions to last them some time, it was true. But even assuming that their foolhardy venture were to succeed, how would they get back? Could they ever get back? Would it be possible to hear from them? These questions discussed by the greatest experts of the time fascinated readers everywhere.

At this juncture a point must be made that should be taken under serious consideration by over-hasty astronomical observers. When a scientist publicly announces a purely theoretical discovery, he can never choose his words too carefully. No one is required to discover a planet or comet or a satellite, but anyone who proves to have made a mistaken claim in such cases can expect to become an object of general derision. Better, then, to wait—and that is exactly what the impulsive J. T. Maston should have done before making the world at large privy to his telegram, which, according to him, said all there was to be said on the matter.

Actually, the telegram contained two kinds of errors, as subsequently transpired. First were errors of *observation* in the calculation of the distance from the surface of the Moon of the projectile, which, on the date of 11 December, was not visible. So what J. T. Maston had seen or thought he saw could not have been the missile launched by the Columbiad. The second, concerning the future fate of the projectile, was an error of *theory*: making it a satellite of the Moon was a flagrant contradiction of the fundamental laws of theoretical mechanics.

Only one hypothesis of the Longs Peak observers had any chance of actually happening: the possibility that the voyagers, if any had survived, might add their own efforts by harnessing the gravitational power of the Moon and in this way succeed in landing on its surface.

Those men, as intelligent as they were bold, had indeed survived the brutal concussive effect of the launch and it is their journey in the projectile that will now be told in its most dramatic moments and all its fantastic detail. This chronicle will dispel many illusions and over-turn many assumptions. But it will give a true idea of the vicissitudes in store for undertakings of this kind and will bring out the scientific instincts of Barbicane, the resourcefulness of the industrious Nicholl, and the good-humoured fearlessness of Michel Ardan.

Moreover, it will show that their worthy friend, J. T. Maston, had been wasting his time when, seated at the great telescope, he had observed the progress of the Moon across the stellar vastness.

1

FROM 10.20 TO 10.40 P.M.

WHEN ten o'clock struck, Michel Ardan, Barbicane, and Nicholl said their last farewells to the many friends they were leaving behind on Earth. The two dogs, which were to acclimatize the canine species on the continents of the Moon, were already in their kennels. The three voyagers approached the mouth of the enormous cast-iron tube and a mobile winch lowered them to the conical nose of the projectile.

There an opening* designed for the purpose gave them access to their aluminium passenger craft. The winch's block and tackle were hauled up and in no time the muzzle of the Columbiad was freed from the remaining scaffolding. Once inside the projectile with his companions, Nicholl set about closing the hatch with a strong metal plate secured by powerful, pressurized bolts. Similar plates, solid and tight-fitting, covered the lenticular glass of the portholes.

Hermetically sealed inside their metal prison, the three voyagers found themselves in total darkness.

'And now, my friends,' said Michel Ardan, 'let's make ourselves at home. I am a domestic sort of man myself and very particular about keeping things neat and tidy. What we have to do is make the best of our new quarters so that we are comfortable here. And our first priority must to throw some light on the scene. Dammit! Gas wasn't invented for moles!'

And so saying, that easy-going fellow caused a flame to spring from a match by striking it on the sole of his boot, and held it next to the gas ring that was screwed into the canister in which carbonaceous hydrogen stored at high pressure would suffice to light and heat the projectile for 144 hours, or six days and six nights.

The gas caught. The interior of the projectile, now illuminated, had the air of a comfortable room, with cushioned walls, furnished with a circular divan, and overhead, the rounded nose had the shape of a dome.

The equipment it contained—the guns, pieces of equipment, utensils—was secured and held fast against the rounded modulations of the padded wall, and would thus come to no harm from the shock of the launch. All the precautions which were humanly possible had been taken so that this bold mission would have every chance of success.

Michel Ardan inspected his surroundings and declared himself satisfied with what he found.

'It *is* a prison,' he said, 'but a travelling prison, and we are allowed to peer out of the window. I wouldn't mind taking out a hundred-year lease on the place! You smile, Barbicane. Having second thoughts? Wondering if this prison might also be our coffin? If a coffin, so be it, but I wouldn't exchange it for Mahomet's, which floats suspended in the air and never goes anywhere!'*

While Michel Ardan stood talking, Barbicane and Nicholl made their last-minute preparations.

Nicholl's chronometer was showing twenty past ten by the time the three voyagers were finally sealed into their travelling carriage. The timepiece was set to within one tenth of a second of the chronometer used by Murchison, the engineer. Barbicane took a look at it.

'Friends,' he said. 'It is now twenty minutes past ten. At ten forty-seven, Murchison will press the switch that sends the electric spark along the cable which connects it to the mass of guncotton in the Columbiad. At precisely that moment, we shall quit our globe. So we still have twenty-seven minutes before we leave Earth.'

'Twenty-six minutes and thirteen seconds,' corrected the methodical Nicholl.

'Well now,' exclaimed Michel Ardan in the best of good humour, 'there are plenty of things you can do in twenty-six minutes! You can thrash out the great problems of morality or politics and even solve them! Twenty-six minutes put to good use are worth more than twenty-six years to people who do nothing at all! For someone like Pascal or Newton, a few seconds are more precious than the entire existence of the revolting class of imbeciles!'

'And what conclusion do you draw from all this eloquent blather . . .?' asked President Barbicane.

'I conclude,' replied Ardan, 'that we have twenty-six minutes left.'

'Twenty-four,' said Nicholl.

'Twenty-four, since you insist, my good captain,' replied Ardan, 'twenty-four minutes during which we could do some deep thinking.'

'Michel,' said Barbicane, 'we'll have all the time we need to think through the deepest questions as we go. But for now, let's think about the launch.'

'Aren't we ready?'

'Of course we are. But there are still a few precautions we need to take to lessen the effect of the initial shock.'

'But haven't we got all that water in collapsible compartments with enough give in them to provide us with adequate protection?'

'I sincerely hope so, Michel,' Barbicane said quietly, 'but I can't be absolutely sure!'

'What a joker!' exclaimed Michel Ardan. 'He says "he hopes" . . . "he isn't sure" . . . And he picks the moment when we are packed in here like sardines before he admits it! Deplorable, I insist on leaving!'

'How would you do that?' said Barbicane.

'True,' said Michel Ardan, 'it wouldn't be easy! We're on the train and the guard's whistle will blow in less than twenty-four minutes.'

'Twenty,' said Nicholl.

For a few moments, the three voyagers looked at each other. Then they started checking the equipment which was also imprisoned with them.

'Everything is where it should be,' said Barbicane. 'What we must do now is decide where it would be best for us to put ourselves to minimize the shock of the launch. Where we are placed is not something of minor importance. We must make sure that the blood does not rush too violently to our heads.

'True,' said Nicholl.

'So,' said Michel Ardan, ready to fit the deed to the word, 'how about standing on our heads, like the clowns at the Great Circus!'*

'No,' said Barbicane, 'but we should lie on one side. That way, we'll have a better chance of withstanding the shock. But remember this: at the moment the projectile is fired, whether we are inside it or in front of it comes almost to the same thing.'

'If it's only "almost" the same thing, I am mightily relieved,' replied Michel Ardan.

'Do you agree with my proposal, Nicholl?' asked Barbicane.

'Unreservedly,' said the captain. 'Still thirteen and a half minutes to go.'

'This Nicholl isn't a man, he's a walking chronometer, with a second hand, an escapement, and eight orifices* arranged—'

But his companions had stopped listening to him and were taking up their final positions with unflustered calm. They behaved like two railway passengers who have stepped into their compartment and are looking for somewhere to settle as comfortably as possible. You have to ask yourself what American hearts are made of, because they refuse to beat a whit faster when confronted by the most appalling danger.

Three well-padded, sturdily constructed settles had been added to the projectile. Nicholl and Barbicane arranged them at the centre of the wooden disc which formed the floating floor. It was on them that the three voyagers would lie down a few moments before the launch.

Meanwhile Ardan, who could never stand still for a moment, prowled around his narrow prison like a wild animal in a cage, chatting to his friends and talking to his dogs, Diane and Satellite, who had clearly been given these suitable names some time before.

'Listen, Diane! Attaboy, Satellite!' he cried, fussing over them. 'You'll show those Moonie pooches what well-brought-up Earth dogs are like! That will do no harm to the honour of the whole canine species! You'll see! If we ever return, I shall want to bring back a crossbreed— *Moondogs*. They'll be all the rage!'

'That's if there are dogs on the Moon,' said Barbicane.

'Oh but there are!' said Michel Ardan confidently. 'Just as there are horses, cows, mules, chickens . . . I bet we'll find chickens!'

'A hundred dollars says we won't,' said Nicholl.

'Done, Captain!' said Ardan, shaking Nicholl's hand. 'Incidentally, you've already lost three bets with the President, because the money needed for the undertaking was raised, the casting of the barrel was a success, and the charge was loaded into the Columbiad without exploding, which in all comes to six thousand dollars.'

'That's right,' said Nicholl. 'And it's now thirty-seven minutes and six seconds past ten.'

'Understood, Captain. Well, a quarter of an hour from now you'll have to hand over nine thousand dollars to the President, four thousand because the Columbiad will not blow up, and five thousand because the projectile will climb to an altitude of more than six miles.'

'I've got the dollars,' said Nicholl, patting his jacket pocket, 'and I'll be only too delighted to pay up.'

'Listen, Nicholl, I see that you are a man of orderly habits, which is something I have never been. But in reality, you made a series of bets which haven't turned out at all well for you, if you don't mind my saying so.'

'Why would I?' asked Nicholl.

'Because if you win the first one, it will be because the Columbiad has blown up and the projectile with it, so Barbicane won't be available to give you your winnings!'

'My stake is deposited at the bank in Baltimore,' said Barbicane simply, 'and if Nicholl cannot collect it personally, it will go to his heirs.'

'Oh, you are such practical men!' cred Michel Ardan, 'So down-to-earth! I admire you all the more for it because I cannot understand you!'

'Ten forty-two,' said Nicholl.

'Just five minutes more,' said Barbicane.

'Yes, five short minutes,' said Michel Ardan. 'And we are shut up inside a cannonball at the firing end of a cannon nine hundred feet long! And under us there is a great pile of 400,000 pounds of guncotton, the equivalent of 1,600,000 pounds of ordinary gunpowder. And in the meantime, our good friend Murchison, chronometer in hand, his eye on the needle and his finger on the electrical switch, is counting the seconds and is about to launch us into interplanetary space . . .'

'That's enough, Michel, quite enough!' said Barbicane in a sobering voice. 'We must brace ourselves. Just a few minutes more separate us from a historic moment. Shall we join hands, my friends?'

'Yes!' said Michel Ardan, more unnerved than he would have wanted to appear.

The three companions joined together in one last handclasp.

'May God preserve us!' said Barbicane, a man of faith.

Michel Ardan and Nicholl lay down on the settles which had been arranged around the centre of the disc.

'Ten forty-seven!' murmured the captain.

Only twenty seconds. Barbicane quickly extinguished the gaslight then took his place next to his companions.

The utter silence was broken only by the ticking of the chronometer as it counted down the seconds.

All of a sudden there was the most brutal shock and the projectile, lifted by the blast from the six billion litres of gas generated by the detonation of the pyroxylin,* rose into space.

2

THE FIRST HALF-HOUR

WHAT had happened? What effect had that tremendous shock created? Had the ingenuity of the men who built the projectile produced the desired result? Had the concussive shock been absorbed by the springs—the four buffers and the water cushioning the collapsible compartments? Had they overcome the awesome thrust of the initial velocity of eleven thousand metres* which would have been enough to power it across Paris or New York in just one second? That obviously is what the thousands of spectators of those dramatic scenes all burned to know. They forgot the purpose of the voyage and thought only of the voyagers! And if one of them—J. T. Maston for example—had been granted a glimpse of the interior of the projectile, what would have he seen?

At that point, nothing. Inside was total darkness. But the cylindro-conical walls of the projectile had coped very well. No splitting or warping or distortion anywhere! The amazing projectile had not been damaged by the force of the exploding guncotton nor, as some had seemed to fear, had it melted and become a shower of aluminium rain.

Inside, there was relatively little mess. A few objects had been rammed up against the nose but the majority of items seemed not to have been damaged by the blast. The restraints holding them in place had held.

On the floating disc, now lying flat on the bottom of the craft after the compartments had collapsed and the water been forced out, were three motionless bodies: Barbicane, Michel Ardan, and Nicholl. Were they still breathing? Was the projectile now no more than a metal coffin carrying three corpses out into space?

A few minutes after the launch, one of the bodies stirred. Its arms moved, it raised its head, sat up, and managed to get onto its knees.

It was Michel Ardan. He felt himself all over, said 'Ahem!' in a loud voice and continued:

'Michel Ardan, all present and correct. Let's take a look at the others.'

The good Frenchman tried to get up but he could not stand. His head lolled and he could not see, blood having filled his eyes during the launch and blinded him. He was like a drunken man.

'Damn!' he said. 'It's had the same effect as drinking a couple of bottles of Burgundy, maybe a Corton.* But they'd be decidedly easier on the palate.'

Then passing a hand across his forehead and rubbing his temples, he called out in a firm voice:

'Nicholl! Barbicane!'

He waited expectantly. There was no answer, not even grunts which might have indicated that the hearts of both his companions were still beating.

He called again.

He got the same reply.

'Devil take it!' he said. 'They both look as if they've fallen from a fifth floor and landed on their heads! No matter!' he continued with that unshakeable confidence which nothing could dampen. 'If a Frenchman can get onto his knees, two Americans won't have any trouble getting to their feet. But first, let's cast some light on the subject.'

Ardan felt life flooding back into him. His blood cooled and began to circulate normally. He made another effort and regained his balance. He managed to remain standing, took a match from his pocket, then a flame spurted from the phosphorus when he struck it. He made for the gas burner and lit it. The canister had not been damaged in any way and no gas had escaped. In any case, its smell would have alerted him—though if it had not, Michel Ardan would not have got off lightly with holding a lit match in a small cabin full of hydrogen.* Gas and air together would have produced a dangerous mixture and the resulting explosion would have finished what the shock of the launch had begun.

Once the burner was lit, Ardan bent over the bodies of his two companions. They were lying stretched out across each other in an inert heap, Nicholl on top and Barbicane under him.

Ardan sat the captain up with his back against the divan, and rubbed him vigorously. The massage, skilfully done, revived Nicholl, who opened his eyes, instantly recovered his composure, grasped Ardan's hand, and, looking around him, asked:

'How is Barbicane?'

'One at a time,' replied Michel Ardan calmly. 'I started with you, Nicholl, because you were on top. Now, let's have a look at Barbicane.'

And so saying, Ardan and Nicholl lifted the President of the Gun Club off the floor and laid him on the divan.

Barbicane seemed to have come off worse than his companions. There had been some bleeding but Nicholl was relieved when he saw that the blood had come from a slight injury to one shoulder, a simple graze, which he bandaged up carefully and securely.

Even so, it took Barbicane some time to come round. This concerned his two friends who did not spare him the rubbing and massaging.

'At least he's breathing,' said Nicholl, pressing his ear to the injured man's chest.

'Yes,' said Ardan, 'he's breathing like a man who has some idea of how it's done on a daily basis. Keep rubbing, Nicholl, let's give it all we've got!'

Both improvised medical orderlies worked so hard and well that Barbicane eventually came to. He opened his eyes, sat up, grasped the hands of his two friends, and spoke his first words:

'Nicholl! Are we moving?'

'Nicholl and Barbicane* looked at each other. They had not yet given a thought to the projectile. Their first concern had been for the voyagers and not the craft.

'Well?' said Ardan. 'Are we moving?'

'Or are we still sitting quietly on the soil of Florida?' asked Nicholl.

'Or lying on the bottom of the Gulf of Mexico?' added Michel Ardan.

'Perish the thought!' cried President Barbicane.

The two possibilities suggested by his companions had the immediate effect of gathering his wits together for him. But the fact remained that there was as yet no way of telling what the precise status of the projectile was. Its apparent immobility and the lack of access to what was outside made it impossible to provide an answer.

Perhaps the projectile was following its course through space as planned? Or perhaps after a brief ascent it had fallen back to Earth or indeed into the Gulf of Mexico, which was a definite possibility given that the Floridian peninsula was relatively narrow.

The situation was serious and the problem worrying and it called for a rapid response. Barbicane, now revitalized and overcoming his physical weakness by the power of his will, got to his feet. He listened. From outside came nothing but silence. But the padded cabin wall was thick enough to block all sounds of earthly origin. All the same, one fact struck Barbicane. The temperature inside the projectile was unusually high. The President drew a thermometer from its protective case and studied it. The instrument read 45° centigrade.

'Yes!' he exulted. 'Yes, we *are* moving! This stifling heat which is infiltrating through the projectile's walls is produced by the friction of our passage through the atmospheric strata. It will soon decrease because we are already entering the void of space and after being suffocated by heat we shall soon be in danger of freezing.'

'Heavens!' exclaimed Michel Ardan. 'So, according to friend Barbicane, it would appear that we are already past the limits of the Earth's atmosphere?'

'There can be no doubt about it, Michel.* Listen. It is now ten fifty-five. We have been travelling for about eight minutes. Now, unless our initial velocity has been slowed by friction, six seconds are enough for us to have passed through the sixteen leagues of atmosphere which surrounds the Earth.'

'Exactly so,' replied Nicholl. 'But by what order of magnitude do you estimate the slowing effect of friction?'

'By a factor of one third, Nicholl,' replied Barbicane. 'This is a significant reduction, but according to my calculations that is the figure. So if we had an initial velocity of 11,000 metres as we moved out of the atmosphere, that speed would drop to 7,332 metres per second. But whatever the figure, we already past the stratosphere . . .'

'Which means,' said Michel Ardan, 'that Nicholl here has lost both his bets: four thousand dollars, because the Columbiad did not blow up, and five thousand dollars because the projectile has reached an altitude of more than six miles. Nicholl, it's time to pay up.'

'Let's consider the facts first,' replied the captain, 'and then we'll pay up. It is quite possible that Barbicane's arguments are correct and that I have lost my nine thousand dollars. But a different hypothesis occurs to me and it would cancel the entire wager.'

'What hypothesis?' asked Barbicane sharply.

'The hypothesis that, for one reason or another, the spark did not set off the explosive and we have not gone anywhere.'

'By God, Captain,' cried Michel Ardan, 'now that's the sort of hypothesis that is beyond the reach of my brain power. But you cannot be serious! Weren't we half-killed by the shock? Did I not bring you round? Is not the President's shoulder still bleeding from being violently thrown about?'

'Agreed, Michel,' said Nicholl, 'but one question.'

'Fire away, Captain.'

'Did you hear the explosion which surely must have been deafening?'

'No,' said Ardan in surprise, 'I certainly did not hear the explosion.'

'How about you, Barbicane?'

'Neither did I.'

'Which means?' asked Nicholl.

'Hm,' murmured the President. 'Why did we not hear the explosion?'

The three friends looked at each other, quite baffled. They had come up against an inexplicable phenomenon. For the projectile had been fired and consequently there must have been an explosion.

'First,' said Barbicane, 'let's find out where we are. We'll uncover the portholes.'

This was a simple task and took no time. The nuts that held the bolts that secured the exterior plates over the porthole on the right-hand side, were easily released with a spanner. The bolts were then expelled and stopples sheathed with India rubber sealed the holes which had let them through. Immediately, the external hatch sprang back on its hinges, like a ship's porthole, and the lenticular glass forming the observation panel was then revealed. An identical porthole was recessed into the thick wall on the opposite side of the projectile, another in the dome of its nose, and a fourth in the centre of its base. It was therefore possible to make observations in four different directions, space through the side panels and, more specifically, at the Earth and the Moon through the lower and upper panels respectively.

Barbicane and his two companions immediately crowded round the panel which they had opened. No glimmer of light showed in it. The projectile was enveloped in profound darkness. Yet this did not prevent President Barbicane from exclaiming:

'No, friends, we have not fallen back to Earth, nor have we ended up on the bed of the Gulf of Mexico! Yes, we *are* rising through space! See the stars that shine in the night and the impenetrable blackness accumulating between Earth and us!'

'Hurrah! Hurrah!' cried Michel Ardan and Nicholl with one voice.

For that dense shadow proved that the projectile had indeed left the Earth because the ground, lit brightly by the Moon's illumination, would have been visible to the voyagers if they had still been on its surface. The darkness also demonstrated that the projectile had passed through the various layers of the atmosphere, because the suffused light distributed through the air would have been reflected by the craft's metal interior and there was no such reflection. Moreover, that light would have been visible in the glass of the porthole, which showed no trace of it. There could no longer be any doubt: the voyagers had left the Earth.

'I lose,' said Nicholl.

'And I congratulate you!' said Ardan.

'Here's the nine thousand dollars,' said the captain, and from his pocket he took a wad of notes.

'Do you want a receipt?' asked Barbicane, as he took the money.

'If it's no bother,' replied Nicholl. 'It would be more business-like.'

And so, soberly, phlegmatically, as if he were sitting at his desk in his office, Barbicane reached for his notebook, tore off a blank page, wrote out a formal receipt, dated, signed, and initialled it and handed it to the captain, who tucked it carefully into his wallet.

Michel Ardan doffed his cap and bowed without speaking a word to his companions. Such formality in the circumstances left him speechless. He had never seen anything quite so 'American'.

Once the transaction was over, Barbicane and Nicholl returned to the glass panel and were looking out at the constellations. The stars stood out like bright pinholes in the black sky. But from that angle nothing could be seen of the Moon, which was moving east to west* and gradually rising towards its zenith. Its absence prompted a question from Ardan.

'Where is the Moon?' he said. 'Is there any chance that it will fail to keep its appointment with us?'

'Don't worry,' said Barbicane. 'Our future destination is where it should be. But we cannot see it from this direction. For that we'd need to open the porthole on the other side.'

Just as Barbicane was turning away from his observation post to see about opening the porthole opposite, his attention was drawn to the approach of a dazzlingly bright object, whose colossal dimensions could not be clearly determined. Its forepart, which was pointing towards the Earth, was blindingly bright.

It might have been a small Moon reflecting light from the larger one. It was travelling at a prodigious speed and seemed to be following an orbit around the Earth which would cross the present course of the projectile. To this orbital motion was added a rotatory movement. In other words, it was behaving like all heavenly bodies abandoned in space.

'Hullo!' exclaimed Michel Ardan. 'What's that? Another projectile?'

Barbicane did not reply. The presence of this very large body astonished and worried him. A collision was possible and it would have a catastrophic effect. The projectile might be deflected from his course, or else a collision, checking its impetus, could send it crashing back to Earth, or, lastly, it could be irresistibly captured by the asteroid's own gravitational field.

President Barbicane had immediately grasped the implications of these three possibilities which, in one way or another, would ineluctably mean the failure of their enterprise. His companions looked out across space in silence. The object grew prodigiously in size the closer it came and some kind of optical illusion gave the impression that it was heading straight for them.

'Great heavens!' exclaimed Michel Ardan. 'Two trains about to crash head on!'

Instinctively, the voyagers had taken a step back. Their fear was very great but did not last long, barely a few seconds. The asteroid passed several hundred metres from the projectile and disappeared,* not because of its speed but because the unlit side, hidden from the Moon, was suddenly swallowed up by the absolute darkness of space.

'*Bon voyage!*' cried Michel Ardan with a sigh of relief. 'Really! Is not infinity big enough for a poor little projectile to wander around without being afraid? But what, I ask, was that highfalutin globe that very nearly crashed into us?'

'I know,' said Barbicane.

'Really? You know everything.'

'It's just a meteor, but a huge one that the Earth's gravity has trapped as a satellite.'

'Is that a fact?' cried Michel Ardan. 'So the Earth has two moons, like Neptune?'

'Yes, Michel, two moons, though usually it is thought of as having only one. This second Moon is so small and its velocity so great that people who live on Earth cannot see it. It was only by taking note of certain celestial disturbances that a French astronomer, Monsieur Petit,* was able to establish the existence of this second satellite and work out its properties and habits. According to his calculations, this particular meteor completes its revolution around the Earth in a mere three hours and twenty minutes.* This suggests that it travels at an enormous speed.'

'Do all astronomers admit the existence of this meteor?' asked Nicholl.

'No,' said Barbicane, 'but if, as we have, they saw it close up, they could no longer have any doubt. Actually, I believe that this meteor, which would have done us huge damage if it had hit us, allows us to pinpoint our position in space with some accuracy.'

'How?' said Ardan.

'Because its distance from Earth is known. At the bearing where we encountered it, we were exactly eight thousand, one hundred and forty kilometres from the surface of the terrestrial globe.'

'That's more than two thousand leagues!' exclaimed Michel Ardan. 'And it knocks into a cocked hat anything the express trains of our poor little globe called planet Earth can do!'

'I should say so,' said Nicholl as he consulted his chronometer. 'It is now eleven o'clock and we left the continent of America just thirteen minutes ago.'

'Only thirteen minutes?' asked Barbicane.

'Yes,' replied Nicholl, 'and if our initial velocity of eleven kilometres a second has remained constant, we should now be doing about ten thousand leagues an hour!'

'Now that's all very well, my friends,' said the President. 'But that still leaves us with an insoluble question: why did we not hear an explosion when the Columbiad was launched?'

There was no answer and the discussion ground to a halt. Barbicane, still thinking about it, busied himself removing the cowling over the other side shutter. It was soon done, and through the uncovered window the light of the Moon filled the interior of the craft with brightness. Nicholl, an economical man, turned off the gas burner, which was now not needed and whose glare in any case interfered with their observation of interplanetary space.

The lunar disc shone with incomparable purity. Its light was not dulled by the vapours which fill the Earth's atmosphere, but flowed unopposed through the glass and saturated the air inside the craft with a silvery glow. The black curtain of the firmament effectively doubled the intensity of the Moon's luminosity, which, in the void of the ether which was hostile to its diffusion, did not eclipse neighbouring stars. As a result, the sky, seen from this perspective, took on an entirely new appearance which human eyes had never even imagined could exist.*

It is not difficult to conceive the degree of interest with which those bold adventurers beheld the Queen of Night, their ultimate destination. In its orbiting trajectory, the Earth's satellite was now slowly but surely approaching its zenith, the mathematical bearing which it would reach about twenty-four hours later. Its mountains, its plains, its entire geographical configuration did not stand out more clearly than if the voyagers had been observing it from some location on the Earth. But seen through the void, its light acquired an unparalleled power. Its disc shimmered like a platinum mirror. Of the Earth, which was fast fleeing under their feet, the voyagers had lost all recollection.

It was Captain Nicholl who was the first to turn their minds back to the globe which they had forgotten.

'But,' said Michel Ardan, 'we mustn't be ungrateful to our native heath. Since we're leaving the old place for good, let's feast our eyes on it one last time. I want to see the Earth again before it is completely hidden from view!'

To satisfy the wishes of his companion, Barbicane set about clearing a way to the porthole in the floor of the craft, the one which gave a clear view of the Earth.* The floating disc which the propellant force had slammed down to the base of the projectile was now removed, not without difficulty, and the resulting debris was carefully stacked against the wall, for it might well come in useful should the need arise. This uncovered a shallow circular aperture 50 centimetres wide drilled out of the base of the projectile. It was filled with glass 15 centimetres thick, held firmly in a brass frame. Underneath was an aluminium plate secured by bolts. When the nuts were removed and the bolts freed, the hatch sprang back and additional visual communication was established between the interior and the outside of the craft.

Michel Ardan knelt, leaning over the viewing panel. It was dark, fogged even.

'Well?' he said. 'So where is the Earth?'

'The Earth,' said Barbicane, 'is *there*.'

'You mean that thin streak of light, a sort of silver crescent?'

'That's right, Michel. Four days from now, when the Moon is full, by which time we will have arrived, the Earth will be new. By then, it will look like a slender crescent which will soon fade and for a few days will be completely enveloped in total darkness.'

'So that's the Earth!' repeated Michel Ardan, as he continued to stare at the thin sliver that was his native planet.

The explanation given by President Barbicane was correct. The Earth, in relation to the position of the projectile, was then entering its last phase. It was in its octant and appeared as a crescent delicately etched against the blackness of the sky. Its light, given a bluish tinge by the density of its atmosphere, was not as luminous as that of a crescent Moon. But this crescent was of a considerable size and resembled a huge arc reaching across the firmament. A few bright areas, especially on the inside of its curve, indicated the presence of high mountains. But these would sometimes disappear, obscured by thick blurred patches of a kind never seen on the surface of the Moon's disc. They were bands of cloud that concentrically girdle the terrestrial globe.

However, as a result of a natural phenomenon, identical to that which features on the Moon when it is in its octants, it was possible to make out the entire shape of the Earth's globe. Its full disc appeared quite clearly by an effect of an ash-grey luminosity which was, however, weaker than the Moon's Earth-shine. The reason for its lesser intensity is not difficult to understand. When this Earth-light occurs on the Moon, it is produced by the light from the sun which the Earth reflects towards its satellite. But here, the opposite was true: it was the product of the sun's rays reflected by the Moon back towards the Earth. Now this Earth-shine is about thirteen times brighter than Moon-shine, because of the difference in size of the two heavenly bodies. Hence the result ensues that in this phenomenon of Earth-shine, the occluded part of the Earth shows less clearly than the relevant obscured part of the Moon's disc, since the intensity of the phenomenon is in proportion to the relative radiancy of the two heavenly bodies. It should also be noted that the Earth's crescent seemed to describe a longer arc than that of the lunar disc. A simple effect of irradiation.

While the voyagers were trying to peer through the blackness of space, they suddenly saw a brilliant burst of shooting stars. Hundreds of meteorites, burning up as they entered the atmosphere, left luminous trails on the gloom and fiery streaks on the ashy-lit part of the disc. At this stage, the Earth was in its perihelion and the month of December is so particularly fertile in producing so many of these shooting stars that astronomers have recorded as many as 24,000 of them each hour. But Michel Ardan, dismissing scientific explanations, much preferred to believe that the Earth was laying on one of its brilliant firework displays as a way of celebrating the departure of three of her sons.

In the event, that was all the voyagers saw of the globe, which scarcely registered in the dark, a minor member of the Solar System which, from the great planets, is seen to set and rise like just another morning or evening star! The globe, where they had left all they loved, was barely visible in space, no more now than a passing lunula.

The three companions, saying not a word but united in friendship, watched for some time while their projectile travelled on deeper into space at a uniformly decreasing speed. Eventually an irresistible need to sleep overcame their brains. Was this an effect of weariness of mind and body? Probably, for after the stimulation of the final few hours they had spent on Earth, there was bound to be a reaction.

'Well,' said Michel Ardan, 'since sleep we must, let us sleep!'

Then all three stretched out on their settles and were soon lost to the world.

But they had not been asleep for more than a quarter of an hour, when Barbicane suddenly sat up and woke his companions with a stentorian cry:

'I have found it!' he exclaimed.

'Found what?' asked Michel Ardan leaping off his settle.

'The reason why we did not hear the detonation as the Columbiad was launched!'

'And why was it . . . ?' asked Nicholl.

'It was because the projectile was going faster than the speed of sound!'

3

SETTLING IN

ONCE this curious but, when elucidated, undoubtedly accurate explanation had been given, the three friends sank back into a deep sleep. Where could they possibly have found a quieter or more peaceful spot to sleep in? On Earth, houses in towns and cottages in the country all feel the effects of the impacts by which the surface of the globe is battered. At sea, a ship tossed by the waves is nothing but constant pitch and roll. In the air, a balloon is endlessly buffeted by ever-shifting, flowing layers of air of varying densities. Alone, this projectile, as it travelled in perfect silence, afforded perfect rest.

And the slumber of the three intrepid voyagers might perhaps have been prolonged indefinitely if an unexpected noise had not roused them at around seven in the morning of 2 December, eight hours after their departure.

This noise was the most emphatic sound of barking.

'The dogs! It's the dogs!' cried Michel Ardan who sprang up at once.

'They'll be hungry,' said Nicholl.

'You're right,' said Michel, 'we forgot all about them!'

'Where have they got to?' asked Barbicane.

They scouted round and found one of the animals crouching under the divan. Terrified and disorientated by the initial shock of departure, it had remained where it was until its voice returned along with the pangs of hunger.

It was the good-natured Diane, still somewhat chastened, who crawled out of her hideaway, though not without a great deal of persuasion. But Michel Ardan coaxed and cajoled her with his gentlest, most reassuring words.

'Here, Diane,' he cajoled, 'come on, there's a good girl, for your destiny shall be inscribed in the annals of hunting! Heathens of old would have given you the god Anubis for a companion, and Christians would have made you friend to St Roch!* You are worthy of being forged in brass by the King of the Underworld, like the pooch Jupiter gave to Europa* in exchange for a kiss! Your fame shall blot out that of the heroes of Montargis and Mount St Bernard!* Winging your way through interplanetary space, you could well turn out to be like

Eve to the dogs of the Moon! And you will vindicate the noble words of Toussenel: "In the beginning, God created Man and, seeing him so weak, gave him a dog!"* So come on, Diane, come here!'

Diane, who may or may not have been flattered, slowly crept out, whimpering plaintively.

'Well and good,' said Barbicane. 'I see Eve but where is Adam?'

'Adam,' replied Michel Ardan. 'Oh Adam can't have gone very far. He's here, somewhere. Let's call him. Satellite! Here, Satellite!'

But there was no sign of Satellite. Diane went on whimpering, but it was clear that she was not injured in any way and they administered a dish of tasty dog food which put a swift end to her whining.

But Satellite was nowhere to be found. They had to spend some time searching before finally discovering him in one of the upper lockers of the projectile where he had been inexplicably thrown by some jolt or shock. The poor creature, severely injured, was in a bad way.

'Devil take it!' said Michel Ardan. 'That's part of our acclimatization programme done for!'*

They carefully lifted the poor creature down. His head had been smashed against the dome of the projectile and it was unlikely that he would recover from such a blow. Nevertheless, they laid him down gently on a cushion and once there he let out a sigh.*

'We'll look after you,' said Michel. 'We're responsible for your existence. I'd sooner lose an arm than see poor Satellite lose a paw!'

So saying, he offered a little water to the casualty who drank it greedily.

Once these matters had been taken care of, the voyagers made observations of the Earth and the Moon. The Earth now appeared as no more than an ashy-lit disc which ended in an arc that was smaller than the night before. But its size was still huge when compared with the Moon, whose shape was now getting closer and closer to a perfect circle.

'What a shame,' said Michel Ardan. 'I am truly sorry that we did not set off when the Earth was full. I mean, when our planet was in opposition to the sun.'

'Why?' asked Nicholl.

'Because then we might have had more light to see Earth's continents and oceans, for the first would have looked brighter when lit directly by the sun's rays, and the latter darker and more as they appear on some maps of the world. I would have loved to see the Earth's poles on which the eyes of men have never rested.'

'No doubt you would,' said Barbicane, 'but if the Earth had been full, the Moon would have been new, that is invisible against the sun's radiancy. So it is more useful for us to be able to see the place we are headed for than our point of departure.'

'You are quite right, Barbicane,' said Captain Nicholl. 'And in any case once we have reached the Moon, we shall have plenty of time during those long lunar nights to gaze our fill on the globe which teems with beings like us.'

'Like us!' cried Michel Ardan. 'But they are no more like us than Selenites are! We now live in a new world inhabited by just ourselves—I mean the projectile! I am like Barbicane and Barbicane is like Nicholl. Beyond us, outside us three, there is no human kind and we constitute the only population of this microcosm until we become common or garden Selenites!'

'Which will be in about eighty-eight hours,' replied the captain.

'Which means . . . ?' asked Michel Ardan.

'That it is now half past eight,' answered Nicholl.

'Well now,' said Michel, 'I cannot possibly find even the shadow of a valid reason why we should not breakfast without further ado!'

Indeed, the denizens of the new star could not live there without eating, for their stomachs were subject to the sovereign laws of hunger. Michel Ardan, by reason of being French, naturally appointed himself chief cook, an important function for which he faced no competition. The gas furnished the few degrees of heat needed for culinary purposes and the provisions store provided the elements of their first banquet.

Breakfast began with three cups of excellent broth produced by dissolving in water the prized Liebig extract* prepared from the choicest parts of the ruminants grazing the pampas. This beef soup was followed by steaks processed by hydraulic press which were as tender and as succulent as if they had come from the kitchens of the Café Anglais.* Michel, a man of imagination, even declared them to be 'rare'.

Preserved vegetables declared by the genial Michel to be 'fresher than fresh' came after the meat course and were themselves followed by cups of tea and bread buttered in the American style. This drink, pronounced delicious, was made by the infusion of best-quality tea leaves of which the Tsar of all the Russias had made several chests available to the voyagers.

Lastly, to round off the meal, Ardan managed to dig out a few bottles of *Nuits* which he 'happened' to find in the larder. The three friends drank to the future union of the Earth and its satellite.

And as if it had not done enough for that heady wine which it had matured on the slopes of Burgundy, the sun itself now joined the party. At that moment, the projectile emerged from the cone of shadow cast by the Earth, and the sun's rays struck the base of the projectile directly, as an effect of the angle made by the orbit of the Moon and that of the Earth.

'The sun!' cried Michel Ardan.

'Of course,' said Barbicane. 'I was expecting it.'

'But,' said Michel, 'doesn't the cone of shadow which the Earth casts into space extend beyond the Moon?'

'It would if we ignore the effect of atmospheric refraction,' said Barbicane. 'But when the Moon is hidden in this shadow it is because the centres of each of the three stars, sun, Earth, and Moon, are in a straight line. The nodes then coincide with the phases of the full Moon and there is an eclipse. If we had started out when there was an eclipse of the Moon, our entire journey would have taken place in shadow—which would have been regrettable.'

'Why?'

'Because as it is, although we are moving through a vacuum, our projectile is now exposed to the full power of the sun's rays, and will therefore take in both light and warmth. This means that we save on gas, always a crucial economy from every point of view.'

Indeed, since the projectile had been exposed to the light of the sun, whose temperature and brilliance were undimmed by having to pass through an atmosphere, it grew warm and bright as if winter had turned instantly into summer. The Moon above and the sun below both flooded it with their fulguration.

'It is very pleasant here,' said Nicholl.

'And so say I!' cried Michel Ardan. 'With a small quantity of soil spread out on our aluminium planet, 'we could raise a crop of green peas in twenty-four hours. There's only one thing I'm afraid of, which is that the walls of our craft might melt in the heat!'

'No need to worry on that score, my friend,' said Barbicane. 'The projectile withstood much higher temperatures as it shot through the layers of Earth's atmosphere. I wouldn't be surprised if it had looked like a flaming meteor to the spectators in Florida.'

'O Lord! J. T. Maston must have thought we'd been roasted alive!'

'What astonishes me,' said Barbicane, 'is that we weren't. It was one hazard we never anticipated.'

'I feared it,' said Nicholl simply.

'And you never told us, doughty captain!' exclaimed Michel Ardan who took his companion's hand and pumped it.

Meanwhile Barbicane busied himself settling into the projectile as though he was never to leave it. It will be remembered that the base of their aerial railway compartment was an area of 54 square feet. Its height to the topmost part of the nose was 12 feet. The cleverly designed interior was largely uncluttered by scientific apparatus and travel appliances, which all had their own appointed places, an arrangement which allowed its three occupants some freedom of movement. The thick glass panel let into part of the base was capable of bearing a considerable weight. So Barbicane and his companions walked on it as though it was all solid wooden flooring. But the rays of the sun, falling directly on it, now lit the interior of the projectile from beneath, thus producing a series of unusual plays of light.

They began by checking the condition of the drinking-water tank and the store containing the provisions, neither of which had suffered any damage thanks to the precautions which had been taken to absorb the initial shock. The stock of victuals was plentiful and sufficient to feed the three voyagers for a whole year. Barbicane had been particularly anxious to take precautions should the projectile land at a totally barren place on the Moon.

As for water and their reserve of brandy, which amounted to fifty gallons, there was only enough for two months. But if reference was made to the most recent astronomical observations, the Moon had a low-lying atmosphere, a dense, thick atmosphere, at least in its deepest valleys where there would no lack of streams and springs. Accordingly, for the entire length of the journey and the first year of their stay on the lunar continent, the intrepid explorers would not be tested either by hunger or thirst.

There remained the question of air inside the projectile. There, too, all was secure. The Reiset and Regnault apparatus,* designed to produce oxygen, had a two-month supply of chlorate of potassium. They were obliged to burn a certain amount of gas because the apparatus had to keep the materials which produced the gas at a steady temperature of over 400°. But in that respect, too, they were in credit.

In fact, the apparatus required little in the way of attention, for it operated automatically. At that high temperature, the chlorate of potassium as it turned into caustic potash released all the oxygen it contained. And how much did eighteen pounds of potassium chlorate yield? The seven pounds of oxygen required for the daily consumption of the occupants of the projectile.

But it was not enough simply to replace the oxygen as it was consumed. The carbon dioxide produced by exhalation also had to be neutralized. And for a dozen hours now, the atmosphere inside the craft had produced high levels of that noxious gas, the end product of the combustion of elements in the blood that were burned up by the oxygen which had been inhaled. Nicholl was alerted to the state of the air when he saw that Diane was panting and in some discomfort. What was happening was that the carbon dioxide, produced as a result of a phenomenon identical to that in the celebrated Grotta del Cane,* was building up in the bottom area of the projectile because it was heavier than air. Poor Diane, because her head was nearer the floor, was being affected by the presence of this gas before her masters were. But Captain Nicholl moved swiftly to remedy this state of affairs. On the base of the projectile he placed various receptacles containing caustic potash and shook them at intervals, so that this substance, which craves carbon dioxide, absorbed it completely and purified the air inside the craft.

They then began making an inventory of the instruments on board. The thermometers and barometers had survived intact except for one minimum thermometer of which the glass was broken. An excellent aneroid was taken out its padded box and hung on one wall. Naturally, it was affected only by the air pressure inside the projectile, which was what it displayed. But it also measured the humidity there present. At that point, its needle registered between 735 and 760 millimetres,* indicating fine weather!

Barbicane had also brought along several compasses, which were found to be undamaged. It should be understood that, given the circumstances, their needles gave the wildest readings, which is to say that they showed no consistent direction. The fact was that at the distance which the projectile now found itself from Earth, the magnetic pole could have no tangible effect on such instruments. But placed on the Moon's disc, these devices might perhaps reveal the existence of unusual phenomena. In any case, it would be useful to check whether the Earth's satellite was also subject to magnetic influence.

A hypsometer* to measure the height of the mountains of the Moon, a sextant for determining that of the sun, a theodolite—a geodesic tool, which is used for making surveys and reducing horizontal angles—glasses, which would come in useful when they got nearer to the Moon, all these instruments were carefully inspected and found to be in working order despite the tremendous stresses of the initial shock effect.

The utensils, picks, mattocks, and other tools which Nicholl had chosen most particularly, plus the sacks of various seeds, the bushes which Michel Ardan wished to plant in lunar soil—all were in their place in the upper section of the projectile where there was a kind of loft full of disparate objects deposited there by the extravagant Frenchman. What these were, no one quite knew, and that carefree man never explained. From time to time, he would use the rungs riveted* to the wall to climb up to his glory-hole as its self-appointed sole inspector. He arranged and rearranged and delved with a brisk hand into certain mysterious boxes while singing in the most discordant of voices some old French refrain which added good cheer to the situation.

Barbicane noted with interest that his rockets and pyrotechnic aids had come to no harm. These important, powerfully charged devices would be used to slow the projectile when, captured by lunar gravitational pull after it had passed the point of nil gravity, it would finally descend onto the surface of the Moon. Its descent, however, would be six times less rapid than it would be on the Earth's surface because of the difference in mass of the two celestial bodies.

The inspection ended greatly to the satisfaction of all. Then they resumed observing space through the side viewing panel and the window in the floor of the projectile.

The view was the same. The entire expanse of the heavens teemed with stars and constellations with quite wonderful clarity. It was enough to turn an astronomer's wits! On one side, the sun, like the open fire-hole of a blazing furnace, a dazzling disc with no halo, standing out starkly against the black backcloth of the sky. On the other, the Moon returning its brilliance by reflection and seemingly immobile in the midst of a world of stars. Then, too, a fairly definite round smudge, rather like a hole punched in the firmament, which was edged with a semi-fringe of silver: it was the Earth. Here and there, nebulous masses like large flakes in a stellar snowfall and, running from zenith to nadir, an immense ring made of insubstantial stardust—the Milky Way—amongst which the sun ranks only as a star of the fourth magnitude!

The observers could not tear their eyes from so novel a spectacle for which there are no words to convey any idea. What thoughts it suggested to them! What unknown emotions it stirred in their souls! Barbicane thought he should begin a chronicle of his journey while the influence of these impressions was still fresh, and hour by hour he noted down the facts which had marked the start of his enterprise.

He wrote steadily in his large square handwriting, adopting a most business-like style.

Meanwhile, the mathematically-minded Nicholl, looked over his records tracking their passage and revised his figures with unparalleled dexterity. Michel Ardan chatted to Barbicane, who largely ignored him, to Nicholl, who did not hear a word he said, to Diane, who did not understand any of his theories, and eventually to himself, asking questions and giving answers, coming, going, busying himself with minor details, at times bent over the window in the floor, at others perched in the nose of the projectile, never ceasing to hum to himself. In this little world, he represented the ebullience and talkativeness of the French and both, you may rest assured, were represented in him to the hilt.

The day, or rather—since the word is inappropriate—the passage of twelve hours which defines a day on Earth, closed with a copious supper delicately served up. Thus far, there had been no incident of a nature to shake the confidence of the voyagers.

And so, fuelled with hope and already assured of success, they slept peacefully, while the projectile, at a uniformly decreasing speed, sailed along the pathways of the empyrean.

4

A LITTLE ALGEBRA

THE night passed without incident, although strictly speaking the word 'night' is incorrect.

The position of the projectile in relation to the sun did not change. Astronomically speaking, it was *day* at the lower half of the craft and *night* at the top. So when these two words are used in this account, they express the period of time which runs between sunrise and sunset on Earth or vice versa.

The voyagers' sleep was all the more tranquil because the projectile, despite its extreme speed, seemed to be absolutely immobile. There was no movement of any kind to suggest that it was passing through space. The fact is that motion, however rapid, cannot have any noticeable effect on the human frame when it is happening in a vacuum or when the ambient air is travelling at the same speed as the body within it. What inhabitants of the Earth are aware of its speed as it hurries them along at 90 thousand kilometres an hour? In such conditions, motion does not make itself felt any more than stillness, which is why bodies in general are not conscious of it. If a body is at rest, it will remain so as long as no external force dislodges it. If it is moving, it will not come to a stop unless some obstacle blocks its path. The indifference to movement and rest is called inertia.

So Barbicane and his companions, being shut away inside the projectile, would have had good reason to believe that they were existing in a state of absolute immobility. However, the effect would have been exactly the same if they had been outside it. Had it not been for the Moon, which grew larger ahead of them as they watched, and for the Earth, which grew steadily smaller behind them, they might well have sworn that they were suspended in a state of complete stagnation.

That morning, 3 December, they were awakened by a glorious but quite unexpected sound. It was the crowing of a cockerel and it echoed around the interior of the craft.

Michel Ardan was first to get up. He climbed into the nose of the projectile and closed a half-opened hutch of sorts.

'Stop that awful row!' he whispered. 'This bird is going to ruin my plans!'

But Barbicane and Nicholl were already awake.

'Is that a cockerel?' Nicholl said.

'No, no!' Michel replied quickly. 'It was just me. I just felt like waking you up with a farmyard impression!'

And so saying, he let out a healthy cock-a-doodle-do which would not have disgraced the proudest of the gallinaceous breed.

The two Americans could not help but laugh.

'A fine talent,' said Nicholl glancing dubiously at his companion.

'True,' said Michel, 'it's a joke where I come from. It's uncouth, but everybody does it just like that in the best company.'

Whereupon he changed the subject.

'I say, Barbicane,' he said, 'do you have any idea of what I was thinking about all night?'

'No,' replied the President.

'I was thinking about our friends at Cambridge. You will have already noticed that I am a complete dunce when it comes to mathematics. So I cannot even guess how those experts in the Observatory were able to work out what muzzle velocity the projectile would need when it was shot out of the Columbiad so that it would reach the Moon.'

'You mean,' said Barbicane, 'to reach the neutral point where the gravities of the Earth and the Moon cancel each other out. For from that point situated at about nine-tenths of the total distance, the projectile will descend onto the Moon powered solely by its own weight.'

'If you say so,' said Michel. 'But I repeat: how did they work out the initial speed?'

'Nothing simpler,' said Barbicane.

'Do you know how to do the calculation?' asked Michel Ardan.

'Oh yes. Nicholl and I could have done it if the reply from the Observatory had not saved us the trouble.'

'But I tell you, Barbicane old man,' said Michel, 'they could have cut my head off, starting with the feet, before I could have been made to do that particular sum!'

'That's because you don't know any algebra,' Barbicane said calmly.

'That's all very well for you $x = y$ types! You think you've explained everything just by saying "algebra".'

'Michel,' said Barbicane, 'do you think that metal can be forged without a hammer or a field tilled without a plough?'

'Hardly.'

'Well, algebra is a tool like a plough or a hammer and a good tool it is for anyone who knows how to use it.'

'Seriously?'

'Very seriously.'

'And could you use that tool for me to see?'

'If you are interested.'

'And show me exactly how they calculated the initial velocity of this capsule of ours?'

'Of course, my dear fellow. By taking all the elements of the problem into account—the distance from the centre of the Earth to the centre of the Moon, the radius of the Earth, the mass of the Earth, the mass of the Moon—I can accurately establish what the initial speed of the projectile needed to be by using a simple formula.'

'Can I see this formula?'

'You shall see it. But I am not going to show you the curve of the actual course followed by the projectile between the Moon and the Earth which takes account of their orbits around the sun. No, I shall assume that both bodies are not moving, which should be enough for our purposes.'

'Why is that?'

'Because it would mean looking for the solution to a problem which is known as "the three body problem" and because integral calculus is currently not sufficiently advanced to deal with it.'

'Ah!' said Michel Ardan in his teasing voice. 'So there really *is* something that maths can't do?'

'It's not that at all,' replied Barbicane.

'Then maybe the Selenites have got further along with integral calculus than you have? Anyway what exactly is this integral calculus?'

'It is a form of calculus which is the converse of differential calculus,' Barbicane answered earnestly.

'Thanks for nothing.'

'Then put it this way: it is a form of calculus used to identify finite quantities of a thing when their differential is known.'

'At least that is clear,' said Michel with every sign of satisfaction.

'Now,' went on Barbicane, 'give me pencil and paper and in less than half an hour I hope to come up with your formula.'

And so saying, Barbicane gave himself completely to the task in hand while Nicholl stared out into space, leaving his companion to prepare the breakfast.

The half hour had not elapsed when Barbicane looked up and showed Michel Ardan a page covered with algebraic symbols in the middle of which the following general formula stood out:

$$\frac{1}{2}\left(v^2 - v_0^2\right) = gr\left\{\frac{r}{x} - 1 + \frac{m'}{m}\left(\frac{r}{d-x} - \frac{r}{d-r}\right)\right\}$$

'What does it mean?' asked Ardan.

'It means', said Nicholl, 'v squared minus v_0 squared, all over two, equals gr multiplied by the difference between r over x and 1 plus m' over m multiplied by the product of r over d minus x minus r over d minus r.'

'You mean x over y mounted on z and cantering over p,' cried Michel Ardan as he burst out laughing. 'And you can make sense of all that, Captain?'

'It's plain as a pikestaff.'

'Good lord!' said Michel. 'Well, if it's so obvious to everybody then count me in too.'

'Always the joker!' said Barbicane. 'You asked for the algebra, you know, and you shall have it to the back teeth!'

'I'd rather be strung up by my neck!'

'Actually,' said Nicholl who had been running an expert eye over the formula, 'this is a pretty fine piece of work, Barbicane. You have established the integral of the live force* and I have no doubt that it gives the result we were looking for.'

'But I'd very much like to understand!' cried Michel. 'I'd give ten years of Nicholl's life to be able to understand!'

'Well, just listen,' Barbicane went on. 'One half of v^2 minus v_0^2 is the formula which gives us the semi-variation of the live force.'*

'Right—and does Nicholl understand what that means?'

'Of course I do, Michel,' said the captain. 'All these symbols which look so cryptic to you are in fact the clearest, most limpid, and most logical language to anyone who can read it.'

'But are you saying, Nicholl,' asked Michel, 'that by using these hieroglyphics, which are more incomprehensible than all those ancient Egyptian ibises, you can find out what initial velocity the projectile needed to have?'

'Absolutely,' replied Nicholl, 'and by using this formula, I could tell you its speed at any point of its journey.'

'Cross your heart?'

'And hope to die.'

'Then you are as wily a customer as our president here?'

'Of course not, Michel. The difficult part is what Barbicane has just done. It meant finding an equation which takes account of every element of the problem. The rest is just arithmetic and requires no more than a knowledge of the four rules.'

'Well, that's something,' replied Michel Ardan, who during his entire life had never added anything up correctly and viewed the operation as a Chinese riddle which allowed him to come up with a different answer every time.

But Barbicane responded by saying that if Nicholl had put his mind to it, he would certainly come up with the right formula too.

'I don't know about that,' said Nicholl, 'because the more I think about it, the more beautifully worked out it seems.'

'But now, just listen,' Barbicane said to his pea-brained comrade, 'and you shall see that all these letters have meanings.'

'I'm listening,' said Michel with a sigh of resignation.

'First,' said Barbicane, 'd is the distance from the centre of the Earth to the centre of the Moon, because we need both centres if we are to calculate their gravitational pulls.'

'That I can understand.'

'r is the radius of the Earth.'

'r is for radius. Got it.'

'm is the mass of the Earth; m^l is the lunar mass. For we must not overlook the mass of each of these gravitational bodies, because their force of gravity is in direct proportion to their mass.'

'I'm with you.'

'g represents gravity, the speed of a body after one second as it descends towards the surface of the Earth. Is that clear?'

'As a mountain stream!'

'Now, I use x to represent the variable distance between the projectile and the centre of the Earth, and v for the velocity at which the projectile is travelling at that distance.'

'Good.'

'Finally the symbol v_o which features in the equation is the speed at which the projectile is travelling when it leaves the atmosphere.'

'Just so,' said Nicholl; 'its speed at that point had to be calculated, because we already know that its speed at launch was precisely 50 per cent more than its speed at the moment it left the atmosphere.'

'You've lost me now.'

'But it's perfectly simple,' said Barbicane.

'Not as simple as me,' replied Michel.

'It means that when our projectile reached the limit of the Earth's atmosphere, it had already lost one-third of its initial speed.'

'As much as that?'

'Yes, my friend, through friction as it passed through the layers of the atmosphere. You can fully appreciate that the faster it travelled, the greater the resistance it encountered from the air.'

'That much I concede,' said Michel, 'and I understand it, although all your v zero two and your v zero squared* are rattling around in my head like nails in a bucket!'

'That's the first thing algebra does for you,' said Barbicane. 'Now, to complete your education, we are going to express in numerical terms what all these symbols mean, that is we shall put a figure on the value of each.'

'Let me have the rest if you must!' said Michel.

'Among all these signs and symbols,' said Barbicane, 'some are known but the rest have to be calculated.'

'Leave the latter to me,' said Nicholl.

'Take r,' said Barbicane. 'r is the Earth's radius which, at the latitude of Florida, our point of departure, measures 6,370 kilometres. Next, d is the distance from the centre of the Earth to the centre of the Moon, which is the same as fifty-six times the radius of the Earth, which comes to . . .'

Nicholl got busy with pencil and paper.

'. . . to 356,720 kilometres at the moment when the Moon is in its perigee, that is when it is closest to the Earth.'

'Good,' said Barbicane. 'Now for m^l over m, which gives us the ratio of the mass of the Moon to that of the Earth, namely 1 to 81.'

'Rather!' said Michel.

'g, for gravity, is 9 m 81* in Florida, which means that gr is . . .'

'. . . 62.426 square kilometres,' said Nicholl.

'Next?' asked Michel Ardan.

'Now that the symbols have been converted into numbers,' replied Barbicane, 'I can calculate the figure for v_o, which is the speed at which the projectile must travel as it leaves the atmosphere so that when it reaches the point at which the two gravitational fields cancel each other, its velocity is nil. Since at that moment its speed is zero, I posit that v_o equals zero and that x—the distance to the neutral point—will be nine tenths of d, which is the distance between the two centres.'

'I seem to think that it may well be so,' said Michel.

'So what I have got now is this: x equals nine-tenths of d and v equals zero. So my equation . . .'—and he began writing furiously on a piece of paper—'. . . looks like this.'

$$v_0^2 = 2gr\left\{1 - \frac{10r}{9d} - \frac{1}{81}\left(\frac{10r}{d} - \frac{r}{d-r}\right)\right\}$$

Nicholl could not wait to read what he had written.

'That's it!' he cried. 'That's exactly it!'

'Is it clear?' asked Barbicane.

'Written in letters of fire!' said Nicholl.

'What a pair!' murmured Michel admiringly.

'Do you understand it now?' Barbicane asked him.

'Do I understand?' exclaimed Michel Ardan. 'My brain is positively reeling with it!'

'So as you see,' said Barbicane, 'v_0^2 equals $2gr$ multiplied by one minus $10r$ over $9d$ minus one 81st multiplied by $10r$ over d minus r over d minus r.'

'And now,' said Nicholl, 'to obtain the speed of the projectile when it leaves the atmosphere, all that remains now is to do the calculation.'

The captain, as an expert equal to any difficulty, began working with alarming speed. Division and multiplication spread and expanded under his fingers. Numbers fell like hail on the white page. Barbicane watched as he worked while Michel Ardan nursed the beginnings of a headache with both hands.

'Well?' said Barbicane, after several minutes of silence.

'Well, with the calculation now complete,' replied Nicholl, 'if the projectile is to reach the point of nil gravity, v_0—its speed as it leaves the atmosphere—should have been . . .'

'. . . yes?' said Barbicane.

'11,501 metres in the first second.'

'What?' said Barbicane, getting to his feet. 'How much?'

'Eleven thousand five hundred and one metres.'

'Devil take it!' cried the President with a gesture of despair.

'Why? What's the matter?' said Michel Ardan in astonishment.

'The matter? If by that instant the speed had already dropped by a third owing to friction, the initial velocity should have been . . .'

'16,576 metres!' replied Nicholl.

'The Observatory at Cambridge said that 11,000 metres would be ample for the launch, and our projectile was fired at that speed!'

'Well?' asked Nicholl.

'Well it won't be enough!'

'I see.'

'We'll never reach the point of zero gravity!'

'Great heavens!'

'We'll not even get halfway!'

'Pesky projectile!' cried Michel Ardan, leaping in the air as if the capsule was about to start falling back towards the terrestrial globe.

'And we'll end up crashing onto the Earth!'*

5

THE BITTER COLD OF SPACE

THE revelation came like a bolt from the blue. Who would ever have dreamed that such a mathematical blunder could be made? Barbicane refused to accept it. Nicholl went over his calculation again. It was correct. As for the formula which had produced the result, they were unable to fault it and, after re-checking, it remained the case that an initial velocity of 16,576 metres in the first second was essential if the zero point of gravity was to be reached.

The three friends looked at each other in silence. All thought of breakfast was forgotten. Barbicane, teeth clenched, brow furrowed, hands working convulsively, stared out of the viewing panel. Nicholl, arms folded, pored over his calculation. Michel Ardan muttered to himself:

'Just typical of these scientific fellows! Humbug, the lot of them! I'd give twenty pistoles* if when we fall we land on top of that Observatory at Cambridge and flatten it and all the adders up and takers away that dwell therein!'

Suddenly, a thought crossed the captain's mind. He approached Barbicane.

'It is now,' he said, 'seven o'clock in the morning. That means we've been travelling for thirty-two hours. More than half the length of our journey has been covered, yet I haven't noticed that we are falling.'

Barbicane did not answer. But after glancing quickly at the captain, he took a pair of compasses for measuring the angular distance of the Earth's globe. Then through the viewing panel in the floor of the craft, he took a reading. This he was able to do with great accuracy, given the perceived immobility of the projectile. Then he stood up, wiped the beads of sweat from his brow, and jotted down a few numbers on a piece of paper. Nicholl saw at once that the President was using the Earth's diameter to deduce how far the projectile was from the Earth's surface. He watched him anxiously.

'No!' cried Barbicane after a few moments. 'No, we are not heading back! We are already more than five thousand leagues from Earth! We have passed the point at which the projectile would have become motionless if its speed at launch had been only 11,000 metres!* We are still moving.'

'Of course we are!' replied Nicholl, 'and we can only conclude that our initial velocity, provided by 400,000 pounds of guncotton, exceeded the required 11,000 metres. I understand now why, after only thirteen minutes, we encountered that other satellite which orbits the Earth at a height of two thousand leagues.'

'And this explanation is made all the more probable,' added Barbicane, 'by the fact that when the projectile expelled the water held in the collapsible partitions, it suddenly shed a considerable weight.'

'You're right!' said Nicholl.

'My dear captain,' cried Barbicane, 'we're saved!'

'Well,' said Michel Ardan calmly, 'if that's settled, let's have lunch.'

Indeed, Nicholl was not mistaken. The initial velocity, very fortunately, had been greater than the velocity recommended by the Observatory at Cambridge. But that did not mean that the Observatory at Cambridge had not made an error.

Having got over this false alarm, the voyagers sat down and downed a hearty lunch. But if they ate a great deal, they talked even more. And their confidence was now greater than it had been before 'the algebra scare'.

'Is there any good reason why we shouldn't succeed?' said Michel Ardan. 'Why shouldn't we get to where we're going? We're on the way. There are no obstacles ahead of us, no boulders blocking the road. Our way is clear, clearer than that of the ship which has to contend with the sea, clearer than the flight of a balloon which has to vie with the wind! And if the ship goes wherever it wishes, if a balloon rises as it pleases, why should our projectile not get to the place to which it is headed?'

'It will get there,' said Barbicane.

'. . . if only to honour the American people,' added Michel Ardan, 'who are the only nation capable of carrying out such an undertaking, the only one that could have produced a President Barbicane! But now that we no longer have to worry, I'm beginning to wonder what is to become of us? Shall we get royally bored?'

Barbicane and Nicholl both threw up their hands to deny the very thought of that prospect.

'But I anticipated the possibility, my friends,' went on Michel Ardan. 'Just say the word. I have for your delectation chess, draughts, cards, and dominos. The only thing that's missing is a billiard table!'

'Good lord,' said Barbicane. 'You brought all those games?'

'I did,' replied Michel, 'and not only to keep us entertained but also with the laudable intention of handing them over to Selenite watering holes.'

'My dear fellow,' said Barbicane, 'if the Moon is inhabited, its first inhabitants appeared some thousands of years before we did on Earth, because there can be little doubt that it is older than our planet. So if there have been Selenites for hundreds of thousands of years then, if their brains are organized like human brains, they will already have invented everything that we have invented, plus whatever we shall invent over the coming centuries.* There won't be anything we can teach them. We shall have to learn everything from them.'

'What!' said Michel. 'So you believe they have had artists like Phidias, Michelangelo, and Raphael?'

'Yes.'

'Poets such as Homer, Virgil, Milton, Lamartine, and Hugo?'

'I'm sure of it.'

'Philosophers like Plato, Aristotle, Descartes, and Kant?'

'I don't doubt it.'

'Men of science like Archimedes, Euclid, Pascal, Newton?'

'I would swear to it.'

'Comic actors like Arnal and photographers like . . . er, Nadar?'*

'Of course.'

'In that case, if those Selenites are as clever as we are, or even cleverer, how come they have never tried to communicate with the Earth?* Why have they never launched a lunar projectile at the terrestrial globe?'

'Who says they have not done so?' Barbicane replied soberly.

'Quite,' added Nicholl. 'It would have been easier for them than it has been for us, for two reasons. First, because gravity is six times weaker on the surface of the Moon than it is on the surface of the Earth. This makes it easier for a projectile to take off. Secondly, they would only have to fire the projectile a distance of 8,000 leagues instead of 24,000, and would require a propulsive charge 10,000 times less powerful.'

'If that is so,' said Michel, 'I repeat: why have they never done it?'

'And I too repeat,' said Barbicane, 'who says that they didn't?'

'When?'

'Thousands of years ago, long before man appeared on Earth.'*

'What about the projectile? Where is the projectile? I demand to see the projectile!'

'My dear boy,' replied Barbicane, 'the seas cover five-sixths of our planet.* That means that there are five good reasons for supposing that this lunar craft, if in fact one was ever launched, is now at the bottom of the Atlantic or the Pacific. Unless it ended up in some crevasse at a time when the Earth's crust had yet to harden.'

'My dear Barbicane,' replied Michel, 'you have an answer for everything and I bow to your superior knowledge. Still, there is one theory that appeals to me more than the rest and it is this: since the Selenites are more ancient than us, are they not also wiser, because they still have not invented gunpowder?'*

Just then, Diane joined the conversation by barking loudly. She wanted her breakfast.

'Oh dear,' said Michel Ardan, 'with all this talk we have forgotten about Diane and Satellite.'

Without further ado, a decent helping of dog food was set before the former, who devoured it with commendable appetite.

'You see, Barbicane,' said Michel, 'we should have turned this projectile into a second Noah's Ark and taken to the Moon a couple of every domestic animal.'

'True,' said Barbicane, 'but there would not have been enough room.'

'There would have,' said Michel, 'if we had all sat closer together!'

'The fact is,' said Nicholl, 'that ruminants like oxen, cows, bulls, and horses would have been very useful to us on the plains of the Moon. Unfortunately, this craft of ours could never have been a stable or a byre.'

'But at least,' said Michel Ardan, 'we might have brought along a mule, just a small one. It is a brave and patient beast which old Silenus* was particularly fond of riding! Mules must be the most ill-favoured creatures in creation. Not only do they get beaten all their lives, but they go on being beaten after they are dead.'

'What do you mean?' asked Barbicane.

'Well,' said Michel, 'because we use them to make drum skins!'

Barbicane and Nicholl could not help laughing at this ludicrous notion. But they were cut short by an exclamation from their jovial companion who, after bending down to look into Satellite's kennel, straightened up saying:

'Ah! Satellite is not sick any more.'

'Good!' said Nicholl.

'No it isn't,' Michel went on. 'He's dead. And,' he added in a doleful voice, 'it makes things awkward. I am very sorry, Diane old girl, but you will not be founding a long line of descendants in those lunar landscapes after all.'

Poor Satellite had not been able to survive his injuries. He had succumbed and was now very dead. Michel Ardan looked at his friends in dismay.

'This creates a problem,' said Barbicane. 'We cannot keep the body of a dead dog here for another forty-eight hours.'

'No, we can't,' said Nicholl. 'But the frames of both of our portholes are secured by hinges* and can be unfastened. We could open one of them and throw the body out into space.'

The President thought for a moment and then said:

'Agreed, and that is what we must do. But only if we are very careful.'

'Why?' asked Michel.

'For two reasons which you will readily understand,' replied Barbicane. 'The first concerns the air enclosed inside the craft. We must let as little of it as possible escape.'

'But surely we can make more air!'

'Only in part. We can only make more oxygen, Michel. And in that regard we must take every precaution to ensure that the apparatus does not produce too much oxygen, because excessive amounts of it would lead to very serious physiological consequences for us. We can replace oxygen, but we cannot replace nitrogen, that element which our lungs do not absorb but must be maintained. Well, our nitrogen would quickly escape through an open porthole.'

'But it wouldn't take long to heave poor Satellite out through it,' said Michel.

'Agreed, but we must be quick about it.'

'And the other reason?' as Michel.

'The second reason is that we must not allow the cold outside, which is extreme, to get into our craft and freeze us to death.'

'But what about the sun?'

'True, the sun does indeed warm the projectile which absorbs its rays. But it does not warm the void through which we are currently travelling. Where there is no air, there can be no heat except from the sun's diffused light, and just as it is dark where the sun's rays do not penetrate, so it is cold where the sun does not shine directly. There the temperature is simply the temperature produced by light from the stars, that is, it would be the temperature to which the Earth would fall should the sun one day cease to shine.'

'There's no fear of that happening,' said Nicholl.

'Who can tell?' said Michel Ardan. 'Anyway, even if we agree that the sun will not stop shining, is it not possible that the Earth might move further away from it?'

'Oh dear,' said Barbicane, 'there goes Michel and his ideas!'

'Well,' Michel went on, 'it is no secret that the Earth passed through the tail of a comet in 1861.* Now, supposing a comet with a gravitational field stronger than the pull of the sun hoves into view, the Earth's orbit would be redirected towards the passing body. Having become its satellite, it could then be dragged so far away that the rays of the sun would not be felt on its surface.'

'That is theoretically possible, of course,' replied Barbicane, 'but the consequences of such a displacement might well not be as deleterious as you think.'

'Why not?'

'Because heat and cold would continue to remain in balance on our planet. It has been calculated that if the Earth had indeed been led astray by the comet of '61, the heat to which it was exposed when it was furthest from the sun would have been at most no more than sixteen times greater than the heat we get from the Moon, and that heat, under the strongest magnifying lens, produces no measurable effect.'

'So?' said Michel.

'One moment,' said Barbicane. 'It has also been calculated that at its perihelion, that is when it is at its closest to the sun, the Earth would be exposed to a degree of heat equal to twenty-eight thousand times that of its summer levels. But such heat, which would turn stone into glass and convert the oceans into steam, would have formed a thick ring of dense cloud which would have moderated such extreme heat. The consequence would be to create compensatory effect between the intense cold of the aphelion and the intense heat of the perihelion which would probably result in bearable average temperatures.'

'And what is the estimated temperature of interplanetary space?' asked Nicholl.

'In the past,' said Barbicane, 'it was thought that it was extremely low. Attempts to calculate its thermometrical floor led to estimates of many millions of degrees below zero. It was Fourier, one of Michel's fellow-countrymen, a respected physicist and member of the French Academy of Science, who brought that figure down to reasonable levels. According to him, the temperature of space does not fall below minus 60 degrees.'*

'Is that all?' said Michel.

'Pretty much,' replied Barbicane. 'Polar temperatures recorded at Melville Island or Fort Reliance gave a figure of 56 degrees below zero.'

'But it still has to be proved,' said Nicholl, 'that Fourier was not mistaken in his estimate. Unless I am mistaken, another French physicist, Monsieur Pouillet, reckons the temperature of space to be 160 degrees below zero. We are in a position to be able to check their figures.'

'But not now,' said Barbicane. 'The sun's rays will be shining directly onto our thermometer and will give us on the contrary a rather inflated reading. When we reach the Moon, where the nights on each of its two faces by turn are a fortnight long, there will be plenty of time to carry out tests, for our satellite moves through the void.'

'But what actually do you mean by the void?' asked Michel. 'Is it a total vacuum?'

'It is a vacuum in which there is no air.'

'And in which air is replaced by nothing?'

'No,' replied Barbicane. 'It is replaced by the ether.*'

'And what exactly is the ether?'

'The ether is an agglomeration of infinitesimally small atoms which in relation to their size—according to the literature of molecular physics—are as far from each other as heavenly bodies are apart in the heavens. But their distance is less than one three-millionths of a millimetre. It is these atoms, through their vibratory behaviour, that produce light and heat by oscillating 430 trillion times per second even though their amplitude does not exceed four to six thousandths of a millimetre.'

'Millions and billions!' cried Michel Ardan. 'So somebody has actually measured and counted those oscillations? My dear Barbicane, this is scientists' talk. It offends the ear and means nothing to the mind.'

'But we have to have accurate figures . . .'

'Not at all. Comparisons are better. A trillion doesn't mean anything. Far better are comparisons which say it all. For example, if you tell me that Uranus is seventy-six times bigger than the Earth, that Saturn is 900 times bigger, Jupiter 1,300 times bigger, and the sun 1,300,000 times bigger, I would be none the wiser. So I myself would prefer, and by a long chalk, the old comparisons you get in the ancient almanacs like the *Double Liégeois*,* which states flatly that: the sun is a pumpkin two feet across, Jupiter is an orange, Saturn a Lady apple, Neptune a heart cherry, Uranus a large cherry, the Earth a pea, Venus a small pea, Mars a large pinhead, Mercury a mustard seed, and Juno, Ceres, Vesta, and Pallas all just grains of sand! Then at least a man would know where he stood!'

After Michel Ardan's outburst against experts and the trillions which they line up without a second thought, they proceeded to the funeral of Satellite. All they had to do was to drop him into space the way sailors consign the dead to the waves.

But as President Barbicane had advised, they had to act quickly so as to lose as little as possible of the air whose fluidity would otherwise have made it quickly escape into the void. The bolts of the viewing panel on the right-hand side, which was 30 centimetres across, were carefully undone while a downcast Michel got ready to launch his dog into space. The glass panel, released by a powerful lever which overcame the pressure inside the craft against the external wall of the projectile, swung open quickly on its hinges and Satellite was propelled through it. Barely a handful of molecules of air were lost and the whole operation was so successful that subsequently Barbicane did not hesitate to use this method to rid the craft of accumulated jumble which cluttered its interior.

6

QUESTIONS AND ANSWERS

On 4 December, the craft's chronometers were showing five o'clock of a terrestrial day when the trio woke, having by then been travelling for fifty-four hours. In terms of time, they had passed the halfway point of the total period scheduled for the craft's journey by only five hours and forty minutes. But in terms of distance, they had already covered seven-tenths of their projected itinerary. This difference is explained by the steady decrease in their speed.

When they observed the Earth through the bottom viewing panel, it now appeared only as a dark patch dimly lit by the glare of the sun. There was no crescent and no ashen illumination. The next day, at midnight, the Earth was due to become new at the exact moment that the Moon would be full. Overhead, the latter was drawing closer and closer to the course followed by the projectile, so that it would soon be on the same trajectory according to the planned timetable. All round, the black canopy was flecked with small bright points of light which seemed to be slowly moving, though from that great distance their relative size did not appear to change. Sun and stars looked exactly as when viewed from Earth. On the other hand, the Moon had grown substantially bigger, but at this stage the voyagers' telescopes were not really powerful enough to allow them to make useful observations of its surface or to identify topographical and geological details.

And so the time passed in endless talk. Their conversation centred particularly on the Moon. Each man brought his particular quotient of knowledge to the table. Barbicane and Nicholl were invariably serious, with Michel Ardan indulging his flights of fancy. The projectile, its position, its course, accidents that might happen to it, the action that their descent onto the Moon would require—all provided subjects for endless conjecture.

More specifically, one breakfast time a question from Michel about the projectile brought a rather curious reply from Barbicane which is worth reporting.

Michel, supposing that their craft might suddenly come to a dead stop while still under the impetus of its initial launch velocity, wished to know what would be the consequences of being halted in their tracks.

'Actually,' replied Barbicane, 'I cannot imagine how the projectile could ever be brought to a sudden halt.'

'Just supposing,' said Michel.

'There is no supposing the impossible,' said the literal-minded Barbicane. 'Unless the power propelling it were somehow to fail. But in that case, its speed would drop gradually and it would not come to an abrupt halt.'

'Let's say it collided with something in space.'

'Like what?'

'Like that very large meteor we saw.'

'In that case,' said Nicholl, 'the projectile would have been smashed to smithereens and the three of us with it.'

'More than that,' said Barbicane; 'we would have been burned to death.'

'Burned to a frazzle!' exclaimed Michel. 'Dammit, I'm sorry in a way that it didn't happen so that we might have seen for ourselves!'

'You would have seen it, all right,' said Barbicane. 'We now know that heat is simply a modification of motion. When you boil water, that is when you add heat to it, it means that you are adding motion to its molecules.'

'Good Lord!' said Michel. 'Now isn't that an ingenious way of looking at it!'

'And the right one, my friend, because it explains all the phenomena of caloric. Heat is merely a form of molecular motion, a simple oscillation of the particles of a body. When the brake of a train is applied, the train will stop. But what becomes of the motion which it had previously possessed? It is converted into heat and the brake becomes hot. Why are axles of wheels kept greased? To prevent them heating up, since heat would be generated by the motion which is lost in exchange for its conversion. Are you with me?'

'With you?' answered Michel. 'Completely! So, for instance, when I have been running for some distance and am in a sweat, why am I forced to stop? It's simple: because my motion has been converted into heat!'

Barbicane could not help but smile at Michel's droll use of theory. Then he took up where he had left off.

'So,' he said, 'if there had actually been a collision, the same thing would have happened to our projectile that happens when a bullet strikes a metal plate: its motion is changed into heat. That is why I can state that if our projectile had collided with the meteor, its velocity, being abruptly terminated, would have released a quantity of heat capable of volatilizing it instantly.'

'In that case,' asked Nicholl, 'what would happen if the Earth suddenly stopped in its orbit?'

'Its temperature would reach such a point', said Barbicane, 'that it would be immediately vaporized.'

'Well,' said Michel, 'at least that would be one way of putting an end to the world. It would simplify a great many things.'

'And what if the Earth collides with the sun?' said Nicholl.

'Calculations', replied Barbicane, 'show that such an event would generate heat the equivalent of that produced by 1,600 pieces of coal each the size of our own globe.'

'So a substantial extra helping of heat for the sun,' replied Michel Ardan, 'and doubtless the inhabitants of Uranus or Neptune would not complain because they must be dying of cold on their planets.'

'In sum,' resumed Barbicane, 'any motion that is ended abruptly will produce heat. This theory also allows us to admit the idea that the heat of the sun's disc is fuelled by the showers of meteors that constantly bombard its surface. It has even been calculated that . . .'

'Take cover,' murmured Michel, 'here come numbers.'

'. . . calculated,' Barbicane went on imperturbably, 'that the impact of each meteor on the sun generates as much heat as 4,000 pieces of coal each the size of the meteor.'

'And how hot is the sun?' asked Michel.

'It is equivalent to that generated by burning a crust of coal covering the sun to a depth of 27 kilometres.'

'And this heat . . . ?'

'Would be capable of boiling 2 billion 900 million cubic myriametres of water an hour.'

'And yet it does not roast us?' exclaimed Michel.

'No,' replied Barbicane, 'because the Earth's atmosphere absorbs four-tenths of the sun's heat. Furthermore, the amount of heat intercepted by the Earth is only one two-billionth of the sun's total output.'

'I can see that this is all to the good,' replied Michel, 'and that this atmosphere of ours is a very useful thing, for it not only enables us to breathe but it also prevents us from being done to a turn.'

'Quite,' said Nicholl, 'but unfortunately it won't be the same on the Moon.'

'Nonsense!' said Michel, ever the optimist. 'If anybody lives there, they must breathe. If there isn't anybody there any more, they will have left enough oxygen for three people, even if it is found only in deep ravines where it has accumulated through its own weight! But we won't be shinning up any mountains! So there!'

And so saying, Michel got to his feet and moved away to stare out at the dazzling brightness of the Moon's disc.

'By George!' he said. 'It must get really hot up there!'

'And that's overlooking', said Nicholl, 'the fact that one day lasts 360 hours.'

'But to even things out,' said Barbicane, 'remember that the nights are just as long, and since heat is restored by direct radiation, the temperature at night can only be the same as that of the rest of inter-planetary space.'

'A homely sort of place!' said Michel. 'Never mind, I wish I was already there! I say, you two, won't it feel odd to have the Earth as our Moon and see it come up over the horizon, and make out the shape of its continents and murmur: that's America, that's Europe, and then follow it as it's lost in the light of the sun! Incidentally, Barbicane, do Selenites have eclipses?'

'Yes, solar eclipses,' replied Barbicane, 'when the centres of all three heavenly bodies line up, with the Earth in the middle. But these are only annular eclipses, during which the Earth is projected like a screen on the solar disc, but leaves most of it visible.'*

'But why,' asked Nicholl, 'aren't the eclipses total? Is it because the cone of shadow cast by the Earth does not extend beyond the Moon?"

'Yes, if you ignore the refraction produced by the Earth's atmosphere. And no, if you include this refraction, with *delta* prime being the horizontal parallax and p prime half of the sun's visible diameter . . .'

'Here we go again!' said Michel, 'two into v_o^2 and all that . . .! Please speak so that everybody can understand, O algebraic man!'

'Very well,' replied Barbicane. 'In layman's terms, the average distance from Moon to Earth being 60 times the radius of the Earth,* the length of the cone of shadow the latter casts is, as a result of refraction, reduced to less than 42 times the radius. As a consequence, during eclipses, the Moon is located beyond the cone of pure shadow and the sun transmits to it not only the light from its edges but also light from its centre.'

'If that is so,' Michel said in a teasing voice, 'why are there eclipses at all since there shouldn't be any?'

'For the simple reason that this light from the sun is dimmed by the refraction and that most of it is absorbed by the atmosphere it passes through.'

'That seems a good enough reason to me,' replied Michel, 'but in any case, we shall see when we get there.'

'And now, Barbicane, tell me,' he went on, 'do you believe that the Moon was once a comet?'*

'What an idea!'

'Yes,' replied Michel, with an affable shrug, 'I often have ideas like that.'

'But actually that particular one isn't Michel's,' said Nicholl.

'So now I'm a plagiarizer!'

'You could very well be,' said Nicholl. 'According to the writings of the Ancients, the Arcadians claimed that their ancestors lived on the Earth before the Moon became its satellite. With that as their starting point, some scholars have argued that the Moon is a comet whose orbit brought it close enough to the Earth at some point to be captured by its gravity.'

'And is there any truth in the idea?' asked Michel.

'None at all,' replied Barbicane, 'and the proof is that the Moon shows no sign of ever having been enveloped in the cloud of gas which invariably accompanies comets.'

'But,' went on Nicholl, 'before it became the Earth's satellite, could it not, in its perihelion, have passed close enough to the sun to have lost all the gas surrounding it by evaporation?'

'It's possible, Captain, but not very likely.'

'Why not?'

'Because . . . actually I don't rightly know.'

'Ah!' cried Michel. 'Hundreds of books could be written about the things that we don't know!'

'True,' said Barbicane. 'But what time is it?'

'Three o'clock,' answered Nicholl.

'How time flies,' said Michel, 'when great minds like ours sit around talking! Actually I feel I'm learning too much! I have the feeling that I'm turning into a walking library!!'

And so saying, Michel climbed up into the nose of the craft, 'to get a better look at the Moon', he said. Meanwhile, his companions gazed out at space through the panel in the floor. There was nothing new to report.

When Michel Ardan climbed back down, he moved to a side porthole and then suddenly gave a loud exclamation of surprise.

'What is it?' asked Barbicane.

The President put his face close to the glass and saw what looked like a flattened sack just metres from their craft. The object appeared to be stationary, like the projectile, and was therefore being propelled by the same ascending power as themselves.

'What the devil is it?' repeated Michel Ardan. 'Could it be some piece of space flotsam which our projectile has picked up in its gravitational field and that will stay with us all the way to the Moon?'

'What I don't understand,' said Nicholl, 'is that the specific weight of that object, which is obviously lower than that of the projectile, allows it to remain so rigidly close to it.'

'Nicholl,' Barbicane said after thinking for a moment, 'I have no idea what that thing is, but I know exactly why it maintains its course on a level with us.'

'So what's the reason?'

'Because, Captain, we are passing through a vacuum and because in a vacuum all bodies fall or move—it is the same thing—at the same speed, irrespective of weight or shape. It is air which creates resistance that generates differences in weight. When you use a pump to create a vacuum in a tube, anything you put into it, be it grains of dust or grains of lead, will fall in at the same rate. Here, out in space, the same cause produces the same effect.'

'Very true,' said Nicholl, 'and everything we throw out of the projectile will also continue to travel with it as it heads for the Moon.'

'Ah! How stupid we were!' exclaimed Michel.

'Why do you say that?' asked Barbicane.

'Because we should have filled the projectile with useful things, books, instruments, tools, and so forth. We could have thrown them all out and the whole lot would have kept coming alongside us. But here's a thought! Why don't we go out and roam around like that meteor? Why don't we jump through a porthole into space? It would be rather fun to feel ourselves suspended in the ether, and better off than birds who have to keep flapping their wings to stay airborne!'

'I agree,' said Barbicane, 'but how would we breathe?'

'Trust air to be in short supply when we need it most!'

'But if it were not in such short supply, Michel, the fact that you are less physically dense than the projectile means that you would soon be left behind.'

'Ah! a vicious circle!'

'As vicious as circles come.'

'So we have to stay shut up in this capsule?'

'We have no choice.'

'Ah! I see!' Michel exulted suddenly.

'What's the matter?' said Nicholl.

'I know! Or at least I can guess what that alleged meteor out there is! It's not a meteor at all! Nor is it a piece of some planet that exploded!'

'So what is it?' asked Barbicane.

'It's our unfortunate dog! Diane's poor spouse!'

And indeed, that shapeless, unrecognizable, collapsed object was the corpse of Satellite, now as flat as a deflated set of bagpipes but still flying, flying!

7

A MOMENT OF MADNESS

AND so a curious but logical, bizarre yet explicable phenomenon was present in these most unusual of circumstances. Every object they threw out of the projectile would follow the same trajectory as it and not stop until they stopped. It was a topic of discussion that could not be exhausted in one evening. The excitement of the three voyagers only grew as they approached the end of their voyage. They now expected the unexpected, were not daunted by new prodigies, and indeed nothing astonished them any longer. Their overheated imaginations ran on ahead of the projectile, whose speed kept dropping, though they were not aware of it. But the Moon grew larger as they watched and they felt that all they had to do was to reach out with one hand and take hold of it.

Next morning, 5 November,* all three were up and about by five o'clock. That day, if their calculations were correct, would be the last of their journey. At midnight that evening, some eighteen hours later, at the exact moment when the Moon became full, they would land on its shining surface. That midnight, then, would see the end of their voyage, the most extraordinary journey ever undertaken in times ancient or modern. So from early that morning, peering out through portholes silvered by its light, they greeted the Queen of Night with a confident, joyful hurrah.

The Moon sailed on serenely across the starry firmament. A few more degrees and it would reach the exact point in space where it was scheduled to encounter the projectile. According to his observations, Barbicane had worked out that they would land in the northern hemisphere, a landscape formed of endless plains where mountains were few. This was a favourable circumstance since, as he believed, what there was of a lunar atmosphere was concentrated in low-lying areas.

'Besides,' remarked Michel Ardan, 'a plain is a better place for a landing than a mountain. A Selenite who landed in Europe on the summit of Mont Blanc, or in Asia on the Himalayas, could not be said to have arrived anywhere!'

'Moreover,' added Captain Nicholl, 'on flat ground the projectile would remain stationary after it landed, whereas on a slope it would slip and slide down like an avalanche and since we are not squirrels, we would not come out of it in one piece. So it is just as well.'

Indeed, the success of their bold venture no longer seemed in doubt. However, one thought haunted Barbicane. But not wishing to worry his two companions, he did not voice it.

For the craft's course towards the northern hemisphere of the Moon indicated that its trajectory had been slightly modified. The firing of the projectile, mathematically calibrated, was intended to deliver it to the exact centre of the lunar disc. If it failed to land there, then it could only be because it had been deflected. What could have caused it? Barbicane could neither imagine nor estimate the size of the divergence for there were no lunar landmarks to go by. But he hoped that it would have no effect except to redirect the projectile towards the upper area of the Moon which was better suited to a landing.

So Barbicane contented himself with saying nothing of his concerns to his friends and instead made frequent observations of the Moon in an attempt to detect any change in their course. Because it would be a disaster if their craft were to miss its target, be drawn outside the disc, and be propelled into interplanetary space.

Soon the Moon, instead of appearing flat like a discus, began to show signs of its convexity. If the rays of the sun had fallen across its face at an angle, the resulting shadow would have highlighted the tall mountains, making them stand out clearly. The eye could have plunged into the gaping hearts of craters and followed unpredictable fissures as they zigzagged across the unending plains. But all relief was levelled by the intense illumination. They could barely make out the huge dark patches which make the Moon look like a human face.

'A face of sorts, I grant you,' said Michel Ardan, 'but I am sorry Apollo's charming sister* should have a phiz as pockmarked as that.'

However, the voyagers, now so close to their goal, never stopped gazing out at this new world. They imagined themselves walking through these new landscapes, climbing up the tall mountains, then clambering down to the bottom of the wide calderas. Here and there in a rarefied atmosphere they saw what they half-thought were vast seas full to overflowing to which water-courses brought the tribute of the mountains. Perched above the abyss, they strained to catch the sounds of the eternally mute orb as it travelled through the solitudes of the void.

This last day left them with thrilling memories. They kept notes of the smallest details. But a vague unease crept up on them as the end grew near. Their anxiety would have been even greater had they realized how much their speed had decreased. It would have seemed to them far too low to get them to the finishing line. The reason was that the projectile was now almost 'weightless'. Its weight was falling inexorably and would drop to nothing at the point where the gravities of Earth and Moon were neutralized and could bring about such astounding effects.

Even so, despite these distractions, Michel Ardan did not forget to prepare their morning meal with his usual promptness. They ate with hearty appetites. There is nothing as good as that jellied soup liquidized by the heat of gas, nothing more satisfying than those preserved meats. A few glasses of good French wine rounded off the meal. Incidentally, Michel Ardan observed that since the vineyards of the

Moon were warmed by such a hot sun surely they must produce the most generous wines—if, that is, there were any. If there weren't, the far-seeing Frenchman had taken good care to include in his collection of samples a few precious plants of the Médoc and Côte d'or varieties for which he entertained the highest hopes.

The Reiset and Regnault apparatus continued to function with extreme efficiency. The purity of the air was kept at a perfect level. Not one molecule of carbon dioxide had resisted the potash while, as for the oxygen, as Captain Nicholl remarked, 'its quality has left nothing to be desired'. The small amount of moisture enclosed inside the projectile mixed agreeably with the air and tempered its dryness. There is no doubt that many apartments in Paris, London, or New York and the auditorium of any number of theatres did not reach such standards of hygiene.

But if the system was to function consistently, it was vital that the apparatus should be kept in perfect running order. So, every morning Michel inspected the flow controls, tried the taps, and used a pyrometer to regulate the temperature of the gas. Everything had functioned well until now and the voyagers, imitating the worthy J. T. Maston, began to put on weight which would have made them unrecognizable if their incarceration had lasted several months. In other words, they were behaving as chickens in a coop do: they were fattening up nicely.

'My dear friends,' said Michel Ardan, 'do you realize that if one of us had died from the recoil shock of our departure, interring him would have been an awkward proposition, or should I say '*etherizing*'* him, since up here ether space has replaced terrestrial ground? Can you imagine it? Can you see now that reproachful corpse stalking us through space like an embodiment of Remorse?'

'It would have been a sad sight,' agreed Nicholl.

'Indeed,' said Michel, 'but I greatly regret that we cannot go out and stretch our legs. Imagine the sensation of floating in all that radiant ether, of bathing or frolicking in the pure rays of the sun! If Barbicane had only thought of bringing some kind of diving suit and an air pump, I would have ventured out onto the roof of the projectile and struck a pose like a chimera or a hippogriff!'

'Actually, Michel,' replied Barbicane, 'you would not have held your pose as a hippogriff for long because despite your diving suit inflated by the expansion of the air in your body, you would have exploded like a shell-burst or rather like a balloon which ascends too far in the atmosphere. So have no regrets and just remember this: for as long as we travel through the void, you must not think of going for pleasant walks outside the craft!'

Michel Ardan allowed himself to be convinced to some extent, accepting that the thing was difficult but not 'impossible', a word he never ever used.

Discussion of this subject then gave way to another and the talk did not lose its momentum. The three friends all had the impression that in their present surroundings, ideas sprouted in their brains as leaves break out in the first warm days of spring. They sensed that their brains were filled with them.

Then, in the midst of the questions and answers which flew back and forth as the morning wore on, Nicholl raised one matter which could not be easily disposed of.

'Look here,' he said, 'it is all very well going to the Moon, but how are we to get back?'

The other two speakers looked at each other in surprise. It was as if it were the first time this problem had been put into words.

'What do you mean, Nicholl?' said Barbicane soberly.

'Worrying about coming back from somewhere, before you've even got there', added Michel, 'sounds rather unsporting to me.'

'I'm not saying I've got cold feet,' answered Nicholl, 'but I repeat the question. I ask: How shall we get back?'

'I have no idea,' said Barbicane.

'Personally,' said Michel, 'if I had known how we would get back, I would not have come in the first place.'

'That's the ticket!' said Nicholl approvingly.

'I fully endorse Michel's sentiments,' said Barbicane. 'And I would add that the question is of no importance at this stage. Later, when we judge the time to return to be right, we will think about it. There might be no Columbiad on the Moon, but the projectile will certainly be there.'

'That won't get us very far! It will be like having a bullet but no gun!'

'The gun can be built,' said Barbicane, 'and we can make gun-powder. There'll be no shortage of metals nor saltpetre and coal in the bowels of the Moon. Besides returning to Earth means over-coming lunar gravity and we shall travel the eight thousand leagues back to Earth's globe simply by being powered by the laws governing mass.'

'Yes, but that's enough of that,' said Michel, becoming impatient. 'Let's have no more talk of going back! We've already said more than enough on that topic. And there won't be any difficulty about communicating with our colleagues back on Earth.'

'Why not?'

'Because we can use the meteorites ejected by the Moon's volcanoes.'

'Well thought of, Michel,' said Barbicane who sounded quite convinced. 'Laplace calculated that a force just five times greater than the firepower of our cannons would be sufficient to propel a meteorite from the Moon to the Earth. Now, there is no lunar volcano there that does not have a greater firepower than that.'

'Bravo!' cried Michel. 'Those meteorites will make useful postmen— and they won't charge us a penny for delivery! It will be one in the eye for those chaps who run the Post Office! It's made me think . . .'

'What do you think?'

'I have this brilliant idea! Why did we not attach a telegraph cable to the projectile? Then we could have exchanged telegrams with the Earth!'

'But dammit!' retorted Nicholl, 'aren't you forgetting the sheer weight of a cable 86,000 leagues long?'

'Not at all! We could have trebled the charge we loaded into the Columbiad! Quadrupled, quintupled it!' cried Michel, whose output was beginning to take on an increasingly excitable tone.

'There's just one small objection to make against your scheme,' said Barbicane, 'which is that as the globe turned on its axis it would have eventually wound us in and towed us back to Earth.'

'By the thirty-seven stars of the Union flag!' said Michel. 'I only seem to be getting impractical ideas today, ideas worthy of J. T. Maston! Still, if we do not get back to Earth, J. T. Maston would find a way of coming to fetch us!'

'True,' said Barbicane. 'He'd come for sure. He is a fine, courageous comrade. Anyway, it wouldn't be difficult to organize. Isn't the Columbiad still sunk in the soil of Florida? Is there not enough cotton and nitric acid to make more pyroxylin? Will the Moon not return to its zenith over Florida? And eighteen years from now, will it not be at exactly the same place it is as today?'

'Yes,' repeated Michel, 'yes, Maston will come and with him will come our friends Elphiston, Blomsberry, all the members of the Gun Club, and they will get a right royal welcome! And later, whole convoys of projectiles will shuttle between the Earth and the Moon! Three cheers for J. T. Maston!'

It is likely that, though the honourable J. T. Maston could not hear those cheers uttered in his honour, at least they would have made his ears tingle. What was he doing at that moment? More likely than not, he was sitting at his post at Longs Peak in the Rocky Mountains trying to locate their invisible craft as it sped through space. If he was thinking of his close friends, it should be said that they were reciprocating: under the influence of a strange elation they too were thinking of him—and in the warmest terms.

But what was the cause of this visibly rising excitement felt by all three of the passengers on board the projectile? That they were sober could not be doubted. Should this strange etherism* of the brain be attributed to the exceptional circumstances in which they found themselves, to their proximity to the Moon from which they were only a few hours distant, or maybe to some unknown lunar effect on their nervous systems? Their faces were flushed as if exposed to the heat of a furnace; their breathing quickened and their lungs worked like a smithy's bellows; their eyes burned with extraordinary fire; their voices exploded in stentorian blasts; their words burst out of them like Champagne corks forced out by carbon dioxide; their gestures became invasive because they took up so much room . . . And odder still, they were totally unaware of the extreme agitation of their minds.

'And now,' said Nicholl curtly, 'now that I do not know if we shall be returning from the Moon, I would very much like to know what we are going to do there.'

'What we will be doing there?' answered Barbicane, stamping his foot though like a fencing master, 'I haven't the faintest idea!'

'Not the faintest idea?' bellowed Michel in a voice which rang loudly through the projectile.

'No, I have not given it any thought whatsoever!' Barbicane roared back at him in a voice that was equally loud.

'Well, I have,' replied Michel.

'Go on then, spit it out,' yelled Nicholl who was quite unable to control the full-throated volume of his voice.

'I'll tell you if I feel like it,' cried Michel grabbing his companion roughly by the arm.

'You'd better feel like it!' said Barbicane, with eyes blazing and one hand raised in anger. 'It was you who dragged us into this tomfool venture and we demand to know why!'

'That's right!' said the captain. 'Now that I don't know where I'm going to, I want to know why I'm going there!'

'Why?' yelped Michel, leaping three feet into the air, '*why?* To lay claim to the Moon in the name of the United States! To add a thirty-eighth state to the Union! To colonize the lunar regions, to cultivate them, to populate them, to bring to them all the wonders of art, of science, and of industry! To civilize the Selenites, unless they are more civilized than we are, and to set them up as a republic, if they aren't republicans already!'

'That is if there actually *are* any Selenites!' retorted Nicholl, who, in the grip of this state of unaccountable exhilaration, had turned most contrary.

'Who says there are no Selenites?' barked Michel threateningly.

'Me! I do!' howled Nicholl.

'Damned insolence!' said Michel. 'Say that again, Captain, and I shall shove the words down your throat!'

The two adversaries were about to square up to each other and the whole incoherent discussion was on the point of descending into fisticuffs when Barbicane stepped peremptorily between them.

'Stop it at once, you crazy fools,' he said, putting the two men in the same category, 'if there are no Selenites, we'll get by without them!'

'Yes!' cried Michel who did not really care much whether there were any or not, 'we'll manage without them. We don't need Selenites! Down with Selenites!'

'The Empire of the Moon will be all ours!' said Nicholl.

'The three of us will form a Republic!'

'I will be the Congress!' said Michel.

'And I will be the Senate!' said Nicholl.

'And Barbicane shall be President!' cried Michel.

'Not a President elected by the people!' said Barbicane.

'Well then, a President elected by Congress,' cried Michel, 'and seeing that I am the Congress, I elect you unanimously!'

'Three cheers for President Barbicane!' cried Nicholl.

'Hip hip hooray!' yelled Michel Ardan.

And then both President and Senate joined together in a raucous rendition of the popular *Yankee Doodle*, while the Congress struck up with the manly tones of the *Marseillaise*.

And then they began to dance wildly, waving their arms madly, stamping their feet like maniacs, leaping about like double-jointed clowns in a circus. Diane joined in, barking frenziedly in her turn, jumping up almost into the nose of the craft. There was the inexplicable sound of wings flapping and the bizarre racket of the cock crowing. Five or six chickens flew around, crashing into the walls of the projectile like demented bats.

Then the three travelling companions, their lungs tested beyond measure by the unaccountable power of some mysterious influence, more than intoxicated, seared by the air which inflamed their airways, fell senseless onto the floor of the projectile.

8*

AT A DISTANCE OF 78,114 LEAGUES

WHAT had happened? What was the origin of the strange wildness whose consequences might have proved disastrous? A casual blunder by Michel which, fortunately, Nicholl was able to correct in time.

After losing consciousness for several minutes, the captain was the first to recover and gather his wits about him again.

Although he had eaten breakfast only two hours earlier, he felt a ravenous hunger which gnawed at his vitals as though he had not eaten for a week. His entire being, from his stomach to his brain, seemed to clamour for attention.

So he got to his feet and asked Michel to provide a second breakfast. Michel, however, was in no fit state and did not respond. So Nicholl decided to make them all a cup of tea which would help wash down a dozen sandwiches. He set about lighting the gas and struck a match.

He was astounded to see the sulphur flare up with an extraordinary brightness which almost dazzled him. And the gas jet also produced a flame comparable in intensity to that of electric light.

Illumination also broke into Nicholl's mind. The brightness of the lights, the physiological troubles he had experienced, the wildness which had overcome his moral faculties and his emotions—now he understood.

'It's the oxygen!'* he cried.

And turning to the air-making apparatus, he saw that the tap was allowing an unimpeded flow of that colourless, tasteless, odourless gas to escape. Though eminently life-giving, in its pure form it could also produce extremely serious reactions in the body. Through sheer carelessness, Michel had left the main tap fully open!

Nicholl quickly turned off the free flow of the oxygen with which the air was saturated and which would have caused the death of the voyagers not by asphyxiation but by internal combustion.

An hour later, the air, less oxygenated now, had restored normal functioning to their lungs. Gradually, the three friends recovered from their recent gas poisoning, but they had to sleep off the fumes the way a drinker sleeps off the effects of wine.

When Michel learned of the part he had played in the incident, he did not appear in any way disconcerted. Their unexpected intoxication had at least interrupted the monotony of the voyage. Many foolish things had been said under its influence but they were as quickly forgotten as they had been spoken.

'Besides,' the cheery Frenchman said, 'I am not at all sorry for having sampled such a heady gas. You know, friends, that someone really ought to open an establishment equipped with oxygen rooms where customers with enfeebled constitutions could live it up for a few hours! Imagine gatherings where the air is saturated with the heroic component. Picture theatres where the management guarantees a supply of a high level of oxygenated air, ah, what passions would then fill the souls of the performers and spectators! What fire in the former! What enthusiasm in the latter! And if, instead of holding public meetings, we could saturate the entire population with it, imagine what energy would be injected into activities, what extra dimension would be added to life! An exhausted nation could be made great and strong again, and I know more than one country in that old Europe of ours which should be put on an oxygen diet in the best interests of its health!'

Michel spoke and warmed to his subject in a way that supposed the tap might well be still fully open. But a word from Barbicane punctured his wild enthusiasm.

'That is all very well, Michel, but can you tell us how these chickens now joining the revels came to be here?'

'Chickens?'

'Yes, chickens.'

Indeed, half a dozen hens and a magnificent cockerel were tottering about, pecking and clucking.

'Oh, those nuisances!' cried Michel. 'It was the oxygen that set them off!'

'But what are you intending to do with those hens?' asked Barbicane.

'Acclimatize them to life on the Moon, of course!'

'So why did you keep them hidden?'

'It was a joke, Mr President, just a joke that went badly wrong. I wanted to release them onto lunar soil without telling you. I wanted to see the look of amazement on your face when you caught sight of chickens from Earth pecking away happily in the meadows of the Moon!'

'Always a wag, always the jester!' sighed Barbicane. 'You don't need oxygen to set you off! You are always the way we all were under the influence of that gas! You're for ever playing the fool!'

'But who's to say that we weren't wise then?' replied Michel Ardan.

After that philosophical observation, the three friends set about clearing up the mess inside the craft; the hens and the cockerel were returned to their cages. But while all that was going on, Barbicane and his two companions were distinctly conscious of a new phenomenon.

Ever since they had left Earth, their weight, that of the projectile and its contents had been gradually decreasing. If they could not be absolutely sure in the case of the projectile, the moment had to come when the loss of weight became obvious in the tools and instruments they used and also their own case.

It goes without saying that a set of scales would not have shown the decrease because the weights used to weigh objects would clearly have lost as much weight as the objects being weighed. But a spring-balance, for example, where the tension of the spring is independent of gravity, would certainly have put a precise figure on the loss.

It is an accepted fact that gravity, another word for weight, is in direct proportion to mass and in inverse proportion to the square of the distances. From this stems the following consequence: if the Earth were alone in the universe and the rest of the heavenly bodies were to be suddenly destroyed, the projectile, according to Newton's law, would have weighed less the further it travelled from the Earth, but without ever entirely losing its weight, since terrestrial gravity would still have been felt whatever the distance.

But in the present case, the time would come when the projectile would no longer be subject to the laws of weight, no account being taken of the other heavenly bodies, whose gravitational effect could be considered nil.

Now the course of the projectile was plotted to take it from the Earth to the Moon. The further it travelled from the Earth, the weaker terrestrial gravity became, being in inverse proportion to the distance between the two. But at the same time the gravity of the Moon increased following the same formula. There had, therefore, to be a point where these gravitational forces cancelled each other out, where the projectile would be without weight. If the mass of the Moon and the mass of the Earth had been the same, this point would be equally distant from the two bodies. But by taking account of the difference between their respective masses, it was an easy matter to calculate that this neutral point would occur at 47/52nds of the journey, that is, in figures, at 78,114 leagues from Earth.

At that point, a body having no autonomous source of speed or motion would remain there, stationary, for all eternity, being held in position equally by Earth and Moon, and with nothing attracting it towards one or the other.

Now if the propulsive force had been correctly calculated, the projectile should reach that point at zero speed, having lost all measurable weight along with everything inside it.

What would happen then? In the general case, there would be three possibilities:

1. The projectile might maintain some speed after all and, passing beyond the point of equal gravitational pull, would then carry on to the Moon, because the power of lunar attraction would be greater than that of the Earth;

2. Or, if its speed failed before it reached the point of equal attraction, it would be dragged back towards Earth, whose gravitational pull would be greater than that of the Moon;

3. Or, finally, having sufficient speed to reach the neutral point but not enough to pass beyond it, it would remain perpetually suspended at that location, like the fabled tomb of Mahomet, between the zenith and the nadir.

These were the possibilities and Barbicane clearly explained the implications to his travelling companions, who hung on his every word. But how would they know when the projectile had reached the neutral point, located 78,114 leagues from Earth? That is, the exact moment when both they and the entire contents of the projectile would cease to be subject to the laws of weight?

Up to now, the voyagers, while they fully recognized that their speed continued to fall, had yet to feel any sense of a total absence of motion. But that morning, at around 11 o'clock, a glass slipped from Nicholl's hand and instead of falling to the floor, it remained suspended in the air.

'Aha!' exclaimed Michel Ardan. 'So physics can be fun after all!'

And all at once other objects left to themselves, such as firearms and bottles, also stayed up miraculously. Diane too, lifted by Michel, needed no sleight of hand to imitate the levitation tricks of Caston and Robert-Houdin. Indeed, the dog did not even seem to be aware that she was floating.

The three intrepid companions, surprised, dumbfounded, despite all their scientific way of thinking, had a sense that they had been transported to a world of miracles, for they felt that their bodies were entirely without weight. They stretched out their arms, which made no attempt to drop to their sides. Their heads wobbled on their shoulders. Their feet did not touch the floor of the projectile. They were like drunkards who had lost control of their limbs. Storytellers have dreamed up men who have no reflection, others who have no shadow. But here reality, in the form of the power of nil gravity, had created men in whom nothing had weight and who themselves weighed nothing!

Suddenly, Michel gave a skip, rose off the floor and remained suspended in the air like the monk in Murillo's *Cuisine des anges*.*

Both his friends immediately did likewise and all three floated like miraculous figures in a painting of the Ascension.

'Is this believable? Is it even plausible? Is it possible?' cried Michel. 'No it isn't. And why is that? Ah, if only Raphael could see us now, he would have all he needed to paint us into an *Assumption*.'*

'The assumption can't last,' said Barbicane. 'If the projectile passes the neutral point, lunar gravity will haul us off to the Moon.'

'And we will be walking around in the nose of the projectile,' said Michel.

'No, no,' said Barbicane. 'Because the projectile has a very low centre of gravity, it will gradually turn round.'

'Which means that everything we arranged so neatly will be turned upside down too, a shambles is the word for it!'

'Don't worry, Michel,' said Nicholl. 'No need to fear that there'll be any mess. Objects won't be flying about because the projectile will come round very gradually.'

'That's right,' said Barbicane, 'and when it has passed the point of zero gravity, its base, which is relatively heavy, will bring its nose round in a line perpendicular to the Moon. But for that to happen we shall first have to pass beyond the neutral point.'

'Pass beyond the neutral point!' exclaimed Michel. 'So why don't we do what sailors do who cross the Equator and drink to our safe passage?'

A swimming movement to one side took him to the padded wall of the craft. Once there, he collected a bottle and three glasses, set them down 'in space' in front of his companions and, clinking merrily, they toasted the neutral point with three loud cheers.

The interaction between the two gravities lasted less than an hour. The voyagers imperceptibly felt that they were being let down onto the floor of the craft and Barbicane observed that its conical nose was beginning to deviate from the direct course to the Moon. And by shifting the other way, the base of the projectile came closer to it. So lunar attraction was winning the tussle with the Earth's gravity. The descent towards the Moon was beginning, still almost unnoticeably. The deviation from their direct course in the first second would be one millimetre and a third, or 590 thousandths of a line. But gradually the pull of gravity would strengthen, their speed would pick up, the projectile, drawn base-first, would have its nose pointing back towards Earth and would proceed towards the lunar surface at an increasing speed. They would therefore be certain to reach their destination. Now, nothing could prevent the mission from being a success and both Nicholl and Michel Ardan shared Barbicane's elation.

Then all three started to discuss the stream of marvels which continued to amaze them one after another. In particular, the neutralizing of the laws of weight was a subject to which they returned again and again. Michel Ardan, always the enthusiast, was minded to draw conclusions from the phenomenon that were pure fantasy.

'Just imagine,' he cried, 'what a step forward it would be for humankind if we could only release the Earth from the shackle of Weight which keeps us chained! Its prisoner would suddenly be free! An end to fatigue! No more weary arms and tired legs! And if it is true that in order to fly above the surface of the Earth and remain airborne by muscle power alone, we would need to possess physical strength one hundred and fifty times greater than that with which we are naturally endowed, then instead, a simple act of will, a mere whim would transport us up into space—if only gravity did not exist!'

'That's true,' laughed Nicholl. 'If we could overcome weight as easily as we deaden pain by the use of anæsthetics, then the whole face of modern society would be changed!'

'Yes!' cried Michel, carried away by his subject. 'If we get rid of weight, there will be no more burdens to carry! There will be no need for cranes, lifting jacks, capstans, cranking handles and all similar tools would have become redundant!'

'Fine words,' said Barbicane, 'but if things weighed nothing, nothing would stay in its place, not the hat on your head, Michel, nor your house, for its stones would no longer be held together by their weight! Boats would lose their stability on water for it is an effect of their weight. There would be no seas because their waters would not remain in their beds courtesy of the Earth's gravity. And finally, there would be no atmosphere, for its molecules would cease to be bound together and would fly off into space!'

'Ah!' said Michel, sadly. 'That would be a pity! There's nothing like sensible people to bring a chap down to Earth with a bump.'

'Never mind, Michel,' went on Barbicane, 'for if no heavenly body exists that is entirely free of the force of gravity, at least you are about to set foot on one where everything weighs less than it does on Earth.'

'You mean on the Moon?'

'Yes, on whose surface things weigh six times less than on the Earth's surface. It is a phenomenon that is easily proved.'

'We will notice the difference?' asked Michel.

'Certainly, because there two hundred kilograms will weigh just thirty.'

'But will our muscles be less strong?'

'Not at all. Instead of being able to jump one metre in the air, you'll be able to clear eighteen metres.'

'So on the Moon we'll all be as strong as Hercules!' cried Michel.

'Especially,' said Nicholl, 'if the height of the Selenites is in proportion to the lunar mass, for then they will be barely a foot tall!'

'Like the Lilliputians!' replied Michel. 'And I'll be like Gulliver! We'll be bringing the fable of the giants to life! That's one advantage of leaving our native planet and gallivanting around the solar system!'

'One moment, Michel,' replied Barbicane. 'If you really want to be like Gulliver, restrict yourself to going to the lesser planets, such as Mercury, Venus, or Mars, whose density is slightly less than that of Earth. But you don't want to venture anywhere near the large planets like Saturn, Uranus, and Neptune, for then the roles would be reversed and you would be a Lilliputian!'

'What about the sun?'

'Though the sun's density is four times less than that of the Earth, its volume is 1,384,000 times greater and its gravity twenty-seven times stronger than on the surface of our planet. When due allowance is made, its inhabitants would be two hundred feet tall on average.'

'Good heavens!' cried Michel. 'I'd be a pigmy, a manikin!'

'Gulliver in the land of giants!' said Nicholl.

'That's the size of it,' said Barbicane.

'And it would do no harm to take along a few cannons for self-defence.'

'Not really,' said Barbicane, 'because your shells would be useless on the sun as they would not carry further than a few metres.'

'That's a bit strong!'

'But it's incontrovertibly true,' replied Barbicane. 'Gravity is so powerful on that massive star that an object weighing 70 kilograms on Earth would weigh 1,900 on the surface of the sun! Your hat would weigh tens of kilograms! Your cigar, half a pound. And if you did land on the surface, your weight would be so great—around two and a half thousand kilograms—that you would be unable to stand up.'

'Goodness gracious me,' sent Michel, 'I should need to have a small portable crane. All in all, my friends, we should make do with the Moon for the time being. At least there we shall cut something of a figure! Later, we'll see if it's worth bothering with the sun, where a man cannot take a drink without having a winch to lift the glass to his mouth!'*

9

THE CONSEQUENCES OF A DEFLECTION

BARBICANE was now free of worries, if not about the final outcome of their mission, at least concerning the power propelling the projectile. Its accumulated impetus was carrying it over the neutral line. The craft would not be pulled back to the Earth nor would it be immobilized on the line of equal attraction. Only one hypothesis now remained to be verified: that the projectile would reach its goal powered by lunar gravity.

This would amount to a descent of 8,296 leagues onto a globe where, it is true, weight had a sixth of its terrestrial value. Even so, it was a dangerous procedure and called for precautions to be taken without delay.

These precautions were of two kinds. The first were designed to absorb the shock at the moment when the projectile settled on lunar soil. The other would slow its descent, thereby lessening the impact.

To soften the landing, it was unfortunate that Barbicane was no longer in a position to use the method that had been so effective in reducing the blast of the launch, that is, by adopting water and collapsible partitions to cushion the effect. The wooden sections still existed but there was insufficient water, because their reserve supply could not be used for this purpose, if it should turn out that the liquid element proved to be unavailable on the Moon's surface for the first few days.

In any case that reserve would have been quite inadequate as a buffer. The amount of water loaded into the projectile when it was launched had been stored under the watertight wooden disc and occupied a space three feet deep and an area of 54 square feet. In volume it measured six cubic metres and its weight was 5,750 kilograms. The partitions now contained not more than one fifth of this quantity. So the idea of using this powerful method of deadening the impact of landing could not be entertained.

Fortunately, Barbicane, not wanting to rely only on the water, had also fitted the moveable disc with heavily sprung shock-absorbers, designed to lessen the effect of the impact on the base after the horizontal partitions had been smashed. These mitigators were still in place and all that was needed now was to reset them and restore the sliding disc to its original position. All these components, easily manipulated because in space they weighed very little, could be quickly reinstalled.

The work was done quickly. The various parts were refitted without difficulty since only nuts and bolts were involved and there was no shortage of tools. Soon, the disc was repaired and sat squarely on its steel buffers, like a table on its legs. The reinstatement of the disc, however, had one disadvantage: the lower viewing panel was now blocked off. It would therefore be impossible for the voyagers to observe the Moon through it as they approached it vertically and they were forced to give up this means of observation. In any case, they still had the side portholes through which they could have sight of the vast expanses of the Moon just as the Earth can be seen from the basket of a balloonist.

Resetting the disc took just one hour's work. It was after noon by the time these preparations were completed. Barbicane then took new observations of the angle of the projectile. But he was somewhat concerned to note that its inclination had not changed sufficiently to make a successful descent. It appeared to be following an inflected course that ran parallel to the Moon's disc. The Moon shone brightly in space while in the opposite part of the sky, the sun blazed on it with all its fire.

The situation was beginning to make them feel uneasy.

'Will we actually be able to land?' asked Nicholl.

'Let's carry on as if we were going to,' replied Barbicane.

'Don't be so spineless!' said Michel Ardan. 'Of course we'll get there—and maybe sooner than we'd like.'

His reaction made Barbicane resume his preparations and he now turned his attention to setting up his system for braking the projectile as it descended.

The reader will recall the mass meeting in Tampa, in Florida, when Captain Nicholl stepped up as Barbicane's enemy and Michel Ardan's opponent. Against the captain, who argued that the projectile would shatter like glass on impact, Michel Ardan replied that he would slow its descent by means of rockets placed in a predetermined pattern.

Indeed, powerful rockets had been arranged around the base of the projectile where they would fire downwards, providing reverse propulsion and to some extent checking its speed. True, these rockets would have to fire in a vacuum, but there would be no lack of oxygen because they would supply their own in the manner of lunar volcanoes whose combustion has never been impeded by the lack of atmosphere on the Moon.

Barbicane had chosen rockets in the form of small steel guns which were grooved so that they could be screwed into the craft's base from within it. Inside they lay flush with the floor; outside each projected by some six inches. There were twenty of them all told. A hole bored in the disc allowed one to light the fuse with which each was supplied. The explosive energy released was confined entirely to the outside. Detonatable charges had been loaded into each gun in advance. All that was needed then was to remove the metal buffers screwed into the base of the craft and replace them with the guns which fitted into the slots they vacated.

This new operation was finished by three o'clock and once these preparations had been made, all they could do was wait.

Meanwhile, the projectile was drawing visibly closer to the Moon and was clearly being influenced to some extent by its proximity. But its own speed was pushing it away on an oblique course. Of these two influences, the outcome was a trajectory which could well move off at a tangent. It was now obvious that the projectile would not land as planned on the Moon's surface, for its base, because of its weight, should by now have been squarely turned towards it.

Barbicane's concerns increased as he watched and saw his projectile resist the power of lunar gravity. What was unfolding before him now was the Unknown, the Great Unknown of interstellar space. He, the scientist, had foreseen the three most likely hypotheses: returning to Earth, continuing on to the Moon, and stagnation on the neutral line. Yet here a fourth hypothesis, which threatened them with all the terrors of the infinite, was unexpectedly emerging. If it was to be confronted unflinchingly, it would take a determined sage like Barbicane, a man as phlegmatic as Nicholl, or a bold adventurer like Michel Ardan.

The conversation was directed to this new prospect. Other men would have considered the problem from the practical point of view. They would have asked themselves exactly where their passenger projectile was taking them. But not these men. They looked for the cause which had produced this effect.

'So we've been derailed?' said Michel. 'But how?'

'I very much fear,' said Nicholl, 'that despite all our precautions, the Columbiad was not pointed in the correct direction. An error, the tiniest of the errors, must have been enough to steer us out of the Moon's gravitational field.'

'You mean our aim was bad?' asked Michel.

'I don't think so,' replied Barbicane. 'The cannon was built absolutely perpendicularly and it was aimed very precisely at the zenith. Now the Moon is moving towards the zenith, so we were timed to arrive when it was full. No, there is another reason, but I cannot put my finger on it; it's on the tip of my tongue.'

'Perhaps we'll be getting there too late?' asked Nicholl.

'Too late?' said Barbicane.

'Yes,' Nicholl went on. 'The report from the Cambridge Observatory said that the journey should take ninety-seven hours, thirteen minutes, and twenty seconds. That means that if it takes less time, the Moon would not yet have reached its predicted station. If it takes longer, it would have moved on.'

'Agreed,' said Barbicane. 'But we started out on 1 December, at thirteen minutes and twenty-five seconds to eleven at night, and we were scheduled to get there on the fifth at midnight, the exact moment when the Moon is due to be full. Well, today is 5 December, at half past three in the afternoon. Eight and a half hours more should be enough to take us to our destination. So why are we not getting there?'

'Maybe we were travelling too fast?' suggested Nicholl. 'Because we know now that our initial velocity was greater than we thought.'

'No! Absolutely not!' replied Barbicane. 'If the course followed by the projectile was the right one, an excess of speed would not prevent us from reaching the Moon. No! There must have been some kind of deflection. We have been knocked off course.'

'By who? By what?' asked Nicholl.

'That I cannot say,' replied Barbicane.

'Listen, Barbicane,' said Michel. 'Do you want know my opinion on the cause of this deflection?'

'Speak.'

'I wouldn't give half a dollar to know! We have been blown off course. That's the long and short of it. Where we are going matters little to me! Anyway, we shall see by and by. Dammit! We have been re-routed into outer space and eventually we'll come down on some centre of gravity or other.'

The indifference shown by Michel Ardan did not appeal to Barbicane. It was not that he was fearful about the future. But what had caused the projectile to veer off course? That was what he would have given anything to know.

In the meantime, the craft continued to move away from the Moon at an angle accompanied by the procession of objects that had been thrown out. By using as reference points the higher landmarks on the Moon, now less than two thousand leagues distant, Barbicane could now even confirm that their speed was becoming uniform. This was further proof that they were not on course for a landing. For the moment, their projectile's own propulsive power was still stronger than the Moon's gravity, yet its trajectory was still taking it closer to the lunar disc, and it was not unreasonable to hope that, as they came nearer still, the effect of the craft's weight would prevail and lead to a definitive descent.

The three friends, having nothing better to do, continued to observe. But they were still unable to identify the topographical features of the satellite. The areas of high relief were levelled by the way the sunlight slanted over them.

So they went on looking out through the side viewing panels until eight that evening. By that time, the Moon had grown so much greater in size that it filled an entire half of the firmament. The projectile was flooded with light from the sun on one side and the Moon on the other.

By then, Barbicane believed he could reliably estimate the distance separating them from their goal as a mere seven hundred leagues. It seemed to him that the speed of the projectile was some two hundred metres a second, or about a hundred and seventy leagues per hour. The base of the craft was tending to incline towards the Moon under the influence of centripetal force, but the grip of centrifugal force was still greater. It looked increasingly likely that its straight course would evolve into a curve of some description whose exact nature could not yet be defined.

Barbicane continued to search for an answer to this intractable problem.

The hours passed by without any solution emerging. The projectile was still getting visibly closer to the Moon. But it was equally plain that it would never reach it. As to the shortest distance by which it would miss, that would be dictated by the twin forces of gravitational pull and push acting on the craft.

'There's just one thing I want,' repeated Michel, 'which is to pass close enough to the Moon to learn all of its secrets!'

'Devil take whatever it is', cried Nicholl, 'that's making our projectile veer off course!'

'Then the devil can also,' replied Barbicane as if he had suddenly been struck by a thought, 'take the meteor we encountered on our way!'

'Why?' asked Michel.

'What do you mean?' asked Nicholl.

'What I mean,' Barbicane went on with conviction, 'is that the reason for our deflection is that wandering fireball!'

'But it did not come anywhere near us!' cried Michel.

'That is of no consequence. Compared to the size of our craft, its mass was enormous and its gravitational pull was sufficient to alter our course.'

'Not by very much,' said Nicholl.

'True, Nicholl, but by however little it was it did not need to be any greater, over a distance of 84,000 leagues, to make us miss the Moon completely!'

10

THE MOON WATCHERS

BARBICANE had clearly found the only plausible cause of the deflection. Small though it had been, it was large enough to have altered the projectile's trajectory. It was a blow dealt by the hand of fate! Their bold initiative had been thwarted by a wholly fortuitous circumstance so that unless something else quite exceptional happened, they could no longer reach their destination. Would they pass close to the Moon and hence solve certain problems of physics or geology which until then had remained insoluble? That was the question, the only issue which now occupied the minds of our intrepid voyagers. As for the destiny the future had in store for them, they refused to give it a second thought. But in the midst of that infinite emptiness, what would become of them there, soon to be without air to breathe? A few more days and they would die, asphyxiated in their voyaging, straying passenger projectile. But a few days were centuries to these dauntless men and they devoted all their waking moments to observing the Moon which they no longer had any hope of reaching.

The distance between the projectile and the satellite was now approximately two hundred leagues. As to the visibility of details on the surface, the three voyagers, despite their current location, appeared in fact to be further from the Moon than Earth dwellers who used powerful telescopes.

For it is known that the instrument designed by John Ross at Parsonstown, with its 6,500 times magnification, makes the Moon seem just sixteen leagues distant. Or again, the huge one built at Longs Peak magnifies 48,000 times and makes it look as if it were less than two leagues away, so that objects with a diameter of ten metres appear clearly enough.

So, at their current distance, topographical details of the Moon observed without the aid of a telescope could not usefully be seen.* The trio might take in the vast contours of the immense depressions incorrectly labelled 'seas' but they were unable to make out their physical make-up or character. The mountainous relief disappeared in the luminous glare produced by the reflected light of the sun so that the human eye, dazzled as if staring into a tank of molten silver, turned instinctively away.

However, the oblong form of the satellite was already emerging. It looked like a gigantic egg whose smaller end faced the Earth. The fact is that when the Moon was first created it was liquid or pliable and appeared as a perfect sphere. But it was not long before it was captured by the Earth's centre of gravity and was stretched towards it by the effect of its attraction. By becoming its satellite, it lost its original pure form. Its own centre of gravity moved forward and beyond its geometrical centre, and from this new arrangement a number of scientists concluded that its air and water had migrated to the opposite side of the Moon which is never seen from Earth.

This change in the original shape of the satellite was visible but only for a few brief moments The distance of the projectile from the Moon was decreasing very rapidly because its speed was considerably less now than its initial velocity, though it was still eight or nine times greater than speeds reached by express trains. The oblique course followed by the projectile—for the very reason that it was oblique—left Michel Ardan with some hope that they might yet come down somewhere on the Moon's disc. He could not believe that they would not make a landing at all. No! He would not believe it and continued to say so. But Barbicane, a better judge in these matters, never wearied of answering him with pitiless logic:

'No, Michel, no! We can only reach the Moon by a descent onto its surface—and we are not descending. Centripetal force is holding us in the grip of the Moon's attractive power, but centrifugal force is pushing us away and there is nothing we can do about it.'

This was said in a voice which denied Michel Ardan's last remaining hopes.

The part of the Moon which the projectile was now approaching was the northern hemisphere, which selenographic charts place in their lower half, for such maps are drawn according to images provided by telescopes and, as is common knowledge, telescope images are inverted. This was the case with the *Mappa selenographica* of Beer and Mädler which Barbicane consulted. This northern hemisphere consisted of endless plains with isolated mountainous outcrops.

At midnight, the Moon was full. Precisely at that moment the voyagers should have been taking their first steps on it if it had not been for that accursed meteor which had altered their course. The Moon had thus arrived at the location meticulously established by the Observatory at Cambridge. It was mathematically at the point of its perigee and at the zenith of the Earth's twenty-eighth parallel. An observer placed at the bottom of the gigantic Columbiad, which was aimed perpendicularly to the horizon, would have seen the Moon framed in the cannon's mouth. A straight line drawn along its axis would have gone straight through the centre of the Eye of Night.

Nothing would be gained by reporting that during that night of 5 December, the voyagers did not rest for one moment. How could they have allowed their eyes to shut, now that they were so close to this new world? No. Their very being was gripped by one thought: they must see! As representatives of Earth, and of the human species past and present, which they embodied in their persons, it was through their eyes that the human race now observed those lunar regions and became privy to the secrets of their satellite! Emotion filled their hearts and they moved from one viewing panel to another in complete silence.

Their observations, noted down by Barbicane, were meticulously recorded. To see, they used binoculars. To verify what they saw, they used charts.

The first man to observe the Moon was Galileo. His primitive telescope had a magnification power of just thirty.* Nevertheless, in the darker patches which are scattered over the lunar disc—'as eyes bespeckle the peacock's tail'—he was the first to find mountains and even measured their height, to which he gave excessive values that made their altitude equal to a twentieth of the diameter of the Moon's disc, which is to say 8,800 metres. Galileo left no chart of his observations.

Some years later, Hevelius from Danzig, using procedures which were accurate only twice a month—during the first and second neap tides—reduced Galileo's height estimates to just a twenty-sixth of the Moon's diameter, which exaggerated in the opposite sense. Yet it is to this man that we are indebted for the first map of the Moon. On it, the light, rounded patches represent circular mountains and the darker areas are immense seas which in reality are flat plains. He gave these mountains and watery expanses terrestrial names. Thus there appears a Sinai in the middle of a new Arabia, an Etna situated on a new Sicily, plus Alps, Apennines, Carpathian Mountains, and also a Mediterranean, a Sea of Azov, a Black Sea, and a Caspian Sea. These names, incidentally, were highly inappropriate for none of these mountains or 'seas' bore any resemblance to their terrestrial homonyms. It is only with great difficulty that in the extensive white area which connects southwards to vaster continents and ends in a point, it is possible to recognize the inverted outlines of the Indian peninsula, the Bay of Bengal, and of Cochin-China. As a result, these names were not retained. Another cartographer, with a better knowledge of the human heart, suggested a new nomenclature which human vanity eagerly embraced.

This observer was Father Riccioli, a contemporary of Hevelius. He drew a crude map full of basic errors. But he gave the mountains of the Moon the names of great men of Antiquity and scholars of his day, an approach which has continued very much ever since.

A third map of the Moon was drawn in the seventeenth century by Dominique Cassini.* An improvement on that of Riccioli in terms of execution, it is inaccurate in its measurements. Several reduced copies of it were published but its plate, conserved for many years at the King's Press, was sold off for the scrap value of its copper.

La Hire, a celebrated mathematician and draughtsman, made a map of the Moon measuring four metres from top to bottom which was never engraved or published.

After him, in the mid-eighteenth century, a German astronomer named Tobie Mayer began publishing a magnificent selenographic map which used lunar measurements which he himself had checked thoroughly. But his death, which occurred in 1762, prevented him from completing his great work.

There followed Schröter of Lilienthal, who drew various maps of the Moon, and a certain Lohrmann of Dresden to whom we are indebted for a chart divided into twenty-five sections, of which four were engraved.

It was in 1830 that Beer and Mädler published their celebrated *Mappa selenographica*, which used orthographic projection. It was an exact representation of the Moon as its appears, though the shape and lie of mountains and plains are accurate only in its central area. Elsewhere, in its northern, southern, eastern, and western regions, such details, given in reduced form, do not allow comparison with those used for the centre. This topographical map, 95 metres from head to foot and divided into four parts, is the culminating master-piece of lunar cartography.

Often quoted, in the footsteps of these experts, are the mountain moonscapes of the German astronomer Julius Schmidt; the topo-graphical works of Father Secchi; the magnificent photographic plates of the British enthusiast Warren de la Rue; and the three-dimensional representation completed by Messrs Lecouturier et Chapuis in 1860, a very fine piece of work, excellent in conception and clarity of detail.

Such, then, has been the nomenclature used by the various charts of the lunar world. Barbicane had two of them to hand, one by Beer and Mädler and the other by Messrs Lecouturier and Chapuis. They were sure to greatly facilitate his task as an observer.

The optical instruments available to him were first-rate marine glasses which had been specially made for the voyage. They should have brought the Moon to within an apparent distance of less than a thousand leagues from the Earth. But now, at around three in the morning, at an actual distance that did not exceed a hundred and twenty kilometres and in a zone where there was no atmosphere to interfere with their working, these instruments could bring the lunar surface to less than 1,500 metres.

11

FANCY AND FACT

'HAVE you ever seen the Moon?' a teacher once sarcastically asked one of his students.*

'No, sir,' replied the pupil even more sarcastically, 'but I can say that I have certainly heard of it.'

Strictly speaking, the boy's witty reply could well be made by the vast majority of the inhabitants of our sublunary world. How many of us have heard of the Moon but never seen it . . . at least not through the eye-piece of a marine glass or a telescope? How many have never looked closely at a map of their satellite?

But anyone who looks at a two-sphere selenographic map is immediately struck by one particular.

Contrary to the manner in which both the Earth and Mars are configured, the continents of the Moon occupy mainly the southern hemisphere of its globe. Its continents do not have the distinct boundary lines which are so clearly marked, so definite and so typical in the case of South America, Africa, and the Indian peninsula. Its coasts, angular, unpredictable, and deeply ragged, have a wealth of bays and jutting headlands. They readily call to mind the clutter and jumble of the Sunda Islands, where the land is excessively broken. If there ever was any navigation on the surface of the Moon, it must have been a singularly difficult and dangerous business, and our sympathies go out to the Selenite sailors and hydrographers, the latter as they surveyed those tormented coastlines and the former when they faced the perils of making landfall.

It will also be noted that on the lunar orb, the South Pole is much more continental than the North Pole. The latter has only a small land cap and is separated from the other continents by vast seas. In the south, land masses cover the hemisphere almost completely. It may therefore be possible that the Selenites have already planted their flag on one of the two poles whereas explorers like Franklin, Ross, Kane, Dumont d'Urville, and Lambert have yet to reach the equivalent pole of the terrestrial globe, on which the foot of man has yet to tread.

As to islands, there are many on the Moon's surface. Virtually all are either oblong in shape or perfectly round as though drawn with a pair of compasses, and they appear lined up as a gigantic archipelago rather like the delightful group of islands that lie between Greece and Asia Minor, which, in times gone by, mythology filled with its most alluring legends. The names of Naxos, Tenedos, Milos, and Karpathos* spring unbidden from the memory and the eye searches in vain for a sight of the ships of Ulysses or the clipper of the Argonauts. It was at the very least exactly what Michel Ardan wanted: what he saw marked on the map was a Greek archipelago. To his less fancifully-minded companions, the look of those shorelines recalled the broken landscapes of New Brunswick or Nova Scotia. And where the Frenchman found traces of the heroes òf fable, the Americans sought locations suitable for setting up trading posts with a view to promoting lunar business and industry.

To complete our description of the continental region of the Moon, a few words on its orographic features are in order. The eye clearly makes out the mountain ranges, the individual peaks, the basins and the rilles. All the Moon's high ground is included in this hemisphere, which is extraordinarily rugged. It is a kind of vast Switzerland, an endless Norway where everything has been shaped by plutonic activity. Its surface, so deeply ridged and uneven, is the product of successive contractions of the lunar crust which occurred when the Moon was in the process of formation. The lunar disc is well suited to the study of large-scale geological phenomena. According to the observations of certain astronomers, its surface, although much older than the surface of the Earth, has remained younger. For there are no streams of water there to erode the original contours and whose mounting power produces a generalized process of levelling. Nor is there any air with its capacity for blasting the face of mountains. There, volcanic activity, free of igneous and aqueous interference, can be observed in its pure, native forms. It is the Earth as it was before the tides of the seas and currents of the air choked it with layers of sediment.

Having meandered over these vast continents, the eye is then drawn to the seas, which are vaster still. Not only do their spatial structures, locations, and appearance recall those of our terrestrial oceans but in addition, as is also the case on Earth, the Moon's seas occupy the greater part of the surface of the globe. And yet they are not spaces filled with liquid but plains whose physical nature our voyagers hoped soon to analyse.

Astronomers, it must be said, have given these supposed 'seas' names which are, to say the least, bizarre but which science has respected until now. Michel Ardan was quite right when he compared their lunar *mappa mundi* to the 'Map of Love'* drawn by some new Mme de Scudéry or a modern Cyrano de Bergerac.

'Except,' he added, 'that it isn't a map of the emotions as in the seventeenth century but a map of reality, very clearly setting it out in two parts, one feminine and the other masculine. The right hemisphere belongs to women; the left, to men.'

And when he spoke in these terms, Michel caused his two matter-of-fact companions to shrug their shoulders. Barbicane and Nicholl examined the map of the Moon from a standpoint completely at odds with that of their whimsical friend. However, that whimsical friend was not entirely wrong—as the reader may judge.

In the left hemisphere is the expanse of the 'Sea of Clouds' in which human reason has so often been shipwrecked. Not far distant from it is the 'Sea of Rains' fed by all the frets and strains of life. Close by is the 'Sea of Storms' where man does battle with his passions, that are all too often victorious. Then, worn down by stratagems, betrayals, perfidies, and all the panoply of terrestrial misery, what does he find at the end of his life's course? That vast 'Sea of Humours' which is barely sweetened by a few drops of the 'Gulf of Dew'! Clouds, rains, storms, humours—does the life of man offer anything else; is it not contained in these four words?

The right hemisphere, 'dedicated to the fairer sex', has smaller seas, with revealing names that punctuate every stage of a woman's life. Here is the 'Sea of Serenity' on which young girls glide and the 'Lake of Dreams' in which they see reflections of future bliss! Next comes the 'Sea of Nectar' with its tender tides and loving breezes! Here are the 'Sea of Fruitfulness', the 'Sea of Crises', and the 'Sea of Vapours' which are perchance too restricted in size, and finally, the vast 'Sea of Tranquillity' which swallows up all false passions, all unrealized dreams, all unslaked desires, whose waters flow peacefully into the 'Lake of Death'!

Such a strange concatenation of names! Such an unlikely division of the two hemispheres of the Moon, joined together as man and woman are joined and forming a single sphere of life in outer space! So was the fanciful mind of Michel not correct in his interpretation of this fantasy world evoked by those astronomers of old?

But whereas his imagination 'sailed the high seas', his sober companions took a more geographical view. They began to get to know this new world by heart. They measured its angles and diameters.

For Barbicane and Nicholl, the Sea of Clouds was an immense land basin which featured a handful of circular mountains and covered a large part of the western section of the southern hemisphere. It occupied 184,000 square leagues and its centre was located at latitude 15° south and longitude 20° west. The 'Ocean of Storms', *Oceanus Procellarum*, the biggest plain on the lunar disc, extended over an area of 328,000 square leagues, its centre being located at latitude 10° north and longitude 45° east. From its vastness rose Kepler and Aristarchus, two superb, shining mountains.

More northerly and separated from the Sea of Clouds by high sierras, was the Sea of Rains, the *Mare Imbrium*, whose mid-point is at latitude 35° north and longitude 20° east; it was more or less circular in shape and covered 193,000 square leagues. Not far away, the Sea of Humours, the *Mare Humorum*, a small depression of just 4,200 square leagues, was situated at latitude 25° south and longitude 40° east. Finally, three further gulfs figured on the shores of this hemisphere: the Torrid Gulf, the Gulf of Dew, and the Gulf of the Rainbows, three small *mares* surrounded by chains of high mountains.

The 'female' hemisphere, more unpredictable by nature, was characterized by smaller and more numerous *mares*. Northwards were *Mare Frigoris*, the Sea of Cold, at latitude 55° north and longitude 0°, with an area of 76,000 square leagues, and bordered by the Lake of Death and the Lake of Dreams; the *Mare Serenitatis*, the Sea of Serenity, at latitude 25° north and longitude 20° west, with a surface of 86,000 square leagues; the *Mare Crisium*, the Sea of Crises, at latitude 17° north and longitude 55° west, with its rounded boundaries clearly delineated and occupying 40,000 square leagues, a second Caspian Sea bounded by a ring of mountains. Then at the Equator, at latitude 5° north and longitude 25° west, sat the *Mare Tranquillitatis*, the Sea of Tranquillity, extending over 121,500 square leagues; to the south, this Sea communicates with the *Mare Nectar*, the Nectar Sea, an expanse of 8,800 square leagues at latitude 15° south and longitude 35° west; and, to the east, it communicates with the *Mare Fecunditatis*, the Sea of Fruitfulness, which is the largest sea in this hemisphere, at 219,300 square leagues, at latitude 3° south and longitude 50° west. Finally, two further seas were also discernible, one in the far north and the other in the far south: the *Mare Humboldtianum*, the Sea of Humboldt, with an area of 6,500 square leagues, and the *Mare Australe*, or Southern Sea. which stretches over 26,000 square miles.

The centre of the lunar disc, at the intersection of the Equator and the prime meridian, is the site of the *Sinus Medii*, the Middle Bay, and forms a kind of hyphenation between the two hemispheres.

It was thus that the still visible surface of the Earth's satellite was envisioned by Nicholl and Barbicane. When they added together their various measurements, they were able to show that the total area of the hemispherical disc ran to 4,728,000 square leagues, of which 3,317,600 were accounted for by volcanoes, mountain ranges, cirques, islands, in short everything deemed to form the solid ground of the Moon, and 1,410,400 by the seas, lakes, marshes, which could be reckoned to constitute its liquid substance. All that, of course, was a matter of complete indifference to the good Michel.

As is now patently obvious, the Moon is in this way thirteen and a half times smaller than the Earth. However, selenographers have already counted 50,000 craters on its disc. Its surface is thus littered with tumours and scarred by crevasses, the nearest thing there is to a sieve, and it amply justifies the unpoetic depiction of it by the British as 'green cheese'.

Michel Ardan gave a start of horror when Barbicane used this unflattering description.

'So that', he exclaimed, 'is how, in our nineteenth century, the Anglo–Saxons speak of fair Diana, blond Phoebe, gracious Isis, the charming Astarte, Queen of the Night, daughter of Latona and Jupiter and sister to Apollo of the Golden Hair!'

12

OROGRAPHIC NOTES

THE projectile's trajectory, as has been noted above, was taking it towards the northern hemisphere of the Moon. The voyagers were a long way off the central point at which they would have landed if they had not been irremediably knocked off course.

It was now half past midnight. Barbicane estimated their present distance from the surface was 1,400 kilometres, slightly more than the length of the Moon's radius. This would decrease as they approached the North Pole. The craft was then not above the Equator, but just crossing the tenth parallel and from this latitude, having first carefully checked their course against the map all the way to the Pole, Barbicane and his two companions were thus able to observe the Moon in the very best conditions.

Indeed, by using their marine glasses, the distance of 1,400 kilometres was brought down to only fourteen, or four and a half leagues. The telescope located in the Rockies brought the Moon nearer, but the Earth's atmosphere considerably reduced its optical effectiveness. So Barbicane, stationed in his projectile, with his glass to his eye, was able to make out several features which are virtually inaccessible to terrestrial-based observers.

'Friends,' the President said gravely, 'I do not know where we are bound, I do not know if we shall ever see our terrestrial home again. Nevertheless, let us proceed as if our work shall one day be of use to our fellow men. Let us keep our minds free of all other concerns. We are astronomers. This craft is an outpost of the Cambridge Observatory transported into space. So let us observe.'

This said, work began with every attention to detail, producing an accurate record of various aspects of the Moon at the changing distances between the projectile and the lunar globe.

At the same time, when the craft reached the latitude of the tenth parallel north, it seemed to be closely following the twentieth degree of longitude east.

At this point an important comment must be made regarding the map they were using for their observations. In selenographic charts where, because of the way telescopes invert the images of what they see, the south is at the top and the north at the bottom, it would seem natural to assume that the east should be on the observer's left and the west on the right. However, that is not the case. If the map were held upside down and showed the Moon as we see it, the east would be on the left and the west on the right, which is the opposite of what happens with terrestrial maps. The explanation of this anomaly is as follows. Observers in the northern hemisphere—in Europe, say—see the Moon in the south in relation to their position. When they observe it, they have their backs turned to the north, which is the opposite of their position when they are looking at a terrestrial map. Now, since their back is turned to the north, the east is now on their left and west

is to their right. In the case of observers based in the southern hemisphere, in Patagonia for instance, the western side of the Moon would
be automatically on their left and its eastern side on their right, since
the south is behind them.*

That is the reason for the apparent inversion of the two cardinal
points of the compass, and it should be borne in mind when listening
to President Barbicane's observation.

With the help of Beer and Mädler's *Mappa selenographica*, the
voyagers would unhesitatingly recognize the part of the lunar disc
framed within the field of their telescope.

'What are you seeing now?' asked Michel.

'The northern end of the Sea of Clouds,' replied Barbicane. 'We
are too far away to make out exactly what it is. Are these plains just dry
sand as the early astronomers claimed? Are they vast forests, which is
the view of Monsieur Warren de la Rue, who reckons that the Moon
has an atmosphere which, though low-lying, is dense. This we shall
see for ourselves in due course. For we must not assert anything until
we are in a position to know it is true.

The outline of the Sea of Clouds is drawn very vaguely on maps.
It is assumed that this enormous plain is strewn with blocks of lava
from the volcanoes Ptolemy, Purbach, and Arzachel on its right side,
But the projectile was still advancing and getting visibly nearer and
soon the peaks bordering this sea at its western end came into view.
Ahead rose a mountain of dazzling beauty, its top seemingly lost in
a burst of solar light.

'This is . . . ?' asked Michel.

'Copernicus,' replied Barbicane.

'Then let's take a look at Copernicus.'

This peak, located at latitude 9° north and longitude 20° east,
reaches a height of 3,430 metres above the level of the Moon's surface.
It is visible from Earth and astronomers are able to study it without
difficulty, especially during the phase between the last quarter and the
New Moon, because then long shadows are cast from east to west and
allow its upper heights to be measured.

Copernicus is the largest hub of radiated solar effulgence on the
entire disc after Tycho, which is located in the southern hemisphere.
It stands alone, like a gigantic lighthouse, on this part of the Sea of
Clouds which borders upon the Sea of Storms, and lights with its
superb radiance two oceans at the same time. It makes a spectacle of

unequalled splendour as it sends forth long, luminous trails, especially brilliant when the Moon is full, which spread across and over the neighbouring sierras and finally fade into the Sea of Rains. At one in the morning, Earth time, the projectile, like a balloon carried up into outer space, looked down on this mountain in all its majesty.

Barbicane perfectly recognized its principal features. Copernicus is part of a series of ring-shaped mountains belonging to the first rank of the class of great cirques. Exactly as Kepler and Aristarchus stand over the Ocean of Storms, it looks at times like a bright spot shining through the ashy light and was at first mistaken for an active volcano. It is in fact an extinct volcano like all the others on this side of the Moon. Its defensive circumference had a diameter of about twenty-two leagues. Visible by telescope were traces of stratification caused by successive eruptions and the area surrounding it looked as if it was strewn with volcanic debris, of which some littered the inside of the crater.

Barbicane said: 'There are several types of these cirques, or basins, on the surface of the Moon, and it is easy to assign Copernicus to the radiant class. If we were closer we would see the cones bristling inside what once were so many fire-breathing mouths. A curious feature, and one which recurs without exception across the entire lunar disc, is that the inner surface of these cirques is significantly lower than the plain that surrounds them, which is the exact opposite of the form of craters on Earth. So it follows that the widespread curved shape of the bottom of these cirques would seem to point to a sphere with a diameter smaller than that of the Moon.'

'But what is the reason for this particular feature?' asked Nicholl.

'No one knows,' replied Barbicane.

'Still, the radiance is quite superb,' repeated Michel. 'I find it difficult to imagine that anyone could see a finer spectacle anywhere!'

'So what would you say,' said Barbicane, 'if the vagaries of our journey were to take us towards the southern hemisphere?'

'I should say that that would be all to the good!' said Michel Ardan.

At this moment, the projectile was passing vertically over the cirque. The raised boundaries of Copernicus formed an almost perfect circle and its steep surrounding walls were clearly visible. The voyagers even sighted a double ring-shaped basin. In all directions a greyish, wild-looking plain stretched away and on it areas of higher ground were marked by their yellow colouring. At the bottom of the cirque, as if kept neatly in a jewel case, two or three eruptive teeth sparkled briefly like two enormous, dazzling gems. To the north, the cirque's walls had been lowered by a sunken area which had probably once allowed access to the crater's interior.

As they moved across the surrounding plains, Barbicane was able to note a large number of not very high mountains and, among them, a small ring-shaped hill, named Gay-Lussac, which was twenty-three kilometres in breadth. Towards the south, the plain grew very flat, without a single protrusion or any sharp rises in the ground. On the other hand, until the surface to the north reached the point where it bordered the Ocean of Storms: it resembled a liquid agitated by a hurricane, but with its peaks and troughs looking like a series of waves which had suddenly been congealed in ice. Over the whole of this expanse and in every direction sped trails of light which converged on the summit of Copernicus. A few were thirty kilometres wide and of a length that could not be estimated.

Our voyagers fell to discussing the origins of these strange beams of light but, no more successful than terrestrial observers, they were unable to establish what they were.

'But why', asked Nicholl, 'is it not possible that they are simply spurs and shoulders of mountains which are reflecting the sun's light with particular intensity?'

'No, no,' said Barbicane, 'for if that were the case, when certain lunar conditions applied, those shoulders and flanks of mountains would cast shadows. But as you see, they are not casting any.'

It was true, for these shafts of light appear only when the sun is in opposition to the Moon and disappear when the sun's rays become oblique.

'But what reasons have been dreamed up to explain these trails of light?' asked Michel. 'Because I cannot believe that experts are ever short of explanations!'

'Indeed,' replied Barbicane, 'Herschel did give an opinion but he was not prepared to claim it was the correct one.'

'Never mind that. What was his opinion?'

'He thought these trails of light might be flows of cold lava which shone brightly whenever the sun shone on them in the usual way. It could be true but it is extremely uncertain. In any case, if we pass closer to Tycho, we will be better placed to establish the cause of this particular radiance.'

'Do you know what that plain seen from our present altitude looks like?' said Michel.

'No,' answered Nicholl.

'With all those lumps of lava shaped like spindles, it resembles an immense set of spillikins that have been dropped on the floor. All we'd need is a hook and we'd be able to haul them in one by one.'

'Do be serious,' said Barbicane.

'Let's be really serious,' said Michel calmly, 'and instead of spillikins, let's say bones. If we do, that plain would be an immense boneyard in which repose the mortal remains of a thousand defunct generations. Do you prefer this more sobering comparison?'

'One is as good as the other,' said Barbicane.

'Dammit, you are a hard man to please.'

'Not really, Michel,' resumed the matter-of-fact Barbicane. 'It does not matter much what it looks like since we have no idea what it is.'

'Well said!' exclaimed Michel. 'That will teach me not to argue with brainboxes!'

Meanwhile, the projectile was proceeding at a more or less even speed as it travelled around the lunar disc. The voyagers, as will be easily imagined, never thought once about getting some rest. Every minute renewed the landscape, which fled away below them as they watched it. At around one in the morning, they glimpsed the top of another mountain. Barbicane consulted the map and identified it as Eratosthenes.

It was a ring-shaped mountain some 4,500 metres high, one of the satellite's very numerous cirques. In this context, Barbicane reminded his companions of the odd opinion of Kepler on the formation of these cirques. According to the famous mathematician, the crater-shaped depressions must have been dug out by the hand of man.

'For what purpose?' asked Nicholl.

'To a very natural purpose,' replied Barbicane. 'The Selenites might well have embarked on such vast works and dug these huge holes in which they could seek refuge and shelter from the sun which beats down on them for fifteen consecutive days.'

'No fools, those Selenites,' said Michel.

'It's a strange idea,' agreed Nicholl. 'Still, Kepler probably did not know how big these cirques were, because digging them out would have been a job for giants and quite unsuitable for Selenites.'

'Why is that, if weight on the Moon's surface is six times less than it is on Earth?' asked Michel.

'But what if Selenites are six times smaller?' asked Nicholl.

'And what if there aren't any Selenites anyway?' added Barbicane, thus ending the discussion.

Soon Eratosthenes disappeared below the horizon before the projectile could get near enough to allow accurate observations of it to be made. The mountain separated the Apennines from the Carpathians.

In lunar orography, several ranges of mountains have been recorded. They are mainly distributed across the northern hemisphere. However, there are a few which occupy certain parts of the southern hemisphere.

The following is a list of the highest peaks in these various mountain ranges, laid out from south to north, with their latitudes and heights:

Montes	Doerfel	84°	S	7,603 metres
–	Leibnitz	65°	–	7,600
–	Rook	20° to 30°	–	1,600
–	Altai	17° to 28	–	4,047
–	Cordilleras	10° to 20°	–	3,898
–	Pyrenees	8° to 18°	–	3,631
–	Ural	5° to 13°	–	838
–	Alembert	4° to 10°	–	5,847
–	Hoemus	8° to 21°	N	2,021
–	Karpathian	15° to 19°	–	1,939
–	Apennine	14° to 27°	–	5,501
–	Taurus	21° to 28°	–	2,746
–	Ripheus	25° to 33°	–	4,171
–	Hercynii	17° to 33°	–	1,170
–	Caucasus	32° to 41°	–	5,567
–	Alps	42° to 49°	–	3,617*

Of these various ranges, the longest are the Apennines, which extend over a hundred and fifty leagues, though this is less than the length of the largest of the Earth's great orographic creations. The Apennines skirt the eastern shore of the Sea of Rains and continue northwards via the Carpathians, which are about a hundred leagues long.

The voyagers were able to manage only a glimpse of the summits of the Apennines, which run from longitude 10° west to longitude

16° east; but they could see the whole of the chain of the Carpathians stretching away from the eighteenth to the twentieth degrees of longitude east, and were able to make out the detail of the configuration of their contours.

One hypothesis seemed plausible to them. Seeing the Carpathians with their intermittent rounded forms and half-open circular hollows in their sides, they concluded that it had once formed a sequence of large cirques. The links of that mountain chain must once have been partly broken by some huge upheaval caused by the Sea of Rains. The Carpathians would then have looked like what the cirques of Purbach, Arzachel, and Ptolemy would become if some giant cataclysm should ever demolish their eastern counterforts and turned them too into a continuous chain. They averaged 3,200 in height, a figure comparable to certain points, like the Port de Pinède in the Pyrenees. Their southern slopes fell away sharply towards the vast Sea of Rains.

At around two in the morning, Barbicane found they were on a level with the twentieth lunar parallel, not far from the small mountain, altitude 1,559 metres, which is known as Pythias. The distance from the projectile to the Moon was then no more than 1,200 kilometres, which, with the aid of a telescope, was reduced to two and a half leagues.

The voyagers were now gazing down at the *Mare Imbrium*, which ran away before them like a vast depression whose detailed topography still eluded them. Closer to their position, to the left, stood Mount Lambert, estimated height 1,813 metres, and further away, at the very edge of the Ocean of Storms and at latitude 23° north and longitude 29° east, glowed the glittering mountain of Euler. This hill, which rises to a height of just 1,815 metres above the Moon's surface, had been the subject of an interesting study by the astronomer Shroeter, who set out to find the origin of the Mountains of the Moon. He wondered if the volume of the crater was always pretty much the same as that of the surrounding mountainsides. He concluded that such a relationship was indeed general and he concluded that a single eruption of volcanic material had sufficed to create those ramparts, since subsequent eruptions would obviously have changed this correlation. Euler alone did not obey this general law, requiring several successive eruptions, since the volume of its cavity was twice that of the ring surrounding it.

Such hypotheses were permitted to observers on Earth who were limited by having to work with imperfect instruments. But Barbicane

was no longer prepared to make do with such aids and seeing that
his projectile was now steadily approaching the rim of the lunar
disc, he had not abandoned hope, even if he himself would never
stand on its surface, of at least uncovering the secrets of its original
formation.

13

LUNAR LANDSCAPES

AT half past two in the morning, the projectile was standing off the
thirtieth lunar parallel at a distance of 1,000 kilometres, reduced to
ten by the craft's optical instruments. It still seemed impossible that
they would ever set down at any point of the Moon's disc. Their craft's
speed of travel was relatively slow, and President Barbicane simply
could not understand it. At this distance from the Moon, it ought to
have been considerably greater so that it could maintain its position
against the pull of attraction. There was therefore some phenomenon
at work here the cause of which still escaped him. Moreover, time was
running out if he was going to find the reason for it. Meanwhile, the
mountains of the Moon were speeding by as the voyagers gazed down
on them, reluctant to miss even the smallest detail.

Seen through the eye-pieces of their viewing glasses, the disc
appeared to be about two and a half leagues away. What would an
aeronaut at this height above the Earth be able to see of its surface? It
is difficult to say, for no ascent to date has exceeded 8,000 metres.*

The following, however, is an exact description of what Barbicane
and his companions saw from that height.

There appeared, in wide swathes, a broad range of colours on the
Moon's disc. Selenographers do not agree about the nature of these
colours. They are varied and sharply delineated. Julius Schmidt
reckons that if the oceans of the Earth were dry, a Selenite observer
would not be able to see, between the oceans and plains of our globe,
any differences as clearly marked as those which a terrestrial observer
finds on the Moon. According to him, the colour most generally
found on the vast lunar plains known as 'seas' is dark grey with hints
of green and brown. Some of the largest craters are also coloured in
the same way.

Barbicane was aware of the German selenographer's views, which were also shared by Beer and Mädler. He noted that observation fully endorsed their conclusion against a number of other astronomers who refused to admit any coloration except grey on the surface of the Moon. In some open areas, the colour green was vividly present and of the same shade as that which according to Julius Schmidt characterizes the Sea of Clouds and the Sea of Humours. Barbicane also observed a number of large craters with no internal cones which gave off a bluish tinge similar to reflections given off by freshly polished steel plate. These colours were inherent in the lunar disc and not the result, as certain astronomers have insisted, of imperfections in the eye-pieces of telescopes or of interference from the Earth's atmosphere. For Barbicane, there was no doubt on this score. He was looking through the void and could not therefore be influenced by optical illusions. He considered that henceforth the various colours had been formally adopted by science. Were those shades of green due to living tropical vegetation which flourished in a low-lying, dense atmosphere? He was not yet in a position to offer an opinion.

Further along, he caught sight of a reddish colour which stood out against the rest. A similar shade had already been seen inside an isolated cirque known as Lichtenberg Crater which is located near the Hercynian Mountains on the edge of the Moon, but he was unable to say exactly what it was.

He was no more successful when confronted by another singular feature of the lunar disc for which he was equally unable to give a reasonable explanation. This particular feature arose as follows.

Michel Ardan was observing next to the President when he noticed a series of long white lines brightly lit by the direct rays of the sun. They were a succession of luminous furrows very different from the radiance which a while previously had been given off by Copernicus. These lines ran parallel to each other.

Michel, with his customary aplomb, coolly remarked:

'Look! Ploughed fields!'

'Ploughed fields?' said Nicholl, with a dubious shrug.

'Marks of ploughs at any rate,' replied Michel Ardan. 'But these Selenites must be mighty workers, and what enormous oxen they must harness to their ploughs to make such furrows!'

'They are not furrows,' said Barbicane, 'they are grooves.'

'All right, grooves then,' Michel replied mildly. 'Only, what does science mean by grooves?'

Barbicane immediately told his companion all he knew about lunar grooves. He knew that such 'furrows' had been observed in all non-mountainous regions of the Moon's disc; that these furrows, single in most cases, were forty or fifty leagues long; that their width varied between a thousand and fifteen hundred metres; and that their banked-up sides were exactly parallel. But he knew no more than that, and nothing of their formation nor of their nature.

Putting his glass to his eye, Barbicane examined the grooves very closely. He noticed that their sides were in fact steeply sloped, forming long parallel ramparts. It took only a little imagination to concede that they must indicate long lines of fortification raised by Selenite engineers.

Of the various grooves, some were absolutely undeviating, as straight as a bow-string. Others were slightly curved though their walls remained parallel. The latter sometimes crisscrossed each other while the former cut straight through craters. Here, they passed over ordinary calderas such as Posidonius or Petavius; there they zigzagged across seas such as the Sea of Serenity.

These naturally occurring furrows could not but rouse the imagination of Earth-bound astronomers. The earliest observations failed to detect these marks altogether. Hevelius, Cassini, La Hire, Herschel . . . none had been aware of them. It was Schröter in 1789 who first drew the furrows to the attention of science. Others followed who studied them, including Pastorff, Gruithuysen, Beer and Mädler. Today, their number has risen to seventy.* But if they have been counted, no one has yet determined what they are. They are not fortifications, that much is clear, nor are they the dried-up beds of ancient rivers because, on the one hand, such quantities of water as exist on the surface of the Moon could never have gouged out such overflow drain-aways and, on the other, the furrows often run across craters situated at high altitudes.

Yet it must be noted that Michel Ardan now came up with an idea and that, unwittingly, his thinking on the subject put him close to that of Julius Schmidt.

'Why', he asked, 'should these inexplicable phenomena not be just manifestations of vegetation?'

'In what way?' Barbicane asked sharply.

'No need to get excited, Mr President,' replied Michel. 'Could it not be that those darker borders which line them are perhaps rows of deliberately planted trees?'

'So you think your vegetation idea is correct?'

'Look,' retorted Michel Ardan, 'I am only trying to explain what you scientific fellows cannot explain at all! At least my hypothesis has the merit of suggesting a reason why those cuts or channels disappear or seem to disappear at such regular intervals.'

'And what is the reason you propose?'

'My reason is that these trees are invisible when they lose their leaves and become visible when they get them back.'

'Your explanation is ingenious, my friend, but it will not do.'

'Why not?'

'Because there are no so-called seasons on the surface of the Moon and because, therefore, the manifestations of vegetation you spoke of simply cannot happen down there.'

It was true. The slight angle of the Moon's axis ensures that the sun remains at a more or less constant height at every latitude. North of the equatorial regions, the sun sits almost invariably at the zenith and scarcely ever moves beyond the limit of the horizon in both polar areas. Therefore, taking region by region, each part has either constant winter or spring or summer or autumn, as also occurs on the planet Jupiter, whose axis is also slightly tilted as it orbits the sun.

So what therefore is the origin of these furrow or channels? That is a question difficult to answer. They are certainly later than the date at which the craters and cirques were formed, for a number pass across them or break through their circular walls. It may therefore be that at around the time of the last geological ages, they were splits or cracks caused by nothing more than the expansion of natural forces.

Meanwhile, the projectile had now crept up to the fortieth degree of lunar latitude, at a distance from the surface which could not have exceeded 800 kilometres. Objects now appeared in the field of glasses and telescopes as though they were only two leagues away. At this point, beneath the feet of the observers and rising to a height of 500 metres, was Mount Helicon, and then, to their left, was the more modestly proportioned, rounded upland which contained that part of the Sea of Rains which is known as the Gulf, or Bay, of Rainbows.

The Earth's atmosphere would need to be seventy times clearer than it is to allow terrestrial astronomers to make optimal observations of the surface of the Moon. But in the vacuum through which the projectile was moving, no veil of mist came between the eye of the observer and the object observed. Moreover, Barbicane was aware that he had been brought closer to his subject than had been possible with the most powerful telescopes—that of John Ross or even the one sited in the Rocky Mountains. He had therefore been handed the luxury of perfect conditions in which to resolve the ultimate question of the inhabitability or otherwise of the Moon. Yet, the answer still eluded him. All he could see were the empty deserts of the vast plains and, to the north, arid mountains. Not one structure to indicate the hand of man; no ruin to mark his passage; no group of animals to suggest that there was life here even if only at a lower level. Nowhere was there movement, nowhere any sign of vegetation. Of the three kingdoms which coexist on planet Earth, only one was represented on its lunar satellite: the mineral.

'Well, there it is,' said Michel Ardan, not a little deflated. 'So there's no one about?'

'No,' said Nicholl, 'nothing so far. Not a single man, not an animal, not a tree. Still, the atmosphere may have taken refuge in holes in the ground, inside cirques, or even on the reverse side of the Moon, so maybe it's too early to tell.'

'In addition to which,' said Barbicane, 'even for anyone with perfect vision, a man is not visible if he is more than seven kilometres away. So if there are any Selenites, they may be able to see our projectile, but we can't see them.'

At around four in the morning, when they were at the fiftieth parallel, their distance from the surface had fallen to 600 kilometres. On their left was a line of freakishly shaped mountains which were bathed in full sunlight. To the right, on the contrary, was a deep hole, like some huge, fathomless, dark pit which had been sunk into the lunar floor.

This was the Black Lake, otherwise known as Plato, a deep, steep-sided, half-open, hollow which may be conveniently studied from Earth during the period between the last quarter and the New Moon, when the shadows lie from west to east.

This solid black coloration is rarely found on the Moon's surface. To date, it has been confirmed only in the depths of Endymion, a cirque located east of the Sea of Cold in the northern hemisphere, and at the bottom of the Grimaldi cirque on the Equator, near the eastern edge of the satellite.

Plato is a ring-shaped mountain situated at latitude 51° north and longitude 9° east. Its cirque measures ninety-two kilometres by sixty-one. Barbicane regretted that they were not passing directly over its vast mouth. Here was a chasm that could be probed and perhaps some mysterious lunar phenomenon might be revealed. But the onward march of the projectile could not be slowed. It was a setback which had to be endured. Being shut up inside their manned craft, they could no more steer the projectile than anyone can manoeuvre an air balloon.

When it got to about five o'clock, they at last cleared the northern limit of the Sea of Rains. The craters of La Condamine and Fontenelle rose on left and right respectively. This sector of the Moon's disc, starting at the sixtieth parallel, was completely filled with mountains. Telescopes brought it to within one league—less than the distance between the summit of Mont Blanc and the level of the sea. The entire region bristled with high peaks and cirques. The approach to the seventieth parallel was dominated by Philolaus, altitude 3,700 metres, topped by an elliptical crater seven leagues long and four wide.

At that point in time and seen from this distance, the lunar disc looked quite fantastical. The landscapes appeared to the eye in conditions very different from those obtaining on Earth but were also distinctly their inferiors.

Since the Moon has no atmosphere, the absence of a protective gaseous layer gives rise to certain effects which have already been pointed out. There is no twilight on its surface: night follows day and day follows night with the suddenness of a lamp which is turned on and off in complete darkness. There is no gradual transition from cold to hot and temperatures drop in an instant from boiling point to the general level of cold that exists throughout space.

Another consequence of the absence of air is that absolute darkness rules wherever the sun's rays do not reach. What is called diffused light on Earth—luminous matter held in suspension by the air—which is created by twilights and dawns and creates shadows and partial shadow and all the magic of *chiaroscuro*, does not exist on the Moon. The result is a brutality of contrasts which admits only two colours, white and black. If a Selenite shades his eyes against the power of the sun, the sky will look totally black to him and he will see the stars shine as brightly as they do on the darkest nights.

Judge, then, the impression produced by this strange spectacle on Barbicane and his two friends. Their eyes were bewildered. They were no longer able to judge the respective distances of the various levels and planes. A lunar landscape unrelieved by the softening effect of *chiaroscuro* could not be painted by a terrestrial landscape artist. It would come out as ink stains on a white page and noting more.

That view did not change even when the projectile, on reaching the eightieth parallel, was no further than a hundred kilometres from the Moon. Not even when, at five in the morning, it passed less than fifty kilometres from the Gioja crater, a distance which telescopes reduced to one eighth of a league. It seemed as if they could reach out a hand and touch the Moon. It seemed impossible that the projectile would not soon hit it even if it were only on its North Pole, whose gleaming backbone stood out starkly against the black of the sky.

Michel Ardan would have liked to open one of the porthole-panels and jump down onto the surface of the Moon—a drop of twelve leagues, a distance which he held to be of no account! A useless gesture, of course, for if the projectile did not land anywhere on the satellite, Michel would be moving at its speed and would not land there either.

Just then, at six in the morning, the lunar pole loomed up very closely. The disc had nothing more to show the voyagers except that one half, brilliantly lit, while the other vanished into shadow. Suddenly, the projectile crossed the line between intense light and pitch darkness, and was suddenly plunged into the blackest night.

14

THE NIGHT OF THREE HUNDRED AND FIFTY-FOUR AND A HALF HOURS

AT the moment when this phenomenon occurred so suddenly, the projectile was passing over the Moon's North Pole by a margin of less than fifty kilometres. A few seconds more and it was plunged into the absolute blackness of space. The transition happened so quickly, so abruptly, with no gradual dimming of luminescence, with no weakening of the light waves, that it was as if the Moon had been snuffed out by some powerful breath.

'The Moon's gone! It's just evaporated!', Michel Ardan cried in disbelief.

Indeed, there was no reflection now, no shadow. Nothing more was seen of the lunar disc which had been so brightly lit. The darkness was complete and appeared even more intense because of the gleaming stars. It was that 'blacker-than-black' of those lunar nights which last 354½ hours at every point on the disc, a long night which results from the equal motions of orbit and rotation, that is between the Moon's circling of the Earth and its turning on its own axis. The projectile, caught in the satellite's cone of shadow, was now no more exposed to the action of the sun's rays than any of the points on the Moon's invisible part.

Inside the craft, the darkness was thus complete. The voyagers could not see each other and this made it necessary to banish the darkness. However sparing Barbicane might wish to be with the gas, of which they had such a small reserve, he was forced to draw on it to supply an artificial glimmer, a profligate illumination, which the sun now refused to give him.

'Devil take the sun,' cried Michel Ardan, 'which is making us use up precious gas, instead of handing out its bright rays for nothing!'

'It's no good blaming the sun,' said Nicholl. 'It's not the sun's fault but the Moon's because it has inserted itself like a screen between us and it.'

'It is the sun's fault!' repeated Michel.

'No, it's the Moon's,' retorted Nicholl.

It was a pointless argument to which Barbicane put an end by saying:

'My friends, the sun is not to blame nor is the Moon. It's the projectile that's at fault, for instead of following its course rigorously it was carelessly deflected from it. Or to be fairer still, it was the fault of that accursed meteor which unpardonably knocked us off our original trajectory!'

'Right!' said Michel Ardan. 'Now that the matter is settled, let us have breakfast. After a full night of observing, we should take in some refreshment.'

The proposal met with no opposition. In a matter of minutes, Michel had prepared a meal. But they ate dutifully, they drank without toasting anyone or anything and without raising a cheer. The bold wayfarers, redirected into dark space and without their customary escort of rays, felt a vague sense of anxiety growing in their hearts. The 'savage' shade, so beloved of Victor Hugo,* gripped them on all sides.

However, they talked for much of the interminable night that lasts 354½ hours, or practically a fortnight, and which the laws of physics have imposed on the inhabitants of the Moon. Barbicane gave his friends some instruction in the causes and consequences of this curious phenomenon.

'Curious indeed,' he began, 'for if each of the Moon's hemispheres is denied light from the sun for two weeks, the one currently passing beneath us is unable to enjoy a view of the brightly lit Earth during the long night. In short, there is never a 'moon'—by which I mean our planet—for one side of the lunar orb. Now, if the same arrangement applied to Earth and if, for instance, Europe never saw the Moon and it was never visible at all except at the antipodes, just imagine how amazed a European would be when he landed in Australia!'

'People would go all the way there just to see the Moon!' said Michel.

'Well,' went on Barbicane, 'that same amazement would be felt by Selenites who lived on the other side of the Moon, the one that is continuously invisible to our fellow creatures on Earth.'

'And which we would have seen,' added Nicholl, 'if we had arrived here a fortnight later when there was a new Moon.'

'Nevertheless,' Barbicane continued, 'I would add that anyone living on the side that is visible is wonderfully favoured by Nature over his fellows who inhabit the side that is not visible. The latter, as you can see, must live through nights that are 354½ hours long, when there is not a single ray to relieve the darkness. But the former, on the contrary, when the sun which has been lighting him continuously for two weeks sinks below the horizon, will see rising out of the opposite horizon a radiant sphere. It is the Earth, thirteen times bigger than the Moon which is so familiar to us; the Earth, which expands until it has a diameter of two degrees and gives off light thirteen times brighter, undimmed here by any atmosphere; the Earth, which disappears only when the sun in turn reappears!'

'Eloquently put,' declared Michel Ardan, 'but perhaps a trifle academic.'

'It follows,' resumed Barbicane without batting an eyelid, 'that the Moon's visible face must be a most pleasant place to live on, because it is perpetually turned to the sun when the Moon is full, or to the Earth when that body is new.'

'But,' said Nicholl, 'against that advantage must be set the intolerable heat which comes with the sunlight.'

'In that respect, that disadvantage is the same for both its sides because the light from the Earth, being reflected, has no heat in it. But the face we do not see is even more tested by the heat than the face we do see. I say this for your benefit, Nicholl, because Michel will probably not understand.'

'Oh thanks very much,' said Michel.

'Actually,' Barbicane went on, 'when the invisible face is receiving both light and heat from the sun, it is because the Moon is new, that is, in conjunction, which means that it is placed between the sun and the Earth. Therefore, given the place it occupies in opposition when it is full, it is nearer to the sun by double its distance from Earth. Now, that latter distance may be estimated as one two-hundredth of the distance between the Earth and the sun,* or in round figures, 200,000 leagues. So when this invisible face is getting its light from the sun, it is 200,000 leagues closer to it.'

'Absolutely right,' said Nicholl.

'On the other hand . . .' said Barbicane.

'One moment,' broke in Michel, interrupting his grave companion.

'What is it?'

'I would very much like to continue the explanation myself.'

'Why?'

'To show that I do understand.'

'Very well,' said Barbicane with a smile.

'On the other hand,' said Michel, imitating the tone of voice and gestures of President Barbicane, 'on the other hand, when the visible face of Moon is full it, is lit by the sun, that is to say that it is positioned opposite the sun relative to the Earth. The distance between it and the radiant sun is therefore increased, in round figures, by 200,000 leagues and the heat it receives must be slightly less.'

'Well said!' cried Barbicane. 'You know, Michel, for an artist you are really quite bright.'

'True,' Michel replied casually. 'And we denizens of the Boulevard des Italiens* are all like that.'

Barbicane solemnly shook the hand of his good-humoured young friend then continued to expatiate on the various advantages that were enjoyed by the inhabitants of the visible face.

Amongst others, he mentioned the observation of solar eclipses which are exclusive to this side of the lunar disc because, if they are to occur, the Moon must be in opposition. These eclipses, caused when the Earth lines up between the Moon and the sun, can last for up to two hours, during which time, on account of the light refracted by its atmosphere, the Earth's globe can appear only as a black spot on the sun.

'So there you have a hemisphere,' said Nicholl, 'an invisible hemisphere that is very badly shared and very badly served by nature!'

'Yes,' replied Barbicane, 'but not entirely so. In fact, through a given movement of oscillation around its centre, the Moon tilts slightly more than half its disc towards the Earth.* It is like a pendulum whose centre of gravity lies towards the Earth's globe and swings regularly. Hence the oscillation I mentioned. Its rotatory movement around its own axis proceeds at a uniform speed, while its motion of translation as it follows an elliptical orbit around the Earth* does not. In perigee, the speed of orbital movement is greater and the Moon displays part of its western edge. At apogee, the speed of rotation is on the contrary greater and what is shown then is part of the eastern edge. At different times, the tilting reaches about eight degrees, to either the west or the east. The upshot is that out of a thousand parts, the Moon lets only 569 be seen.'

'No matter,' said Michel Ardan, 'if we ever become citizens of the Moon, we shall live in the visible part. I like the light!'

'Unless,' replied Nicholl, 'the atmosphere has condensed on the other side, as some astronomers think.'

'Ah yes,' Michel replied thoughtfully. 'That's a consideration!'

Meanwhile, with breakfast over, the observers returned to their posts.

They tried to see out of the black viewing ports, extinguishing the light inside the projectile. Not an atom of light passed through the blackness.

Barbicane was wrestling with one inexplicable fact. How, after passing so close to the Moon—at about fifty kilometres distance—why had the projectile not been pulled down onto it? If it had been travelling at high speed, he would have understood why there had been no landing. But at their relatively low velocity, the craft's resistance to lunar gravity was not explicable. Had the projectile been subjected to some external influence? Had some heavenly body or other kept it up in the ether? It was obvious that it would not now reach any part of the Moon. So where was it going? Was it moving away from or towards its surface? Was it being carried away into the profound night of infinity? How could they tell? How could they chart their movement surrounded as they were by blackness? All these questions nagged at Barbicane, who, however, was quite unable to find answers to any of therm.

Of course, the invisible heavenly body in question was perhaps there, just a few miles off, but neither he nor his companions could see it. Sounds might have been coming from its surface, but they could not hear them:* there was no air, which carries sound, to convey the groans of the Moon, which is depicted in Arabic legend as 'a man already partly turned to stone but still a-quivering'!

It was all enough to try the temper of the most patient observer, as will be readily agreed. It was precisely this unknown half of the Moon which was eluding their scrutiny! Two weeks earlier or two weeks later, this now hidden side had been or would be brilliantly lit by the sun's rays, whereas it was now shrouded in the darkest of dark nights. Where would the projectile be two weeks from now? Whither would it have been led by the vagaries of attraction? Who could say?

It is generally thought, on the basis of selenographic observations, that the constituent parts of the Moon's invisible hemisphere are identical to the visible hemisphere's. And indeed about one seventh* of it has been identified through the oscillating libration movements of which Barbicane had spoken. But the zones they had seen from a distance had been only plains and mountains, cirques and craters similar to those found on maps. It was thus possible to predict the same structural features on its reverse side, the same kind of world, arid and dead. Yet what if the atmosphere had migrated there? If, along with air, water had brought life to those regenerated continents? What if plants still grew there and animals populated those lands and seas? What if man, in such inhabitable regions, still lived there? So many questions to which it would have been interesting to have answers! What insights might have been extracted from studying that hemisphere! What a delight it would be to pause and let the eye wander over a world which no human had ever glimpsed!

It is not difficult therefore to understand the dismay of the voyagers, stranded as they were in the depths of blackest night. Observation of the lunar disc was out of the question—there were only the starry constellations to attract the eye now. And it must be admitted that no astronomer, not Faye nor Chacornac nor Secchi, ever found himself in circumstances so favourable for observing them.

Indeed, nothing could equal the splendour of that astral world bathed in limpid ether. Diamonds set in the vault of heaven emitted the most brilliant light. The eye spanned the firmament from the Southern Cross to the North Star,* two constellations which, within the next 12,000 years, and as a result of the precession of equinoxes, will lose their role as pole stars, one to Canopus in the southern hemisphere and the other to Vega in the northern hemisphere. The imagination was lost in that sublime infinity through which the projectile moved like a new star created by the hand of man. By a natural effect, these constellations shone with suffused intensity. They did not twinkle, for there was no atmosphere, and it is the intervention of the unevenly dense and variously humid layers of an atmosphere which causes the effect of scintillation. Those stars were soft eyes staring out of the pitch blackness in the absolute silence of space.

For some considerable time, the voyagers, unspeaking, looked out at this starry firmament in which the huge bulk of the Moon left a vast black hole. But eventually they were torn from their contemplation by the intensest cold which very quickly covered the interior of the craft with a thick layer of ice. For since the sun no longer shone directly on the projectile and warmed it, their craft had gradually lost the heat which had built up inside it. This heat, through radiation, had quickly evaporated into space and this had resulted in a substantial reduction in temperature. On contact with glass, the moisture inside the craft had thus turned to ice and ended all observation.

Nicholl looked at the thermometer and saw that it had fallen to seventeen degrees centigrade below zero. Therefore, despite the very good reasons for using it sparingly, Barbicane, though he had already turned to gas for light, was also forced to turn to it for heat. The low temperature of the projectile was no longer bearable. Its occupants would have frozen to death.

'We mustn't ever complain about how monotonous our journey has been!' remarked Michel Ardan. 'We have had huge variety at least of temperatures! There are times when we are blinded by light and bombarded with heat like Indians on the Pampas! At others we are surrounded by total darkness and enveloped in Arctic cold, like

Eskimos at the Pole! No, we really have no right to grumble about nature, for nature does what it does in our honour!'

'But,' asked Nicholl, 'what is the temperature outside?'

'It is exactly that of planetary space everywhere,' replied Barbicane.

'So,' Michel Ardan continued, 'would this not be a good moment to try the experiment we couldn't carry out when we were being drenched in scalding hot sunshine?'

'It's now or never,' said Barbicane, 'because we are in the right place to verify the temperature of space and check if the calculations made by Fourier and Pouillet are correct.'

'Either way, it's pretty cold,' replied Michel. 'Look! The humidity inside is condensing on the glass of the viewing panels. The temperature won't need to drop much more before the steam from our breath will be falling around us like snow!'

'Let's set up a thermometer,' said Barbicane.

Naturally, an ordinary thermometer would have supplied no information at all in the conditions to which it was going to be exposed. The mercury would simply have frozen solid in the reservoir because it ceases to be liquid in form at forty-two degrees below zero. But Barbicane had brought with him a discharge thermometer of the Walferdin type, which registers exceptionally low minimum temperatures.*

Before embarking on the experiment, this instrument was compared with an ordinary thermometer, and then Barbicane made ready to use it.

'How are we going to set about it?' asked Nicholl.

'Nothing simpler,' replied Michel, who was never at a loss for an idea. 'We open a porthole quickly; we put the thermometer outside; it follows the projectile with commendably uncomplaining docility; then a quarter of an hour later, we bring it back in.'

'How?' asked Barbicane. 'With your hand?'

'With my hand,' replied Michel.

'Well, my friend, don't risk it,' replied Barbicane. 'When you bring your hand back in, it would be nothing more than a frozen stump twisted out of shape by the cold!'

'Really?'

'You will feel a terrible burning sensation, the same as would be caused by a white-hot iron. For whether heat is removed brutally from our bodies or whether it is suddenly driven into it is one and the same. Besides, I am not at all sure that the objects we threw out of the projectile are still travelling with us.'

'Why not?' asked Nicholl.

'Because if we are passing through an atmosphere, however thin it might be, those objects will have been slowed down. Now, the darkness makes it impossible to check whether they are still there, alongside us. Therefore, to avoid running the risk of losing our thermometer, we will attach it so that we can bring it back inside without difficulty.'

Barbicane's advice was followed. The porthole was quickly opened, Nicholl tossed out the instrument, to which a short length of string had been attached so that it could be hauled in just as quickly. The porthole was open for just one second and yet that one second had been enough to allow a blast of perishing cold to enter the projectile.

'Hell's bells!' gasped Michel Ardan. 'It's cold enough to freeze polar bears!'

Barbicane waited until half an hour had ticked by, which was more than enough to allow the instrument to go down to the temperature of space. Then, when the time was up, the thermometer was quickly retrieved.

Barbicane calculated the quantity of mercury that had settled into the small reservoir at the bottom of the instrument and said:

'One hundred and forty degrees centigrade below zero!'

Monsieur Pouillet was right and Fourier was wrong. This was the terrifying temperature of interstellar space! Perhaps it was also the temperature on the continents of the Moon once it had lost through radiation all the heat with which two weeks of sunshine had flooded it!

15

HYPERBOLA OR PARABOLA?

No one should be surprised to find Barbicane and his companions so unconcerned about what future their metal prison, now launched into the infinity of the ether, had in store for them. Instead of wondering where they were going, they spent the time working on experiments as if they were tranquilly ensconced in their observatories.

It might be said on their behalf that men of such mettle were above such petty concerns, that it would take a great deal more to worry them, and that they had more important things to do than be bothered about their coming fate.

The simple fact is that they were not masters of the projectile. They could neither slow its forward motion nor steer it. A sailor changes his ship's course when he sees fit and an aeronaut can make his balloon rise and fall. But they, on the contrary, had no control over their vehicle. They had no room for manœuvre. This was at the heart of their present frame of mind, which meant giving their craft its head or, as sailors say, 'letting her run'.

So where were they now, at eight in the morning of the day which, on Earth, was dated 6 December? Clearly, they were somewhere near the Moon, indeed near enough for it to loom up like an immense black screen against the firmament. As to the exact distance which separated them from it, it was impossible to calculate. Their projectile, held in the grip of inexplicable forces, had skimmed past the North Pole of the satellite by less than fifty kilometres. But for the last two hours, ever since they had entered the cone of shadow, had this distance been getting smaller or bigger? There were no landmarks or reference points they could use to estimate the projectile's course and speed. Perhaps they were rapidly getting further away from the disc so that they would soon emerge from the cone of undiluted shadow. But perhaps, on the contrary, they were moving steadily towards it and would shortly collide with a high mountain peak on the invisible hemisphere, which would evidently put an end to the voyage, surely to the voyagers' detriment.

A discussion arose on this very point and Michel Ardan, always quick to offer an explanation, expressed the view that the projectile, held in the grip of the Moon's gravity, would end up on its surface, just as a meteorite invariably falls onto the surface of the Earth.

'First of all, my friend,' replied Barbicane, 'not all meteors end up on Earth. Only a small proportion of them do. So even if we became one, it does not follow that we should necessarily reach the surface of the Moon.'

'Still,' said Michel, 'if we get close enough . . .'

'A mistake,' said Barbicane. 'Have you never seen shooting stars which at certain times streak across the sky in their thousands?'

'Yes I have.'

'Well, those stars, which are in reality small objects, only shine because they heat up by friction as they pass through the layers of the atmosphere. Now, if they travel through the atmosphere, they must be less than sixteen leagues from the Earth and yet they rarely reach its surface.* The same must be true of our projectile. It may get close to the Moon but still not reach it.'

'In that case,' said Michel, 'I would be interested to know how exactly this wayward craft of ours will behave in space.'

'I see only two possibilities,' replied Barbicane after a few moments' reflection.

'Which are?'

'The projectile has a choice of two mathematical curves and it will follow one or the other depending on the speed at which it is travelling, and that, currently, I have no way of estimating.'

'That's right,' said Nicholl, 'its path will be either a parabola or a hyperbola.'

'Quite,' replied Barbicane. 'At one speed it will follow a parabola but, at a higher speed, a hyperbola.'

'I am thrilled by such grand words,' said Michel Ardan. 'Everyone knows at once what they mean. Still, could you say what exactly this parabola of yours is?'

'Dear boy,' said Nicholl, 'a parabola is a second-order curve, produced by the cross-section of a cone intersected by a plane running parallel to one of its sides.'

'I see,' said Michel, with every sign of satisfaction.

'It is more or less,' Nicholl went on, 'the trajectory described by a shell fired by a mortar.'

'Wonderful,' said Michel. 'And the hyperbola?'

'The hyperbola, Michel, is a second-order curve produced by the intersection of a conical surface and a plane that runs parallel to its axis and is made up of two distinct branches separated from each other and continuing indefinitely at both ends.'

'Is it possible?' cried Michel Ardan earnestly, as if he had just been informed that something serious had happened. 'In that case, Captain Nicholl, think on this: what I like about your definition of the hyperbola—I almost said hyperbunkum—is that it is even more obscure than the word you are explaining!'

Nicholl and Barbicane were not greatly taken with Michel Ardan's jokes and at once launched into a heated scientific argument. The question that gripped them was about which curve the projectile would follow. One thought it would be the hyperbola and the other the parabola. They supplied reasons for their choices which bristled with the letter x. Their views were set out in language which made Michel quail. The debate was lively and neither man was prepared to sacrifice the curve he was championing.

Their scientific dispute went on and on and eventually Michel became impatient and broke in:

'Come, ye lords of the cosine, when are you going to stop lobbing parabolas and hyperbolas at each other? What I want to know is the only interesting thing in this great debate. We are going to follow one or other of these curves. Agreed. But where would they take us?'

'Nowhere,' replied Nicholl.

'What do you mean nowhere?'

'It is clear,' retorted Barbicane. 'They are both open curves which can therefore be prolonged indefinitely.''

'Know-alls!' snorted Michel, 'I love you both but why are you worrying about parabolas and hyperbolas when at any minute one or the other is about to shoot us into space towards infinity?'

Barbicane and Nicholl could not repress smiles. They had just performed 'art for art's sake'!* Never had such a trivial topic been discussed at a more inappropriate moment. The awful truth was that the projectile, borne off hyperbolically or parabolically, would never see either Earth or Moon again.*

What would happen to these bold voyagers in the very near future? If they did not die of hunger, if they did not succumb to thirst, the fact was that a few days from now, when their supply of gas was all used up, they would die of lack of air—if the cold did not finish them off first.

Yet however vital it was to be economical with their gas, the extremely low level of the ambient temperature left them no choice but to use a certain amount of it. Strictly speaking, they could manage without light but not without heat. Fortunately, the caloric output of the Reiset and Regnault apparatus contributed a little to raising the internal temperature of the projectile which, without undue extravagance, could be maintained at a bearable degree.

But making observations through the portholes had become very problematic. The humidity inside the craft condensed on the glass and froze at once. The resulting cloudiness had to be removed from the glass by rubbing it at frequent intervals. Even so, the voyagers were able to make out enough to register a number of highly significant phenomena.

Now, if the invisible Moon did indeed have an atmosphere, would they not have seen the bright tails of shooting stars as they passed through it? And if the projectile itself was moving through various layers of an atmosphere, might not sounds, transmitted as lunar echoes, be detectable, like the growl of a storm, the roar of an avalanche, or the blast of an active volcano? And if ignivomous mountains were decked out with plumes of leaping flames, would not their fiery intensity be seen? Facts like these, meticulously recorded, would have done a great deal to clear up the intractable question of what the Moon was made of. Consequently, Barbicane and Nicholl, stationed like astronomers at their viewing panel, kept watch with scrupulous patience.

But up to this point, the lunar disc remained silent and dark, refusing to provide answers to the many questions asked of it by those two keen minds.

It was this that prompted a reflection, apparently reasonable, from Michel:

'If we ever embark on this journey again, we would be well advised to choose a time when the Moon is new.'

'Indeed,' said Nicholl. 'Doing so would be much to our advantage. I concede that the Moon fully lit by the sun would not be visible during the voyage, but on the other hand, the Earth would be in view because it would be full. Furthermore, if we were to circle round the Moon as is currently happening, we at least would have the advantage of seeing its invisible side splendidly lit up!'

'Well said, Nicholl,' replied Michel Ardan. 'What do you think, Barbicane?'

'This is what I think,' the President said gravely. 'If we ever repeat this journey, we will set off at the same time and under the same conditions. Suppose we had reached our goal; would it not have been better to discover brightly illuminated continents rather than a land in the deepest darkness? Would our initial settling in not have been managed in better conditions? Yes, of course it would. As for the hidden face of the Moon, we would have explored it as we reconnoitred the various parts of the lunar globe. Therefore, the period of the full Moon was well chosen. Of course, we should have arrived at our destination and to do that we should not have been deflected in our course.'

'There's no answer to that,' replied Michel Ardan. 'Still, it was a lost opportunity for observing the other side of the Moon! Who can say if the inhabitants of other planets know any more about their satellites than scientists on Earth do about ours?'

There was, of course, an easy answer to Michel Ardan's question, which would have been as follows. Yes, the fact that other satellites were nearer would have made it easier to study them. The inhabitants of Saturn, Jupiter, and Uranus, if they exist, would be in a position to establish contact more easily with their moons. Jupiter's four satellites orbit at a distance of 108,260, 172,200, 274,700, and 480,130 leagues respectively. But these distances are calculated from the centre of the planet and the length of the planet's radius needs to be subtracted, which is between seventeen and eighteen thousand leagues. Thus the first satellite mentioned is less distant from the surface of Jupiter than the Moon is from the surface of the Earth. Of the eight moons of Saturn, four are also nearer: Dione is 24,600 leagues away, Tethys 62,966, Enceladus 48,191, and lastly Mimas, at an average of a mere 34,500 leagues. Of the eight satellites of Uranus, the first, Ariel, is barely 51,520 leagues from the planet.

Thus an expedition from the surface of any of these three planets, of the kind carried out by President Barbicane, would have met with fewer difficulties. So if their inhabitants did ever actually try the experiment, they may have seen the anatomy of the half of its disc which the satellite keeps constantly hidden from their sight. But if they have never left their planet, they are no further forward than the Earth's astronomers.

Meanwhile, the projectile followed the unchartable trajectory for which no points of reference were available. Had its course been altered either by the influence of lunar gravity, or by the pull of some unknown body? Barbicane could not answer that question. But a change had in fact occurred in the relative position of the craft as Barbicane was able to confirm at about four in the morning.

The alteration was this: the base of the projectile had turned towards the surface of the Moon and had stayed that way, that is, with its axis now perpendicular to it. Attraction, or to give it its other name, weight, was responsible for this modification. The heaviest part of the craft was drawn towards the invisible disc exactly as if it had been falling towards it.

But was it falling? Were the voyagers about to reach their long-desired goal? No . . . but then the sight of a seemingly unaccountable point of reference informed Barbicane that his projectile was not getting any closer to the Moon and that it was in fact following a curved, more or less concentric course.

The reference point in question was a flash of bright light which Nicholl suddenly brought to his attention at the very edge of the horizon which was the black disc of the Moon. The point of light could easily have been mistaken for a star. It was a red incandescence which grew steadily larger, a sure sign that the projectile was moving towards it and was not descending onto the surface of the Moon.

'A volcano! A volcano, and it's erupting!' cried Nicholl. 'A spillage of fiery matter from inside the Moon! So this body is not totally extinct!'

'Yes, it's an eruption,' replied Barbicane, who was carefully studying the phenomenon with the aid of his night glass. 'What could it be if not a volcano?'

'If it is,' said Michel Ardan, 'then to be able to burn, it needs air. So there *is* an atmosphere on this part of the Moon!'

'Perhaps,' replied Barbicane, 'but not necessarily. A volcano, as a result of the decomposition of certain kinds of matter, can supply its own oxygen and send flames up into space. It even seems to me that this conflagration has the intensity and brilliance of objects which burn in an atmosphere of pure oxygen. Let us not be too hasty in declaring the existence of a lunar atmosphere.'

The ignivomous mountain was probably located at about the forty-fifth degree of latitude south on the invisible part of the disc. But to Barbicane's intense annoyance, the curve followed by the projectile was carrying them away from the spot pinpointed by the eruption. So he was unable to say more accurately what it was. Half an hour after it was first seen, the source of the light fell below the dark horizon. However, the fact that the phenomenon had occurred at all marked a point in the annals of selenographic studies. It proved that all heat had not disappeared from the entrails of the globe, and wherever there is fire who can say for sure that the realms of vegetable, mineral, and even animal have not fended off the destructive power of natural forces? The existence of an erupting volcano, once acknowledged beyond doubt by Earth's scientists, would produce many a theory favourable to the vexed question of whether the Moon was inhabitable or not.

Barbicane surrendered to his thoughts. He was lost in a silent reverie in which the mysterious destiny of the lunar world agitated his mind. He was attempting to make sense of the facts they had observed up to that moment when a new incident abruptly called him back to reality.

This incident was more than a cosmic phenomenon, it was a threat of danger whose consequence might well prove disastrous.

For out of the ether, from the depths of sable night, a huge mass had suddenly surged. It was like a Moon, but an incandescent Moon, a Moon so brilliant that it was even more unbearable to look at because it contrasted with the unyielding blackness of space. This mass, circular in form, cast light that filled the projectile. The faces of Barbicane, Nicholl, and Michel Ardan, brutally bathed in sheets of white light, took on the spectral, livid, pallid look which doctors produce using the artificial light of alcohol impregnated with salt.

'By all that's holy . . .!' cried Michel Ardan, 'We look dreadful! What on earth is this new damnable Moon?'

'A meteor,' said Barbicane.

'A meteor in flames? Here, in the void?'

'Yes.'

Barbicane was not wrong. The fiery sphere was indeed a meteor. Now when such a cosmic meteor is seen from Earth, it generally gives out a light that is slightly less bright than that of the Moon. But here, surrounded by dark ether, it was resplendent. These wandering bodies carry within them the source of their incandescence. The ambient air is not necessary for their combustion and flame propagation. Indeed, while some of these meteors pass through the atmosphere merely two or three leagues from the Earth's surface, others on the contrary follow their trajectory at heights beyond the limits of our atmosphere. Such was the meteor of 27 October 1844, which was recorded at a height of 128 leagues, and another on 18 August 1841 which vanished at an altitude of 182 leagues.* Some of these meteors can be three or four kilometres wide and travel at speeds reaching seventy-five kilometres a second as they travel in a direction that is the opposite of the Earth's rotation.

This shooting meteor which had suddenly burst out of the dark just a hundred leagues away probably had, according to Barbicane's estimate, a diameter of some two thousand metres. It moved at a speed of about two kilometres a second, or thirty leagues a minute. And it was on a course to meet the projectile and would be on them in the next few minutes. As it got nearer, it swelled to enormous proportions.

One should imagine—if one can—the predicament of the three voyagers, for it cannot be described in words. For all their courage, composure, and coolness in the presence of danger, they were silent, motionless, their limbs tense, victims of blind panic. Their craft, whose course they could not alter, was running directly into the path of that igneous mass that glowed more intensely than the open mouth of a reverberatory furnace. The projectile seemed to be rushing towards an abyss of fire.

Barbicane had taken the hands of his two companions and the three of them stared out at the white-hot asteroid through half-closed eyes. If all thought had not been suspended, if their brains continued to work despite the horror, they had to believe that all was lost!

The two minutes following the unexpected appearance of the meteor were two centuries of pure anguish! The projectile seemed about to crash into it, when the ball of fire exploded like a bomb,* but made no noise in the void, where sound cannot be produced, since it is nothing more than a disturbance of air waves.

Nicholl had given a cry. He and his companions had rushed to the viewing portholes. What a sight met their eyes! No pen could describe it in words, no palette is rich enough in colour to reproduce so magnificent a spectacle!

It was like a crater gaping open, it was like the leaping blaze of an immense inferno. Thousands of burning fragments lit up space and hung broad swathes of flame on the void. Sparks of all sizes and colours and shades were sprayed outwards. There were irradiations of yellow, red, green, and grey: a crown of multicoloured pyrotechnics. Of the enormous, fearsome globe nothing remained except shards blown out in all directions which in turn became asteroids, some of which gleamed like swords while others were wrapped in whitish cloud and the rest fled, leaving behind them glittering trails of cosmic dust.

These incandescent blocks crisscrossed each other, collided and sprayed out smaller fragments some of which struck the projectile. Its portside viewing panel was actually cracked by a mighty glancing hit. The craft seemed as though it was floating in a hail of cannon shells of which the smallest might blow it to smithereens at any moment.

The light which saturated the ether grew and spread with incomparable intensity, for the sheaf of asteroids was dispersing in every direction. Once it was so bright that Michel called Barbicane and Nicholl to his viewing panel, exclaiming:

'The invisible side of the Moon! Visible at last!'

Peering through the luminous debris, all three caught for a few seconds a glimpse of the mysterious disc which the eye of man now saw for the very first time.

What could they see of it at this distance that they could not evaluate?

A small number of elongated strips across the surface—actual clouds formed in zones with highly limited atmospheres out of which rose not only all the mountains but also all high ground of any significance, the cirques, the gaping craters, all haphazardly arranged just as they were in the visible disc. Then there were vast empty spaces, which were not arid plains but real seas and widely distributed oceans in whose liquid mirrors was reflected the mass of the dazzling display which filled the fiery space above them. Finally, on the surface of continents, huge dark masses, as endless forests would appear when lit in a brief flash of lightning.

Was it a mirage, an optical illusion, a trick played by their eyes? Could they provide a conclusive scientific affirmation for this observation so sketchily come by? Would they dare claim to have the answer to the question of the Moon's habitability after such a slight glimpse of the invisible disc?

Meanwhile, the pyrotechnic display in space died away little by little; its chance brightness faded; the asteroids fled in different directions and were extinguished in the distance. The ether resumed its habitual cloak of darkness; the stars, momentarily eclipsed, shone out once more in the firmament and the disc, barely discerned, was once more lost in impenetrable night.

16

THE SOUTHERN HEMISPHERE

THE projectile had just avoided a terrible peril, a peril that had not been anticipated. For who could have foreseen any such encounter with a meteor? Those journeying bodies could place the projectile in

serious danger. For voyagers, they were the equivalent of reefs scattered throughout the interplanetary ocean which they, less fortunate
than seafarers, could not avoid. But did our space-farers complain?
They did not, because nature had offered them the magnificent
spectacle of a cosmic meteor exploding from a build-up of pressure,
because the incomparable firework display, which not even a Ruggieri*
could match, had lit the invisible glory of the Moon for a few seconds.
In that rapid glimpse, continents, seas, forests had been revealed. So,
did an atmosphere bring its life-giving molecules to that face of the
Moon? Such questions were still unanswerable, but were eternally
posed by the curiosity of man!

It was then half past three in the afternoon. The projectile was following its curvilinear course round the Moon. Had its trajectory been
further affected by the meteor? It was to be feared so. Nevertheless,
their craft should be moving along a curve solidly determined by the
laws of rational mechanics. Barbicane was inclined to think that this
curve was a parabola rather than a hyperbola. But if the hypothesis of
a parabola was to be credited, the projectile should have emerged very
quickly from the cone of shadow created in the space opposite the
sun, because this cone is actually quite narrow, the Moon's angular
diameter being small when compared with the diameter of the sun.
Until now, however, the projectile had remained in its deep shadow.
Whatever its speed—and it could not have been insignificant—it was
continuing to be held within the cone. That much was clearly a fact.
But it would have not been so if the trajectory was rigorously parabolic. It was another problem to preoccupy Barbicane's brain, which
was trapped in a circle of unknown possibilities from which it could
not escape.

None of the voyagers once thought of getting any rest. Each man
remained on the alert for some unexpected fact that might throw new
light on the sum of uranographical knowledge. At about five o'clock,
Michel Ardan handed round, in the guise of dinner, a few hunks of
bread and some cold meat, which were quickly devoured without any
of them leaving his observation window whose glass was constantly
being covered by condensation from the vapour inside the craft.

At around a quarter to six, Nicholl, his glass to his eye, spied,
towards the southern edge of the Moon and in the direction being
followed by the projectile, a succession of small bright lights which
stood out against the dark screen of the Moon. They could have been

a series of sharp peaks strung out in profile on a bobbing line. They were very bright. A similar feature marks the linear edge of the Moon when it is in one of its octants.

There was no mistaking it. Here was no straightforward meteor, of which this group of illumined peaks had neither the colour nor the mobility, nor on the other hand did it have the traits of an erupting volcano. Consequently, Barbicane did not hesitate to give his opinion:

'The sun!' he cried.

'The sun? Really?' replied Nicholl and Michel Ardan.

'Yes, my friends! It is the radiant body which is lighting the tops of those mountains which stand on the southern rim of the Moon. It is clear that we are approaching the South Pole!'

'After passing over the North Pole,' said Michel. 'So we have circumnavigated our satellite!'

'Correct!' said Barbicane.

'So no more hyperbolas, no more parabolas, no more open curves to fear?'

'No, but there is one closed curve . . .'

'Does it have a name?'

'It's called an ellipse. It means that instead of running straight on and disappearing into interplanetary space, the projectile will probably travel in an elliptical orbit around the Moon . . .'

'Is that so!'

'. . . and become its satellite.'

'A moon of the Moon!' cried Michel Ardan.

'Only I would point out, my dear fellow,' said Barbicane, 'that we shall be no less lost for all that.'

'True, but in a different way and one that is infinitely more pleasant!' replied the devil-may-care Frenchman with his most winning smile.

President Barbicane was right. In following this elliptical course, the projectile was about to start travelling round the Moon and become a sub-satellite. It would be a new body added to the Solar System, a microcosm occupied by three inhabitants—who would soon die from lack of air. So Barbicane was in no mood to rejoice at their new but permanent predicament which had been thrust on them by the double influence of centripetal and centrifugal forces. He and his companions were about to see the lighted face of the lunar disc once more. Perhaps their lives would be prolonged sufficiently for them to enjoy one last sight of a full Earth brightly lit by the rays of the sun! Perhaps they might even have time to bid a last farewell to the globe which they would never see again! But then their craft would become an extinct mass, dead and no different from the inert asteroids which circulate throughout space. There was just one consolation for them: they would at last emerge from the fathomless gloom and would return to the world of light, to zones bathed in the radiance of the sun!

Meanwhile, the mountains which Barbicane had seen were looming larger as they emerged from the ubiquitous blackness. They were the Montes Doerfel and the Montes Leibnitz which paraded their bristling, spiky ranges across the circumpolar region of the south.

The heights of all the mountains of the visible hemisphere have been measured with meticulous precision. Readers will doubtless be surprised by such accuracy and yet hypsometrical methodology is rigorous. It can even confirm that the altitude of the mountains of the Moon is not less accurately determined than that of the mountains of planet Earth.

The method most generally used is to measure the shadows cast by the mountains, allowance being made for the height of the sun at the moment when the observation is made. This measurement is easily obtained by means of a telescope fitted with a reticule with two parallel hairs, for it is generally accepted that the diameter of the disc is accurately known. This method is also used for measuring the depth of the Moon's crater and cavities. Galileo used it as, subsequently, have Beer and Mädler and with the greatest success.

Another method, known as Tangent Rays, may also be applied to the task of measuring the height of lunar uplands. It is initiated at the exact moment when mountain tops become luminous points detached from the line separating light and dark, and shine against the black part of the disc. These illuminated points are produced by rays of the sun which are higher up than the rays which determine the limit of the current phase. Thus measurement of the dark gap left between a given bright point and the nearest part of the lit phase gives the height of that point.* But as will be appreciated, this procedure is suitable only with mountains actually on or close to the line separating light and dark.

A third method consists of measuring the profile of lunar mountains which stand out against their background using a micrometre.

But this technique is best suited to mountains that lie close to the edge of the globe.

In all these cases, it will be noted that the measurement of shadows, gaps, and outlines can be carried out only when the rays of the sun fall on the Moon obliquely, relative to the observer. When they fall perpendicularly, that is, when it is full, the disc is completely free of shadow and this makes observation impossible.

Galileo, after establishing the existence of these lunar mountains, was the first man to use the method of cast shadows to calculate their height. As has already been said,* he attributed to them an average altitude of 8,800 metres. Hevelius lowered the figure significantly, which on the contrary Riccioli then doubled. All these measurements were exaggerated, being too high or too low. Herschel, equipped with improved optical instruments, came nearer to hypsometrical reality, which was finally achieved through the work of modern observers.

Beer and Mädler, the finest selenographers in the whole world, have measured 1,095 of the Moon's mountains. From their calculation, it emerged that six hundred of these mountains were higher than 5,800 metres and twenty-two were above 4,800 m. The highest peak of all measured 7,603 m and is thus below the altitudes reached by mountains on Earth, some of which exceed it by fifteen or eighteen hundred yards. But one reservation must be made. If we compare the respective mass of both heavenly bodies, the Moon's mountains are relatively higher than terrestrial mountains. The first form 1/470th part of the diameter of the Moon, while the second just 1/404th part of the Earth's diameter. For a terrestrial mountain to reach the relative proportions of a lunar mountain, its height above sea-level would need to be six whole leagues and a half. In fact, the altitude of the highest is less than nine kilometres.

And so, to proceed by comparison, the chain of the Himalayas contains three peaks that are higher than any peaks on the Moon: Mount Everest at 8,837 m, Kanchenjunga at 8,588 m, and Dhaulagiri at 8,187 m. The Montes Doerfel and Montes Leibnitz are equal in altitude to that of Djawahir* in the same chain, that is 7,603 m. Newton, Casatus, Curtius, Short, Tycho, Clavius, Blancanus, Endymion, as well as the summits of the Caucasus and the Apennines, are all higher than Mont Blanc, which is 4,810 m high. As high as Mont Blanc are Moretus, Theophilus, and Catharina; equal to Monte Rosa (4,636 m) are Piccolomini, Werner, Harpalus; to Mont Cervin (4,522 m) are

Macrobe, Eratosthenes, Albategnius, Delambre; to Pic de Teide (3,710 m) are Bacon, Cysatus, Philolaus, and the highest Alps; as high as Mont Perdu (3,351 m) in the Pyrenees are Roemer and Boguslawsky; and equal to Etna, at 3,237 m, are Hercules, Atlas, and Furnerius.

These are points of comparison which allow us to have a clear notion of the height of the mountains of the Moon. Now as it happened, the trajectory of the projectile was directing it towards this mountainous region of the southern hemisphere where proudly stand the finest specimens of lunar orography.

17*

TYCHO

AT six in the evening, the projectile passed near the South Pole at a height of sixty kilometres, the distance at which it was when it passed near the North Pole. The elliptical curve was thus being strictly adhered to.

It was now that the voyagers felt once more the benevolent effects of the sun's rays. Once again they could see the stars sail slowly from east to west and the radiant body was greeted with three cheers. Along with its light, it also beamed down its heat which soon passed through the craft's metal sides. The viewing panels resumed their habitual transparency as their covering of ice melted as if by magic. The gas was turned off at once as an economy measure. Only the air-making machine consumed it in the usual quantities.

'Ah!' said Nicholl, 'how pleasant it is to feel the warm rays! Can you imagine the impatience with which the Selenites must wait to see the sun reappear after such a long night?'

'Absolutely!' said Michel Ardan, sniffing, as it were, the glowing ether. 'Heat and light, all of life is there!'

Just then, the base of the projectile was shifting slightly away from the Moon's surface, to follow its markedly elongated orbit. From that point, if there had been a 'full Earth', Barbicane and his companions would have been able to see their globe once more. But, overcome by the brilliant light directed on it by the sun, it remained absolutely invisible. However, another spectacle was about to attract their attention, namely that of the southern part of the Moon, which their telescopes brought closer, to approximately half of a quarter of a league. They remained at their observation panels and took note of all the details of that bizarre continent.

The mountains of the Doerfel and Leibnitz ranges emerge from two distinct groups which rise more or less at the South Pole. The first group runs from the Pole to the 84th parallel on the eastern side of the Moon. The other, outlined against its eastern edge, extends from the 65th degree of latitude to the Pole.

Along their irregularly contoured spines, appeared areas of dazzling sheets, as Father Secchi described. With greater certainty than the illustrious astronomer from Rome, Barbicane was able to say exactly what the whiteness was:

'It's snow!' he cried.

'Snow?' said Nicholl.

'Yes, Nicholl, snow the surface of which has been frozen to a considerable depth. Do you see the way it reflects the sun's rays? Cooled lava flows would never give off such intense reflections. There must be water, there must also be air on the Moon. It may be hard to credit, but the plain fact of it can no longer be contested!'

No, it certainly could not! And if Barbicane ever sees the Earth again, his notes will bear testimony to a fact of considerable significance in the annals of selenographic observation.

The Doerfel and Leibnitz ranges terminate in the middle of plains of limited extent bordered by an indefinite number of cirques and ring-shaped ramparts. These two ranges are the only ones to be found in an area of cirques. Not markedly uneven or rugged, they nevertheless boast a few needle peaks, the highest of which measures 7,603 m.

But the projectile was high above the scene and the landscape was flattened by the intensity of the light falling on the disc. As the voyagers watched, the archaic look of lunar landscapes re-emerged: crude tones, with no colour variation and no nuances of light and shade, only brutal whites and blacks, with no diffused light to modify them. Yet the sight of this desolate world could not do other than feed the voyagers' curiosity by its very strangeness. They were moving through the space above this whole chaotic region as though they were being blown away by the breath of a hurricane, seeing mountain peaks parade under their feet, their eyes peering into pits and pockets, gliding down rilles, rising up the bulk of the hills, probing mysterious cavities, and levelling the fractured terrain. But no trace did they find

of vegetation nor of the remains of cities. There was only stratification, old lava spills, rocky outcrops, outflows as polished as immense
mirrors which reflected back the sun's rays with overpowering brilliance. No hint of a living world but every sign of a world that was
dead. But there were avalanches that careered down from the summits of mountains in silence only to be lost in the depths of chasms;
they had movement but still no roar, no thunder.

Time and time again, Barbicane noted in his observations that the
endless high ground on the edges of the disc, although subjected
to forces different from those shaping the central region, presented
a generally uniform appearance: the same circular formations, the
same ridges and outcrops. However, it might be thought that their
character could not be analogous. Indeed, at the centre of the disc, the
still malleable crust of the Moon has been subjected to the attraction
of both Moon and Earth, acting in opposite directions along an
imaginary line extending from one to the other. On the other hand,
at the edges of the disc, lunar attraction has been, so to speak, perpendicular, to the forces of Earth's attraction. It would seem therefore that the formations in the ground resulting from the action of
these two kinds of attraction should have been very different in
appearance. But that was not the case. Therefore, the Moon must
have found in itself the origin that shaped its outward formation and
the inner arrangement of its constituent parts. It thus owed nothing
to external influences and this confirmed the proposition advanced
by Arago:

'No force external to the Moon has had a hand in the creation of
its relief.'*

Be that as it may, and given its present state, the Moon presented
an image of death, though it was not possible to assert that it had
never been inhabited by any form of life.

Still, Michel Ardan was convinced that he could make out a collection of ruins that he brought to Barbicane's attention at a location
more or less on the eightieth parallel and 30° longitude. A heap of
stones, arranged in some sort of order, gave the effect of a vast fortification which looked down over one of the long rilles that formed the
beds of rivers in prehistoric times. Close by, the ring-shaped Short
Mountain rose to a height of 5,646 m, which made it as high as the
Caucasus mountains of Asia. Michel Ardan, with his customary passion, swore it was 'obvious' that here was a fortress. Below it, he could

make out the dismantled ramparts of a town; here was the still intact arch of a portico; there, two or three columns lying under their stylobates; further along, a series of soffits which must have supported the channels of an aqueduct; elsewhere, the collapsed pillars of a gigantic bridge built over the widest part of the rille . . . All this he could see, but he did so with such an imaginative eye and through such a fantastical lens that one must be wary of his observations. And yet who could say for certain that the brave Michel did not really see what his two companions did not wish to see?

These moments were too precious to be wasted in idle argument. The Selenite city, hypothetical or not, had already disappeared in the distance. The height of the projectile above the lunar disc was beginning to increase and the detail of what lay below was starting to be lost in a confused blur. Only the high ground, the craters, the plains remained, their boundaries clearly marked.

Just then, to the left, stood out one of the finest cirques in lunar orography and one of the most noteworthy features of that continent. It was Newton, and Barbicane identified it without difficulty by referring to the *Mappa selenographica*.

Newton is situated at exactly latitude 77° south and longitude 16° east. It forms a ring-shaped crater with ramparts 7,264 metres high, apparently unclimbable.

Barbicane pointed out to his companions that the height of the mountain above the surrounding plain was nowhere as great as the depth of its crater. It was a vast hole eluding all attempts to measure it: it was a gloomy abyss whose floor never saw the rays of the sun. In it, according to Humboldt, reigns absolute darkness that neither the direct light of the sun nor the reflected light of the Earth can pierce. Mythologists might well have named it the Mouth of Hades.

'Newton', said Barbicane, 'is the best specimen of these annular or ring-shaped mountains of which there is no example on Earth. Their existence proves that the formation of the Moon came about as a result of violent causes during a process of cooling. Because mountains, forced up by pressures of internal fires, rose to considerable heights, the depths grew deeper and became much lower than the rest of the Moon's surface.'

'I don't deny it,' replied Michel Ardan.

A matter of minutes after they had left Newton behind, the projectile was passing over another annular mountain, Moretus. It skirted the heights of Blancanus, some distance off, and, towards half past seven that evening, it reached the cirque of Clavius.

This cirque, one of the most remarkable anywhere on the Moon's disc, is located at latitude 58° south and longitude 15° east. Its height is estimated to be 7,091 metres. The voyagers, at a distance of 400 kilometres (shortened to four by their telescopes) were thus able to admire the full extent of the vast crater.

'Volcanoes on Earth', intoned Barbicane, 'are mere molehills compared with the volcanoes of the Moon. By measuring the ancient craters formed by the earliest eruptions of Vesuvius and Etna, it was discovered that they are scarcely six thousand metres wide. In France, the cirque in the Cantal is ten kilometres across; in Ceylon, the island's cirque is seventy kilometres wide and is reckoned to be the largest on the planet. But what are their dimensions next to the diameter of the Clavius cirque which is now beneath us?'

'How wide is it then?' asked Nicholl.

'Two hundred and twenty-seven kilometres,' said Barbicane. 'True, it happens to be the biggest cirque on the Moon. But there are many others that reach two hundred, a hundred and fifty, or a hundred kilometres!'

'Listen, friends!' cried Michel. 'Can you imagine what the serene Moon must have been like when its craters were filled with thunder and all simultaneously spewing out great gouts of lava, showers of stones, clouds of smoke, and huge sheets of flame? What a prodigious sight that must have been! And see now how the mighty have fallen! The Moon is now only the skin-and-bone carcass of a great firework display of squibs, rockets, pharaoh's serpents, and Catherine wheels of which, after putting on a superb show, nothing survives but remnants of the torn cardboard packaging they came in! Which of you can tell me the cause, the reason, the scientific rationale of such catastrophic upheavals?'

But Barbicane was not listening to Michel Ardan. Instead, he was staring out at the ramparts of Clavius, broad mountains spread out over several leagues. On the floor of its immense basin were a hundred or so small extinct craters which formed holes in ground and left it looking like a colander—all under a tall peak five thousand metres high.

All round, the plain had an abandoned look. Nothing could be as barren as these crags, nothing so sad as these ruins of mountains, nothing quite as forlorn, if it may be so expressed, as those broken remnants of peaks and summits which littered the ground! It was as if the Earth's satellite had burst open at this place!

The projectile travelled onwards but the chaos below did not lessen. Cirques, craters, and toppled peaks continued in an unbroken succession. No more empty plains now, no more seas. It was like a never-ending Switzerland, an interminable Norway. Finally, in the heart of this creviced place, and at its culminating point, stood the most magnificent mountain on the entire face of the Moon, the dazzling Tycho, to which posterity will always continue to give the name of the celebrated Danish astronomer.

When one observes the full Moon in a cloudless sky, there is no one who has failed to notice this brilliant point in its southern hemisphere. When Michel Ardan set out to describe it, he used all the similes his imagination could supply. For him, it was a fire of bright coals, a centre of radiance, a crater blasting out rays. It was the hub of a wheel that gave off sparks, a starfish gripping the lunar disc with silver tentacles, an immense eye filled with flames, a halo designed to fit the head of Pluto!* It was like a star thrown by the hand of the Creator which had smashed into the face of the Moon!

Tycho is such a site of concentrated luminosity that Earth-dwellers can see it without a glass or telescope—even though it is a hundred thousand leagues away. Imagine, then, what its intensity would be to any observer located at a distance of just one hundred and fifty leagues! Through the pure ether, its fulgurance was so unbearable that Barbicane and his friends were forced to darken the eye-pieces of their telescopes with smoke from the gas jet before they could tolerate its brightness. Then, in silence, barely muttering a few admiring interjections, they looked and they watched. All their emotion, all their impressions were concentrated in the act of looking, just as life, when buffeted by some violent emotion, is wholly concentrated in the heart.

Tycho is part of a system of light-emitting mountains, like Aristarchus and Copernicus. But as the most complete, the most distinctive of them all, it provides irrefutable evidence of the terrifying volcanic activity to which the formation of the Moon owes its being.

Tycho is situated at latitude 43° south and longitude 12° east. At its centre is a crater eighty-seven kilometres wide. It is slightly elliptical in shape and is set in an enclosure of annular ramparts which, to the east and the west, rise over the outer plain to a height of 5,000 metres.

It is a collection of Mont Blancs arranged around a common centre and coiffed with brilliantly shining coronets.

What this incomparable mountain actually is, together with the high peaks which converge on it and the extumescences within its crater, has proved beyond even the ability of photography to capture. It is only when the Moon is full that Tycho is revealed in all its splendour. For then there is no shadow so that there is no foreshortening of perspective and the developed proofs come out perfectly blank. This is most unfortunate because this strange region would be a curious sight if reproduced with all the exactness of detail of a photograph. It is basically a vast agglomeration of holes, craters, and cirques, a dizzying crisscrossing of crests, plus, rolling away into the distance, a vast volcanic network which covers the rutted, pitted ground. It is easy to grasp how the ebullitions of the central eruption have kept their original shape. Crystallizing as they cooled, they fixed in stone the way the Moon looked in times gone by, when it was undergoing the impact of the murky devastation.

The distance between the voyagers and the ring-shaped peaks of Tycho was not so great as to prevent them from noting its major features. On the great embankment which forms the bulwarks of Tycho, the mountains cling to the slopes of both the internal and external flanks in tiers, like gigantic ledges. In the west they appear to be higher by some three or four hundred feet than in the east. No terrestrial system of castrametation could be compared to this naturally fortified place. A city built in the bowl of this circular crater would be totally inaccessible.

Inaccessible but also wondrously filling the broken terrain with picturesquely exposed formations! Nature had not left the floor of this crater flat and empty. It had its own orography, a mountain system which made it seem like a world apart. The voyagers could see the cones, the hills at the centre, and the remarkable variations in the terrain which seemed expressly designed to display the masterpieces of selenite architecture. There, a site for a temple, here, place for a forum; in this area, the sub-foundations of a palace, in that, the ideal spot for a citadel. And all this was overlooked by a central mountain fifteen hundred feet high. A vast circle, then, where ancient Rome might have been accommodated ten times over!

'My word!' exclaimed Michel Ardan, enthused by the sight. 'What a splendid city could be built inside that ring of mountains! A city of peace, a tranquil refuge, a place beyond the reach of human misery! What calm, sheltered lives the misanthropists, the haters of human-kind and those revolted by community spirit would lead if they lived there!'

'But,' said Barbicane drily, 'it would be too small to contain them all!'

18

GRAVE CONCERNS

MEANWHILE the projectile had passed beyond the ramparts of Tycho and Barbicane and his two friends now gave their full attention to observing the shining streaks which the celebrated massif sends out so strangely in all directions.

What exactly was the nature of its pulsating corona? What geological phenomenon had created that blazing mane? This question now filled Barbicane's mind, and rightly so.

He could see, stretching to all points of the compass, illuminated furrows which were raised at the edges and concave in the middle. Some were twenty kilometres wide and others fifty kilometres. These shafts of bright light ran in some directions over distances of three hundred leagues from Tycho, and appeared to cover, particularly to the east, north-east, and north, half of the southern hemisphere. One shaft reached as far as the Neander cirque on the fortieth meridian. Another, broadening out as it furrowed the Sea of Nectar, was brought up short against the Pyrenees range after travelling four hundred leagues. Others, in the west, spread a net of light over the Sea of Clouds and the Sea of Humours.*

What was the origin of these shimmering spokes which ran out across plains and over hills whatever their height? They all sprang from a common source: Tycho's crater. It was from there that they emanated. Herschel attributed their brilliance to ancient extrusions of lava solidified by the cold, a theory which has not been taken up. Other astronomers have seen these inexplicable streaks as a type of moraine, or lines of unstable blocks of matter released at the time when Tycho was being formed.*

'And whyever not?' Nicholl asked Barbicane, who summarized these various hypotheses only to reject them all.

'Because the uniformity of the light lines and the violent force needed to project volcanic matter over such great distances are both inexplicable.'

'Oh I don't know,' said Michel Ardan, 'it seems easy enough to me to explain the source of those spokes.'

'Really?' said Barbicane.

'Yes, really,' went on Michel. 'All you need say is that it is a vast star-shaped break-up, like the one you get when a bullet or a stone hits a pane of glass.'

'I see,' said Barbicane with a smile. 'And what hand would have been mighty enough to throw a stone that could produce such an impact?'

'A hand is not necessary,' answered Michel, not backing down; 'the stone could well have been a comet.'

'Ah,' exclaimed Barbicane, 'those comets are abused! Listen, Michel, your explanation is not at all bad, but your comet does not add anything. The force which caused the surface to rupture could easily have come from inside the Moon itself. A violent contraction of the lunar crust, caused by the loss of heat, would have been enough to cause this star effect.'

'I'll go along with the contraction, which would be a kind of lunar stomach ache.'

'Actually,' added Barbicane, 'that argument was put forward by a British astronomer named Nasmyth* and to my mind it adequately explains the spreading out in all directions of those mountains.'

'Well, this Nasmyth is no fool!' replied Michel.

For a long time, the voyagers, who never wearied of the spectacle below, gazed admiringly at the splendours of Tycho. Their craft, flooded by the glow of the light from the twin sources of sun and Moon, must have looked like an incandescent globe. It also meant that they had moved out from deep cold into intense heat. Nature was clearly grooming them to become Selenites.

Becoming Selenites! The idea brought them back once more to the question of whether the Moon was habitable. Could the voyagers, after all they had seen, come up with an answer now? Could they say one way or the other? Michel Ardan challenged his two friends to state their opinion, inviting them to be direct and say whether they thought that animals and humans were represented in the lunar world.

'I think we are now in a position to give an answer,' said Barbicane, 'though in my view the question ought not to be put in that form. I would like it to be framed differently.'

'Frame it as you wish,' replied Michel.

'This is what I think,' said Barbicane. 'The problem is in two parts and calls for a two-part answer. Is the Moon habitable? Has the Moon ever been inhabited?'

'Well then,' said Nicholl. 'First, we should decide if the Moon is habitable or not.'

'To be frank,' said Michel, 'I have no idea.'

'My answer,' said Barbicane, 'is in the negative. In its present condition—an atmosphere which is clearly very restricted, seas that are mostly dried, with a supply of water that is extremely limited, scarce vegetation, the abrupt transition from extreme heat to extreme cold, and nights and days that last 354 hours—the Moon does not appear to me to be habitable, being apparently unsuitable for the animal kingdom. Nor does it sufficiently furnish the essentials of life as we know it.'

'I agree,' replied Nicholl. 'But is the Moon not habitable for people who are not made as we are?'

'Now that is a question,' said Barbicane, 'which is more difficult to answer. Still, I shall try—but first let me ask Nicholl this: does movement seem to you to appear the necessary result of *life* regardless of its physical constitution?'

'Most certainly,' replied Nicholl.

'Well then, my friend, my answer is that we have observed the continents of the Moon down to a distance of at most five hundred metres, and we have seen nothing that seemed to be moving on its surface. The presence there of some form or other of humankind would have been revealed by its impact on its surroundings, by traces of various constructions, even ruins. But what have we seen? Everywhere and constantly the geological handiwork of nature and never the hand of man. So if representatives of the animal kingdom do exist on the Moon, they must be hidden away in the endless caverns which the human eye cannot plumb. But even that I cannot grant you, for they would have left traces of their passage on those plains necessarily covered by some scanty atmosphere, however low it lies. But no such traces are visible anywhere. Which leaves but one hypothesis, that of the existence of a race of living creatures to whom movement—which is life itself—is unknown.'

'Which is tantamount to saying living creatures who are not alive!' said Michel.

'Exactly,' said Barbicane, 'and that would make no sense to us.'

'So now we can decide what our opinion is,' said Michel.

'Yes,' said Nicholl.

'Well then,' Michel Ardan resumed, 'the Scientific Committee, meeting in the projectile of the Gun Club, after hearing arguments based on newly observed facts, hereby delivers its unanimous judgement on the question of the current habitability of the Moon as follows: no, the Moon is not habitable.'

The decision was formally recorded by President Barbicane in his notebook where the full minutes of the meeting of 6 December may be found.

'And now,' said Nicholl, 'let us turn to the second question, the indispensable extension of the first. I now therefore put it to the honourable committee; if the Moon is not inhabitable, has it ever been inhabited?'

'Citizen Barbicane has the floor,' said Michel Ardan.

'My friends,' said Barbicane, 'I did not wait for this voyage to form an opinion on whether our satellite was inhabited in the past. I would add that our first-hand observations have served only to confirm that opinion. I think, nay assert that the Moon was once inhabited by a race of humans living in a society organized in ways not unlike our own, that it had animals anatomically similar to terrestrial animals, but I further add that those human and animal species have had their day and that they are now and forever extinct!'

'It would seem, then,' said Michel, 'that the Moon is a world that is older than the Earth.'

'Not so,' replied Barbicane with conviction, 'but a world which has aged more quickly, whose rise and decay have occurred at a faster rate. In relative terms, the forces that shape matter were far more violently active at the centre of the Moon than at the centre of our terrestrial globe. The present state of the Moon, fissured, ravaged, and rutted, furnishes ample proof of that. Originally, both Earth and Moon were clouds of gas. The gases underwent various interactions turning them into liquids. Their mass became solid much later. But it is certain that our globe was still at the gaseous or liquid state when the Moon had already become solid as a result of cooling and was already becoming habitable.'

'That I can believe,' said Nicholl.

'At that stage,' Barbicane went on, 'it was surrounded by an atmosphere. The water, being contained within this envelope of gas, could not evaporate. Supplied now with air, water, light, and warmth both from the sun and from its own internal fires, vegetation took hold on land masses which were now ready to receive it. Life first surely appeared at about this time, for nature does not expends its bounty to no purpose, and a world richly habitable must necessarily have been inhabited.'

'And yet,' said Nicholl, 'many phenomena inherent in the development of our satellite must have placed limits on the spread of the vegetable and animal kingdoms—like, for example, those days and nights that last three hundred and fifty-four hours?'

'At the poles on Earth,' said Michel, 'they last six months!'

'That's not a point that carries much weight because the poles are not inhabited,' replied Nicholl.

'But remember,' Barbicane went on, 'that if under the present dispensation these long nights and long days created differences in temperature which are inimical to living organisms, it was not so at that period of historical time.* The atmosphere covered the entire disc with a fluid mantle, and the moisture in it took the form of clouds, which formed a natural screen that tempered the rays of the sun and restricted nocturnal heat radiation: light and warmth were freely diffused through the air. There resulted a state of balance of the two which no longer exists now that the atmosphere has virtually disappeared. But wait, I shall now amaze you . . .'

'Please do,' said Michel.

'For I am inclined to believe that at that period, when the Moon was inhabited, night and day did not last 354 hours!'

'But why not?' asked Nicholl keenly.

'Because very probably at that stage the rate at which the Moon turned on its axis was not equal to the rate at which it circled the Earth, the two needing to be the same if each point on the Moon's disc is to remain exposed to the rays of the sun during its two-week orbit.'

'Agreed,' said Nicholl, 'but why should both speeds have not been the same then given that they are now?'

'Because they could be settled definitively only by the strength of the Earth's attraction. Now what tells us that this pull was strong enough to modify the motion of the Moon at a period when the Earth was still in a state of flux?'

'But,' said Nicholl, 'what tells us that the Moon has always been a satellite of Earth?'

'And what tells us,' exclaimed Michel Ardan, 'that the Moon did not exist before the Earth?'

Their imaginations began to take flight into the clouds of the infinite. Barbicane tried to rein them in.

'Such matters belong to the lofty realm of speculation, of problems to which there are no solutions. Let us not get embroiled in them and let us just accept that the pull of primordial attraction was in fact inadequate. The result was that, owing to the lack of synchronicity of the rates of rotation and revolution, night and day could have followed each other on the Moon as they did on Earth. But even without these conditions, life was still possible.'

'So,' said Michel Ardan, 'humans could have disappeared from the Moon?'

'That's right,' said Barbicane, 'after most probably existing there for thousands of centuries. Then little by little, as the atmosphere grew thinner, the disc would have become uninhabitable as Earth too will become one day, through the process of cooling.'

'Cooling.'

'Of course,' answered Barbicane. 'As the Moon's internal fires went out, the incandescent matter became compacted and the lunar crust became cold. Gradually the consequences of this process became apparent: living organisms became extinct and vegetation disappeared. Soon the atmosphere was impoverished, probably drawn off by Earth's attraction; the breathable air disappeared, and the water by evaporation. At that point, the Moon, having become uninhabitable, ceased to be inhabited. It was a dead world and as we see it today.'

'And you say that a similar fate awaits the Earth?'

'Most probably.'

'But when?'

'When its crust has cooled sufficiently to make it uninhabitable.'

'Has anyone worked out how long it will take our wretched planet to cool down?'

'Of course.'

'And have you seen the figures?'

'I have.'

'Well, out with them, you uncooperative scientist,' cried Michel. 'You're making me boil with impatience!'

'As you wish, Michel,' Barbicane replied calmly. 'We know by how much temperatures fall over a period of a century. Well, according to some calculations, the average temperature will fall to zero 400,000 years from now.'

'Four hundred thousand!' cried Michel. 'Ah! I can breathe again! I was struck all of a heap for a moment! Listening to you, I imagined that we only had fifty thousand years left!'

Barbicane and Nicholl could not help chuckling at their companion's fears. Then Nicholl, in an effort to cut the debate short, repeated the second question which had been raised.

'So, has the Moon ever been inhabited?'

The response was affirmative and unanimous.

But while this discussion—so rich in somewhat dubious theorizing, though it did summarize general ideas which had been added to the sum of scientific knowledge—was proceeding, the projectile had rapidly moved nearer to the lunar Equator while steadily gaining in height. It had left behind Wilhelm's cirque and the fortieth parallel was now 800 kilometres behind them. Then leaving on their right Pitatus on the thirtieth parallel, it followed the southern end of the Sea of Clouds which it had previously approached from the north. Various cirques then appeared in an irregular profusion in the blinding whiteness of the full Moon: Bullialdus, Purbach—almost square in shape with a central crater—and then Arzachel, with a mountain inside it which shone with an indefinable glow.

As the voyagers gazed down and the projectile continued to gain altitude, the clear shape of things faded, individual mountains became blurred and merged in the growing distance, and soon, of that whole wondrous world of the Earth's satellite, so bizarre, so strange, all that remained was an unforgettable memory.

19

FIGHTING IMPOSSIBLE ODDS

FOR a considerable time, Barbicane and his companions, silent and pensive, gazed back at that world which they had seen only from a distance—like Moses and the Land of Canaan*—but were now leaving never to return. The angle of the projectile relative to the Moon had changed. Its base, now, was turned to face the Earth.

This change, which was pointed out by Barbicane, did not fail to surprise him. If the projectile was to revolve around the Moon in an elliptical orbit, why did it not have its heaviest side turned to it, as the Moon turns hers to the Earth? There was something unaccountable about this.

Observing the progress of their craft, they could see that by moving away from the Moon, it was embarked on a curving trajectory similar to the course it had followed when heading towards it. In other words, it was keeping to a very elongated ellipse which would presumably lead to the point of equal attraction, the point at which the forces of the Earth and its satellite are neutralized.

Such was the conclusion correctly reached by Barbicane on the basis of his observations, a view which was heartily endorsed by his two friends.

But then the questions started.

'So when we reach the neutral point, what becomes of us then?' asked Michel Ardan.

'We'll be in uncharted territory!' replied Barbicane.

'But I assume we can explore the possibilities?'

'There are two,' said Barbicane. 'Either the speed of the projectile will be inadequate, in which case it will remain eternally immobile on the line of double attraction . . .'

'I think I'd prefer the other possibility, whatever it is,' replied Michel.

'. . . or its rate of speed will be sufficient,' Barbicane continued, 'in which case it will pursue its elliptical course and continue to revolve around the Moon for ever.'

'As revolutions go, an orbit is no comfort,' said Michel. 'Ah! to become lowly minions of a Moon which we are used to thinking of as our handmaiden! So that's the fate in store for us!'

Neither Nicholl nor Barbicane spoke.

'Cat got your tongues?' went on the impatient Michel.

'There's nothing to say,' replied Nicholl.

'So there is nothing we can do?'

'No,' said Barbicane. 'Do you think you can fight odds that are impossible?'

'Why not? Since when do one Frenchman and two Americans retreat from the word impossible?'

'But what do you intend to do?'

'Get control of the movement that's carrying us off!'

'Control it?'

'Yes,' said Michel, with increasing excitement, 'change it, slow it down, use it to do what *we* want to do!'

'And how will you do that?'

'That's where you come in. If artillerymen aren't masters of the shots they fire, they are not artillerymen. If the shell dictates to the gunner, the gunner deserves to be stuffed down the barrel in its stead! Oh these great minds! Look at you: you have no idea what's to become of us after inducing me . . .'

'Inducing you?' cried Barbicane and Nicholl. 'Inducing? What the devil do you mean by that?'

'No recriminations!' said Michel. 'I'm not complaining! I'm loving our outing! The projectile agrees with me! But let us do everything that's humanly possible to ensure that if we are to land anywhere, it's not on the Moon!'

'We ask for nothing more, Michel, my dear fellow,' answered Barbicane, 'but we haven't got the means.'

'Is there nothing we can do to alter the direction of the projectile?'

'No.'

'Nor slow it down?'

'No.'

'Not even by lightening it the way an overloaded ship is lightened?'

'What do you propose to jettison?' said Nicholl. 'We're not carrying any ballast. Anyway, I have a feeling that by lightening the projectile we shall only make it go faster.'

'More slowly,' said Michel.

'Faster,' repeated Nicholl.

'Neither slower nor faster,' said Barbicane to extract agreement from his two friends, 'because we are moving through a vacuum where any specific weight is of no account.'

'Well in that case,' cried Michel Ardan in a resolute voice, 'there is only one thing we can do.'

'And what is that?' asked Nicholl.

'Have breakfast!' was the bold reply of the irrepressible Frenchman, who always relied upon this solution in the most trying of circumstances.

So although this proposal had no effect on the direction of the projectile, it could nevertheless be taken up without detriment and indeed with advantage, gastrically speaking. Decidedly, Michel had only good ideas.

And so they breakfasted. It was then two in the morning, but the time was largely irrelevant. Michel served up his customary menu rounded off with a rather pleasant bottle which he produced from his secret reserve. If ideas did not spring into their minds now, they never would—and Chambertin 1863* was not what it was cracked up to be.

Once the meal was over, they resumed their observations.

Around the projectile, at various distances, were stationed the disparate objects which they had thrown out of the craft. It was clear that during the time the projectile had spent travelling around the Moon, it had not passed through an atmosphere of any sort since the specific weight of those objects would have modified their respective speeds.

As regards the terrestrial globe, there was nothing that could be seen. The Earth was just one day older, having been new at twelve midnight the previous night. Another two days would have to pass before its crescent, freed from the sun's rays, could be used by Selenites as a clock. This was because, as it rotated on its axis, each point on its surface always came round twenty-four hours later to the same meridian on the Moon.

As regards the Moon, the view was different. It shone out in all its splendour against a background of countless constellations whose light could not detract from its purity. On its disc, the plains were already taking on the darker hues which are seen from Earth. The rest of its halo remained radiant and in the middle of the general luminescence, Tycho stood out yet more dazzlingly still, like a sun.

Barbicane was still not able to work out a way of estimating the speed of the projectile, but reflection demonstrated that it should steadily reduce in accordance with the laws of mechanics.

Indeed, once it was conceded that their craft would follow an orbital course around the Moon, it followed that its orbit must be of necessity elliptical. Science shows that it must be so. No moving object circling a body endowed with the power of attraction can escape this law. All orbits in space are elliptical—those of satellites around planets, those of planets around the sun, that of the sun around the unknown star which acts as the central pivot on which it turns. Why should the Gun Club's projectile be exempt from this natural dispensation?

Now, in all elliptical orbits, the attracting body always occupies one of the focuses of the ellipse. Its satellite is therefore at times nearer to and at other times further away from the body which it is orbiting. When the Earth is closest to the sun, it is in perihelion and when furthest away, in aphelion. To adopt analogous expressions which can enrich the language of astronomy, if the projectile continued to exist as a satellite of the Moon, it can be said that it is in 'aposelene' when it is furthest away and in 'periselene' when closest.

In the latter case, the projectile would reach its maximum speed, and in the former its minimum. In the event, it was clearly heading towards its aposelenitical* point and Barbicane had good reason for thinking that its speed would slow until it reached that point and would then regain it little by little as it approached the Moon. But if that point coincided with the point of equal attractions, its speed would be reduced to nothing.

Barbicane explored the consequences of each of these situations and was searching for how they might be best turned to their advantage when he was suddenly interrupted by a shout from Michel Ardan.

'By Jove!' cried Michel. 'You won't deny that we are total blockheads!'

'I don't deny it,' said Barbicane, 'but why?'

'Because there is a very simple way of slowing our speed which is taking us away from the Moon and we have not thought of using it!'

'And what would that way be?'

'To use the recoil power of our rockets!'

'That's true!' said Nicholl.

'We have not used any of them,' said Barbicane, 'you are quite right. But use them we shall!'

'When?' asked Michel.

'When the time is right. Remember, my friends, that given the angle at which the projectile is presently inclined—it is still obtuse in relation to the Moon—firing the rockets would change our course and might well shift us away from, rather than closer to, the Moon. At least, I assume that it's the Moon you are aiming to reach?'

'Basically,' said Michel.

'Best wait, then. For some unaccountable reason, the projectile is tending to bring its base round towards the Earth. It is likely that at the point of zero gravity its conical nose will be pointing straight at the Moon. At that moment we can hope that its speed will have dropped to nothing. That will be the moment when we should act. With the impetus supplied by our rockets, we might be able to begin a long descent onto the surface of the Moon.'

'Capital!' said Michel.

'We did not attempt it on our outward journey,' Barbicane went on, 'when we reached the neutral point, nor could we have done, because the projectile's speed was still too high.'

'Well thought through!' said Nicholl.

'So let's be patient and wait,' Barbicane went on. 'We must do all we can to ensure that the odds are on our side. So, after abandoning all hope of success, I'm beginning to think once more that we shall reach our destination.'

This conclusion prompted cheers and hurrahs from Michel Ardan. And not one of that crazily bold trio had lost sight of the question which they themselves had answered in the negative: no, the Moon is not inhabited! No, the Moon is probably not habitable! And yet they were about to do their best to go there!

Only one question now remained to be answered: at what precise moment would their craft reach the point of zero gravity when the voyagers would play their ace card?

To work out the moment to the last few seconds, all Barbicane had to do was refer to his journal notes and take account of the various heights he had measured between them and the lunar parallels. The reason being that the time spent covering the distance between the neutral point and the South Pole had to be equal to the distance which separated the North Pole from the neutral point. The hours they had spent travelling were carefully noted and the calculation then became straightforward.

Barbicane found that the projectile would reach the neutral point at one o'clock during the night of 7 to 8 December. It was then three in the morning of the night of 6 to 7 December. So, provided that nothing interfered with its progress, the projectile would reach the rendezvous in twenty-two hours' time.

The rockets had originally been intended to slow the descent of the projectile onto the Moon, but now the intrepid voyagers were about to use them to produce the exact opposite effect. Be that as it may, they were ready and now they only had to wait for the time to come when they would fire them.

'Since we've got nothing to do,' said Nicholl, 'I have a suggestion to make.'

'What is it?' asked Barbicane.

'I propose we should get some sleep.'

'Perish the thought!' exclaimed Michel Ardan.

'It's forty hours since we closed our eyes,' said Nicholl. 'A few hours' sleep will restore our strength.'

'Never!' replied Michel.

'Very well,' Nicholl resumed. 'Let each man make up his own mind. As for myself, I'm going to sleep.'

And lying down full length on a divan, Nicholl was soon snoring like a forty-pounder cannonball.

'Nicholl has the right idea,' soon said Barbicane. 'I shall follow his lead.'

Moments later he was accompanying the captain's baritone with his bass.

'Actually,' said Michel Ardan, finding himself alone, 'these practical men do sometimes have good ideas.'

With his long legs stretched out, his great arms folded under his head, Michel in turn fell asleep.

But sleep could not be peaceful or long-lasting. Too many thoughts kept rolling round in the minds of the three men and a few hours later, at about seven in the morning, the voyagers were up and about at the same time.

The projectile was still travelling away from the Moon, with its nose tilting more and more towards it. This phenomenon was as puzzling as ever but it suited Barbicane's plans perfectly.

Another seventeen hours and the time to act would be upon them.

That day seemed very long. Intrepid though they were, the voyagers were nevertheless acutely aware of the approach of the moment which would decide whether they would soon be heading down to the Moon or be permanently locked into a never-changing orbit. So they counted off the hours, which passed too slowly for their taste. Barbicane and Nicholl tenaciously buried themselves in their calculations while Michel paced to and fro between the narrow walls and gazed eagerly out at the impassive Moon.

Sometimes, memories of Earth passed quickly through their minds. They again saw their Gun Club friends and, dearest of them all, J. T. Maston. At that very moment, the honourable secretary was

surely at his post in the Rocky Mountains. If he could see the projectile via the mirror of his gigantic telescope, what must he be thinking?
After seeing it disappear behind the Moon's southern pole, he would
have seen it reappear via the North Pole!* It had become the satellite
of a satellite. Had J. T. Maston given out this unexpected news to the
whole world? If so, would the announcement be the final act of their
great enterprise?

Meanwhile the rest of the day went by without incident. Midnight
(Earth-time) struck and the day of 8 December was about to begin.
One more hour and they would be at the point of equal attraction. At
what speed would the projectile then be travelling? There was no way
of estimating it. But Barbicane's calculations could not possibly be
mistaken. At one in the morning its speed should be, nay would
be, zero.

But another phenomenon was to mark the arrival of the projectile
at the neutral point, the line at which the attractions of Earth and
Moon cancelled each other and objects would be 'without weight'.
This strange fact which had so peculiarly surprised Barbicane and his
companions on the outward journey would arise again, under identical conditions. And it would be precisely at that moment that they
would have to act.

Already the conical nose of the projectile was tilted markedly
towards the Moon's disc. The craft was now in the position which
would maximize the recoil of its rocketry. The odds thus seemed to
favour the voyagers. If the speed of the projectile was cut to zero by
the neutral point, one decisive movement towards the Moon, however
slight, would be enough to commit it to a descent.

'Now five minutes to one,' said Nicholl.

'Everything is ready,' said Michel Ardan holding out a prepared
wick near the flame of the gas jet.

'Wait,' said Barbicane, chronometer in hand.

At that moment, weight ceased to have any effect. The voyagers
sensed its absence within themselves. They had to be near the neutral
point if they were not there already!

'One o'clock!' said Barbicane.

Michel held the lit wick to a device which set off the rockets instantly.
No explosions were heard inside the craft where the air was depleted.
But through the viewing panels Barbicane saw the long process of
ignition and a burst of flame which was extinguished immediately.

The projectile was rocked by a jolt which was definitely felt inside the craft.

The three friends looked and listened, saying nothing and scarcely breathing. The beating of their hearts could have been heard in the total silence.

'Are we descending?' Michel Ardan asked eventually.

'No,' said Nicholl, 'because the base of the projectile is not turning towards the Moon!'

At that moment, Barbicane, stepping away from his observation window, turned to his two companions. He was ghastly pale, his brow furrowed and his lips drawn tightly together.

'We're descending!' he said.

'Really?' cried Michel Ardan. 'Towards the Moon?'

'Towards Earth!' replied Barbicane.

'Heavens above!' cried Michel Ardan, adding philosophically: 'Ah well. When we got into this projectile, we did think that it wouldn't be easy to get out of it again!'

But the terrifying descent was now beginning. The projectile had maintained enough speed to carry it across the neutral point. The detonation of the rockets had not significantly slowed it. Its speed, which had pushed it over the neutral line on the outward journey, was doing the same on its way back. The laws of physics required that during its elliptical orbit, it should again pass through every point it had already passed through.

It was a terrifying prospect, a descent from a height of 78,000 leagues, which could not be cushioned by any sort of shock-absorbing spring. According to the laws of ballistics, the projectile would crash into the Earth at a speed equal to that with which it had been fired out of the Columbiad, that is, a velocity of sixteen thousand metres in the final second.

To give some figures for the purpose of comparison, it has been calculated that an object dropped from the top of the towers of Notre Dame, which are a mere 200 feet high, would hit the ground at a speed of 120 leagues an hour.* Here the projectile would hit the Earth with a speed of 57,600 leagues an hour.

'It's all up with us,' said Nicholl coolly.

'Well, if we die,' replied Barbicane with a sort of religious fervour, 'the result of our voyage will be magnificently expanded! God will reveal His very secret! In the life that is to come, our souls will have no need of machines and engines in their pursuit of knowledge! They will be at one with eternal wisdom!'

'Actually,' said Michel Ardan, 'the entire world to come would not be a bad exchange for the piffling orb we call the Moon!'

Barbicane folded his arms across his chest in a gesture of sublime resignation.

'May Heaven's will be done!'

20

THE *SUSQUEHANNA* TAKES SOUNDINGS

'Well, Lieutenant, what news of the sounding?'

'I'd say, sir, that the operation is almost done,' said Bronsfield. 'But who would ever have dreamed of finding depths like these so near land, just a hundred leagues from the American coast?'

'Indeed, Bronsfield, it is a very deep depression,' said Captain Blomsberry. 'Just here, there's a valley scooped out by the Humboldt current which runs down the entire coast of America all the way to the Magellan Strait.'

'Depths like these,' went on the Lieutenant, 'are not much use for laying telegraphic cables. A level seabed is better, like the one that carries the American cable between Valentia and Newfoundland.'

'I agree with you, Bronsfield. 'But, with your permission, Lieutenant, how deep have we got now?'

'Sir,' replied Bronsfield, 'at this time we have 21,500 feet paid out over the side and the ball that takes the sounding lead down has still not reached the sea floor, because if it had the lead would have come back up to the surface by itself.'

'This Brooke apparatus* is most ingenious,' said Captain Blomsberry, 'as it enables one to take highly precise soundings.'

At that moment, one of the for'ard helmsmen overseeing the operation sang out: 'Bottom!'

The captain and the Lieutenant moved to the quarterdeck.

'What depth do we have?' asked the captain.

'Twenty-one thousand seven hundred and sixty-two feet,' replied the Lieutenant as he entered the number in his notebook.

'Good, Bronsfield,' said the captain. 'I'll add the result to my chart. Now you can haul up the line. It'll take a good few hours. While that's going on, the engineer will light the boilers and we'll be ready to leave as soon as you are done. It's 22.00 hours now and, with your permission, Lieutenant, I shall turn in.'

'Of course sir,' said the obliging Bronsfield.

The master of the *Susquehanna*,* a good man if one ever lived and the kindly servant of his officers, returned to his cabin, and reached for his brandy grog, which drew from him interminable expressions of appreciation to his steward. Then he took to his bed but not without commending his servant for the way his bed had been made, and slept peacefully.

It was ten o'clock and dark. The eleventh day of the month of December was soon to end in a magnificent night.

The *Susquehanna*, a corvette of 500 horsepower belonging to the United States Navy, was then taking soundings in the Pacific at about one hundred leagues from the American coast, off the elongated peninsula which runs along the shores of New Mexico.*

The wind had eased down and the air was calm. The corvette's flag was still and hung limply from the topgallant mast.

Captain Jonathan Blomsberry—first cousin to Colonel Blomsberry, one of the keenest members of the Gun Club, who had married a Miss Horschbidden, who was the captain's aunt and daughter of a worthy Kentucky merchant—Captain Blomsberry could not have wished for better weather in which to complete this delicate sounding operation. His corvette had not even felt a breath from the huge storm which, by sweeping away the clouds piled high over the Rocky Mountains, at last allowed observers to follow the progress of the celebrated projectile. Everything was going his way and he did not forget to thank heaven for it with all the fervour of a Presbyterian.

The series of soundings taken by the *Susquehanna* was intended to chart the seabed and identify the most suitable areas for laying an underwater cable which would connect the Hawaiian Islands with the American coast.

It was a huge project, the initiative of a huge company. Its managing director, the highly intelligent Cyrus Field,* designed to eventually connect all the islands of the Pacific in one vast electrical network, an immense undertaking and one worthy of American genius.

It was the corvette the *Susquehanna* that had been entrusted with the first active soundings. During this night of 11 to 12 December, its position was precisely latitude 27° 7′ north and longitude 41° 37′ west of the Washington meridian.

The Moon, then in its last quarter, was just beginning to show on the horizon.

After Captain Blomsberry had departed, Lieutenant Bronsfield and a few other officers had assembled on the poop deck. When its first light appeared, their thoughts turned to the Moon, to which the eyes of an entire hemisphere were already turned. The finest marine glasses could not have picked out the projectile as it wandered across the half of the Moon that was visible, but each one was trained on that bright disc which millions were contemplating at the same time.

'They've been gone ten days,' said Lieutenant Bronsfield. 'What can have happened to them?'

'They've got there, Lieutenant,' cried a young midshipman, 'and they are doing what all voyagers do when they arrive in a new land: they've gone for a walk!'

'I believe it because you say so,' smiled Lieutenant Bronsfield.

'Still,' said another officer, 'there's no doubting that they got there. The projectile must have reached the Moon when it was full, on the 5th at midnight. Here we are, on 11 December, six days later. Now those six times twenty-four hours, when there is no darkness, give ample time to settle in comfortably. I seem to be able to see in my mind's eye our brave countrymen camped in a fold of the hills by a selenite stream with the projectile close by, half-buried in volcanic debris since it landed, and Captain Nicholl making a start on his surveying operations, President Barbicane writing up the notes he made during the voyage, and Michel Ardan filling the empty lunar spaces with the fragrance of one of his havanas . . .'

'Yes, it must be like that, it must!' cried the midshipman, thrilled by his superior's golden description.

'I'd like to think so,' replied Lieutenant Bronsfield, with no great enthusiasm. 'Unfortunately, no direct news from the lunar world will ever be possible.'

'Excuse me, Lieutenant, said the midshipman, 'but can't President Barbicane write?'

A burst of laughter greeted the words.

'No, I don't mean write letters,' said the young man. 'This has nothing to do with postal services.'

'Maybe it's got something to do with telegraph wires?' one of the officers asked sarcastically.

'Not that either,' replied the midshipman, not backing down. 'But it is easy to establish a form of written communication with the Earth.'

'How?'

'By using the telescope on Longs Peak. As you know, its lens brings the Moon to within two leagues of the Rockies, which means that objects nine feet in diameter on its surface can be seen clearly. So, why not get our ingenious friends up there to make a giant alphabet! Then they could write words a hundred fathoms long and sentences a league long! Then they can let us know how they are getting on!'

The young midshipman, who had shown that he was not lacking in imagination, was loudly applauded. Lieutenant Bronsfield himself agreed that the idea was feasible. But he added that signals using parallel light beams reflected by parabolic mirrors would also establish direct communications. The light beams would be as visible on the surface of Venus and Mars as the planet Neptune is from Earth. He added that the bright points of light which had been observed on the nearest planets to us could very well be signals directed at the Earth. But he did concede that though it might be possible to receive news from the lunar world by these means, there was no point in the terrestrial world transmitting news if the Selenites had not developed some way of observing distant objects.

'That's true of course,' said one of the officers, 'but what's happened to the voyagers, what they've done, what they've seen—that is what interests us most. And if their experiment has succeeded, which I do not doubt for one moment, it will be tried again. The Columbiad, embedded in the soil of Florida, is still serviceable. All that is needed now would be another projectile and some more gunpowder. Every time the Moon is due to reach its zenith, we could fire off a cargo of visitors.'

'And it is certain,' replied Lieutenant Bronsfield, 'that one of these days J. T. Maston will be off to re-join his friends up there.'

'If he'd have me,' cried the midshipman, 'I'd be ready to go with him!'

'Oh, there'll be no shortage of volunteers,' replied Bronsfield, 'and if they let them, half the Earth's population will soon have emigrated to the Moon!'

This conversation among the officers of the *Susquehanna* went on until almost one on the morning. There is no way we can report all the startling systems and revolutionary theories that were bandied about by these bold thinkers. Ever since Barbicane had announced his plans, it seemed that for Americans nothing was impossible any longer. They were already planning to send, not just a committee of scientists, but an entire colony to settle on those Selenite shores, together with a complete army of infantry, artillery, and cavalry with which to conquer the lunar world.

At one in the morning, not all the sounding-line had been hauled in. The ten thousand feet that still remained over the side would require several hours more work. Following the captain's orders, the ship's furnaces had been lit and the pressure in the boilers was building up. The *Susquehanna* was ready to leave at any time.

At one particular moment—it was seventeen minutes past one in the morning—Lieutenant Bronsfield was about to leave the watch and return to his cabin, when his attention was caught by a screeching sound. It was some distance away and totally unexpected.

He and his companions thought at first that the drawn-out screech was the sound of steam escaping. But on looking up, they were able to ascertain that the noise was coming from a long way up in the air.

They did not have time to think before the screeching assumed a terrifying intensity, and suddenly, before their bedazzled eyes, there appeared an enormous meteorite wrapped in flames produced by friction in the upper reaches of the atmosphere due to the speed of its descent.

This blazing mass grew bigger and bigger as they watched until it crashed with a noise like thunder onto the bowsprit of the corvette, snapping it off at the base of the stem-post* before vanishing below the waves with a deafening roar! A few feet more and the *Susquehanna* would have gone down with all hands.

Caption Blomsberry appeared half-dressed and rushed onto the fo'c'sle where his officers had gathered.

'With your permission, gentlemen,' he said, 'what has happened here?'

The midshipman, acting as a spokesman for them all, cried:

'It's *them*! They've come back, captain!'

21

J. T. MASTON RECALLED

THE excitement ran high on board the *Susquehanna*. Officers and sailors forgot all about the terrible danger they had just escaped—of being broken up and sinking in the deep waters. They were thinking only of the catastrophe which had ended the great experiment. And so it was that the boldest venture in ancient and modern times was costing the lives of the bold men who had dared to undertake it.

'It's *them*, coming back!' the young midshipman had said and every man knew at once what he meant: no one doubted that the meteorite was the Gun Club's projectile. As for the fate of the voyagers inside it, opinion was divided.

'They're dead!' said one.

'They're alive!' said another. 'The water is deep here and that deadened their fall!'

'But they didn't have any air,' said the first man, 'they'll have died of suffocation!'

'Burned to a crisp!' said the second man. 'The projectile was an incandescent mass as it came down through the atmosphere.'

'What does it matter?' said a third man. 'Alive or dead, we've got to get them up from there!'

Meanwhile Captain Blomsberry had called his officers together and, with their permission, he was canvassing their advice. It was vital to act at once. The first thing was to haul up the projectile. It would be a difficult but not impossible operation. However, the corvette did not have on board the machinery with the required strength and precision. So it was decided to make for the closest port and alert the Gun Club that the projectile had come down.

This decision was arrived at unanimously. The choice of port was then discussed. The nearest coast could offer no facilities for a landing on the twenty-seventh degree of latitude. Further north, above the Monterey peninsula, was the good-sized town which gave it its name. But it was situated on the edge of what was virtually desert and was not connected with the hinterland by the telegraphic network; only electricity was capable of transmitting this important news quickly enough.

But a few degrees further north was the Bay of San Francisco. From the capital of gold-rush country, communications with the heart of the Union would be easy. By piling on the steam, the *Susquehanna* could reach the port of San Francisco in less than two days. They should set off without delay.

The boilers were now up to pressure which meant they could leave immediately. Two thousand fathoms of sounding-line were still not hauled up. Reluctant to waste precious time winding it in, Captain Blomsberry decided to cut what remained and drop it over the side.

'We'll attach the end to a buoy,' he said, 'and the buoy will mark the precise location where the projectile came down.'

'Right,' said Lieutenant Bronsfield, 'but we also have our exact position: latitude 27° 7′ north and longitude 41° 37′ west.'

'Excellent, Mr Bronsfield,' replied the captain. 'Now, if you please, give the order to cut the line.'

A robust buoy, reinforced by a floating drag of wooden spars, was dropped onto the surface of the ocean. The end of the line was securely lashed to the top and, left to the action of the swell, it would not drift much.

At that moment, the chief engineer informed the captain that steam was up and that they could now move. The captain sent his thanks for the excellent report, then gave out their course: north-north-east. The corvette came round and made for the bay of San Francisco at full steam.

It was now three in the morning.

Two hundred and twenty leagues were nothing to a pacy vessel like the *Susquehanna*. In thirty-six hours, it had eaten up the distance and on 14 December, at twenty-seven minutes past one in the afternoon, it entered the Bay of San Francisco.

When this vessel of the national navy was seen making full speed, with its bowsprit sheared off and its foremast shored up, the curiosity of the public was swiftly aroused. A dense crowd quickly assembled on the quayside and waited for disembarkation.

After dropping anchor, Captain Blomsberry and Lieutenant Bronsfield stepped into a boat with a crew of eight oarsmen who rowed them quickly ashore.

They leapt out onto the wharf.

'The telegraph office!' they demanded, without answering any of the countless questions that were being fired at them.

The harbour master escorted them personally to the telegraph office through an army of onlookers.

Blomsberry and Bronsfield entered the building while the throng crowded round the door.

Minutes later a dispatch had been sent to four destinations: 1. the Navy Secretary, Washington; 2. the Vice-President of the Gun Club, Baltimore; 3. the honourable J. T. Maston, Longs Peak in the Rocky Mountains; and 4. the Deputy Director of the Observatory at Cambridge, Massachusetts.

It read as follows:

At 27° 7′ north and 41° 37′ west, at 01.17 hours today, projectile from Columbiad came down in Pacific. Wire instructions. Blomsberry, Commander, *Susquehanna*.

Five minutes later, the entire city of San Francisco had heard the news. Before six that evening, the various States of the Union had been made aware of the unparalleled tragedy. After midnight, via the Cable, the whole of Europe knew the result of the great American experiment.

No attempt will be made to describe the effect produced throughout the world by this unexpected news.

On receipt of the dispatch, the Navy Secretary telegraphed the *Susquehanna* ordering the vessel to remain in San Francisco Bay and not let its boilers go cold. It must be ready, night and day, to take to sea.

In Cambridge, the Observatory met in extraordinary session and, with the cool composure which characterizes all learned bodies, the scientific aspects of the question were debated.

But the reaction of the Gun Club was explosive. All the artillery-men were there. Its Vice-President, the honourable Wilcome, was reading out an untimely dispatch in which J. T. Maston and Belfast announced that the projectile had been seen by the huge reflector at Longs Peak. The wire also reported that the projectile was in the grip of the Moon's gravity, and so acting as a sub-satellite in the Solar System.

The truth about that precise matter is now known.

However, on the arrival of Blomsberry's dispatch, which explicitly contradicted J. T. Maston's wire, two groups emerged within the Gun Club. In the first were those who accepted that the projectile had come down and consequently that the voyagers had returned. In the second were those who, preferring to trust to the Longs Peak sighting, concluded that the captain of the *Susquehanna* was mistaken. For this second group, the supposed projectile was a meteorite and nothing more, a shooting star of sorts which, as it had come down, damaged the bow of the corvette. No one knew what to say to counter their argument, given that the speed at which the object was travelling must have made it extremely difficult to get a proper sighting of it. The captain of the *Susquehanna* and his officers could easily have been mistaken, though in good faith. One idea, however, militated in their favour: if the projectile had landed anywhere on Earth, its collision with the terrestrial globe could only have occurred on the twenty-seventh degree of latitude north and—if account was taken of the time it had been away and of the rotation of the Earth—between the forty-first and forty-second degree of longitude west.

Despite this difference of opinion, it was unanimously agreed by the Gun Club that Blomsberry's brother,* plus Bilsby and Major Elphiston, would travel at once to San Francisco and there make arrangements for retrieving the projectile from the bottom of the Ocean.

These dedicated men left immediately and the railway (which will soon be completed all the way across the middle of America*) took them as far as St Louis, where express mail carriages were waiting for them.

At virtually the same moment that the Navy Secretary, the Vice-President of the Gun Club, and the Deputy Director of the Observatory received the telegram from San Francisco, the honourable J. T. Maston was experiencing the greatest shock of his life, more violent even than when his famous cannon had burst, and once again almost proving fatal.

It will be recalled that a few moments after the departure of the projectile—and almost as quickly—the Gun Club's secretary had rushed away to the Longs Peak station in the Rocky Mountains. The astronomer J. Belfast, Director of the Observatory at Cambridge, had gone with him. When they arrived, the two friends had settled in hurriedly and thereafter never left their seats high on their enormous telescope.

It is well known that this gigantic instrument had been built in the style of what the British call 'front-view'* reflectors. By this system, objects were viewed only via a single reflection and thus appeared at higher levels of clarity. As a result, when J. T. Maston and Belfast were observing, they were positioned in the upper part of the instrument and not at its foot. They reached it by a spiral staircase, a masterpiece of airy, gracious design. Below them—with the metal mirror at its base—was the huge metal tube 280 feet long.

Thus it was on the narrow platform situated above the telescope that the two scientists spent their time, cursing the daylight whose brightness hid the Moon from their eyes and the clouds which stubbornly obstructed their view at night.

So their delight may be imagined after waiting for several days when, during the night of 5 December, they saw the projectile which was carrying their friends through space! Their relief was followed by deep disappointment when, trusting to an incomplete set of observations, they fired off their first telegram all over the world, containing their mistaken claim that the projectile had become a satellite of the Moon and was circling it in a permanent orbit.

After that moment, they never saw the projectile again, a disappearance made all the more understandable because it was then passing behind the Moon's invisible disc. But predicting the moment when it would reappear on its visible face was frustrating to a degree which may be judged by the exasperation of the excitable J. T. Maston and his colleague, a man no less impatient than him! Not a moment passed that night but they thought they could see the projectile! This gave rise to endless discussions and violent arguments. Belfast said that the projectile was not visible while J. T. Maston insisted that it was 'as plain as the nose on his face!'

'It *is* the projectile!' repeated J. T. Maston.'

'It is *not*!' replied Belfast. 'It's an avalanche sliding down a mountain on the Moon!'

'Ha! We'll see it tomorrow!'

'We won't! We shan't see it again! It's been carried off into space!'

'We shall!'

'Shan't!'

And at these times when claim and counter-claim came down like hailstones, the well-known combustibility of the Gun Club's secretary represented a permanent danger for the honourable J. Belfast.

Being yoked together like this soon made life impossible. But an unexpected event cut short their constant bickering.

During the night of 14 to 15 December, the two irreconcilable friends were busy observing the face of the Moon. In his usual manner, J. T. Maston was berating the learned Belfast, who rose to the challenge. The secretary of the Gun Club asserted for the millionth time that he had just caught sight of the projectile, even adding that the face of Michel Ardan had just appeared in one of its portholes. He backed this sighting with a series of gestures which his fearsome hook made all the more intimidating.

At that juncture, Belfast's manservant appeared on the platform—it was ten at night—and handed him the telegram from the captain of the *Susquehanna*.

Belfast tore open the envelope and gave a cry!

'Well?' asked J. T. Maston.

'The projectile!'

'What about it?'

'It's come back to Earth!'

He was answered by another exclamation, a scream this time.

He turned to face J. T. Maston. But the poor man, imprudently leaning over the metal tube, had fallen into the huge telescope! A drop of 280 feet! Appalled, Belfast rushed to the mouth of the reflector.

He breathed again. J. T. Maston, caught by his metal hook, was dangling from one of the braces which supported the barrel of the telescope. And he was yelling blue murder.

Belfast shouted for help. His aides came at a run. Pulleys were installed and, not without difficulty, the reckless secretary of the Gun Club was hauled to safety.

He reappeared without further alarums at the upper opening of the telescope.

'Dammit!' he said. 'I could have broken the mirror!'

'And you'd have had to pay for it!' Belfast replied tartly.

'So that blasted projectile is back?' asked J. T. Maston.

'Came down in the Pacific!'

'Let's go!'

A quarter of an hour later, both savants were careering down the slopes of the Rocky Mountains. Two days later, they arrived in San Francisco at the same time as their friends from the Gun Club, having killed five horses on the way.

Elphiston, Blomsberry (the captain's brother), and Bilsby had rushed to greet them on their arrival.

'What are we going to do?' they cried.

'We're going to fish up the projectile,' answered J. T. Maston, 'and as quick as we can!'

22

THE RESCUE

THE exact position at which the projectile had come down was known. The means required to locate, attach a line, and bring it up to the surface of the Ocean were still not to hand. They would have to design equipment then build the machinery. But those American engineers were not going to let themselves be beaten by such trifles. When grappling hooks were ready and with the aid of steam power, they would be able to raise the projectile, despite its weight, though it would in any case be offset by the density of the water it had displaced.

But simply bringing it up was not enough. They needed to act quickly for the sake of the voyagers inside. No one doubted for a moment that they were still alive.

'Of course they are!' kept repeating J. T. Maston, whose confidence was infectious. 'Our friends are skilled fellows and they won't have let themselves be snuffed out like witless birdbrains. They are alive, very alive, but we must act quickly if we are to find them while they're still breathing. Provisions, water . . . I'm not worried about that. They have supplies which will last them a good long time! No, it's air! That is what they'll soon run short of. So roll up your sleeves!'

And roll them up they did. The *Susquehanna* was fitted out for its new destination. Its powerful engines were adapted to operate haulage chains. The aluminium projectile weighed no more than 19,250 pounds, which was much less than the transatlantic cable that was raised in similar conditions. The only difficulty lay therefore in how to pull up a cylindro-conical object whose smooth sides made it difficult to hook onto.

With this in mind, the engineer Murchison, who had rushed to San Francisco, devised a huge automatic grab which, when in place, would not release the projectile once it had managed to get its powerful claws onto it. He also prepared diving suits which had a tough waterproof outer layer, and so allowed divers to reconnoitre the

seabed. In addition he loaded on board the *Susquehanna* several cleverly designed compressed-air bathyscaphs. They were pressurized
craft, with portholes in the sides. When selected compartments were
filled with water, they could descend to great depths. Manned diving
chambers of this type were already in use in San Francisco, where
they had been involved in the construction of an underwater seawall.
And it was well that it was so, for there would have not been time to
construct them from scratch.

However, despite the excellence of these various kinds of equipment and the ingenuity of the experts entrusted with making them
work, the success of the operation was far from guaranteed. The odds
could not indeed be calculated, given that it involved hauling up
a projectile lying in 20,000 feet of water. And then, even if the projectile could be brought to the surface, would the voyagers have survived
the violent impact of their return from space, which 20,000 feet of
water had perhaps not sufficiently cushioned?

But they had to act fast. J. T. Maston urged on his workers night
and day. He was ready to get into a diving suit or a compressed-air
chamber himself, so that he could help discover what had happened
to his brave friends.

But for all the diligence displayed in making the equipment, and
despite the considerable funds made available to the Gun Club by the
government of the Union, five long days—five centuries!—went by
before their preparations were complete. During that time, public
opinion rose to the highest pitch of excitement! Telegrams never
stopped crisscrossing the whole world along electric wires and cables.
The rescue of Barbicane, Nicholl, and Michel Ardan was now a focus
of international attention. All the populations which had subscribed
to the Gun Club's appeal took a direct interest in the fate of the
voyagers.

In due course, the hauling chains, the air tanks, and the automatic
grab were loaded onto the *Susquehanna*. J. T. Maston, the engineer
Murchison, and the delegates from the Gun Club were all settled in
their cabins. All that remained now was to leave.

At eight o'clock on the evening of 21 December, the corvette
weighed anchor and began moving over a calm swell into a north-
easterly breeze and sharp, cold air. The entire population of San
Francisco had turned out on the quayside, excited but silent, reserving
their cheers for the vessel's return.

Full steam ahead was ordered and the *Susquehanna*'s propeller took the ship quickly out of the Bay.

Nothing would be gained by repeating the onboard conversations of the officers, crew, and the passengers. All these men had but one thought; every heart beat with the same emotion. And as they raced to the rescue, what were Barbicane and his companions doing? What had happened to them? Were they capable of devising some bold plan to regain their freedom? No one could say. The truth is that any plan was bound to fail! Submerged almost two leagues under the Ocean, their metal prison would have defeated their best efforts.

At eight on the morning of 23 December, after a rapid navigation, the *Susquehanna* was on station at its planned destination. They were obliged to wait for midday to get a precise reading of their position. The buoy to which the sounding-line had been lashed had yet to be sighted.

At noon, Captain Blomsberry, assisted by his officers who were overseeing the operation, took the reckoning in the presence of the delegates from the Gun Club. There was a moment of anxiety: when the *Susquehanna*'s position was determined, it was found to be a few minutes west of the place where the projectile had sunk below the waves.

The corvette was given a new course that would bring it directly to the precise spot.

At forty-seven minutes past noon, the buoy was sighted. It was intact and had probably drifted very little.

'At last!' exclaimed J. T. Maston.

'Shall we begin?' asked Captain Blomsberry.

'Without wasting a second!' replied J. T. Maston.

Every care was taken to keep the corvette completely stationary.

Before any attempt was made to attach a line to the projectile, engineer Murchison wished to know its exact position on the seabed. The diving chambers to be used for the search were given a supply of air. Operating these craft is not without its dangers because at 20,000 feet below the surface of the Ocean they are subjected to intense pressure. They have been known to spring a leak, the consequences of which would be unthinkable.

J. T. Maston, Colonel Blomsberry, and Murchison the engineer, heedless of the dangers, took their places in the diving chambers. Captain Blomsberry took his place on the bridge and directed operations, ready to halt or rewind the chains at the first signal. The vessel's propeller had been disengaged and the full power of the ship's engines, now directed to the capstan, could quickly haul a craft back on board if needed.

The descent began at twenty-five minutes past one o'clock that same afternoon. The diving chamber, pulled down by its full water-tanks, disappeared beneath the waves.

The emotions of officers and the crew were divided between the prisoners in the projectile and the men imprisoned in the submarine capsule. These last, with no thought for themselves, were glued to the glass of the portholes, attentively gazing out at the great volume of water through which they were descending.

It did not take long. At seventeen minutes past two, J. T. Maston and his companions were at the bottom of the Pacific. But they saw nothing, only barren desert undisturbed at this depth by marine fauna and flora. By the light of their lamps, to which were fitted powerful reflectors, they were able to see through the dim waters over a considerable distance—but of the projectile there was no sign.

Words cannot describe the impatience of those brave divers. Their vessel being connected electrically to the corvette, they sent a signal and the *Susquehanna* dragged them for a mile in their craft suspended a few metres above the ocean bed.

In this way they explored the flat floor of the Ocean, constantly deceived by tricks of the eye which broke their hearts. Here a rock, there a mound on the seabed resembled the projectile they were seeking, and then they realized they were mistaken and their hearts sank.

'Where have they got to? Where are they?' cried J. T. Maston.

And the poor man called out loudly to Barbicane, Nicholl, and Michel Ardan, as if his unfortunate friends could hear or answer him in that inhospitable environment!

The search continued in this fashion until the air began to grow bad inside the capsule and this forced them to return to the surface.

The process of hauling them up started at about six in the evening and was not ended before midnight.

'We shall resume in the morning,' said J. T. Maston, setting foot on the deck of the corvette.

'Indeed we will,' said Captain Blomsberry.

'And at a different location.'

'Yes.'

J. T. Maston was quite convinced they would succeed. But already his companions, no longer buoyed up by the excitement of those first hours, were aware of the enormous difficulties facing their efforts. What had seemed simple in San Francisco appeared almost impossible here in the middle of the Ocean. The prospects of success had fallen substantially and it now was to chance alone that they had to trust if they were to find the projectile.

Next morning, 24 December, despite the fatigues of the previous day, operations were restarted. The corvette moved several minutes to the west and the capsule, resupplied with air, again carried the same explorers into the depths of the Ocean.

The entire day passed in fruitless searching. The seabed was barren and empty. The 25th brought no result, nor did the 26th.

It was a desperate situation. They pictured the three wretched men who had now been shut up inside the projectile for twenty-six days. Even at that very moment they might well be feeling the first effects of asphyxiation—if, that is, they had survived the dangers of their cataclysmic return. Their air-supply would be running low and doubtless with it their courage, their good spirits.

'It's possible they might be running out of air', was J. T. Maston's invariable answer to that, 'but good spirits—never!'

On 28 December, after two more days of fruitless searches, all hope was gone. The projectile was an atom in the vast immensity of the Ocean. They would have to accept that they would never find it.

But J. T. Maston would not hear any talk or suggestion of leaving. He refused to go anywhere without having at least found the last resting-place of his friends. But Captain Blomsberry was unable to maintain his obstinate searching and despite the pleadings of the worthy Gun Club secretary, he was obliged to give the order for their departure.

On 29 December, at nine o'clock, the *Susquehanna* set a north-easterly course to return to San Francisco Bay, and headed back.

It was ten in the morning, and the corvette was proceeding at half-speed, as if reluctant to leave the site of the tragedy, when a sailor who had climbed to the cross-tree of the topgallant, suddenly cried out:

'Buoy on the lee beam!'

The officers scoured the sea as directed. Through their marine glasses they could see that the object sighted looked like the kind of buoy used to mark out channels in bays and rivers. But the odd thing was that a flag, flapping in the breeze, was fixed to a cone projecting five or six feet above the waves. The buoy glinted in the morning sun as if its sides were made of silver plate.

Captain Blomsberry, J. T. Maston, and the delegates of the Gun Club had climbed onto the bridge and were inspecting the object which was drifting aimlessly over the surface of the water.

They all watched it in a fever of anxiety but without speaking. Not one of them dared voice the thought that had entered the mind of every man.

The corvette steered a course that brought it to within two cables of the object.

A frisson ran through the entire crew.

The flag was an American flag!

At that moment, there was a loud yell. It was the loyal J. T. Maston, who had just fallen like a dead weight. Forgetting, first, that his right arm had been replaced by an iron hook, and second, that a protective gutta-percha skull cap covered his cranium, he had just given himself a tremendous crack on the head.

They all went to his aid, lifted him up, and brought him round. And what were his first words?

'Triple jackasses! Quadruple fools! Idiots five times over! That's what we are!'

'What do you mean?'

'What is it?'

'Well, out with it!'

'What I mean, you clown,' bawled the explosive secretary, 'what I mean is that the projectile weighs only 19,250 pounds!'

'And?'

'And that it has a displacement in water of twenty-eight tons, in other words, 56,000 pounds and that as a result, it *floats*!'

And he placed huge stress on the verb 'float'! And he was right! All—yes all!—those clever experts had forgotten one fundamental law by which, given the projectile's specific lightness, after its descent had taken it down to the lowest depths of the Ocean, had simply returned it to the surface unaided! And now it was floating gently wherever the waves chose to take it.

The lifeboats had been lowered. J. T. Maston and friends had leapt into them. The excitement had reached a peak: every heart raced as the boats bore down on the projectile. What did it contain? People who were alive or dead? Alive, yes! Alive—unless death had struck down Barbicane and his friends after they hoisted their flag!

A deep silence hung over the lifeboats. Hearts beat faster, eyes grew bleary. One of the portholes was open. A few pieces of glass remained in the frame, proving that it had been smashed. The port-hole was then some five feet above the level of the sea.

One boat tied up alongside, the one carrying J. T. Maston. J. T. Maston made straight for the porthole with the broken glass.

And then they heard a clear, cheerful voice. It was the voice of Michel Ardan who gave a cry of triumph:

'Double zero, Barbicane, double zero!'*

Barbicane, Michel Ardan, and Nicholl were playing dominoes!

23

TO FINISH OFF

THE reader will recall the great warmth of feeling which had attended the voyagers at the time of their departure. If at the start of their enterprise, they had attracted such sympathies from both worlds—the Old and the New—what kind of welcome would they be given on their return? Would the millions of spectators who had invaded the Floridian peninsula not rush back to greet those fabulous adventur-ers? Would those same legions of foreigners, who had already flocked to the shores of America from all points of the compass, leave the territories of the Union without seeing Barbicane, Nicholl, and Michel Ardan again? The fervour of the public would rise worthily to match the greatness of what had been achieved. Human beings who had left the terrestrial globe, and now returned after their unusual excursion into the space of the heavens, could not fail to be received as the prophet Elijah will be when he too returns to Earth.* See them and hear what they said: that was what people wanted.

And their wish would soon be granted to virtually the entire popu-lation of the Union.

Barbicane, Nicholl, Michel Ardan, and the Gun Club delegates, having returned promptly to Baltimore, were greeted there with indescribable enthusiasm. President Barbicane's systematic annota-tions were now ready to be laid before the public. The *New York*

Herald bought the handwritten notes for a sum which has not yet
been divulged but was assuredly substantial. When it serialized
instalments of this *Journey to the Moon*, its circulation rose to five
million. Three days after the return of the voyagers, the minutest
details of their expedition were known. All that remained now was to
see in person the heroes of this superhuman enterprise.

The exploration of Barbicane and his friends around the Moon
had enabled the various existing theories about the Earth's satellite to
be reviewed. The voyagers had made their observations with the
naked eye and under exceptional conditions. It was now known which
theories were to be excluded, and which retained. These covered the
formation of the Moon, its origins, and the question of whether it
was habitable or not. Its past, present, and future had all yielded up
their deepest secrets. What objections could be raised against these
meticulous observers who had, from a distance of less than forty
kilometres, delineated the curious mountain of Tycho, the strangest
instance of lunar orography? What possible argument could be put
up against these scholars whose eyes had looked into the abysses of
Plato's cirque? How could anyone contradict these audacious men
who, through the vicissitudes of their enterprise, had been carried
away above the hidden side of the lunar disc which no human eye had
ever seen before? It was now their right to decide the parameters of
selenographic science which had reconstituted the lunar world (just
as Cuvier had reconstructed the skeleton of a fossil) and say: 'The
Moon *used to be* an inhabitable world which was inhabited before
the Earth!' or 'The Moon *is* this: a habitable world which is now
uninhabited'!

To celebrate the return of its most illustrious member and his two
companions, the Gun Club gave a banquet in their honour, a banquet
which would be worthy both of these heroes and of the American
people, and take a form which would allow the entire population of
the Union to participate directly.

All the terminuses in the country were accordingly linked by temporary rail tracks. Then in all the stations, decked out with the same
flags and garlanded with the same decorations, tables were uniformly
set up and laid. At fixed times, calculated according to a timetable and
advertised by an interconnected series of electric clocks which marked
each second simultaneously, residents were invited to take their places
at the banqueting tables.

For four days, from 5 to 9 January, all trains were cancelled—as they are on railways in the Union on Sundays—and all rail tracks remained clear.

During those four days, only one locomotive, an express hauling a triumphal carriage, was allowed to run on the rail network of the United States.

The locomotive was operated by a train driver and an engineer and, as a signal mark of recognition, carried on its footplate the honourable J. T. Maston, secretary of the Gun Club.

The carriage was reserved for the exclusive use of President Barbicane, Captain Nicholl, and Michel Ardan.

After the hurrahs, hip-hips, and the other admiring hosannas in the American lexicon had faded, the engineer sounded his whistle and the train pulled out of Baltimore station. It travelled at a speed of eighty leagues an hour.* But what was such speed compared with the velocity at which the three heroes had shot out of the muzzle of the Columbiad?

In this way they went from one town to the next, seeing residents sitting at tables as they passed and waving at them and giving the same ovations without sparing the bravos. In this manner they toured the east of the Union through Pennsylvania, Connecticut, Massachusetts, Vermont, Maine, and New Brunswick;* they passed through the north and the west via New York, Ohio, Michigan, and Wisconsin; they turned south by way of Illinois, Missouri, Texas, and Louisiana; they branched off south-east through Alabama and Florida; they turned north again through Georgia and the Carolinas; from there they visited the centre, taking in Tennessee, Kentucky, Virginia, and Indiana; then after Washington station they returned to Baltimore. And so, during those four days, they could well believe that the entire United States of America, sitting down to the same colossal banquet, was welcoming them home with the simultaneous chorus of the same hurrahs!

Their apotheosis was worthy of those three mythological heroes who would have the rank of minor gods!

But would their great initiative, which was without precedent in the annals of travel, lead to some practical outcome? Will direct communication ever be established with the Moon? Will there be a system of space travel which will serve the entire solar system? Will people move from one planet to another—from Jupiter to Mercury—and later, from one star to another—from the North Star to Sirius? Will some means of locomotion ever allow humans to visit those suns which swarm in the firmament?

There are no answers to these questions. Yet, knowing the bold ingenuity of the Anglo-Saxon race, no one should have been surprised when the Americans tried to make the most of President Barbicane's audacious enterprise.

Indeed, some time after the return of the voyagers, the public reacted with marked enthusiasm to the creation of a limited company, with a capital of a hundred million dollars to be constituted by a hundred thousand shares of a thousand dollars each, and known as the 'National Company for Interstellar Communication': President, Barbicane; Vice-President, Captain Nicholl; secretary, J. T. Maston; director of operations, Michel Ardan.

And since it is part of the American position in business to take precautions covering all eventualities, even bankruptcy, the honourable Harry Troloppe, as official receiver, and Francis Dayton, public trustee, were appointed in advance!

APPENDIX 1
INCEPTION AND DEVELOPMENT OF THE NOVEL

'From the Earth to the Moon'

IN seeking the best nineteenth-century edition of *The Moon*, one can start by studying Verne's own views on the matter. The evidence is indeed clear: he invariably indicated his preference for the modest unillustrated 16mo editions of all of his novels: he gave copies to colleagues, friends, and relatives; cited their titles when they differed from the octavo ones; quoted from *From the Earth to the Moon* by referring to the small-format page number; and referred only to this unillustrated edition in what was probably his introductory footnote in the serials of *Around the Moon* published in the *Débats*.

Verne also showed two other preferences: a belief that the two lunar volumes form a single work; and a reluctance to use their published titles.

In contrast, the official announcements of whether one or two works were involved were far from consistent.[1]

Below the title '*From the Earth to the Moon*' in its manuscript of 1864, Verne writes the words '*Around the Moon*' in the same style, presumably words added after completion. The second manuscript of the second volume carries no title but immediately launches into a chapter heading which purports to 'rectif[y] the previous one', probably meaning the last chapter of the first volume ('A New Celestial Body'); and which also refers back to 'the first part of this work'. It is indeed clear that there is just one story: each of the volumes is incomplete on its own, for the first one ends

---

[1] The two volumes were published four years apart, without a common title. (The footnote in the serial of the 2nd part attributes the delay to the author: 'Many readers from all countries asked the author for this sequel, this conclusion. He was finally able to deliver it to us.') At the end of the 1st volume, there is no hint of a sequel, no words like 'End of the first part', unlike for instance in the two-volume *Adventures of Captain Hatteras* (1864). Even when the two parts were published together with *Around the World* (only in octavo editions), they were simply juxtaposed, with no indication of a connection. In volumes consisting of only the two parts, however, the cover, the half-title page, and the title page read '*From the Earth to the Moon* . . .', with 'followed by *Around the Moon*' in smaller characters. The unsigned footnote at the beginning of the *Débats* publication, however, refers repeatedly to the 'first part' and the 'second part'. In fact the only formal link, almost imperceptible, is the numbering of the issues printed individually before the octavo editions, in a tiny font at the bottom of every 8th page: only in these large-format editions, the numbering in the 2nd volume, for example, runs from '23' to '45'.

with the launch of the projectile and the second one starts with the events following it. Both have the same characters.

Among the 'works in preparation' listed at the end of the first volume of Hetzel's *Magasin d'éducation et de récréation* in September 1864 is a *Voyage dans la lune* (literally: Journey into the Moon). In the correspondence with Hetzel, Verne normally refers to '*The Moon*', whether meaning the first volume alone or the two combined. In 1868–9 the novelist's letters speak of *Return from the Moon* (*Retour de la Lune*) and in 1877 of *The Journey to the Moon* (*Le Voyage à la Lune*).[2] In French interviews with Verne in 1875 and 1902, the title is again *Le Voyage à la lune* or *Voyage vers la Lune* (. . . towards . . .); and in an English interview of 1896 he similarly refers to *Voyage to the Moon*—these forms being conciser and more accurate descriptions than the official ones.

The title *Voyage à la lune* was in fact first used by Hetzel: he wrote it into the final manuscript of the 2nd volume, as the name of the lunar story *within* the fictional universe. It thus plays the same self-referential, story-within-a-story and slightly inaccurate role as the definitive fictional title he incorporated into the final chapter of *Journey to the Centre of the Earth* in 1864. Similarly, in the other case of a novel with a misleading title, *Twenty Thousand Leagues under the Seas*—where Verne seems to have preferred 'Twenty-five Thousand Leagues'—the first use of the title may have been the publisher's, again in the margin of the final manuscript.

For Verne himself, in sum, the two lunar volumes form a single work. To respect his wishes, it seems incumbent to publish it in a single volume, under his preferred title, while also sometimes referring to '*The Moon*' or the 1st and 2nd volumes as abbreviated forms.

THE ORIGINAL EDITIONS

From the Earth to the Moon appeared in the *Débats* as sixteen serials from 14 September to 14 October 1865, as a 16mo volume on 25 October 1865, and in octavo form only on 31 July 1868.[3] The latter two went through numerous re-editions, more than thirty in the case of the small-format one.

The octavo editions were recomposed in about the 1870s. However, there do not seem to be any significant differences between large-format editions. The mid-career one of 1880 can accordingly be taken to typify the octavo version.

---

[2] In the 'Publishers' Notice' in *Hector Servadac*, for which Verne provided the draft, the work is cited as 'the *Journey to the Moon* and *Around the Moon*'.

[3] The octavo edition was first printed in the form of twenty-two short 'issues' from 12 June 1868 onwards.

The 16mo editions are far from identical.[4] Although responsibility for the changes is not known, it is possible to observe an overall but not uniform improvement up to the 10th edition of 1871, but a slight general deterioration thereafter.[5] This 10th edition may therefore be considered the best small-format text of *From the Earth to the Moon*.[6]

Between this 16mo edition of 1871 and the octavo one of 1880, there are a considerable number of variants, some substantial. In some cases, particularly where stylistic variants are concerned, it would be difficult to express a preference for one or the other form.[7] In rare instances, the octavo version benefits from updated information, such as the identification of ninety-seven orbiting fragments between Mars and Jupiter, compared with eighty-two in the 16mo editions, the galley proofs, and the manuscript.[8] However, the 16mo appears superior more often, as in: 'the oceans of the Earth', compared with '*the oceans of the* Moon' in 1880; 'the thin sheet of cast-iron melt which lay on the top of Stone's Hill' vs '*the sheet of cast-iron melt*'; 'the eclipse of 18 July 1860' vs '*of 8 July*'; or 'direct journey in 97 hours' in the novel's subtitle, compared with '*direct flight in 97 hours* 20 minutes' in 1880, a figure contradicted in the text of all the editions.

The 16mo edition of 1871 is therefore selected here as the base text for *From the Earth to the Moon*, even if doubt may be allowed about the accuracy of a few of its variants.

THE PROOFS

The surviving set of cut and bound galley-proof pages, numbered from 1 to 100 by Verne, contains chapters 1 to 17, with the chapter titles already in place. The layout is the same as in the early 16mo editions, with generally the same line breaks. Although a number of variants can be observed vis-à-vis the

[4] The 2nd 16mo edition in particular contains a list of nine 'Errata', most of which were later corrected, for example: 'Read: *knife* instead of *kniff* . . . *o'possum* instead of *kanguroo* . . . [Much] *Ado* instead of . . . *Abo*'.

[5] Including, for example, the erroneous replacement in some editions of 'twenty thousand pounds' as the weight of the projectile with 'five *thousand pounds*', of '1832' as the date of discovery of xylidine with '1833', and of 'cellulose' with 'celluse'.

[6] The first few 16mo editions, more often than the octavo ones, 'follow' the text of the *Journal des débats politiques et littéraires* (henceforth *Débats*)—'follow' in inverted commas because the serial publication was prepared either from 16mo proofs prepared by Hetzel or, more probably, from the aborted first impression, and the order of the various proofs is therefore unclear.

[7] As in the following example: in the 16mo edition, 'I fully agree that it is an admixture which has produced excellent results', as opposed to '*I* admit *that*. . .' in the octavo one. (Roman type is used for text absent from the base edition, italic for text shared with it.)

[8] The 82nd fragment, named Alcmene, was discovered in November 1864 and the 87th, Sylvia, in May 1866.

corrected manuscript, the corrections to the proofs, in Verne's hand, are modest in scale and number; and between these corrected proofs and the published texts, there are usually only slight stylistic and typographical adjustments.[9]

In the printing of Verne's manuscripts, if [symbols, placed to indicate the start of the work of new typesetters, correspond to line breaks in a given edition, then the first proofs must have been of the same format. In this case, three of the relevant symbols correspond to ends of lines in the 16mo editions, meaning that the first proofs were very probably also 16mo.

On a sheet of the manuscript of *From the Earth to the Moon* (253— unadorned Arabic numbers refer to manuscript pages), there is a fragment of nine lines of mirror-image printed text, presumably accidentally transferred from the first proofs.[10]

THE MANUSCRIPT

The last page of the sole surviving manuscript shows a great deal of pen cleaning, wear, and dirt. In the second half of the document gaps of several lines are left for later completion, especially in the astronomical sections and the dialogues.[11]

In some places the manuscript is longer than the published texts. For example, after the description of the luxuriant vegetation of central Florida, it presents giant spiders, including a passage where one of them 'devour[s] like a mere fly a poor little bird inextricably tangled up in its nets' (127). Again, the difficulty of giving an adequate description of the Columbiad's detonation is emphasized much more in the manuscript (264).

Four chapter titles will change for the better.[12]

[9] They may be an intermediate set of proofs, since they seem to pre-date the edition in the *Débats*, reading for example '*only* one *leg for six men*' (ch. 1), amended in all the editions to '*two legs*', perhaps slightly more suggestive.

[10] The lines, which, like sheet 253 itself, deal with the events leading to the launch of the projectile, appear to be slightly longer than in the 16mo editions; but the size of the tabs at the beginnings of lines seems to resemble that of the 16mo more than that of the octavo edition. The minor variants in the fragment unfortunately do not coincide with any of the variants *between* the editions.

[11] Opposite another blank, Ardan ventures a pun that will not survive in the book (195).—The ms and the proofs are conserved at the Nantes Municipal Library, under references mjv 83–14 and mjv B 13. Sincere thanks are due to the Library and its then director Agnès Marcetteau for enabling online access to these precious documents and for granting permission to reproduce them.

[12] '*The Moon*'s History' in the manuscript becomes the published 'The Romance of the Moon'; 'The First Committee Meeting: The cannon', 'A Paean of Praise to the Cannonball'; 'The Second Committee Meeting: *The cannon*', 'The Chronicle of the Cannon'; and 'The Third Committee Meeting', 'The Matter of the Propellant'.

The Margins

The right-hand halves of the manuscripts of *Les Voyages extraordinaires*, designed for annotations and modifications, form an almost unexploited field of research to date, although they transform our understanding of the works.

Throughout the margin of *From the Earth to the Moon*, Verne writes notes not intended for publication, perhaps added after the return of the manuscript from typesetting. Most are simple arithmetical operations designed to estimate the quantity of cast iron required or to calculate periods of time or the 'circumference of the lunar orbit' (217).

A few traces of external hands also seem to have survived, perhaps those of scientific readers, undoubtedly including his cousin Henri Garcet.[13] Also in the margin are some sixty interventions by Hetzel, often incoherent or illegible, which Verne crosses out, re-copies, or writes over, sometimes identically letter by letter. Since the publisher annotates the manuscript at least twice, his large scribbles in blue crayon and his neat small italic comments in black ink presumably correspond to successive readings.[14]

Nearly all of the editorial interventions concern details, sometimes aiming to refine or clarify the meaning, like 'this word doesn't seem right to me', 'What's this . . .?' or 'say . . . cannon' (51, 52, 96). When Hetzel asks '. . . in what way', concerning 'nothing as embarrassing as a man who . . .', Verne adds 'in private' (45), phrases which will nevertheless both disappear in the following stages of production. Sometimes the publisher suggests adding text, such as: '. . . *Phoebe* . . . and *Jupiter* . . .', '*sudden*' before '*subjection of a people*', or 'useless' before 'projectile to the Moon' (46, 30, 66). (The reader may deduce how much manuscript text survives until the published book from the proportion of italic text in the transcription.) Sometimes he questions the arithmetic, like the conversion of foreign currencies into francs; sometimes he makes convoluted practical suggestions—'why 1,000 workers try—to dig a pulley 900 [big ones]' (115, 132).

Only some of the longer remarks, aiming to remove or water down text, are acted on by the author, for example those commenting: on the idea of '*being* [one of the] *the Columbuses of that unknown world*' (19); on a passage about the variation of the distance from the Earth to the Moon (36); on the biting phrase, '*the Bastille, a place where the mad locked up the wise*' (69),

---

[13] For instance, the margin contains information written in an unusual hand: 'the unit of the Moon's atmosphere is probably less than one 2,000th the density of the Earth's atmosphere' (218).

[14] However, more than half of the manuscript (119–276) contains almost no remarks by the publisher, only rare entries in faint pencil, which may conceivably constitute his third revision. On about fifty of these sheets (147–57 and 167–210), Verne crosses out much or all of the original text, and writes a new version in the right-hand section.

which provokes Hetzel's incoherent exclamation; or on about fifteen lines of dialogue concerning the construction of the cannon, which produce further disjointed indignation—'You make of this Maston who is a scientist a fool so do that with some gravity'—causing them to be deleted (79).

In Verne's other manuscripts, Hetzel shows himself to be sensitive about anything to do with France or her international relations, above all social or political comments. Here he deletes an acerbic remark about Fontenelle's book: '*La Pluralité des mondes*, a masterpiece in its time, but science marches on, and crushes even masterpieces' (20).[15] Where Verne dares to quote statistics—'*France, where the accident rate is one for every 200,000 francs worth of work*'—the publisher exclaims: 'what [land] is this figure for? It's a lot of accidents . . .' (140). Finally, when Michel Ardan claims to know a controversial author—'*If I were a naturalist, I would . . . tell him following* my friend Flammarion . . .'—Hetzel downgrades it to: '. . . *would tell him, following many illustrious men of science* . . .' (183).

The publisher intervenes most intensively at the beginning and end of the volume. Only in the manuscript is the Gun Club characterized as 'very American' and an irreverent aphorism is offered: 'it was proved, once again, ~~that the art of war, like all the arts, can manage without teachers~~' (1). As in the proofs, the subtitle, 'Direct journey in 97 hours', has not yet been added, words that in the published versions will reinforce the impression of a landing on the surface of the Moon.

Dates

Neither in the manuscripts nor in the published versions of *From the Earth to the Moon* (1865) and *Around the Moon* (1869) is the year of events made explicit, the indirect indications not being entirely consistent. In the manuscript of *From the Earth to the Moon* (13), and in the published versions of *Around the Moon* (preliminary chapter, henceforth ch. o), the year is given as '186–'. Clues in the first volume, present at all stages of composition, are the functioning of the transatlantic cable, which in reality broke on 31 July 1865, and the absence from Italy of the autonomous territory of Veneto, which was incorporated *de facto* in July 1866. The transcontinental railway, opened in May and September 1869, remains unfinished in *Around the Moon*.

In the manuscript of the first volume, Lincoln, born in 1809, is still president, albeit ageing, which projects the work a few years into the future. As might be expected, the galley proofs also contain these remarkable lines,

---

[15] Similarly, he crosses out more than 300 words on the subject of the negligible British contribution to the cost of the projectile, writing at length about Verne's '~~failure~~', and suggests: 'write a scene' (117–18).

including: 'Lincoln is getting old . . . He's been on the throne in Washington for too long . . . We need a younger president who still has his reputation to make!' (8).

In the published first volume, the Gun Club is established 'during the . . . Federal War' (I 1),[16] which ended in reality on 26 May 1865, but 'after' it in the second volume (II 0). In the manuscript, there seems to be a small gap between the end of the War and the formation of the Gun Club, 'on 3 May' (11)—but this is inspired anticipation, as it was written in about September 1864.[17] (Verne was perhaps trying to synchronize the events of the novel with its publication, initially planned for the first half of 1865.)

From the first pages of the manuscript, Verne goes to great lengths to try to make the internal dates consistent, a task he will return to several times. The planned interval between the launch, on 1 July (267), and the landing on the Moon, on 4 July (38), is at this stage three days. The 16mo editions propose the same interval, between a launch on 1 December and arrival at the Moon at midnight on 4 December. (This revision to the launch date means that most of the preceding dates are put back by five months.) In *Around the Moon*, however, Verne says that the latter date is a mistake, without admitting that the error is his own: 'their arrival on the surface of the lunar disc could only take place on 5 December . . . and not on the 4th, as a few ill-informed newspapers had announced' (II 0). To remedy the inconsistency, he also inadvertently adjusts the launch date, writing '30 November' (II 1).

The last chapter

Chapter 28 of the first volume undergoes major changes. The manuscript still highlights the firm aim of walking on 'the surface of the Moon' (271). Although Maston mentions the possibility that the projectile became 'deformed by the explosion', at the same time 'he only regretted one thing, not to be with [the three voyagers], to increase the population of this new world to four' (273–4). However, by concluding that the projectile seems to have entered a lunar 'orbit', the possibility is also raised that the three men will simply return to Earth, an unappealing if practical idea that, like the others, will not survive as far as publication.

---

[16] Reminder: chapter numbers in the first or second volume are cited as 'I 1' or 'II 10'. Unadorned numbers like '23' refer to sheets in the relevant manuscript.

[17] The ageing of president Lincoln seems to imply that at this stage the War was projected to continue a few years after 1865. In contrast, in *Sans dessus dessous (Topsy-Turvy)* (1889), where the American characters reappear and which describes the first two volumes as 'the improbable attempt . . . made to establish direct communication between the Earth and the Moon', Verne places the founding of the club 'a few years after the American Civil War' (ch. 4).

The narrator closes the manuscript with the words: the aim of Ardan and his companions is '*to broaden the circle of human knowledge*'; they are heading for the 'solar world'; and they will find their 'eternal' reward in 'posterity'. In short, they have no thought of returning, having even '*gambled their lives*'. This moral perfectly reflects the philosophy of the great pioneering heroes of Verne's first period, including Captain Hatteras and Dr Lidenbrock, who give up everything, do not fear death, are prepared to sacrifice themselves for the cause of discovery and exploration. At the end, in short, Verne may simply be planning to abandon the lunar martyrs to their heroic fate.

In the published book, in contrast, the paragraph is weakened and moved to the middle of the chapter, and it is Maston who closes the volume, expressing confidence that the three men will emerge unscathed: 'We will correspond with them . . . as soon as circumstances allow. We'll get news from them and we'll send them our news . . .! they'll come through right as rain in the end!' This resolutely optimistic conclusion, supported by a mysterious hope, chimeric in fact, of establishing bilateral communication between the Earth and the projectile, perhaps allows for a sequel, but is devoid of substance, and wholly didactic, in the worst sense of the word, filling young heads as it does with empty ideas and unjustified confidence.

'*Around the Moon*'

THE ORIGINAL EDITIONS

As with the previous volume, the first galley proofs of *Around the Moon* (published in 1869) must have been of 16mo format.[18] Also as before, the text of the various octavo editions, for example those of 1872, 1880, and 1893, does not show any significant variants, only a few minor typographical adjustments. The middle one of 1880 may accordingly be taken to represent this series of editions.

The small-format editions are again surprisingly varied.[19] Up to a certain date, most of the changes are positive. While the 17th edition of about 1875 in particular shows an improvement on its predecessors, a comparison with the 30th one of about 1899 is inconclusive. In the absence of evidence as to the origin of the variants, caution is advisable: it will accordingly be

---

[18] Since the typographical symbols in the manuscript corresponding to changes of typographer: for instance, 'par[sèment' (116) or 'pieds res[taient dehors' (229), coincide with line endings in the 16mo editions.

[19] A 16mo copy of *Around the Moon* in the French National Library, without an edition number but with '1870' in pencil on the title page, contains a list of 'Errata' (p. 319), indicating only the corrected form. The corrections were incorporated in the octavo and subsequent 16mo editions.

assumed that this 1875 edition comes closest to representing the author's wishes.

Comparing the octavo version of 1880 and the 16mo one of 1875, some variants amount simply to a reformulation, neither clearly superior nor inferior. But in a few cases, the large-format edition is preferable, with for instance a past participle agreeing with its preceding direct object.[20] In a larger number of cases, however, compared with the 1880 or the *Débats* editions, the 16mo appears to show a greater level of accuracy, elegance, or clarity. It contains fewer agreement and spelling slips; and has fewer substantial problems, reading for example: 'the tides . . . and currents' (vs '*the* marshes *and* . . .' in 1880—'tides' and 'marshes' sound similar in French), 'Cooled lava flows would never give off such intense reflections' ('. . . elections'), or 'the thirty-seven stars' of the Union flag ('thirty-nine').[21] In sum, the 16mo of 1875 seems to be the best edition available, and has accordingly been adopted here.[22]

The clean copy

The second manuscript of the final lunar volume, written in April and May 1869, with 260 pages, or almost seven times the untitled first manuscript, is a legible document used for preparing proofs.[23] It underwent a number of revisions, apparently resulting in the replacement of sheets, particularly those at the beginning and end, but also perhaps including pages 84 to 112, which contain a fair number of modifications in the margin, but no visible interventions by Hetzel. Between June and September 1869, the publisher corrected *Around the Moon* at least four times, on this final manuscript and the proofs.

Margins

The right-hand halves of the manuscript pages contain various entries, in pencil or large blue or sometimes orange crayon; it is not always easy to distinguish those written by Verne himself, external readers, the publisher, or the printers.

Hetzel's scrawled entries become denser during the return to Earth and its aftermath. He points out text that seems to him unclear, awkward,

---

[20] The phrase 'in this country that loves difficulty' (I 1), describing the United States, is present only in the octavo editions.

[21] In 1869 the American flag contained 37 stars, the 39th not being added until 1889.

[22] Because this operation of establishing the text was not carried out, modern editions, even the Pléiade, maintain some of the errors of the octavo editions, for example: '*I'm afraid, my poor Diane, that you won't make your mark in the lunar* legions' (the 2nd ms, *Débats* and 1875 have 'lunar regions').

[23] The two mss of vol. II are conserved under references 'mjv 83–15' and 'mjv 83–16' in the Nantes Municipal Library, to whom thanks are recorded.

implausible, frivolous, or too technical. To explain the 'star effect' of an impact on the lunar surface, for instance, Ardan says '*I'll go along with the contraction*', to which Hetzel adds '*or* even *a lunar stomach ache!*' (199). Where Verne writes a clear and concise telegram, '. . . *projectile came down in Pacific*' (234), the publisher adds a dozen or so superfluous words. Pessimistic ideas, especially references to death, particularly annoy him: for instance, a passage that presents the certainty of not returning to Earth; the possibility of the astronauts dying during the splashdown in the Pacific; or the phrases '*It was a terrible fall*', 'Any means would have failed!', or 'perhaps, at this very moment, ~~they were succumbing,~~ *asphy*xiated' (216, 251, 221, 244, 248). Opposite another passage citing the various ways in which the astronauts might perish (166), the publisher inscribes, in vain, more than fifty words of criticism.

In other cases, he adds slightly conventional affectivity—'Emotions were running high. Every heart was palpitating . . .' or predictable comments: in response to a remark about the lack of a close-up view of the Moon, he adds '. . . *seen from a distance . . . like Moses and the Land of Canaan*', or '*Gosh! . . . when we got into the projectile we did think that it wouldn't be easy to get out of it again!*' (251, 208, 221).

Verne responds by making numerous corrections of variable length, often simply copying out Hetzel's text, but sometimes either weakening his original position or adding reasoning to support it, or, more rarely, simply crossing out the publisher's intervention.

The draft manuscript

The first manuscript is one of only five of Verne's true novel drafts to survive, with the unpublished text probably constituting more than half the volume. Written in a tiny, barely legible hand, its lines reach all the way to the left margin, contain few corrections, and are relatively incoherent and repetitive, with an informal style and faulty punctuation. Several sheets at the beginning and end are torn or worn at the bottom edge.

As in the other drafts, apparently in order to reach a target, Verne counts the number of new lines at the end of each page, sometimes reaching 120, or a thousand words. Nevertheless, the document contains fewer than 4,900 lines (in comparison the first manuscript of the two-volume *Twenty Thousand Leagues* has 16,640) and only twenty chapters, compared with twenty-four in the published book.

Although the content will not change radically before publication, the order of the scenes is altered between the two manuscripts. Verne gives the impression of struggling to write enough episodes to fill a volume, of writing passages of less than gripping interest, almost all of which, however, end up being retained.

The titles at this stage are simple and descriptive. Among those that will disappear are 'Ardan's Projects' and three with a negative tone, 'Goal Missed', ~~A Dead World~~ and ~~Barbarian Landscapes~~', a heading that Hetzel dislikes intensely: 'Delete this/vulgar' (11, 14, twice—18 and 20, 22). In '*The* Other Side' (30), which will be replaced by 'The Southern Hemisphere', the intention can be seen of devoting an entire chapter to the dark side of the Moon. The title, 'A Passing Ship' (39), underlines the coincidence of seeing the projectile splash down next to a vessel.

Verne inserts reminders to himself in the margins of some pages, noting that the dead dog floating in space is '*like a deflated set of bagpipes*', or writing 'turn off *the gas*' or a simple underlined 'no' (11, 31, 32).

As in the first volume, the margin contains simple sketches, such as one showing the rotation of the Earth or one of the Moon with five time markers around it (30). Others are more complex. A first drawing shows the Earth, the Moon, twice the projectile, and the triangular shadow of the sun's rays (7).[24] The following sheet contains a revised version, which adds a sun and is personalized with a nose, eyes, and hair-rays. Seen from a distance, it resembles a woman's body: the Earth seems to form the head, the orbit a broad hat, the sun a massively rounded belly—a visual pun on the fullness of the Moon and the woman? Below, the Moon, superimposed with an arrow aimed at the lower abdomen, forming an approximate crotch, bears at the same time an equivocal protuberance.

Lost texts

Unusual notes appear in the margins of the mathematical sections, often written in pencil, suggesting improvements on very minor details; almost all will be implemented at later stages of publication. These appear to be the author's, noting down suggestions by Henri Garcet or another adviser.

The initial chapter, provocatively entitled 'Which Rectifies the Previous One . . .' (1), attempts to summarize and update the first lunar volume. The opening lines make striking generalizations about scientists who take risks.[25] Hetzel, probably, annotates this incipit harshly.[26]

A soliloquy by Ardan that compares the lunar seas to the stages of a woman's life will go through intensive revision, more than half

---

[24] Reproduced in *Jules Verne inèdit*, 215.

[25] 'One should never be in a hurry to make *a discovery* when one is not absolutely sure to have made it, as regards a new heavenly body even less than any other . . . And when one makes one such, one must be certain that it is correct' (1): the passage, in a watered-down form, will be moved to a less prominent position in the middle of the chapter.

[26] 'The chapter that begins the second part of these surprising adventures must be [modulated better] in view of the too [precise] observations . . . /No one will [extend] any [welcome to the lessons]/And these discoveries are of no use to it' (1).

disappearing before publication: '*It is . . .* the Sea of Happiness and Love, it is *the Sea of Fertility of* the young woman who has become a mother . . .'[27] Even the slimmed-down version in the final draft—'in which the woman plunges into the ineffable joys of motherhood' (123–4)—attracts the publisher's ire: without comment, he crosses out the first four lines, although Verne declines part of the correction.

The few unpublished words in the key passage giving tantalizing glimpses of oceans and forests on the far side of the Moon are not very distinctive: 'certainly water . . . at a distance they could not assess', 'like low *clouds* in a rarefied atmosphere', the only exception being the regular shape of the 'entirely conical *mountains*' (30). Lower down on the same page, Verne plans to increase the number of glimpses of the dark side by providing additional illumination—'<seas . . . another aspect of vegetation, a few shooting stars>' (the < > indicate an addition to the original text)—but does not follow up.

The last page of the manuscript, with about twenty blank lines, is very sparse, although the closing words are already there: '*Double zero'* /Nadar [*sic*] *Barbicane and* Niccoll [*sic*] *were playing dominoes!*' Then comes the title of chapter 23, followed only by an anguished question, unpunctuated and unanswered: 'Conclusion/Is there a conclusion possible to this book'. The tension of universal emptiness continues in the final draft, where the last page contains the same sentence, and then merely a corresponding 'Chapter 24/Conclusion' and a closing horizontal line (252). Hetzel scribbles 'Upon my soul/Why not a banquet'; and accordingly a new chapter, entitled '~~A monster banquet~~ *To finish off*', will be added to the manuscript at a later stage (2nd series, [1]–6).

References in the margin

As usual in the drafts, Verne makes numerous calculations in the margins. But the great interest of this part is his quotation of sources, which are all popular astronomical works.[28]

Immediately after the words 'no, ether—atoms', for example, Verne notes 'Mgo 204' and writes a summary in telegraphic style of how solar heat is propagated, followed by a discussion of the '*trillions*' of vibrating

[27] Variants noted and analysed by Sainlot (pp. 54–5). The peroration continues: 'It is *the Sea of Crises*, this moment of doubt that comes to every woman who glances at her past, then at her future! It is lastly *the Sea of Tranquillity*, when all has been said of her role on Earth, when it is over, when the play has finished, and she has but to vanish into *the Lake of Death*' (21).

[28] The exception is the words, '~~Illustration no~~ 737—1857', opposite '*the dazzling Tycho*' (33), a reference to the periodical *L'Illustration*, which features this lunar peak in issue no. 737 (pp. 234–8).

constituents of the '*ether*', culminating in the words '*molecular physics*' and a new reference, 'Mgno' (5). Page 204 of Abbé François-Napoléon Moigno's *Molecular Physics* (1868) does indeed contain identical information about the transmission of the heat of the sun, which will be largely reproduced in Verne's book.

Again, the origin of the dialogue about the immense weight of objects on the surface of the sun is added in the margin, as '<Liais 67>' (16), meaning Emmanuel Liais's *L'Espace céleste* (1865), from which nearly all the passage is drawn. To fill the six closing blank lines of the dialogue, Verne writes himself a reminder: '~~not . . . stand up~~'; and in the second manuscript he duly writes in the rest of the discussion. The likelihood of water having existed on the Moon is attributed to the same book: 'it is probable that there was water on the other side, but see Liais' (30). Similarly, the novelist writes 'Lunar asteroids L. 524' (13), referring to Liais's idea that large bodies could have been projected into space by the Moon's volcanoes: '*L Laplace calculated that a force just five times greater than the fire-power of our cannons . . .*' (p. 524).[29]

The information on the '*three* [Himalayan] *peaks that are higher than any peaks on the Moon*' is copied from '<Lec. 97>' (31), or Henri Lecouturier, co-author with Adolphe Chapuis of *La Lune: Description et topographie* (1860) (p. 97); their detailed relief map of the Moon shows 232 named peaks.

On the subject of the greater number of shooting stars visible when the Earth veers away from the sun, Verne cites an observation made by 'Dr Burton' (4), or Charles Edward Burton (1846–82), an assistant to the celebrated astronomer William Rosse from February 1868 to March 1869.

The description of the two methods of calculating the height of lunar mountains comes from '<Ar. 15 414>' (32), or the fifteenth volume of Arago's *Complete Works*, p. 414. However, borrowings from this author are not always indicated: when the asteroid, about to hit the projectile head on, explodes into a shower of burning fragments, Verne gives the statistics and dates of comparable exploding bodies near the Earth, reproduced from Arago, pp. 424–6 (32).[30] Similarly, he draws much of his mini-monograph on the 'grooves' or furrows of the lunar surface from the same volume.[31]

In two places in the margin, Verne writes an identical 'see Hatteras' (8, 28). In the first case, he later adds 'about fifty-six degrees centigrade below zero'. *The Adventures of Captain Hatteras* contains the corresponding

---

[29] However, a passage on chiaroscuro in the lunar landscape gives three references that are difficult to trace precisely: 'Li[a] 60–1' and '<*Dictionnaire illustré*/Liais 123>' (26).

[30] References to Arago without a volume number are to his vol. 3. Further down on the same sheet Verne writes: 'the meteorite lighting up like that of Kinsbourg [Kingsburg?], 12 Feb. 1836', surely linked to the passage of Halley's Comet on that date.

[31] However, Verne states that the number of grooves is '70', whereas this figure refers to the number of *new* grooves 'reported by Messrs *Beer and Mädler*' (Arago, p. 426).

figure, '−56°7 centigrade' (vol. II, ch. 9), information derived in turn, according to a reference in the first manuscript—'Ar. 8 205' (28)—from Arago, who gives the same figure of '. . . −56°.7' (vol. 8, p. 205).

Chaotic pages

Rather than attempting the huge task of transcribing or synthesizing all the unpublished passages of the first manuscript, it may be simpler to look at a condensed version, in the form of a few pages which illuminate Verne's creative process and in which deletions, insertions, summaries, corrections, and elementary calculations abound (5–7).

Verne starts by depicting the first night of the voyage, where the voyagers contemplate space before turning in: 'Our heroes slept without taking any kind of watch' (7).[32] He then tries out five versions of the key first awakening in space. The opening one, which forms the beginning of the chapter '*Settling in*', emphasizes the voyagers' calmness, due to the silence and absence of worries: they have a 'very cheerful' and 'very tipsy' breakfast, generously washed down with '*Nuits* [St George]' and 'brandy' (5), an episode that will not survive Hetzel's scissors intact. (Similarly, the publisher will criticize the words '*good French wine*' (2nd ms 81).) The second and third attempts give lengthy explanations, perhaps designed to satisfy Hetzel's wish for more hard science, of 'the Moon and the Earth being *in conjunction* as regards *the sun*' (7), as well as of the consequences of an eclipse of the Earth; passages that are leavened with 'a cockerel crowing [that] woke them up, as on farms' (7). A fourth scene deals mainly with saving fuel for the lighting and central heating—'compressed gas, with hot water pipes like in workshops'—and with finding objects in the dim interior of the projectile, 'a relative darkness cut only by the bare rays of the Moon' (6). In the last passage, after a short dialogue about Ardan's 'culinary functions'—'the journey whets our appetites'—the passengers easily open the porthole covers. The reduced form of the Earth, seen for the first time, resembles 'one of those crescent moons that artists of mythological scenes sometimes suspend in a corner of their paintings', illuminated by the 'ashen light' coming from 'a few shooting stars' (7). A description of the Moon follows: 'all resplendent with the rays of the sun, already distended, with its barely recognizable patches of light and shadow; it seemed to boil in the coloured rays, and its disc was white-hot, making its brilliance difficult to bear.' The sun's rays in fact blind the three men.[33]

[32] The scene is transcribed in *Jules Verne inédit*, 214–15.

[33] 'Arrows of fire rushed at their eyes and stabbed them, for there was no atmosphere to reduce the brilliance, and whenever their eyes happened to turn in that direction, they again felt a severe pain; after several attempts, the voyagers had to avoid this agonizing result completely' (7).

In the published book, instead of these imaginative cultural and scientific passages—unsuitable, however, for placing in young hands, given the danger of imitation—there will appear long technical (and educational?) explanations, not only of the means used to open the porthole covers, but also of the changes in the Moon's light and the appearance of the Earth's crescent.

In short, although certain ideas, such as the death-throes of the dog, are transferred to other sections, more than three-quarters of these pages differ significantly from the published book. The order is logical: peace at night, the warmth of the sun, the absence of lunar eclipse, the abolition of day and night, the view, especially of the Moon, and lastly lunch, eaten while chatting about crossbreeding terrestrial and selenite dogs.

APPENDIX 2

PROPER NAMES CITED BY VERNE

(in order of appearance)

Robert *Parrott* (ms: 'Parrots') (1804–77) introduced rifled armaments, although his guns sometimes exploded. John *Dahlgren* (1809–70), admiral who designed a more precise and powerful cannon. Thomas *Rodman* (1815–71), general who designed a water-cooled cannon with a greater range.

Sir William *Armstrong* (1810–1900) designed a reinforced gun, which still sometimes exploded but usually provided warning. Cavalry officer Sir William *Palliser* (1830–82) developed projectiles that pierced armour effectively, as well as a method of adding rifling to cannons. General Antoine Hector Thésée *Treuille de Beaulieu* (1809–86) designed high-performance rifled guns.

Jean Baudoin (c.1590–1650), writer and proof-reader, in fact the French translator in 1649 of *The Man in the Moone . . . By Domingo Gonsales* (1638), written by Francis Godwin, featuring goose-wing-powered travel to a Moon inhabited by giants.

Savinien de *Cyrano de Bergerac* (1619–55), author of *Histoire comique des États et empires de la Lune et du soleil* (1657 and 1662). Bergerac attaches steam-filled bottles to his belt, which act as primitive rockets when heated by the sun; on his second flight, he is propelled by real three-stage rockets.

Bernard Le Bouyer de *Fontenelle* (1657–1757), playwright and author of *Entretiens sur la pluralité des mondes* (1686), in which the Selenites are hidden in deep wells.

Phoebe is the virgin goddess of the Moon and hunting.

William Cranch *Bond* (1789–1859) discovered the Andromeda nebula (galaxy) and photographed the Moon. American painter and telescope maker Alvan Graham *Clark* (1832–97) discovered Sirius B in 1862. His telescope was in fact transported shortly afterwards to Evanston, Illinois. (All the scientists quoted here are astronomers unless otherwise indicated.)

Endymion, simple shepherd or mythological king, lover of Selene on Mount Latmos.

Selene, Greek goddess of the Moon, who crosses the sky in a silver chariot.

Greek philosophers: *Simplicius*, flourished in the 6th century AD. Achilles *Tatius*, 2nd or 3rd century AD, author of *Introductio in Aratum*. *Clearchus* of Soli (Cyprus), 4th century BC.

Thales of Miletus, mathematician who died in the 6th century BC. Arago reads: '*Thales* . . . already professed *the opinion that the Moon was illuminated by the sun*' (p. 390). (Reminder: unless otherwise indicated, references to Arago are to his vol. 3.)

Aristarchus of Samos, 3rd century BC, another borrowing from Arago, who notes that he 'found *the true explanation* of lunar *phases*' (p. 390).

Berossus, astrologer born in Babylon in the 4th century BC.

Hipparchus, mathematician born in Anatolia in the 2nd century BC, who studied lunar movements and built the first astrolabe.

Ptolemy Claudius (*c*.100–*c*.168), Greek author of astronomy and geography. *Abul-Wafa* (940–98), Persian author of astronomy.

Nicolas *Copernicus* (1473–1543), Polish or German, promoted the theory that the Earth revolved around the sun. *Tycho Brahe* (1546–1601), Danish author of *Astronomiae Instauratae Mechanica* (1602), who proposed that the Moon and the sun revolved around the Earth.

Galileo Galilei (1564–1642) perfected the telescope and observed the craters and 'seas' of the Moon; he also promoted heliocentrism, but was forced to recant by the Inquisition.

Johannes *Hevelius* (1611–87) created an astronomical telescope and drew the first comprehensive map of the Moon (1647). The encyclopaedia *Almagestum novum* (1651) by Giovanni *Riccioli* (1598–1671) contains a lunar map, whose nomenclature, often based on the names of astronomers, grouped by affinity, largely survives today. In *Around the Moon* (henceforth II or vol. 2), Verne describes his map as 'full of crude errors' (II 10).

Wilhelm *Beer* (1797–1850) and Johann *Mädler* (1794–1874), authors of *Der Mond* (1837) and *Mappa selenographica* in four volumes (1830, 1834). Almost a metre wide and identifying thousands of craters, the most influential lunar publication of the time, the map is described by Verne in vol. 2, ch. 10. Johann Hieronymus *Shroeter* (1745–1816), author of a topographical study of the Moon. Scottish engineer James *Nasmyth* (1808–90) invented a telescope bearing his name. Priest Francesco *Bianchini* (1662–1729), Mars and Venus specialist. Johann Wilhelm *Pastorff* (1767–1838) studied sunspots. Mathematician Wilhelm Gotthelf *Lohrmann* (1796–1840) drew 'Topography of the Visible Surface of the Moon' (1836).

According to Arago (p. 382), Pierre-Simon de *Laplace* (1749–1827) concluded in 1787 that the Moon was undergoing a very slight deceleration, but was also moving imperceptibly away from the Earth.

Richard *Mead* (1673–1754), physician to the king and author of *De Imperio Solis ac Lunae in Corpora humana* . . . (1704). Verne mentions him again later (II 22), following Arago, who writes: '*Mead* cites *a child who* always experienced *convulsions when* this heavenly body was in opposition' (pp. 508–9).

Possibly Confederate general John Hunt *Morgan* (1825–Sept. 1864). *Major Elphiston*: a Major Elphinston accompanied Queen Victoria to Brussels in October 1862.

Unionist artilleryman Thomas Jackson *Rodman* (1815–71) designed innovative cannons (1861–4); those used at *Fort Hamilton* were of 20-inch calibre.

Mahomet II, or Mehmet II the Conqueror (1432–81), sultan who took Constantinople in 1453 and conquered several countries in Eastern and Central Europe.

Henri *Braconnot* (1780–1855), pharmacist and naturalist; chemist Théophile-Jules *Pelouze* (1807–67); Christian *Schönbein* (1799–1868), Swiss chemist who invented the fuel cell and discovered guncotton.

Samuel Houston (1793–1863), President of the Republic of Texas, whose independence he defended against the United States. General Antonio Lopez de *Santa Anna* (1794–1876), President of Mexico.

Explorer and conquistador *Juan Ponce de León* (1474–1521) landed in Florida in fact in April 1513.

Jean de Bade (1434–1503), Prince of Trier and Margrave of Baden-Hachberg. In *Le Rhin, Lettres à un ami*, Victor Hugo quotes 'the famous fort of Ehrenbreitstein [containing] . . . a *well* five hundred and eighty *feet* deep, *dug by Margrave Jean de Bade*' (p. 267). However, most sources give its depth as at most 300 feet.

Johann Kaspar *Lavater* (1741–1801), Swiss phrenologist; Louis-Pierre *Gratiolet* (1815–65), physiologist, fellow student with Hetzel, and author of *De la Physionomie et des mouvements d'expression* (Hetzel, 1865).

German Peter Andreas *Hansen* (1795–1874) studied the perturbations of the planets.

Probably alchemist and philosopher Roger *Bacon* (*c*.1210–*c*.1292). Arago reads: '*21 January* . . . the *eclipse* . . . *the* illustrious *Bacon fainted during* all *lunar eclipses and* only recovered his senses as *the heavenly body* came back into the light' (p. 507).

Franz Joseph *Gall* (1758–1828), physician and phrenologist.

Karl von *Reichenbach* (1788–1869), chemist who believed in a vital force in everything, author of a dissertation on aeroliths published in *Annales de Poggendorf*, vol. 111 (1860).

Marie-Joseph Motier, *Marquis de la Fayette* (1757–1834) fought alongside the insurgents in the US War of Independence.

Noël Paymal *Lerebours* (1807–73) produced daguerreotypes.

Lord Rosse: in 1845 William Parsons, Earl of Rosse (1800–67), built a 183-cm-long telescope, the largest in the world. Guillemin: 'the telescope built *by Lord Rosse in his park at Parsonstown, Ireland*' (pp. 601–2—all references to Guillemin are from his book *Le Ciel* unless otherwise indicated).

Léon *Foucault* (1819–68), physicist and inventor. Guillemin observes that '*a scientist . . . Léon Foucault . . .* imagined constructing telescopes with mirrors made of *silvered glass, which* would make it . . . extremely *easy to polish the lenses*' (p. 601).

The polymath Robert *Hooke* (1635–1703) lived more than 'a few years' ago.

Heinrich Daniel *Ruhmkorff* (1803–77), physicist living in Paris, the inventor of an induction coil (1850–1), which transformed a low-voltage direct current into a high-voltage alternating current to ionize gases and so produce light, a coil which plays an important part in *Journey to the Centre of the Earth*. However, the coil had low efficacity and required a separate device to generate electricity. Verne generally underestimates the usefulness of alternating current.

Robert Wilhelm *Bunsen* (1811–99), physicist and chemist who improved the battery and the spectroscope, and perfected the Bunsen burner. The cell, or Bunsen battery (1841), with opposing cathodes made of carbon and zinc, produced less than 2 volts.

The soldier Henri de La Tour d'Auvergne, known as *Turenne* (1611–75), took a quick sleep before the Battle of Westphalia (1673).

Robert *FitzRoy* (1805–65) accompanied Darwin on his decisive circumnavigation on board the *Beagle* (1826–30) and was promoted vice-admiral in 1863; he committed suicide on 30 April 1865.

Mathematician and physicist Joseph *Fourier* (1768–1830), author of the Fourier series, which he used to decompose periodic functions and hence apply them to the propagation of heat.

Physicist and politician Claude *Pouillet* (1790–1868), author of *Mémoire sur la chaleur solaire . . . et sur la température de l'espace* (1838).

Alfred de *Caston*, pseudonym of illusionist and author François Léon Antoine Aurifeuille (1822–82); Jean-Eugene *Robert-Houdin* (1805–71), conjuror and magician, who gave 'Harry Houdini' his surname.

'*John Ross*', here and in ch. 13, must in fact be William Parsons, Earl of Rosse.

Philippe de *La Hire* (1640–1718). Arago reads: 'a *4-metre* painting . . . *La Hire's map* was not *engraved*' (p. 444).

Tobie Mayer (1723–62), author of *Tables de la Lune* (1770).

Like William Herschel and Gruithuysen, Johann Hieronymus *Schröter* (1745–1816), claimed to have seen signs of life on the Moon.

Engraver *Warren de la Rue* (1815–89) photographed the Moon in the 1850s.

Julius Schmidt (1825–84), author of *Der Mond* (The Moon, 1856) and *Rillen auf dem Monde* (Grooves on the Moon, 1866); specialist in astronomical spectroscopy; priest Angelo *Secchi* (1818–78), mapped the Copernicus crater; journalist and scientist Henri *Lecouturier* (1819–60) and Swiss Adolphe *Chapuis* (b. 1812) were co-authors of *Carte générale de la Lune* (c.1859) and *La Lune: Description et topographie* (1860).

John *Franklin* (1786–1847), John *Ross* (1777–1856), and American Elisha *Kane* (1820–57) were polar explorers, often mentioned in *Captain Hatteras*. Admiral *Dumont d'Urville* (1790–1842) studied terrestrial magnetism, mapped the South Seas, and published *Voyage de découvertes autour du monde et à la recherche de La Pérouse* (1832). *Lambert* was either a Dutch whaler who in 1670 saw Lambert Land at about 78° 30′ N; or perhaps Gustave Lambert (1824–71), hydrographer and navigator who in 1867 proposed an expedition to the North Pole.

Diana is the goddess of the Moon and hunting, *Isis* an Egyptian goddess, *Astarte*, the Phoenician name for either Venus or the Moon, and *Latona*, the mother of Apollo and Artemis.

Johannes *Kepler* (1571–1630) studied Mars, formulated laws of planetary motion, and wrote *Somnium* (1634), about a dream featuring travel to a populated Moon.

Johann W. *Pastorff* (1767–1838), specialist in sunspots; Franz von *Gruithuysen* (1774–1852), physicist who observed fortifications around a lunar city in *Découverte de traces évidentes d'habitants dans la Lune* (1824).

Hervé *Faye* (1814–1902), author of 'Remarques sur l'hypothèse de l'atmosphère de la Lune', *Comptes rendus hebdomadaires des séances de l'Académie des sciences*, vol. 51, pp. 445–8; Jean *Chacornac* (1823–73) published an atlas and discovered six asteroids.

Politician and physicist François *Walferdin* (1795–1880), whose thermometer dates from 1836.

Explorer and naturalist Alexander *Humboldt* (1769–1859), author of *Cosmos* (1845–58). Guillemin writes that: 'The hollow of *Newton's crater* is such, according to *Humboldt*, that *the bottom is* never illuminated by either *the Earth* or the *sun*' (*Éléments de mécanique*, 174).

Georges *Cuvier* (1769–1832), a founder of comparative anatomy and palaeontology, author of *Discours sur les révolutions de la surface du globe* (1822); he claimed to be able to reconstruct an extinct animal from a single bone, but in fact used detailed knowledge from extant species to do his reconstructions.

Chemist and physicist William Hyde *Wollaston* (1766–1828), who in fact attributed to Sirius a diameter of 4,500 leagues (Guillemin, 380).

EXPLANATORY NOTES

7 *the Federal War in the United States*: (12 April 1861–26 May 1865), fought mainly over the abolition of slavery and the secession of the South from the Union. [Selected parts of the critical material are due to appear in W.B.'s edition of *The Moon* for Gallimard (in press).]

that people of shipowners, merchants, and engineers: for Verne, America is the land of engineers, where 'practical difficulties melt away before they even arise' (p. 36), and who dream of 'plant[ing] on its highest peak the star-spangled banner of the United States of America' (p. 35).

'the art of war': without capital letters, perhaps nonetheless a reference to the treatise on military strategy of that name by Sun Tzu (544–496 BC), translated into French in the 18th century; the title was also used by Machiavelli in 1521.

8 *Newton's law of universal gravitation*: the force of gravity between two masses is proportional to each mass and inversely proportional to the square of the distance, law enunciated by physicist Isaac Newton (1643–1727).

9 *Coutras . . . Kesselsdorf . . . each time it was fired*: in all three cases, the cannons did indeed make a decisive contribution. At Coutras, north-west of Bordeaux, an outnumbered Protestant force defeated Catholics. At Zorndorf in Poland, the Prussians overcame the Russians. Kesselsdorf was a Prussian victory over Saxons and Austrians, in fact in 1745.

Iena or Austerlitz: victories by Napoleon I over respectively Prussia (1806) and Austria and Russia (1805).

Gettysburg: decisive Union victory (1863), which saw the Confederates retreat across the Potomac.

J. T. Maston: from *masse-tonne*? In *Sans dessus dessous* (1889) he is called James T. Maston.

Exterminating Angels: four angels sent to avenge the violation of God's law, who introduce the tenth plague to Egypt (Exodus 11: 1–12).

10 *Sherman or McClellan*: Unionist generals: William Tecumseh Sherman (1820–91), a bold officer who took Atlanta; George Brinton McClellan (1826–85), cautious commander-in-chief of the Army from November 1861 to March 1862, later a politician.

12 *Bowie knife*: popularized by Colonel James Bowie (1796–1836).

13 *Impey Barbicane*: authentic first name, perhaps taken from the geologist and cartographer Roderick Impey Murchison (1792–1871). *Barbicane* may be an anglicized form of *barbacane* (fortified gateway) or *barbican* (a type of bird).

straining to get to the front: the manuscript (henceforth ms) of *From the Earth to the Moon* adds '~~with typically American intrepidity~~'. (Reminder: text common to the base text and a source or a different version of the work appears in italics; text not in the base edition, in roman.)

15 *punctual as a stopwatch*: the ms adds: 'even in the most minor matters'.

Roundheads . . . Cavaliers: Roundheads was the informal name given to the Puritans, supporters of Parliament, headed by Oliver Cromwell in the First English Revolution (1642–51), which led to the execution of Charles I, a Stuart. The royalists, of ornate appearance, were nicknamed Cavaliers. This contrast, between the Protestant farmer–artisans of the North-East and the aristocratic rentiers of the South, is often seen in contemporary commentaries.

16 *the thirty-six states*: in the ms Verne writes: ' . . . *of the thirty*-four *states* that make up *our great Union*'. Hetzel scribbles 'what union' and largely illegible words; and Verne crosses out this phrase and replaces it with: '*thirty*-four . . . the *Union* and we will talk about the State of the Moon, as we talk about the State of Louisiana!'

17 *David Fabricius*: (1564–1617), German theologian who, along with his son Johannes, was the first to note the existence of sunspots and the rotation of the sun on its axis. Flammarion says: '*David Fabricius* . . . claimed to *have seen with his own eyes inhabitants of the Moon*' (p. 29). The list of voyages to the Moon that follows is highly selective; all reach the Moon by fanciful means—birds, heated light bulbs, fireworks—and all discover inhabitants. (Until the beginning of the 19th century it was believed that there was an atmosphere between the Earth and the Moon.)

the New York American . . . Herschel: this Democrat newspaper, established in 1819, merged with the *New York Courier* in about 1846. Philosopher Sir John Herschel (1792–1871) wrote *A Treatise on Astronomy* (1833).

Locke: the six articles by Richard Adams Locke (1800–71), called 'The Great Moon Hoax', in fact appeared in *The Sun* in New York in 1835, before being reprinted as a brochure. Painter, art critic, and revolutionary Gabriel Laviron (1806–49) translated and published Locke's work (Lyon: Aimé, 1835).

18 *Hans Pfaall*: in Edgar Allan Poe's 'Unparalleled Adventure of One Hans Pfaall' (1835, translated by Baudelaire in 1856), a balloon filled with an ultra-light gas is propelled by gunpowder, with Pfaall carrying pure oxygen. Verne analysed the hoax in 'Edgar Poe and his works' (*Musée des Familles*, 1864), declaring the means used to reach the Moon 'too implausible'.

colossal geometrical shapes using luminous reflectors: the idea of Karl Gauss (1777–1855), who did not in fact propose using illuminated shapes. Verne's source may be Flammarion: 'Arago recounted . . . [the idea] of *a German geometer* . . . on the immense *steppes* of *Siberia a team of scientists* charged with arranging . . . *geometric shapes* . . . mirrors . . . *reflectors*' (p. 258).— Famous physicist and liberal politician François Arago (1786–1853) measured a terrestrial meridian and worked on electricity and optics. His

Œuvres complètes in thirteen volumes, together with the four volumes of *Astronomie populaire*, which Verne owned, form the largest source for the Moon volumes.

19 *12,000 yards a second*: or about 11.2 km/s, not far from the modern escape speed of 11.4 km/s. In Part II ch. 4, it is pointed out that this calculation fails to take air resistance into account.

20 *Jones Falls Street*: perhaps an amalgamation of Jones' Falls and Fall Street, both in Baltimore.

21 *ten times the size of France*: this figure seems to apply only to the States in the narrow sense, not including the unincorporated territories.

fifteen hundred . . . took up the story: a number which according to Miller does not include specialist magazines.

22 *Impey Barbicane . . . George Washington of science*: the ms adds: 'his portrait cards were printed in several million copies, and took pride of place in every album'.

23 *Observatory at Cambridge*: founded in 1823, part of Harvard College.

24 *247,552 . . . 218,657 miles*: now quoted as 252,700 and 221,500 miles. There is often a ratio of 0.98 between the distances given by Verne and modern ones, a discrepancy perhaps due to his use of French miles.

eighty-three hours and twenty minutes . . . thirteen hours, fifty-three minutes, and twenty seconds: or the 'ninety-seven hours, thirteen minutes, and twenty seconds' of the following sentence.

25 *in its perigee . . . at its zenith*: in other words, the cannon will have to aim for the vertical, at the moment of the shortest trajectory, conditions applicable to the planned time of arrival on the Moon, not to those of the departure.

3,919 miles: '218,657' minus '214,976' gives 3,681 miles.

next year: probably 1866. According to Miller, the first year of the coincidence would be 1876.

between 0° and 28° latitude north or south: it might have been simpler to determine the site before choosing the date.

eleven degrees: 'six degrees' may be more accurate.

26 *on 1 December next year at 13 minutes and 20 seconds before 11 p.m.*: or at 22.46 40 seconds, derived by subtracting the journey time of 97 hours 13 minutes and 20 seconds from the scheduled lunar landing, at midnight on 4 December. In fact, the subtraction gives 30 November, an error that will only be partially corrected later (p. 154).

another eighteen years and eleven days: in the ms, 'every fourteen months or so'.

J. M. Belfast: until February 1865 the director was George Phillips Bond (1825–65).

27 *eighteen million stars*: modern estimates of the number of stars in the Milky Way range from 100 billion to 400 billion.

28 *the first days of the world*: perhaps 'world' in the sense of universe; in Hugo's paraphrase of the Old Testament (*Les Contemplations* (1856), 334), Genesis similarly describes the '*first days of the world*'. Verne presents the formation of the Earth as the result of the aggregation of scattered matter; the theory that it was formed by the sun encountering a second star is no longer proposed nowadays.

1,400,000 times larger than the Earth: the modern figure is usually 1,300,000. In the galley proofs, Verne crosses out 'it is 357,290 leagues wide', a figure taken from Guillemin's *Le Ciel* (p. 28).

Neptune: we now know that Pluto is beyond Neptune.

Saturn eight, Jupiter four: information on the number of satellites given in Guillemin's *Le Ciel* (p. 14).

the lion of Nemea: a fantastic creature in the Peloponnese whose killing was the first Labour of Hercules. Plutarch quotes a fragment of the work of *Agesianax* in *De Facie in Orbem Lunae*.

29 *the Arcadians . . . images of the oceans*: information taken from Arago, who writes not only '*The Arcadians* . . . maintained that their ancestors had inhabited the Earth *before* it had a satellite' (p. 455) (given the preponderant number of borrowings from vol. 3 of his *Astronomie populaire*, this volume number will be omitted from references), but also '*Tatius* . . . [maintained that] the Moon [came] from *a fragment* of *the sun*' (p. 411) and '*Clearchus . . . a disciple of Aristotle*, said . . . that the Moon was . . . "the sharpest mirror in plain polish" and . . . that "the *images . . . of the* great *ocean* appeared . . . as in a *mirror*"' (p. 412).

Cleomenes: although borrowed from Arago—'*Cleomenes* . . . only made it *shine* with *reflected* sunlight' (p. 391)—this name, given to kings of Sparta and several scholars, is probably meant to be Cleomedes (dates unknown), the author of *On the Circular Motions of the Celestial Bodies*.

30 *Herschel*: whereas earlier Verne referred to John Herschel, here he is referring to his father, the German William Herschel (1738–1822), the discoverer of Uranus.

over 14,400 high: a peak of almost 30,000 feet has now been identified. Arago observes that according to '*Messrs Beer and Mædler . . .* out of 1,095 measured *heights of mountains on the Moon*, there are *six above* 5,800 m, and *twenty-two above* 4,800 m' (p. 417). In writing '1,905', Verne reverses Arago's two middle digits; and he is not consistent in his conversion from metres to feet.

31 *300,000 times weaker than sunlight*: a figure put forward in the 18th century by Pierre Bouguer (1698–1758), although Guillemin gives 'the 801,072nd part' (*La Lune*, 33).

Barbicane's proposal: the idea of sending a projectile to the Moon, proposed at the end of ch. 2.

32 '*sun of the wolves*': expression used from the beginning of the 19th century, for example in a French translation of *Don Quixote*.

70 miles (30 leagues): the two conversions are given in notes in the ms, but, following a comment by Hetzel, Verne transfers them to the main text.

354⅓ hours long: later on, the figure is '354½ hours' or simply '354 hours'. Guillemin notes: '354½ *hours* . . . is the *length* of its *night*' (p. 194).

33 *'that pale brightness that drops down from the stars'*: this quotation can be found both in Corneille's *Le Cid* (IV, 3) and in Dumas's *La Comtesse de Charny* (1852–3), ch. 7.

the same length of time . . . Cassini and Herschel: Guillemin reads 'Equality of duration of the two movements *of rotation and revolution*' (*La Lune*, 150). Giovanni *Cassini* (1625–1712) was a specialist on Saturn and Jupiter. Arago similarly reads: 'Observations made by *Cassini*, repeated and perfected by *Herschel*, seem to indicate that the *satellites of Jupiter* always present the same face to the planet' (p. 487).

to be exact 57 hundredths: in fact about 59% of the disc. Whereas the small-format editions read '*47 hundredths*', the octavo editions more accurately read '*57 hundredths*'.

34 *lunation*: or lunar month, approximately 29.5 days long.

35 *the time of the Caliphs*: in the five centuries following the death of Mahomet in 632, a succession of Caliphs ruled over the Muslims.

Boys are born mostly during a New Moon and girls during its last quarter: a belief that can be seen in Jacques Barthelemy Salgues, *Des erreurs et des prejugés répandus* . . . (vol. 1 (1828), 77), which refers however to the moment of conception, rather than to the moment of birth.

37 *800,000 times more slowly than electricity, 640,000 times slower than the speed of light*: since electricity travels about 20% more slowly than light, these two figures must have been reversed.

40 *The Knights of St John . . . Fort St Elmo*: the Knights occupied Malta from 1530 to 1798; the fort dates from 1552–6.

the Bastille . . . landed at Charenton: a distance of more than 7 km, as reported by several historians, who attribute it variously to Philippe de Commines (*c.*1445–*c.*1515), to a contemporary 'Saint-Rémy', or to a 'Scandalous Chronicle' (late 15th century). According to the *Encyclopédie nouvelle* (1811), 'The cannonballs fired by the Emperor *Mahomet at the siege of Constantinople weighed* two *hundred pounds*. Louis XI had a *500* calibre cannon cast that fired the cannonballs from the tower of *the Bastille* to *Charenton*' (vol. 3, p. 11—reminder: text borrowed by Verne is quoted in italics). In the octavo editions, 'lock up' is replaced by 'locked *up*', less forceful.

Columbiads: large-calibre, smooth-bore, muzzle-loading artillery pieces (1811–*c.*1900).

42 *aluminium in a compact mass*: it was in 1853 that Deville (1818–81) succeeded in making aluminium in small quantities, which he exhibited in 1854.

francs: the ratio to the dollar used by Verne varies from 4.8 to 5.4.

42 *cast iron, 67,440 pounds . . . aluminium . . . 19,250 pounds*: underestimates, according to Miller.

eighteen dollars a pound: five paragraphs earlier, aluminium cost 'nine dollars a pound'.

44 *the impulse force which has been imparted to it*: in fact, this force will act on the projectile for only a few seconds.

forty miles: although nowadays the Karman line at 100 km is often cited as the limit of space, atmospheric effects are perceptible up to 120 km.

about one twelfth of an inch: according to Miller, this should be increased by a sixth.

45 *30,000 pounds*: elsewhere in the work, except in ch. 9, the projectile weighs '20,000 pounds'.

900 feet long: not long enough to give the required impetus. What is more, the air trapped in a tube of this length could not escape in time and would crush the projectile.

47 *siege of Atlanta*: from 22 July to 1 September 1864, a turning point in the Civil War.

48 *Schwartz*: inventor Berthold Schwartz (*c.*1318–*c.*1384); in fact firearms existed before then.

sulphur and saltpetre: in reality Greek fire also contained naphtha and usually pitch.

52 *guncotton*: effectively the most powerful explosive in 1865.

54 *Merrimac . . . Weehawken*: in the American Civil War, the Northern *Monitor* (1861–2) and the *Virginia* (ex-*Merrimac*, 1855–62) fought the first battle between ironclads, described by Verne in *North versus South* (1887), I 13. The Confederate *Ram Tennessee* sailed to Mobile Bay in August 1864. The *Weehawken* took part in the Unionist blockade of Charleston Harbor, bombarding its fortifications, but in December 1863 sank in a storm.

55 *impenetrable suit of armour . . . a cannonball which went clean through him*: according to Miller, this paragraph contains homosexual innuendo of penetration.

57 *Richmond Enquirer:* (founded in 1804, closed in 1867), Democrat and pro-Confederate.

58 *19 May*: date also present in the manuscript, error for '19 October'. The '20 October' below was '20 May' in the ms.

Florida and Texas: the ms reads: '*Florida* versus *Texas*' (101).

a copy of the magnificent Z. Belltrop map: the ms reads 'H. Fridson [Friedson?] and Belletrop' (101).

in these terms: in the margin of the ms, Hetzel writes: 'experiment in the projectile with launching animals in it', an idea adopted only in ch. 22: it is thus possible that he was the first to propose this idea.

60 *southern parts of both Texas and Florida*: in the margin of the ms, Hetzel suggests a launch from 'adjoining countries [*sic*]' and criticizes the 'angry atmosphere' of the passage (103), although Verne does not change the text.

Rio Bravo: the Mexican name for the Rio Grande.

61 *the New York Herald and the Tribune . . . the Times and the American Review*: respectively: pro-Democrat (founded in 1835); the *New York (Daily) Tribune* (1841); the *New York Times* (1851); and the *North American Review* (Boston, 1815–1940) or perhaps *The American Review: A Whig Journal* (New York, 1844–52). The *Tampa Observer* (p. 140) seems to have been invented.

vomito negro: yellow fever.

Bay of Espiritu Santo: now Tampa Bay.

63 *sarcastic threat at their opponents*: the ms has: '*sarcasm towards* the deputies from Florida, which earned them a response worthy of ancient times' (109); but Hetzel disapproved of even indirect references to bad language.

64 *urbi et orbi*: allusion to the Pope's blessing of all humanity ('to the city and to the universe').

Buda: now Budapest.

'to all men of good will on Earth': quotation from Luke 2: 14.

66 *the French had once paid heavily for singing a song*: Cardinal Jean Mazarin (1602–61) wrote: 'They sing, they will pay' and 'Let them sing, they will pay for the violins'.

Christiania: or Christiana, capital of Norway, was renamed Oslo in 1948.

Norwegians dislike sending money to Sweden: at the time the King of Sweden also reigned over Norway. In his Scandinavian travel diary of 1861, Verne twice notes Norwegian resentment of the Swedish yoke.

the Sublime Porte: the seat of government of the Ottoman Empire, in Constantinople.

Denmark, though territorially somewhat restricted: Holstein and Schleswig had been ceded to Prussia in 1864.

67 *fledgling empires invariably have little cash to spare*: an allusion to Maximilian's Second Mexican Empire, founded in 1863 under the aegis of Napoleon III?

'the principle of non-intervention': allusion to the British position during the American Civil War, of not giving support to either side, which features in Verne's short story 'The Blockade Runners'.

68 *Cold Spring*: factory (1818–1912), under the name of West Point Foundry, which supplied a major part of the nation's artillery after 1861.

69 *Bartram's Travels . . . East Florida*: motley selection of relatively old volumes: William Bartram, *Travels Through North & South Carolina, Georgia, East & West Florida . . .* (1791; French translation, 1799); Bernard Roman, *A Concise Natural History of East and West Florida* (1776); John Lee Williams, *The Territory of Florida, or Sketches of the topography, civil and*

natural history of the country (1837); and John C. Cleland, *The Superior Advantages to be derived from the culture of the sugar cane in East Florida* (1836).

70 *between America and the Gulf of Mexico*: a slip for 'between the Atlantic and . . .'.

71 *Murchison*: the name may be derived from the geologist Roderick Impey Murchison, whose surname is borrowed for the director of the Cold Spring works.

72 *a hundred dollars a day . . . for eighteen years and eleven days . . . 658,100 dollars*: Verne forgets to include the four leap days.

By about ten . . . dazzling, feathered brilliance: this paragraph, together with the caimans and horses of the following paragraphs, probably derives from Bartram.

73 *Stone's Hill*: instances of this name are attested in southern England and New England; some translators have replaced it with 'Stony Hill'.

1,800 feet above sea-level: in fact the highest point in Florida is less than 350 feet. Three positions are given for Stone's Hill: the coordinates cited here, those shown on the map, and those implied by the text, more than 'a dozen miles . . .' from the west coast (p. 72).

76 *Father Joseph's Well . . . Sultan Saladin*: a misunderstanding by Verne, Joseph being the first name of Saladin (1138–93), the ruler of Egypt and Syria who fought against the Third Crusade. According to Joseph d'Avenel, '*Joseph's well, dug by Saladin* in the living rock, is *three hundred feet* deep' (*Rome et Jerusalem* (1841), 334).

79 *silicon:* Verne probably means silica.

80 *a mixture of clayey soil and sand to which hay and straw were added*: no explanation is given as to how the cylinder will be built.

amalgamated into the liquid metal: it is not clear whether the 'iron bands' will also be 'amalgamated into the liquid metal' during the melting process; if not, they must form part of the cylinder, so that the inner wall can become smooth.

83 *the Gun Club's members chafed at the bit*: the 'Univerne' has two parts, living and inanimate, with each constantly metaphorizing into the other. If the vessel is identical to the man, then the man must be identical to the vessel. If suns 'swarm' and locomotives 'whinny', Vernian characters 'chafe at the bit', as here, or boil with impatience, as if there were fires within them. Sometimes, as in the traditional metaphor, curiosity, ambition, anger, impatience, jealousy, or desire make a character 'devour' his fellows or else these feelings 'devour' the character himself from the inside.

84 *Herostratus*: Herostratus (or Erostratus) was a 4th-century Greek arsonist who destroyed the second Temple of Artemis in order to achieve posthumous notoriety.

87 *the 'peaceful courier of the heavens'*: perhaps an approximate quotation from *Religious and Prophetic Meditations on the end of time* (1836), by Pierre-François Delestre-Boulage, who, in a fantastic vision of an eclipse of the Moon on 'the last day', describes 'the *heavens* . . . How beautiful was that lamp, *peaceful courier of the* nights', adding a reference to the Book of Revelation (6: 12).

88 *From Valentia . . . down the coast of America*: attempts to install a telegraph cable in 1858 and 1865 quickly failed: it was not until July 1866 that lasting transatlantic communication was established, financed by Cyrus Field and installed by the *Great Eastern* under James Anderson's command.

89 *Atlanta*: a Confederate battleship of this name forced the blockade but was captured by the *Weehawken* in 1863.

   Ardan: an anagram of Nadar, the *nom de guerre* of caricaturist, photographer, aeronaut, and self-publicist Gaspard Félix Tournachon (1820–1910). The first illustration in the original 2nd volume shows Ardan with a camera, in a pose often adopted by Nadar, and with the same grandiose moustache. Similarly both men are short-sighted, and while Ardan declares himself a 'friend' of Flammarion (the 1st ms of the 2nd volume (henceforth 1st ms), 183), Nadar often photographed the astronomer and dedicated a book to him. In 1863 Verne was not only a founder member and then '*censeur*' of Nadar's Society for the Promotion of Air Locomotion, which met at his house every Friday in 1864, but he also published an article about his friend's huge balloon titled 'About the *Géant*'. Verne sent him about fifteen extant letters, although only two date from the 1860s. Nadar wrote a brief, generally positive article, 'Loose Leaves: M. Jules Verne', in *Le Moniteur des eaux et des courses* (no. 6, 17 June 1866, p. 2), pointing out the novelist's lack of female characters and discreet promotion of religious values.

90 *But no one wished to take the notion any further*: the ms adds: 'to spare him all the nonsense he would have spouted in the heat of the discussion' (162).

92 *flyboats*: flat-bottomed coasters.

93 *'more forged in a smithy than cast in a mould'*: meaning one of a kind.

94 *'a sublime ignoramus'*: perhaps an allusion to Christopher Marlowe's *Faust*, as translated by Victor Hugo (1858): 'that *sublime ignoramus* who did *The Winter's Tale*' (p. 210). According to Miller, it was Voltaire who first described Shakespeare in this way. Nadar similarly liked to call himself 'ignorant', but at the same time ahead of the scientists.

   Phaeton . . . Icarus: Phaeton, the child of the sun in Greek mythology, borrows his father's chariot, loses control, and sets the sky and Earth ablaze. Icarus's wings, made of wax and feathers, melted when he got too close to the sun.

   Agathocles: king of Syracuse (*c.*361–289 BC) who burned his ships after landing in Africa, to force his men to fight to the bitter end.

94 *Pope's fine words, his 'ruling passion'*: Alexander Pope (1688–1744) used both the phrases 'ruling passion' and 'master passion'. Verne cites the former, but translates it in a footnote as 'maitresse passion' (mistress passion).

95 *'The forest is only burned down by its own trees'*: this proverb, supposedly from Tunis, is quoted in *Le Magasin pittoresque*, which paraphrases it as 'One is never betrayed except by one's own people' (1859, p. 202).

The thoughts which filled the mind of the President of the Gun Club: this lengthy revelation of Ardan's thought process, in the manner of Fenimore Cooper or Walter Scott, interrupts the external point of view.

99 *5,000 leagues an hour . . . perihelion*: these speeds are given by Francois Moustey, *Exposition élémentaire du système du monde* (2nd edition, 1856, p. 313); in fact the approximate average speed of Uranus is 15,200 m.p.h., and that of Mercury 106,000 m.p.h.

a circle of Popilius: to prevent the Syrian king, Antiochus Epiphanes, from consulting his advisers, consul Popilius Laenas (2nd century BC) drew a circle around him.

Rothschild . . . 147 million short: James de Rothschild (1792–1868) headed the French branch of this famous bank, where Verne purchased a banker's order for his 1861 visit to Scandinavia. The final figure is derived from the facts that '5 sous a kilometre' is equivalent to a franc a league and that the distance is '1,147 million leagues'.

100 *Alpha Centaurus . . . Capella 170,000 billion*: these figures differ considerably from modern figures. Although similar information appears in Arago (vol. 1, p. 436), it is also visible, in rounded form, in other authors, for example Guillemin (p. 418).

resumed his message: the paragraph is more developed in the ms: 'There, in spite of all the theories, the reality of distances was rigorously demonstrated to him by a vigorous contusion which marked his kidneys for a long time'.

101 *Plutarch . . . Bernardin de Saint-Pierre*: writers: Plutarch (*c.*46–*c.*120), Greek author, notably of 'The Face that Appears in the Disc of the Moon'; Emanuel Swedenborg (1688–1772), mystic Swedish mathematician and naturalist, author of *Des Terres dans notre monde solaire* (1758); and Bernardin de Saint-Pierre (1737–1814), naturalist and novelist of *Paul and Virginia* (1787). All three are mentioned in Flammarion's *La Pluralité des mondes . . .* (1864), the bibliography of which may have provided Verne with other names of authors who had written about the Moon.

102 *of animal origin*: carbon alone does not imply that organic matter is present; and we now know that, while meteors do indeed contain complex carbon compounds, they can form without the presence of life. The vocabulary of 'aeroliths . . . living organisms . . . animal origin' may have come from Flammarion (p. 187).

divine redemption . . . in all celestial worlds: St Paul speaks of 'the glory reserved for us on Earth itself, which . . . is promised to us in the *celestial worlds'* (Rom. 8: 18). However, the worlds are those of Heaven, rather than the firmament, so Ardan's claim is far-fetched, perhaps humorously so.

103 *the best of all possible worlds*: phrase coined by philosopher and mathematician Gottfried Wilhelm Leibniz in *Essais de Théodicée* (1710), and ridiculed by Voltaire in *Candide* (1759).

let's . . . straighten up the Earth's axis: the idea of righting the axis—which generates *Sans dessus dessous*, using the Gun Club's cannon and characters— may derive from Auguste Comte's *Traité d'astronomie populaire* (1844), which also draws a comparison with Jupiter's axis (p. 161).

104 *Archimedes*: scientist (287–212 BC) who wrote: 'One point of support, and I move the Earth' (*Archimedis Opera, de aequiponderantibus*, 150).

105 *not made to live in water*: Jules Seguin wrote that since they 'cannot rest in the air', '*birds* are not made to live in it' (*Projet d'établissement d'un système de locomotion aérienne . . .* (1863), 8). However, he added: '*Fish are made to live in water*'. Ardan sometimes distorts quotations to pour ridicule on arguments from authority.

a poor ignoramus: the ms adds: '*a poor* man like me, an *ignoramus* in the absolute sense of the word, or rather, an ass, a wretched ass!'

106 *the Moon is not enveloped by an atmosphere*: a thesis amply demonstrated by Arago (p. 436).

the Moon's atmosphere: Ardan's argument, at first glance a *non sequitur*, is nonetheless also taken from Arago: 'This method has only one disadvantage, that of supposing that *the angular diameter of the Moon* is known with very great precision' (p. 436). The truth lies in between: the absence of refraction of starlight on the edges of the Moon indeed shows that there is not a significant atmosphere. But to calculate the precise degree of refraction, one does need to know the Moon's exact angular diameter (its apparent width in degrees, seen from Earth).

Louville and Halley . . . in fact purely terrestrial: mathematician Colonel Jacques de Louville (1671–1732) studied eclipses of the Moon; Edmond Halley (1656–1742) determined the periodicity of comets. Their erroneous deductions in 1715 are noted by several authors including Arago, who, like Verne, cites Herschel's observations of 1787 (p. 492). He also writes: '*Messrs Beer and Mädler . . .* say positively that . . . they have never . . . seen . . . a *lunar* atmosphere' (pp. 496–7).

107 *the horns of the solar crescent*: Aimé Laussedat (1819–1907) was co-author of *Report on the Observation of the eclipse of 18 July 1860, made in Algeria* (1860). But it is more likely that Verne is borrowing from Guillemin, who wrote that in '*the eclipse of 18 July 1860 . . .* one *of the horns of the solar crescent* appeared *rounded and truncated*' (pp. 209–10).

112 *a less ceremonious entrance*: in the ms a lengthy dialogue follows between Ardan and Maston about the danger of a duel between Barbicane and Nicholl—an idea impossible to get past Hetzel: ' "What the devil!"

exclaimed the secretary of the Gun Club. "They are bound to kill each other . . . not a moment to lose".'

117 *'Nicholl!' cried Barbicane*: the ms, where the preceding dialogue between Ardan and Nicholl is much longer, underlines the aggression of the two men, a behaviour that the publisher Hetzel rarely allowed: 'whose eyes were inflamed, when he found himself face to face with his rival. The two enemies were glaring at each other with hatred, their hands instinctively twisting their rifles butts, when Michel Ardan stepped in . . .'.

119 *sober-sided holders of public office . . . bear her along in triumph*: allusion either to the Swedish diva Jenny Lind (1820–87), who made a triumphant tour of the United States in 1850–2, but was not in fact a dancer; or to the Irish dancer and courtesan Lola Montez (1821–61), who lived in America in the early 1850s.

E pluribus unum: 'From many, one', the unofficial motto of the United States.

120 *King Charles VI . . . either new or full*: text taken word for word from Arago (p. 505), as is the vocabulary of '*quiet, sane . . . whenever they think of the Moon*' (p. 503) and that below of '*fainting fits, malignant fevers, sleepwalking*' (p. 509).

Perhaps it's because it isn't true!: Arago claimed to be borrowing his quip on the links between the Moon and mental disturbances and his scepticism from Plutarch: '*Perhaps it's because* that *isn't true*' (p. 510).

Barnum: Phineas Taylor Barnum (1810–91) was an American showman; Verne visited his theatre in New York on 9 April 1867.

121 *in all imaginable poses*: Nadar photographed himself in twelve different profiles in about 1865.

122 *32-inch . . . (75 cm)*: in fact 81 cm, part of the difference being explained by the use of French feet.

123 *no squirrel*: originally it was a dog that went into space: 'The animal experiment will also be carried out . . . The dog will eat the squirrel' (Verne's letter of October 1864).

President of the Union: Andrew Johnson (1808–75) was president from 15 April 1865.

125 *The Little Clay Cart*: in ten acts, also known as the *Mrichchhakatika*, attributed to the king and poet Sudraka (4th or 5th century); a five-act adaptation by Joseph Méry and Gérard de Nerval was staged at the Odéon on 13 May 1850.

132 *the mirror sixteen feet in diameter*: Verne's telescope, placed in an elevated position, derives from those of Lord Rosse (with a mirror 1.83 m wide— not 1.93, as Verne writes) and of Léon Foucault, but hugely extrapolating their dimensions; however, he could probably have achieved the same power with a smaller mirror and a shorter telescope.

133 *10,700 . . . 26,776 feet above sea level*: while some of the difference between these measurements and modern ones can be explained by the

use of French feet, there are in fact many peaks in the Rockies that exceed 14,000 feet.

Longs Peak in Missouri Territory: from 1861 Longs Peak, 4,345 m, was located in Colorado Territory.

135 *workmen who wore no footwear*: to avoid sparks.

137 *the eastern portion of the Moon's disc*: in fact the Leibnitz mountains lie to the west; Verne often confuses east and west.

138 *wretched terraqueous globe*: a phrase used by Hugo in *Les Misérables* (1862), vol. 3, book 5, p. 288.

139 *another eighteen years*: the ms reads: '~~many months~~ <*more* than a year>' (reminder: the '< >' indicate text added after first composition).

141 *turn European stomachs . . . raccoon steaks*: and yet frogs' legs are a French speciality. The ms has 'kanguroo'.

cribbage and faro: card games.

142 *Yankee Doodle*: (= Northern/American lowlife) if this British song united the rebels during the War of Independence, in the 19th century it applied only to Northerners. There was no national anthem.

145 *the Childe Harold*: 1,036 tons. The ms adds politician and scientist 'Mathieu de la Drôme' (1808–16 March 1865), who describes lunar phases in his *De la Prediction du temps*.

146 *atmospheric conditions . . . suddenly changed by the discharge of many cannons*: a general illusion in the 19th century.

148 *an elliptical orbit around the Moon*: in the absence of atmosphere or intervention, the projectile will either head for interstellar space or return to Earth. The ms adds: 'It is therefore behaving round the night star as that body does round the Earth's globe'.

154 *longitude 5° 7' west*: according to the Washington meridian, like the coordinates in the following chapters.

157 *an opening*: although here located in 'the conical nose of the projectile', previously it was 'in the side of the cone' (p. 127); it is explained later that there are four portholes. If in the 1st volume, the covers are on the outside of the portholes, henceforth they are on the inside.

158 *Mahomet's, which floats suspended in the air and never goes anywhere*: the coffin of the prophet, soldier, and politician who founded Islam (*c.*570–632) is believed by some to remain suspended in the air.

159 *the clowns at the Great Circus*: in the 'Empress's Circus', 'the clown Boswell . . . with his head at the bottom and feet in the air, fires two pistol shots and swallows a glass of wine' (*L'Illustration*, vol. 22 (1853), 276).

160 *an escapement, and eight orifices*: in addition to the double entendre of something 'escaping', the 'orifices' are presumably nostrils, ears, mouth, navel, and two located at the 'South Pole', to adopt Verne's euphemism in a letter to his mother.

162 *pyroxylin*: or fulmicoton.

eleven thousand metres: per second; equivalent to the 'twelve thousand yards' in the first volume.

163 *Corton*: wine of the Côte-d'Or.

full of hydrogen: lighting gas was at the time extracted from coal, and contained hydrogen.

164 *Barbicane*: a mistake for Ardan.

165 *Michel*: the 2nd ms reads 'my good *Michel*', an epithet criticized by Hetzel.

167 *east to west*: in fact this apparent movement of the Moon seen from Earth is due to the rotation of the Earth, no longer a factor if the projectile is heading for the Moon.

168 *The asteroid . . . disappeared*: in a summary of this scene in the 1st ms of the 2nd volume, the body, not yet the 'second Moon', collides with the projectile:

They stood there breathing heavily. It [the asteroid] struck them with its South Pole, which hit the base of the projectile (perhaps changing its course), but in any case affecting its speed . . .

'Is it possible' . . .
'It's even certain' . . .
'But it also proves one thing'
'That we are'
'*8,140 kilometres from the Earth's surface* . . . Well, you have to travel to find out.'

169 *Monsieur Petit*: in 1846, to explain irregularities in the Moon's movements, Frédéric Petit (1810–65), the author of *Traité d'astronomie* (1866), erroneously deduced the existence of a second Moon orbiting the Earth, with a period of 2 hours and 45 minutes. Here the body is strangely orbiting in the opposite direction to the Moon.

three hours and twenty minutes: in fact, with the figures quoted by Petit of an apogee of 3.57 km and a perigee of 11.4 km, the object would have a period of 4 hours and 48 minutes. Verne took his figures—'*three hours and twenty minutes*' and '*eight thousand one hundred and forty kilometres*'—from Guillemin's *La Lune* (pp. 192–3), who nevertheless cites them as extreme values, unachievable at the same time. In fact, the asteroid should be in eclipse like the Moon and therefore invisible.

170 *The black curtain . . . had never even imagined could exist*: Hetzel writes largely illegible comments opposite these sentences, but Verne does not change his text.

the porthole . . . view of the Earth: words added to the ms by Hetzel.

173 *Anubis . . . St Roch*: Anubis was the Egyptian god of death, depicted with a jackal's head; St Roch (1350–c.1378), from Montpellier, is the patron saint of pilgrims and animals, usually depicted with a dog.

King of the Underworld . . . Europa: in Greek mythology Hades is master of the three-headed watchdog Cerberus, and Europa is a Phoenician princess, to whom Roman master of the gods Jupiter gives a dog as his first mortal love.

Montargis and Mount St Bernard: in a story from the 15th century, popularized by the play *Le Chien de Montargis*, staged continuously from 1814 to 1834, a dog fights a duel with the murderer of his master. The large and intelligent St Bernard dog was bred by the monks of the hospice of Grand-Saint-Bernard for rescue purposes.

174 *'In the beginning . . . gave him a dog!'*: this quotation from farmer, politician, and journalist Alphonse Toussenel (1803–85) is from *Esprit des bêtes: Mammifères de France*, with a preface by P.-J. Stahl (pseudonym of Hetzel, Librairie Phalanstérienne, 1847; new edition, Hetzel, 1868, p. 3).

our acclimatization programme done for: in the 2nd ms, Hetzel twice tries to correct the original wording, 'peace *done for*'. The publisher also inserts, three pages later, 'with the *tea*' after '*bread buttered in the American style*'; but then half erases his insertion, adding 'good'. His remark about 'saving gas' (35) is also ignored.

he let out a sigh: in the 1st ms, Ardan tries in vain to save the dying dog:

As for his [illegible], it was sad again!
'Good!' said Nadar [*sic*], 'he *is* not *ill*.'
'Ah!' said Barbicane.
'No! *he died* is dying.'

Indeed, the poor beast had only a few hours to live, and would soon meet the fate of dead animals in planetary space. However, he was looked after with the utmost care, Nadar despairing that the male would fail to take part in his colonization experiments.

'We'll have to cross-breed our bitch with lunar dogs,' he said.
'There are some?'
'By Jove yes! My poor Diane, I'm afraid she won'*t breed.*' (7)

In the 2nd ms, Hetzel criticizes at length, but in vain at this stage, a shortened scene of caring for the dog.

175 *Liebig extract*: popularized in 1856 by Justus Liebig (1803–73), it condensed the nutritional values of lean meat.

Café Anglais: famous restaurant located at 13 Boulevard des Italiens, a meeting place for writers.

177 *the Reiset and Regnault apparatus*: invented by Jules Reiset (1818–96) and Victor Regnault (1810–78), authors of *Sur la respiration des animaux des diverses classes* (1849).

178 *Grotta del Cane*: near Lake Agnano in Campania. Verne visited it on 29 June 1884.

735 . . . millimetres: various editions give '735', '730', or '765' (e.g. the octavo of 1872); 2nd ms: '753'.

179 *hypsometer*: instrument that deduces altitude from the boiling point of a liquid.

179 *use the rungs riveted*: following a question from the publisher, 'How . . . ?',
Verne inserts these four words. For the same reason, he adds '*doing* the
asking and responding' after '*Ardan was chatting to*' Barbicane and Nicholl
(41) and copies Hetzel's '*nails in a bucket*' (50).

184 *the integral of the live force*: the famous three-body problem, that of predicting the paths in space of three bodies with interacting gravitational
forces: it still cannot be solved, so requires numerical approximation
methods. However, given the negligible mass of the projectile, the three
bodies in fact virtually reduce to two, making a solution possible.

the live force: an obsolete and inaccurate expression, corresponding to
kinetic energy, or $\frac{1}{2}mv^2$.

186 *Your v zero two and your v zero squared*: Ardan is pointing out that both
expressions correspond to v_0^2.

9 m 81: the unit should be m/s^2.

188 *crashing onto the Earth*: in what follows, the accuracy of the Observatory's
figure will not be questioned, but a new explanation is offered: 'when it
expelled the water held in the collapsible partitions the projectile became
suddenly lighter as a result of shedding a considerable weight' (ch. 5).

pistoles: gold coins from Italy or Spain.

189 *if its speed at launch had been only 11,000 metres*: Barbicane seems to be
confusing the speed required at launch with the speed required on leaving
the atmosphere.

190 *if there have been Selenites . . . over the coming centuries*: this dialogue exists
in heavily abbreviated point form in the 1st ms: '<"*If* Moon [is] inhabited,
[it must have been] inhabited long before"/"*Therefore, its hab. invented*
[all] that . . . and better."/ "*If* [they had a] *brain*."//"Then, if [so], I'm
surprised they haven't *achieved . . . what we have*">' (38).

Comic actors like Arnal . . . Nadar?: self-referring line added to the final
draft by Hetzel—who also adds Corrège to the list of painters, then crosses
it out (58). Étienne Arnal (1794–1872) was a comic actor at the Vaudeville
theatre in Paris.

never tried to communicate with the Earth?: a question also asked by
Fontenelle.

191 *before man appeared on Earth*: in the 1860s Verne's thinking evolves,
accepting the existence of increasingly long prehistoric periods without
humans, hence perhaps the slight discrepancy between the appearance of
man, here implied to be less than 'thousands of years ago' and the 'hundreds
of thousands of years' of imputed Selenite existence at the beginning of
the discussion.

five-sixths of our planet: the sea was previously said to cover 'three-quarters'
of the globe (I 27).

still have not invented gunpowder: phrase added to the 2nd ms in an unknown
hand, then copied by Verne.

Silenus: minor Greek god who gets drunk, mingles with mortals, and rides a donkey.

192 *secured by hinges*: the 1st ms emphasizes the strength of the portholes, 'made in Chartres and laminated from top to bottom' (7).

193 *a comet in 1861*: the Great Comet, discovered on 13 May 1861, remained visible for three months.

194 *60 degrees*: while in the 1860s some authors continued to support Fourier's figure, lower values were proposed from the 18th century onwards: −130° in 1845 by Faraday, and finally −273° by Kelvin in 1848.

ether: Verne adheres to the scientific theory of this universal and highly elastic but imponderable fluid, the medium through which light and heat are transmitted, a theory that was discredited towards the turn of the 20th century. In fact, there was no way of evaluating the speed or 'amplitude' of the ether's 'undulations'.

195 *Double Liégeois*: popular almanac published between 1820 and 1840 giving predictions of catastrophes, derived from the *Almanach liégeois* of 1626. The analogy with grains of sand is present almost word for word in Herschel's *Nouveau manuel complet . . .* (p. 271).

199 *leaves most of it visible*: from the Moon the sun appears much smaller than the Earth, so is not seen during eclipses.

60 times the radius of the Earth: identical information appears in Guillemin (p. 172).

200 *the Moon was once a comet?*: very unlikely, since the large comets that pass close to Earth are never captured.

203 *5 November*: error for 5 December.

204 *Apollo's charming sister*: Diana, Apollo's twin, Greek god of the arts and male beauty.

205 *etherizing*: ('éthérer'), word used especially in oenology, palmistry, and the treatment of venereal diseases, sometimes employed by Dumas.

208 *etherism*: a possible innuendo, since 'erethism' means 'morbid excitation of an organ'.

210 *8*: In the serial publication, the following chapters are incorrectly numbered ('10' etc.): the error goes back to the 2nd ms, where a printer mistakenly introduces two instances of 'Chapter 6'.

211 *It's the oxygen*: in Poe's short story, 'Conversation of Eiros with Charmion' (1839), a comparable atmosphere of pure oxygen generates a 'frenzy . . . of humanity'.

214 *Cuisine des anges*: painting (1646) by Bartolomé Esteban Murillo (1617–82) that shows St Giles floating in mid-air.

Assumption: an irreverent allusion to Raphael's *Sistine Madonna: The Assumption of the Virgin* (1513), in which Mary is shown standing on a cloud.

217 *to his mouth*: the rest of this passage in the 1st ms, discussing the trajectory of the projectile, is surprisingly different: 'The conversation continued like this, jumping from subject to subject, often broken up by observations to see if the projectile would turn round, or if they had gone past the neutral line; then the descent towards the surface of the Moon began in earnest' (16).

224 *could not usefully be seen*: Verne has set things up to avoid having to provide information about the Moon going beyond current knowledge.

226 *just thirty*: earlier Galileo's telescope magnified 'at most seven times' (p. 130). According to Moustey (p. 178), Galileo's first telescope magnified four times, the second seven times, but the third one, 32 times.

Dominique Cassini: rather than the Frenchman (1748–1845), Verne is referring here to his Italian great-grandfather, Giovanni Domenico Cassini (1625–1712).

228 *asked one of his students*: according to Arago, a Jean-Henri Hassenfratz called a student named Leboullenger to the board to ask him: '"... *have you seen the Moon?*", to which came the reply: "I would be lying if I told you *that I had* not *heard of it*, but I have never seen it"' (vol. 1, p. 13).

229 *Naxos, Tenedos, Milos, and Karpathos*: islands in the Aegean Sea that feature in the *Odyssey*.

230 '*Map of Love*': a '*Carte de Tendre*', drawn by François Chauveau, in the first part of *Clélie, histoire romaine* (1654–60) by Madeleine de Scudéry (1607–1701), includes a feature called Tendre and the successive topographic and allegorical stages of a woman's life.

234 *since the south is behind them*: Verne's explanation is repetitive and unclear. The vital information is that the direct image of the Moon viewed from Earth is inverted left–right compared with chart representations of it.

238 *Leibnitz . . . 3,617*: the information in this table, except for '*D'Alembert*', '*Humus*', and '*Hercynians, from 17° to 29°*', appears in identical form in Arago (pp. 445–6): Verne seems to have mistakenly taken '*33°*' from the previous line. Other figures from Arago are: '*Lambert . . . 1,812 . . . Euler . . . 23° . . . 29° E*' (p. 449).

240 *It is difficult to say, for no ascent to date has exceeded 8,000 metres*: horizontal observations might nevertheless allow the question to be answered.

242 *risen to seventy*: in fact 90, Verne having misread Arago (pp. 424–46). The rest of this paragraph is also taken from the same source (p. 426).

248 *The 'savage' shade, so beloved of Victor Hugo*: a phrase he often uses, e.g. in *Les Misérables*, vol. 4, book 4.

249 *double its distance . . . between the Earth and the sun*: the reference 'G. 194' (27) appears in the 1st ms, the text of which, paraphrased in the published version, is virtually identical to Guillemin (p. 194).

denizens of the Boulevard des Italiens: Hetzel replaces the phrase in the 2nd ms, '. . . *we are all like that* in photography!', with the published words

(Sainlot, p. 52). Nadar's photography studio was located at no. 35 of this boulevard.

250 *movement of oscillation . . . half its disc towards the Earth*: the source seems to be Garcet (*Cosmographie*, pp. 255–6).

an elliptical orbit around the Earth: the source is given in the margin of the 1st ms as 'H. 206' (27), meaning Henri Garcet, who discusses '*the speed of translation*' and provides an illustration of the elliptical path of the Moon (*Leçons nouvelles de cosmographie*, 4th edn (1861), 206).

251 *they could not hear them*: the 1st ms reads: '~~And this was happening in the midst of that deep silence, that absolute silence of which we have no idea in our noisy hemisphere~~ G. 139' (27), apparently a reference to 'No *air* and no water! . . . eternal stillness and silence' (Guillemin, *La Lune*, 140).

about one seventh: the more correct '57 hundredths' was cited previously (p. 33).

252 *the firmament from the Southern Cross to the North Star*: so close to the Moon, the whole firmament would not be visible.

253 *exceptionally low minimum temperatures*: in the 1st ms, an 'alcohol *minimum thermometer*' is used (28), followed by six blank lines; the margin reads 'Ar. 8 205', referring to Arago's '*alcohol* Fahrenheit *thermometer*' (vol. 8, p. 205). In fact even a Walferdin thermometer would take longer than 'half an hour' to register in the absence of an atmosphere; and would not in any case work in space.

256 *they rarely reach its surface*: because small objects normally burn up.

257 *'art for art's sake'*: expression associated with the Romantic Movement from 1840, which declares that art has an intrinsic value, with no necessary didactic, moral, or practical purpose.

would never see either Earth or Moon again: an example of unreliable narration, although perhaps a transcription in 'free indirect style' (unmarked reported speech) of the thoughts of Barbicane and Nicholl.

261 *27 October 1844 . . . 18 August 1841 . . . 182 leagues*: Arago, reporting Petit, gives the same two dates and distance (p. 270). As the 'meteors' could have disappeared only after encountering the Earth's atmosphere, the large heights given cannot be correct.

262 *The projectile . . . exploded like a bomb*: the publisher twice amends this passage, as well as the third paragraph below, but only starting from the serial publication does he manage to remove the pessimistic idea of 'The wretches . . . thought they were lost' (2nd ms 175–6). In fact, in the absence of an atmosphere, the meteor would not explode; and, having originally been on 'a course to meet the projectile', its explosion should probably have made a collision more likely.

264 *Ruggieri*: family of French firework makers, including Désiré-François (1818–85).

266 *gives the height of that point*: it is in fact difficult to calculate the height of a mountain from only the diagonal distance between a bright point on it and the nearest part of the lit section of surrounding terrain.

267 *As has already been said*: words suggested by Hetzel.

Djawahir: now Nanda Devi.

268 *17*: all the Hetzel editions erroneously read '18'.

270 *'No force external . . . its relief'*: as confirmed by Verne's note ('Ar. 424', 1st ms 32), a quotation from Arago, who adds: 'At the edges of the disc, the action of the Moon on matter will be more or less perpendicular to the attraction of the Earth on this same matter' (p. 424).

273 *Pluto*: the god of the underworld.

275 *Pyrenees . . . the Sea of Humours*: information taken from Guillemin (*La Lune*, 52–3).

Herschel . . . Tycho was being formed: information derived from Arago (p. 421).

276 *Nasmyth*: James Nasmyth (1808–90), Scottish artist and engineer; Arago similarly states that this author 'assimilates . . . [in] *Tycho's crater* . . . the divergent rays . . . to those starshaped patterns in *glass* panes when they have been struck by *a stone* . . . or even by *a bullet*' (pp. 421–2).

279 *historical time*: in fact prehistoric times.

281 *Canaan*: the land promised to Moses by God, but which he never reaches (Deut. 32: 49).

284 *Chambertin 1863*: grand cru from the Côte-d'Or.

285 *aposelenitical*: neither this term nor 'aposelene' in the previous paragraph (*apo* = outside) is attested in French or English in the 1860s.

288 *reappear via the North Pole*: in the previous chapters, the projectile went from the North Pole to the South.

289 *120 leagues an hour*: in fact 120 km/h. It is not clear where the speed of '57,600 leagues an hour' comes from, or whether it takes into account the changes due to the two periods of air friction and the in-flight firing of rockets.

290 *Brooke apparatus*: Confederate officer and inventor John Mercer Brooke (1826–1906) took soundings of the ocean floor to map its shape: because of the underwater currents, he used a heavy device that released ballast when it touched bottom.

291 *the Susquehanna*: a corvette sent to Japan in 1853, which laid a telegraph cable in about 1856 (see the following paragraphs) and was decommissioned in January 1868.

New Mexico: Verne is probably thinking of California.

Cyrus Field: American businessman and engineer Cyrus (West) Field (1819–92) laid the definitive transatlantic cable in 1867. His fictional compatriots Cyrus Smith (*The Mysterious Island*, 1875) and Cyrus Bikerstaff (*Propeller Island*, 1895) share traits with him.

294 *snapping it off at the base of the stem-post*: in the 1st ms, the projectile misses the ship by 'a few metres' (40).

298 *Blomsberry's brother*: Captain Blomsberry was previously Colonel Blomsberry's 'first cousin' (p. 291).

across the middle of America: since the railway opened on 10 May 1869 as far as Sacramento, and to the Pacific on 6 September, Verne seems to be anticipating the final connection to the Californian coast.

'front-view': a term used by Guillemin: 'W. Herschel's *front-view* telescopes have the advantage . . . of not blocking some of the rays of light' (pp. 600–1).

307 *double zero*: placing a blank domino at both ends of the board wins the game.

the prophet Elijah . . . when he too returns to Earth: Elijah (9th century BC) ascends to heaven in a whirlwind; he will return at the end of time (Rev. 11: 3–12).

309 *eighty leagues an hour*: or 320 km/h . . .

New Brunswick: either Verne is anticipating the incorporation into the Union of Canada or he means New Hampshire; he omits the West of the United States, not yet linked by railway.

American Literature

British and Irish Literature

Children's Literature

Classics and Ancient Literature

Colonial Literature

Eastern Literature

European Literature

Gothic Literature

History

Medieval Literature

Oxford English Drama

Philosophy

Poetry

Politics

Religion

The Oxford Shakespeare

A complete list of Oxford World's Classics, including Authors in Context, Oxford English Drama, and the Oxford Shakespeare, is available in the UK from the Marketing Services Department, Oxford University Press, Great Clarendon Street, Oxford OX2 6DP, or visit the website at www.oup.com/uk/worldsclassics.

In the USA, visit www.oup.com/us/owc for a complete title list.

Oxford World's Classics are available from all good bookshops.

ANTHONY TROLLOPE

2 04